Economic Policies for Sustainable Development

Economy & Environment

VOLUME 7

The titles published in this series are listed at the end of this volume.

Economic Policies for Sustainable Development

edited by

Thomas Sterner
Department of Economics,
University of Gothenburg,
Sweden

KLUWER ACADEMIC PUBLISHERS
DORDRECHT / BOSTON / LONDON

A C.I.P. Catalogue record for this book is available from the Library of Congress

ISBN 0-7923-2680-6

Published by Kluwer Academic Publishers,
P.O. Box 17, 3300 AA Dordrecht, The Netherlands.

Kluwer Academic Publishers incorporates
the publishing programmes of
D. Reidel, Martinus Nijhoff, Dr W. Junk and MTP Press.

Sold and distributed in the U.S.A. and Canada
by Kluwer Academic Publishers,
101 Philip Drive, Norwell, MA 02061, U.S.A.

In all other countries, sold and distributed
by Kluwer Academic Publishers Group,
P.O. Box 322, 3300 AH Dordrecht, The Netherlands.

02-0896-150 ts

First published 1994, Reprinted 1996.

Printed on acid-free paper

Printed in the Netherlands

CONTENTS

Preface

This book focuses on describing policy instruments in different countries. Its purpose is not only descriptive but also, to some extent, advocatory. We believe that economic instruments can make an important contribution to an environmentally less disruptive path of development. The design of economic instruments is however a fine art and depends among other things on their political acceptability and this acceptability is of course influenced by experience. It is therefore important to provide information on the use of policy instruments in other countries. Policies are currently developing quite fast and thus a book such as this one can inevitably not capture more than a "snapshot" view at a single moment of time. We would hope that the book encourages more experimentation with economic instruments and that countries will make a fuller use of the whole arsenal of economic policy instruments. If the book does succeed in this sense then it will soon become dated as policies change - but that would be a price well worth paying!

The book combines a dozen country monographs together with a few international surveys on particular topics (gasoline pricing, vehicle regulations, acid rain, deforestation and global warming). These papers are intended to illustrate the diversity of policy options available. The actual policies adopted depend on economic as well as ecological conditions. The country studies cover two "Western" countries and then concentrate on formerly planned and developing countries. They show that economic instruments are still generally thought of as new and innovative. They have however passed the experimental stage and are now being implemented on a larger scale but still mainly in the OECD countries.

Working on this topic has engaged me rather heavily. Apart from writing or co-authoring four chapters, I have been stubborn enough to want to get a good cross-section both by subject and geographically. It is easier to get articles from some regions than others and there has thus been quite a painstaking process of searching for and selecting papers to form a natural entity and in some cases some very far-reaching editing and rewriting. Luckily I have had help from a number of colleagues and I would particularly like to thank those who have helped me referee various chapters. I have had each chapter refereed, sometimes anonymously but to encourage communication among the various chapters I have also asked some chapter authors to help me referee other chapters. Most of the chapters have the usual acknowledgments but I would again like to thank all those who have helped me and very particularly Tomasz Żylicz, Katarina Katz, Jorge Buzaglo, Milford Aguilar, Martin Linde and Gunnar Köhlin for many valuable comments. I would also like to thank Ulla Mellgren and Mimi Möller for help with proof-reading and copy editing.

Finally I would like to thank two organizations that have made this project possible. Firstly the Swedish Council for Planning and Coordination of Research (FRN) who provided initial finance that resulted in a survey article and the start-up of this project. Secondly the Swedish International Development Assistance (SIDA). SIDA has since three years been financing the set up of an Environmental Economics Unit at our department. Together with some other donors, SIDA is very concerned for the connections between aid, development and environment and in fact this book is a product of this interest since SIDA has supported it not only through finance to cover some of my working time but also with considerable intellectual stimulus.

Gothenburg

Thomas Sterner

CHAPTER 1

Policy Instruments for a Sustainable Economy*

by

Thomas Sterner

Abstract

This chapter is intended to introduce the subject and provide an overview of the relevant aspects of environmental policy making. It starts with some general reflections on environmental economics and the formulation of environmental policies as a means of copying with the underlying conflict between economic growth and the limited carrying capacity of the environment. Section 4 provides a brief overview of the contents of the book but without summarizing individual chapters (such summaries are provided in the abstracts of each individual chapter). Sections 5-8 contain an attempt at summarizing some reflections emanating from the various chapters analyzing policy instruments in industrialized, transitional and developing countries as well as on the global arena.

* Thanks are due to Thomas Żylicz for comments.

T. Sterner (ed.), Economic Policies for Sustainable Development, 1–19.

1 INTRODUCTION

Environmental economics has always, in principle, been a central part of economics. Economists such as Ricardo, Marshall, Pigou or Hotelling made significant contributions to the subject. Using modern terminology, we might say that these economists considered that the market needs to be corrected for externalities, public goods and for the short-sightedness of economic agents. Practically all economists presumably accepted their principles but, with a few notable exceptions such as Malthus, most economists have seen market failures and particularly negative externalities as minor aberrations. We have all heard how the laundry costs in Manchester increased because of soot or how the orchards benefitted from the bee-hives but this didn't seem to be such a major issue. It is only very recently that it has started to dawn on us that external effects on our living environment are a major and even crucial aspect of all modern societies and that our economic policies must be designed to manage conflicting demands on an increasingly scarce habitat.

During the last decade there have been some important developments concerning the relationship between economics and ecology. The most basic of these is that the economy is a subsystem of an ecological system that is finite, complex and possibly instable. Although simple and in a sense obvious, the general acceptance of this fact should have profound implications on the way economists think of environmental issues since it goes to the heart of questions of economic growth, sustainability and the optimal scale of the economy, see Daly & Cobb (1989).

When we turn to the policy arena itself we should remember that modern environmental protection is barely three decades old. The early countries enacted their first vaguely comprehensive legislation and set up their "EPAs" starting in the sixties. Since then the perceived problems have gone from local to national and then global, solutions have changed from being purely technical fixes to becoming more societal, perspectives have become more ecological and policy instruments more sophisticated. It is fair to say that there has been a good deal of success in attacking problems of sanitation and even the worst smog problems. However, other problems have loomed to take their place. Concerning the change during this period, the Swedish biologist Arne Jernelöv has noted:

"25 years ago the typical picture around the outlets from industrial or municipal sewage works in the Baltic Sea was an area of about a square kilometer which was practically void of all macroscopic life. A number of miles away there would be a practically untouched area that could be used as a reference point and between the two places there would be a sharp gradient of both pollution and biological effect. Today these heavily polluted sites are gone and the visible improvement at the sewage outlets is in fact drastic. However, if you try to find your reference points they too are gone and it is practically impossible to find a completely unpolluted area anywhere" (Jernelöv (1989) translated, and slightly abridged, by T. Sterner).

What has been described at an exact level for the Baltic sea would appear to hold, in a more general sense, for the whole Planet. In the more affluent countries, many of the most striking environmental problems such as the famous smogs in

London, Los Angeles or Tokyo have been tackled with varying but generally quite impressive results. However, we have hardly come any closer to solving - and in fact it seems on the contrary that we have exacerbated - a number of other more global problems such as global warming, depletion of stratospheric ozone and perhaps acid rain. The new chemicals invented by man have also found their way across the globe from the penguins of the Antarctic to the upper layers of the stratosphere and may be the cause of as yet unidentified problems which might possibly turn up as future environmental issues. Thus environmental problems are shifted further away rather than really being solved. To some extent this is due to the increasing scope of industrial activity in general but it is also specifically due to earlier policies of hiding, diluting or just dumping rather than really tackling the fundamental problems of our interaction with the environment.

Partly this must be due to ignorance: we think of "cleaning", forgetting that material (like energy) is conserved. When people wash (themselves or their clothes) they use chemicals and water to get rid of unwanted dirt. But the dirt particles do not vanish; they are merely moved from one place to another (for instance to the sewers and ultimately to the sea). Similarly filters remove particles from the air, but we must learn to ask where they go afterwards! Most likely they go to a waste disposal site and then get leached by rain into the groundwater.... If instead the particles are "disposed" of by mixing them into cement then their final release into the biosphere is delayed by a few decades, until the cement withers away. So the externality is moved further away not only in space but in time too. We are gradually beginning to learn the lessons but as recently as 1974, Article 1 (d) of the OECD **Guidelines for actions to reduce emissions of sulphur ...** set out "to encourage the confinement of high polluting fuels to large installations equipped with tall chimneys ..".

The conclusion of this should not be that the traditional approaches to environmental management (the "end-of-pipe" approach) with subsidies for filter technology, licensing of plants, the building of municipal waterworks and sewers etc. is unnecessary. Quite to the contrary such policies are urgently needed in many third world countries and formerly planned economies. Indeed much of the material of this book deals with policies designed exactly to further such measures. We must however now start to face the fact that such policies may not actually suffice to deal neither with the purely national nor with the global environmental problems we face. These questions are particularly relevant for the transitional and developing countries who are already deeply concerned at the prospect of having to invest the very sizeable (but still maybe conceivable) resources to copy "clean Western" technology: but what if these Western technologies themselves are unsustainable - what if even more draconian measures are required?

2 RECONCILING GROWTH AND ENVIRONMENT

The human dilemma is now that we desperately need growth but uncontrolled economic growth may ruin the very basis for our survival. Arguments as to whether "growth" is positive or detrimental for "the environment" are already far too common. These debates are superficial, the important factor from an environmental standpoint is not the (average) rate of growth of GDP but its composition: the choice of production techniques and the relative importance of various sectors and activities.

There are broadly speaking two ways in which growth can be made more acceptable from an ecological point of view. Firstly technologies of production (and consumption) must be improved, in many cases by substitution of hazardous materials or processes by less dangerous ones. The second, and equally important mechanism, is that our patterns of consumption must be modified so that we avoid those products that degrade the environment or use very scarce environmental resources.[1]

To influence both the sectoral composition of the economy and the choice of production technologies with respect to scarce natural or environmental factors, the economist immediately thinks in terms of rising Hotelling prices: In some way society must find a way of communicating increasing natural resource and environmental scarcity to the economic agents. The trouble is often that there has traditionally been free access to a number of resources such as the seas and the atmosphere which now appear more limited. One obvious policy is to impose increasing taxes on various environmental services but even if regulation is done through some other mechanism, the effect will still have to be a rising cost for those who use natural resources.

As an example we can think of policies to reduce emissions of carbon dioxide in order to slow down global warming. Assume the atmosphere can only support x% of current emissions and the income elasticity of fossil fuel combustion (for heating, industry and transportation) is α while the corresponding price elasticity is β (which is usually smaller in absolute size). Then present growth levels for the overall economy can only be maintained if specific fuel use (per unit of GDP) can be reduced more than proportionately. This could conceivably be done by many different policies but we conjecture that all of them would in some sense imply higher costs to the user. Basically the real price of fossil fuels must increase immediately by P% in order to bring down consumption to x% of present levels. If we then assume economic growth of g% per year we also need an additional, permanent, yearly increase of q% in real fuel prices in order to counteract the effect of growth and high income elasticity. The required price increases P and q are given in (1-2)[2], see Sterner (1990).

(1) $$(1 + 0.01P)^{\beta} = (1 - 0.01x)$$

(2) $$(1 + 0.01q)^{\beta}(1 + 0.01g)^{\alpha} = 1$$

Environmental economics often analyses cases when the resource concerned has no owner and it may even be inconceivable to have an owner. The establishment of "property rights" for global commons must then be taken to mean the implementation of international agreements on policies such as taxes or tradeable emission permits that ensure a sustainable intertemporal allocation of this resource.

---

[1] And when we speak here, of degrading the environment, we naturally refer to the whole life-cycle of production, through use to disposal.

[2] With income and price elasticities of 1.1 and -0.8 respectively a 70% emission target **would require a 56% immediate price hike** ($1.56^{-0.8} = 0.7$). If income grows at 2% we would need a **further annual price rise of 2.76%** since $(1.0276^{-0.8})(1.02^{1.1}) = 1.0$. Note that the scarce "resource" here is neither oil nor oxygen but "absence of excess carbon dioxide in the atmosphere".

3 ENVIRONMENTAL POLICY INSTRUMENTS

Experience with environmental policy making is rapidly increasing due to increased application in various countries. The scope of the policies we have at our disposal is also being widened and now ranges from the rather obvious and basic to some very sophisticated schemes. It may be convenient to think of these as four different layers.

Starting at the basic end, *information* is actually the most essential element of all policy making and in fact the requirements as to its accuracy, timeliness and appropriateness are daunting. The policy makers and the researchers that advise them have an urgent need for exact, swift, detailed and scientifically correct data, but in addition to this the decision makers in companies and their technicians have their specific information needs. Finally it is also vital that the public has access to sufficiently detailed - and yet understandable - information to provide the electoral support without which no policies would be possible. The metering and monitoring equipment necessary is often fairly expensive which implies that in many countries with little prior experience, the first priority must be to raise the funds (perhaps through inspection fees or very modest taxes) to acquire the necessary equipment and to man the necessary organizations for environmental protection. These are needed in order to investigate local problems, set priorities and provide information to foster a democratic debate on environmental issues.

Another very fundamental arena for policy making is the creation of institutions and rules for the economy and this applies equally to property rights and codes of civil law on the one hand to specific institutions on the other; such as insurance systems, courts, environmental or health protection agencies and so forth. Although we can never in practice allocate all the "perfect" property rights that some textbook theories would suggest (to the air, water quality, silence, fish, birds etc.), experience has shown clearly that the absolute lack of appropriate property institutions can cause incentives for massive environmental disruption as has been witnessed for instance in both Soviet and Amazonian forestry.

However, experience shows that the governing of local commons is an area in which state involvement in general is very inappropriate. There was a time when people used to lament the "tragedy of the commons" concluding that private ownership is the only solution while common property appeared as synonymous with waste. This fails to explain how people have actually managed to use certain local common property resources sustainably in some cases, for many centuries. In fact it is free access that leads to "overgrazing" not common property as such since management of the latter may well be ruled by very strict and complex codes of conduct. The allegory of the commons is still very relevant to our predicament. The trouble is not really common property rights but simply lack of property rights to such things that have always seemed abundant and self evident - such as clean water, forests or even air. With Ostrom (1990) we believe that neither privatization nor state control is the general panacea for the commons. Often enough the only appropriate solution is through self-governance. Ostrom shows convincingly that the administrative and transaction costs for monitoring, control, allocation of work and distribution of benefits may be much lower in local self-governing, traditional, institutions than in either state-controlled or private-property type solutions.

The above applies to local commons. We are now coming up against limits for what are often called the global commons such as the oceans and the atmosphere. In these cases we can hardly rely on traditional mechanisms but when trying to devise new mechanisms such as international treaties, we can possibly learn from the experience of long-lasting local institutions.

Our third layer of policy making concerns the direct set of regulations which must be the basis of every attempt at regulating and improving environmental conditions. The whole area of environmental protection actually comprises an enormous diversity of issues from the many health hazard issues to nature and animal protection, forestry, fishing and agricultural practices to the whole energy field and various "global" issues such as the greenhouse effect which do not readily fit into the above (although they do have a bearing on health and other issues). In each of these areas we expect to find market failures with respect to various environmental factors and thus there will be a need for a good deal of detailed regulation.

It is only when we get to the fourth layer of policy instruments that we actually discuss the policy instruments normally associated with environmental economics: firstly taxes, charges or subsidies levied with respect to emissions, ambient levels or simply products, secondly various kinds of marketable pollution permit or deposit-refund schemes and then other forms of market creation or market influencing mechanisms such as liability insurance schemes. Finally we should also remember that government does not only influence the economy through this type of instruments which are all designed to affect the behaviour of other agents in the economy: Governments' perhaps most powerful tool is through the direct use of economic resources, through public spending and investments for example in infrastructure such as roads, railways, telecommunications and also research etc.

The exact design of policy instruments for different environmental problems may in fact be quite complicated; thus "tax-differentiation", "credit-subsidy" or "tax-holiday" mechanisms are sometimes described as separate instruments although they are rather obvious extensions of standard instruments such as taxes and subsidies. There are multiple criteria for the choice of policy instruments: static and dynamic efficiency, transaction and administrative costs, equity, fairness, "Polluters Pay" and income distributional effects, sensitivity to underestimates of environmental damage and the presence of irreversible effects, flexibility in the face of change and so forth. Many real-World problems require a combination of policy instruments including ordinary regulations, subsidies, taxes, charges and Tradeable Emission Permits (TEPs). The design of policy instruments to satisfy the criteria mentioned above has indeed evolved into a fine art that requires a detailed understanding not only of the environmental problems but also of the ecological system and its variation in time and space as well as of the social and economic context[3].

One traditional controversy over environmental policies concerns the use of quantity or price instruments to regulate economic activities. Generally academic

---

[3] The phasing out of CFCs is an interesting example of how different layers of policy instruments can be combined. First the international community agrees on a physical phase-out (percentage reductions at various dates) leaving each country to choose instruments. The US has chosen to use tradeable emission permits but found that in the process windfall gains are being produced and so the TEPs have been supplemented with taxes, see Chapter 2.

economists have emphasized the superior efficiency of market instruments and only conceded a role for physical constraints in rather special circumstances (for instance when the damage function is very steep, when damages occur stochastically over time or space or for monopolies). Actual practice is, however, only recently turning to the use of economic instruments and then as a complement to, not a replacement for regulations. In some countries there is still a compact resistance against them and the reasons for this remain an important area of research. Apparently transaction costs, incentive effects and moral perceptions of rights are more complex than first realized. The choice of policy instrument furthermore depends crucially on both the institutional setting of the country involved and on the exact nature of the environmental problem at hand. As we will see in several chapters the tradeoffs may be particularly complicated in developing or transitional economies.

4 OUTLINE OF THE BOOK

After this introductory chapter the book starts off with two chapters intended to give the reader a flavour of the industrialized country experience. For this purpose we have chosen the USA and Sweden, two countries that have both been fairly early in implementing environmental policies although in different areas and with different policy instruments. One notable difference is in the pioneering of tradeable emission permits in the US and the reliance on environmental taxes in Sweden.

Chapters 4-7 describe the environmental situation and analyze policies in a number of transitional (formerly planned) economies of the East. We start, naturally, with the former USSR itself and then move in Chapter 5 to Poland which is a country that appears to be combining a fairly swift and successful transition to market economics with a rather ambitious environmental program. Chapter 6 gives an overview of the smaller, more fragile and still very dependent Baltic states and 7 concentrates on the design of policy instruments in Estonia which gives some interesting insights into the difficulties inherent in the introduction of market-like policy instruments in a planned economy.

The next block of chapters, from 8 to 15 focus more on the developing country experience. Some of these are country monographs describing different aspects of the environmental situation and environmental policies in a diverse range of countries, from the poor and agricultural Tanzania (Chapter 8) to the slightly wealthier but still agricultural Uruguay (Chapter 9), the industrializing, heavily polluted oil exporter Mexico (Chapter 10) and finally to the giant China (Chapter 12) which is both an LDC and a "transitional" economy at the same time.

Some of our chapters broadly cover all the general environmental policies in a country while others concentrate on one particular dimension related in some way to energy, forestry or land use. This applies for instance to Chapter 12 on environmental aspects of Chinese energy policy and Chapter 9 which explores the energy and forestry policies designed to meet a pending fuelwood shortage in Uruguay. Chapter 11 provides a survey of policy implications of deforestation in a number of African countries. Chapter 13 discusses the policy implications of acid rain in Asia; Chapter 14 covers environmental regulation of transport vehicles following how legislation and policy instruments to deal with vehicle emissions spread across the globe, from Japan and California to Europe and various developing countries, primarily in L America and SE Asia. Chapter 15 is even broader, at least geographically, since it in principle covers all the LDCs, concentrating on energy and in particular on the electricity sector.

Finally the last two chapters are more global. Chapter 16 discusses the design and implementation of policy instruments to come to grips with global climate change and Chapter 17 discusses the experiences of gasoline taxation in various countries which presumably will be one of the concrete ways of implementing any global policy for reduction of carbon emissions.

5 THE "WESTERN" EXPERIENCE

Since the use of economic policy instruments as a means towards environmental goals was initiated in the industrialized market economies, it is natural to start with an overview of their experience. According to the OECD (1992) the use of economic instruments is most widespread in the US, Sweden, Norway, Denmark and the Netherlands[4]. Chapters 2 and 3 survey the first two of these countries which share many basic aspects of their efforts at environmental protection, but still have rather opposite experience with respect to economic policy instruments. Presumably the most important innovation from US experience is the use of Tradeable Emission Permits (TEPs). One of the reasons why the TEPs are such a major breakthrough is because they show how the cost saving potential of the market can be harnessed even within quite a strict quantity-based control regime. In other countries TEPs have so far found little use but there is a similar program in Germany where neighbouring companies can agree jointly to implement pollution reductions and TEPs are being given serious consideration for domestic policies in Poland (see Chapter 5) and for global issues such as climate change (Chapter 16). For the first time, they are also being considered in Sweden (although, admittedly, only for a single isolated application). In the US, on the other hand, tax proposals have a very hard time getting accepted and there are only a few exceptions such as the tax on ozone-depleting chemicals (halons and CFCs). The resistance to Clinton's proposed fuel tax (in 1993) was so considerable that the final tax increase is only a fraction of the original proposal. However it is worthy of notice that at the time of writing, the financing of his health reforms appears to imply a major increase in tobacco tax.

In other countries where economic policy instruments are used, various forms of tax, charge, subsidy and deposit-refund are the most commonly used instruments. The case of Sweden is fairly typical for the group of countries that have been keen on introducing these more fiscal instruments. In these countries, subsidies are generally regarded with some caution but still quite common both with respect to industrial and municipal clean-up, particularly of sites contaminated by historic emissions or when there is no obviously responsible "polluter" who can pay (as with long-distance transboundary pollution). Sometimes new technology that is cleaner or more energy efficient has been subsidized as is the case with insulation of housing, or the introduction of catalytic converters, for instance in the Netherlands and the Nordic countries, etc.

---

[4] According to the same source, economic policy instruments are used the least in the UK, Japan, Switzerland, Canada and Italy.

Deposit-refund systems are typically used for beverage and food containers, bottles and cans but there are some other interesting applications such as deposit-refunds for car hulks in Sweden. Other examples include certain older types of lamps in Austria and lubricating oils, batteries, plastics etc. in several countries . Deposit-refunds can in principle be used to ensure the return of any noxious substances such as cadmium from batteries etc. There is even an example of refundable "reforestation deposits" in Malaysia.

Charges are particularly used for wastewater discharge but increasingly their use is being considered for solid wastes and air-borne emissions. Industrial emissions are often subject to control or inspection charges mainly intended to finance public control itself. With respect to energy and transport related emissions, it is quite common to use product charges, and taxes on the goods or services (such as petroleum products) that are identified as problematic or even on complementary goods (such as "gas-guzzling" cars) instead of directly taxing the emissions (such as CO_2 or NO_x). In an even more indirect manner it is also quite common to use subsidies or tax differentiation etc. for substitutes such as "alternative" sources of energy (windpower, eolic power, solar energy etc.), public transport and so forth. Thus product charges and taxes are more common than emission taxes in spite of the fact that the latter deal more directly with the negative externalities (emissions) concerned. However up till now the greater administrative simplicity of product charges appears to have been decisive. Among the products most commonly taxed in the OECD countries we particularly find fossil fuels including lead in gasoline and sometimes sulphur in fuel, waste oil, NO_x and VOC (Volatile Organic Compounds) etc. Turning to other areas of the environment we find taxes on pesticides, fertilizers, packaging materials, plastics, wastes (hazardous and household) and water, CFCs/halons and even, in a few countries, on (aircraft) noise (in the form of differentiated landing fees), gravel, sand and other building materials and so forth.

Recently there has also been quite an increased interest in the use of environmental or green taxes as part of a general tax reform. In the past, many natural resources or environmental services have either been provided at very low cost or even free by the state. Examples include water, electricity, refuse collection and so forth. It is becoming quite evident that such zero or low flat rate pricing does not provide the individual with correct incentives for environmentally responsible behaviour. The state and local governments are now beginning in many countries to levy charges that more closely reflect marginal social costs for this type of service or good. By green taxes, we however refer to something rather more far-reaching than the ordinary Pigouvian taxes which are intended to correct for externalities. The idea (see for instance the seminal article by Sandmo 1975) is that all forms of taxation imply excess burden of some kind and in an economy which needs to finance a state (in other words, in all real economies) optimal taxes on pollution should be much higher than the compensatory (Pigouvian) level because taxing pollution is an excellent way of helping finance joint consumption (the state) at a lower allocative cost than other forms of taxation. The latest tax reform in Sweden when high marginal tax rates on income were reduced in exchange for increased environmental taxes did at least partly apply these principles.

If one doubts of the efficiency of economic policy instruments it should suffice to look at the evidence from gasoline taxation, Chapter 17. There are very substantial differences in tax level, and consumer price of gasoline between countries, both in the OECD and in developing countries. Although this is only to a small degree due to explicit environmental policies, it can be analyzed *as if* it were a result of such policies. Dahl and Sterner (1991) show that gasoline demand is indeed more sensitive to consumer price (as well as to income) than many observers seem to believe, with long run price elasticities not too far from -1. The significance of this is illustrated in Sterner et al (1992) which shows that total OECD carbon emissions from transport use of gasoline could vary by a factor 1:3 depending on the tax rate adopted.

6 POLICY MEASURES IN TRANSITIONAL ECONOMIES

The formerly planned economies which we will refer to as transitional are of considerable importance in the context of environmental policy analysis because they are heavily polluted and because each new institutional setting and each type of economic condition requires us to analyze anew the optimal design of policy instruments. It is interesting to note that in some cases (see Chapter 4 and 7 on the USSR and Estonia respectively) at least the experts had quite an early awareness of environmental problems and very sophisticated mechanisms were designed including taxes on emissions that were differentiated by type of pollutant and by the ecological sensitivity of the area affected. This was, however, all make-believe paperwork and in reality there was no enforcement at all - in fact, there was often no monitoring of pollution at all. Even if there had been payments the system of "soft budgets" made all such charges or taxes irrelevant to management since it did not affect the fulfillment of plans, the "profits" or other indicators that management really cared about. The overriding concern was always with plan targets and although the Soviets enacted numerous environmental laws, created environmental bodies high up in the political and administrative hierarchy and used environmental policy instruments, in the end physical production goals always seemed to dominate. There were simply no incentives for cleaner production. One of the fundamental reasons may have been the absence of sufficiently free and informed public debate and press.

In fact, as pointed out by Salay in Chapter 6, centralization went so far that responsibility at the level of the enterprise was not clearly defined. The enterprises were legally subordinate to the ministries who had the ultimate power and thus responsibility. It could thus be hard to judge, in many concrete cases, who should be held accountable for environmental damage - the enterprise or the ministry. The system provides a sadly clear illustration of the importance of property rights. Since natural resources (all of them - not just esoteric ones like clean air, but even forests, water and raw materials for energy) lacked ownership and were allocated to households and enterprises as "free goods", overuse was quite uncontrolled.

These countries cannot just adopt the now so popular market mechanisms when there is no underlying legal and control structure on which to build. All Western economies have built up the bulk of their environmental control on physical regulations and are now looking to introduce some degree of market-type flexibility basically to reduce compliance costs. Hughes (1991) suggests the East European countries will imitate this 30 years of experience and that they should expect, with some patience, to be equally (if not more) successful in reducing the environmental hot-spots that now characterize Eastern Europe (such as the Katowize and Krakow area) as Western countries were in dealing with, for instance, the London smog.

Hughes probably has a very important point when he argues against the worst catastrophe scenarios for Eastern Europe (by comparing them to already solved problems in the West), because exaggeration of the already difficult situation is not likely to help. However, in some respects, the Eastern economies face a tougher economic and political situation within which to carry out these environmental improvements. Furthermore we have, as already mentioned above, the worry that simply imitating the West may not be enough - particularly not with respect to various global problems.

The transitional countries today face extremely severe difficulties of simultaneously providing fairly rapid economic growth to satisfy the (sometimes unrealistic) aspirations of the electorate, and at the same time cleaning up after decades of mismanagement. The difficulties are compounded by the very structure of these economies with their bias towards large centralized units of heavy industry. As shown in Chapters 6 and 7 the smaller countries, for instance of the Baltic, tend to have extremely lopsided industrial structures which are practically unmanageable in isolation. Even the bigger economies, including Russia, are so marked by centralization and the (probably futile) quest for economies of scale, that there is often only one single company or even plant in each branch that serves a vast geographical region. This implies, of course, that privatization will not automatically result in a market economy but just a set of private monopolists which will turn out to be all the more powerful since they often occupy very dominating positions not only sectorally but also in regional labour markets and so forth.

These giant companies, producing energy, steel, machine tools, transport equipment etc. are used to "administration through negotiation" and an essential element in the transition to a market economy is that this type of behaviour is discontinued in favour of general rules and legislation to be followed by all. If companies do not feel that they are ultimately responsible for their own fate, but can always turn to ministries to solve economic problems then the economy will still be stuck with "soft budget constraints" and in essence policy instruments will have little incentive effect.

In Chapter 5, Żylicz, raises some very fundamental criticisms against the undue enthusiasm some of his compatriots show for economic instruments in general and environmental taxes in particular. These points are presumably equally relevant in the context of all the transitional economies and to some extent for a number of developing countries as well.

One of these criticisms against the undue reliance on economic instruments has been mentioned above. When the authorities lack physical control and even capacity to measure or monitor pollution then economic instruments are pointless. A first set of prerequisites is a market economy with properly allocated private property rights and public authorities that have the means and authority to impose standards, control emissions and enforce sanctions. Then, as is well known from the literature in environmental economics, there are still a great number of conditions under which physical restrictions will be preferred to economic policies. One such condition is when the environmental damage curve is steeper than the cost of abatement curve which implies that the potential cost of errors in the environmental tax can be very expensive (compared to mistakes in the emissions standards), see Weitzmann (1974) or a standard textbook such as Baumol & Oates (1988). Another condition is when variations due to geography or other variables such as time of day or year, height, velocity, weather etc. are crucial for the environmental impact. Under such conditions environmental taxes are generally thought of as being far too inflexible and direct regulations are, again, preferred.

Żylicz also argues strongly in favour of the advantages of TEPs compared to environmental taxes. The main advantage, in a transitional setting, seems to be that the true Pigouvian taxes (set equal to marginal abatement costs at the target level of pollution) would bring most of the polluting companies to immediate bankruptcy. They would thus either ruin the economy or end up being considered as unrealistic thus discrediting the whole environmental policy (and bringing us back into the realm of the earlier discretionary policies) if the companies manage to get their tax payments waived or deferred.

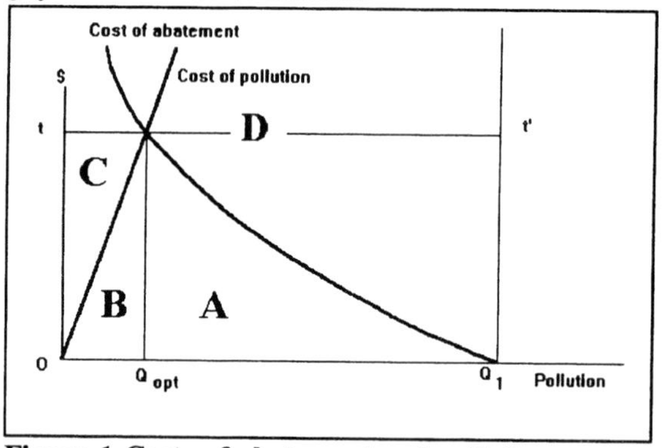

Figure 1 Costs of abatement and pollution.

There are actually two dilemmas, one of distributional effects and one of timing. Starting with the distributional or equity issue, illustrated in Figure 1, we see that the polluting company causes considerable damage to society through its pollution (the costs of which D, may considerably outweigh the cost of abatement, A) and consequently pollution ought to be cut back from Q_1 to Q_{opt}. There is no disagreement (in principle) that the firm should pay most of the pollution abatement costs A. This is the minimum interpretation of the Polluter Pays Principle. The idea of the Pigouvian tax t is that they will do this automatically in their own self interest. However, if they have trouble finding the finance for the cost A, they may simply have no chance to find the money to pay the tax B+C in addition. Obviously the relative sizes of A and B+C depends on the assumptions made about abatement and damage costs. In some examples B+C may be relatively small so that the problem does not arise. However, in other cases B+C may be very sizeable and in fact if abatement takes a long time, then the initial tax will be $OQ_1t't$ which is even more than B+C.

Of course one could say that if the company cannot support its full social costs (including environmental ones) then it should indeed be closed down. There are, however, numerous problems with this approach. Firstly it is not likely to gather political support. We could interpret this by saying that the costs associated with an excessive decrease in employment outweigh all the other factors in our analysis. Secondly we might observe that our argument above is strictly speaking only true for the cost A+B. The part of the tax corresponding to C is actually not a payment for a social cost but just an excess tax[5]. Finally, we should see the problem of abatement costs in a dynamic perspective which brings us to the issue of timing.

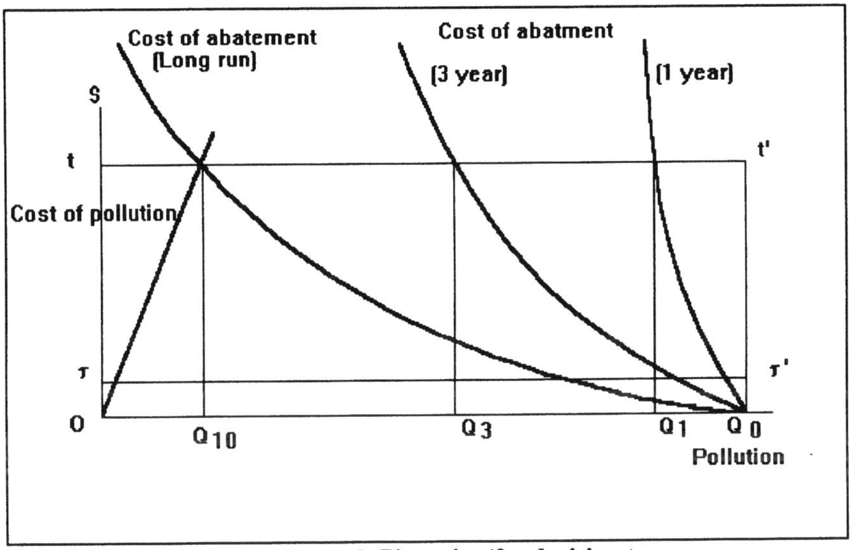

Figure 2 Long run abatement & Pigouvian/fundraising taxes.

As shown in Figure 2, it may very well be the case that pollution abatement is prohibitively expensive in the short run but affordable in the longer run. In this case it could clearly be premature to cause an immediate closedown of the plant - what it needs is instead a realistic timetable within which to clean up its pollution to required levels. The policy instruments chosen in the Polish content seem to focus on realistic emission permits which in some cases may be made tradeable (TEPs) to further stimulate least cost pollution abatement strategies and innovations. This can, as in Poland, be combined with subsidies for abatement technology, These subsidies come from specialized funds which in their turn are financed by pollution charges. The charges (although fairly high by international standards) are far from the Pigouvian level t. Pigouvian taxes at this level would be clearly uncollectible but we note that, since initial pollution levels are so extremely high, this implies that even quite moderate tax levels such as τ can generate very considerable funds that actually can play a significant role in the financing of abatement. As an example Tiit Kallaste writes in his chapter on Estonia that the environmental tax is decided not by pollution costs but by the funds currently needed for abatement!

Although taxes have a number of inherent problems TEPs also have their disadvantages. For instance if grandfathered (as is current practice in the US) they benefit already existing companies, who may use their permits as barriers to entry for new firms (this risk would seem to be acute in the case of heavily monopolized

[5] On the other hand, this extra cost is quite analogous to the corresponding extra costs paid for water, land, labour or on any other market. In many cases it is of little concern and often overlooked.

economies). Furthermore there is the problem of how to finance pollution abatement (and indeed the more general problem of excess burden when searching for other sources of taxation). Grandfathered permits also fail to fulfill the Polluters Pay Principle. However, a certain number of permits might initially be grandfathered and later additions auctioned. Various mixed forms of policy instruments are also conceivable and may in fact be very useful. Note also that the problem of the unaffordabilitiy of the Pigouvian tax could be solved by allowing a certain amount of pollution "for free" (or at a low tax rate) but charging the full Pigouvian tax at the margin (since it is the marginal level which affects behaviour). This is rather like the idea of social tariffs for electricity used in some countries. Effectively these suggestions amount to the imposition of a step-shaped tariff structure. Note, however, that this is equivalent to granting a limited number of (grandfathered) emission rights and then charging a Pigouvian tax as the fee for noncompliance (ie pollution in excess of permits). All this goes to show that TEPs and charges can be modified and combined in many ways. There is not necessarily such a clearcut distinction between them. Our discussion has, however, hopefully made clear the importance of careful reflection on the full consequences of various policy instruments before any final choice is made. The implementation of any rapid but simple-minded policies may be extremely dangerous.

7 POLICY MEASURES IN DEVELOPING COUNTRIES

Turning to the developing countries we find a large number of similarities, most LDCs and particularly the ones with a more or less socialist orientation, share the bureaucratic allocation mechanisms, soft budgets and other characteristics described in the formerly planned economies. Depending on the type of economic system, some of them also share the ensuing inefficiency. However, there are also enormous differences between the transitional countries and the LDCs and among the latter countries themselves. The "newly industrializing" countries of SE Asia and Latin America share the pollution problems (but not necessarily all the inefficiency) with Eastern Europe. On the other hand many countries for instance in Africa share the inefficiency but have relatively little industrial pollution: Their environmental problems are more concerned with the basic management of sensitive natural resources such as soil, water, forest cover and biodiversity. Their top priorities focus on food, drinking water, energy, sanitation and shelter. Often their economies are organized around raw material extraction either in the form of oil and minerals or export agriculture. These sectors can be very disruptive for the environment as is the case with, for instance, salt production from areas that are dominated by sensitive mangrove ecosystems. This example from Tanzania is taken from Chapter 8 which also describes how even the relatively minute industries such as textiles in this country can pose severe environmental threats because of the complete lack of resources for abating, controlling or even monitoring pollution. If industrial pollution in the classic sense is somewhat less prevalent in most LDCs, natural resource problems related to food, water, health and so forth are often more serious compared to the transitional countries and the same obviously goes for the general economic situation since most of the latter countries do have considerably greater economic resources.

There are now a number of industrializing countries in Latin America (for instance Chile and Mexico) and in Asia (Singapore, Honk Kong, Malaysia and so forth) that are striving quite actively (in at least some areas) to adopt modern environmental regulations and even to experiment with modern economic instruments (such as road tolls, differentiated tax for leaded/unleaded gasoline or for different types of vehicle and various schemes for area pricing of traffic). Chapter 14 describes in some detail the spread of auto emission controls. There are conceivably several reasons for new countries to adopt modern controls including a desire to integrate as quickly as possible into the industrialized World (and to this end it can be appropriate to set ambitious technological standards) coupled with high levels of population density and in some cases extreme pollution. It is just possible that these countries might be able to benefit from experience in the West and avoid some pitfalls in environmental regulation by immediately going in for market based policy instruments. Some developing countries seem very pragmatically to be adopting Western vehicle emission standards, generally with a 5 or 10 year lag, which presumably is a cheap, effective and quick way of deciding on regulations instead of going through the painstaking work of designing new regulations in each country - regulations that furthermore run the risk of acting as future trade barriers.

In the poorer LDCs, however, the use of economic instruments for environmental policy as such is still quite rare. There is, however, an increased awareness of the importance of getting incentives right. Gradually, outrageously overvalued currencies and extremely cheap energy are being abolished. The worst cases of perverse incentives (as in Brazil when you had to burn down the forest in order to claim it, see Binzwanger (1989)) have also received attention. Still, we note in Chapter 8 that land in Tanzania is state property and only leased to individuals or groups. Obviously such leases do not generally give the security of tenure needed for long term investments and there is now a growing understanding of the need for more security in property rights.

Another important area of progress is in project evaluation where environmental (as well as social) impacts are receiving greater attention. Chapters 8,11 and 12 show that for many of the developing countries, environmental policy making entails some very difficult choices in the area of energy, agriculture and forestry. In the oil-importing countries, the market forces have, themselves, since 1973 tended to reduce energy waste and induce a substitution for oil of waste, biomass and other non-conventional energy supplies. Often enough however, the general lack of resources may imply that these options in themselves imply other sets of problems such as deforestation. It is therefore essential to combine energy and environmental policies with suitable policies in agriculture and forestry, see Chapter 9 on Uruguay for an apparently positive experience along these lines.

Ironically we may find that countries such as Uruguay where forests are badly needed for energy and raw materials will look after them better and thus have less deforestation (and more afforestation) than countries such as Mexico where oil abundance implies that forests are not quite as "necessary" for fuelwood and where cattle ranching is steadily being extended to the detriment of forests. As Chapter 10 shows Mexico is a country that is privileged at least as far as energy is concerned and Mexico is one of the prime examples of the costs, not just environmental but social and economic of subsidized energy, oil-boom and "Dutch disease". Recently, however, Mexico is becoming pressed into taking environmental issues more and more actively into account. The prime force behind this is the severity of environmental problems in Mexico City and other centres. However, there are also other forces such as the North American Free Trade Association (with the US and Canada) that inevitably imply a force towards harmonization of environmental (as well as other) legislations.

It is extremely hard to generalize about environmental policies and the potential use of economic policy instruments since not only the character of the countries' economies but also of their ecological conditions vary so considerably. However, a few general principles would seem to apply both to the transitional and developing countries alike:

The first requirement for a successful environmental policy is to have the appropriate technical (and ecological) knowledge in order to analyze the problems and formulate the appropriate alternatives technically. This knowledge must to some extent be shared between the government agencies, the polluting enterprises and the general public in order to foster a democratic debate on alternatives and priorities.

Secondly the economy as such must to some reasonable extent be characterized by competitive markets for economic incentives to work and waste to be avoided. Although state involvement is indeed heavily needed in the formulation and implementation of environmental policies, it is also important to emphasize that unnecessary state intervention in the actual running of many economic activities can have very detrimental effects both economically and for the environment, see for instance, Chapter 15 which describes the counterproductive state influence on the electricity sector in many LDCs. State dominance here, just like in the formerly planned economies removes any local accountability and thus weakens incentives for environmentally responsible management.

Thirdly, there must be an appropriate legal structure and set of institutions that define property rights and establish the framework within which an environmental authority can function. The political leadership must have the electoral backing, as well as the financial and legal means to implement the most efficient policy instruments possible with respect to the individual conditions of the country. In order to do this and build up institutions with the necessary power and integrity, an initial, moderate taxation (see Section 6 and the discussion related to Figure 2) of natural resources and pollution specifically designated for the build-up of these institutions may be an appropriate first step.

At a later stage, the type of green tax reform discussed in Section 5 might also be particularly relevant for many Third World countries where people are not likely to fill in detailed tax forms (as in Sweden) about their income and where most finance ministers are desperate to find anything to tax[6]. Currently many LDCs subsidize roads, dams, fuel and many other goods which at least in some cases are closely related to serious pollution. Considering that these countries also need to subsidize health care, education, staple foods and many other more urgent items and have nothing to tax there is a strong case for including the concept of green taxation in the

[6] The poor are too poor to tax and it is hard to tax the rich or "capital" or profits because you want to attract investors. Nor can you tax imports for fear of distortions. The only ideal taxables are luxury goods such as perfume but they do not make much of a tax base.

tax reform process going on in many countries.

It is however crucial that environmental policies are properly designed with respect to both environmental, fiscal and distributional or social effects. The finding, in Chapter 8, that one of the few instances of an economic instrument was the tax exemption on electric cookers "to diversify to electricity as an alternative source of electricity" is clearly worrying. The marginal electricity will in Tanzania often be inefficiently produced with imported oil and consumed by the relatively wealthy consumers so the environmental or other gains are not all that clear!

8 GLOBAL ENVIRONMENTAL POLICIES

We have up to now concentrated on local (or regional/national) environmental problems. However, as we suggested through the citation of Jernelöv in Section 1, there is a tendency for environmental problems to go from the local to the national and then global arena. As shown in Chapter 13 intra country problems of acid rain are becoming quite a major problem throughout large parts of Asia. Very often the "solving" of a local environmental problem entails moving it away or creating another type of environmental problem further away, see also Sterner (1992). If environmental policy making with the allocation of property rights and selection and implementation of appropriate policy instruments is difficult on the local or national scale it is not going to be easier on a global scale.

For global issues we inevitably need truly global agreements. As pointed out by Grubb in Chapter 16, the very size of the environmental problems and the costs they entail as well as the difficult issues of distribution of costs and benefits make it essential that we make use of the most effective policy instruments available. Obviously it is particularly important that the OECD countries themselves take the lead in this policy implementation precisely because they are the leading market economies and furthermore since they are often the major sources of emissions. It is essential that the OECD countries themselves start with a much more convincing effort to apply effective policy instruments including green taxes, Tradeable Emission Permits, new Deposit Refund schemes and to encourage the build-up of institutions to manage common property resources.

Naturally the implementation of effective policies is also needed in Third World countries but in these cases we should distinguish very carefully between local or national problems on the one hand and global ones on the other hand. For global problems this implementation should be accompanied by massive resource transfers from North to South. The reason for this is that these transfers can be seen as a "purchase" of environmental services by the North from the South. The rich countries of the North are objectively more likely to be affected and worried by, for instance, skin cancer from increased ultra violet radiation due to a thinner ozone layer, while many inhabitants in the South are naturally more interested in access to cheap refrigeration. This is an unusually clear example since the ozone hole appears most serious over the poles, since ultraviolet radiation is more dangerous to people of light colored skin and cancer is more of a risk to those with a long expected life. However, the main argument will apply, with varying strength, to most long-run global problems simply because they are problems we in the North want to solve while people in the South have other and more immediately pressing priorities. This has the important implication that financial transfers related to these environmental problems should be seen as "purchases" of environmental services and thus in no way be mixed up with development assistance.

For local environmental problems, however, such as access to clean water and sanitation, the situation is quite different. As already mentioned above many LDCs and transitional economies are currently implementing environmental policies in these areas and for instance for vehicle emission control. Here the implementation of environmental policies is directly in the material interests of the local population and there is not the same reason for side payments from the richer countries. The design of these instruments and the financing of related projects can thus be part of "ordinary" development assistance. Just as one can build dams or industries so aid can be used to conserve biodiversity, create conditions for sustainable fisheries, agriculture or provide better drinking water or cleaner urban air. These are all very important areas that should be seen as integral parts of development assistance as long as the main beneficiaries are the local people. Similar examples include soil conservation, water management, sanitation and so forth. Quite a number of development agencies including the World Bank and many national donor agencies such as SIDA in Sweden are heavily increasing their involvement with environmental issues and natural resources. They are also including assistance in the build-up of suitable institutions and policies for the environmental area including systems of green taxation or common property management. Naturally all this is subject to the usual condition that the recipient countries agree that these are areas of priority.

Quite often we find technical connections between local and global environmental issues. Global warming, energy use, smog and urban pollution go at least partly hand in hand. As Foell shows, increased fuel efficiency in China is probably more effective than direct sulphur scrubbing etc. for abatement of the acid rain precursors in China. At the same time China's use of coal is one of the major issues for global warming in the future.

When global and national environmental issues are interlinked in this way, it becomes all the more natural for the richer nations to commit themselves to assisting in programmes to deal with environmental threats in the poorer countries. In some fortunate cases efforts to deal with a global problem will have additional local benefits on the side and vice versa. As we will discuss in the last two chapters however, there are still many substantial hurdles to be overcome. Although the convening of the Rio conference was a step forward in itself, the actual agreements reached show that the World Community is not quite prepared for any major steps. The GEF (Global Environmental Facility)[7] definitely is an interesting tool. It may be seen as a global transfer of resources for environmental services partly along the lines discussed above but it is still on quite a limited scale compared to what will be needed in the future.

---

[7] For a further discussion of the various problems related to GEF and to Debt-for Nature Swaps, another interesting mechanism in this connection, see Köhlin & Sterner (1992). As with all projects, the essentials of good, individual, project appraisal and solid local participation at all stages must never be forgotten.

REFERENCES

Baumol, W.J. and W. E. Oates. 1988 . *The theory of environmental Policy*, 2nd ed, Cambridge University Press.

Binzwanger, H.P. 1989."Brazilian Policies that Encourage Deforestation in the Amazon", *World Bank Working paper no 16.*

Dahl, C. and T. Sterner. 1991. "Analyzing Gasoline Demand Elasticities", *Energy Economics,* vol. 13, no. 3, July.

Daly, H.E. and J.B. Cobb. 1989. *For the Common Good*, Beacon Press, Boston.

Hughes, G. 1991. "Are the Costs of Cleaning up Eastern Europe Exaggerated?", *Oxford Revue of Economic Policy*, vol. 7, no. 4.

Jenelöv, A. 1989. "Ecology and Environmental Politics", (in Swedish), *Värdera Miljön,* ed L. Bergman, SNS, Stockholm.

Köhlin, G. and T. Sterner. 1992. "Making the Rich Pay for the Global Environment", Presented at the Cracow Conference of the EEARE, July.

OECD 1974. "Resource Managment: Air. Guidelines for actions to reduce emissions of sulphur dioxides and particulate matter from fuel combustion in stationary sources", C(74)16 adopted 18 June.

OECD 1991. "Recent Developments in the Use of Economic Instruments", *Environment Monograph* no 41, February.

OECD 1992. *Taxation and Environment: Final Report*, Paris 29 December.

Ostrom, E. 1990. *Governing the Commons. The Evolution of Institutions for Collective Action,* Cambridge University Press.

Sandmo, A. 1975. "Environmental Taxation", *Scandinavian Journal of Economics.*

Sterner, T. 1990. *The Pricing and Demand for Gasoline,* ISBN 91-87246-57-0. Swedish Transport Research Board, Stockholm, May.

Sterner, T, C Dahl and M Franzén. 1992. "Global Environmental Policies and Carbon Emissions", *Journal of Transport and Economic Policy*, May.

Sterner, T. 1992. "Economic and Environmental Policies for Sustainability" in *Society and the Environment: A Swedish Perspective*, eds., Svedin, U. and B. Aniansson, Kluwer.

Weitzmann, M. 1974. "Prices vs Quantities", *The Review of Economic Studies* XLI.

CHAPTER 2

Market-Based Mechanisms for Controlling Pollution: Lessons from the U.S.

by

Tom Tietenberg

Abstract

As recently as a decade ago environmental regulators and lobbying groups with a special interest in environmental protection looked upon the market system as a powerful adversary. That the market unleashed powerful forces was widely recognized and that those forces clearly acted to degrade the environment was widely lamented. Conflict and confrontation became the battle cry for those groups seeking to protect the environment as they set out to block market forces whenever possible.

Among the more enlightened participants in the environmental policy process, the air of confrontation and conflict has now begun to recede in many parts of the world. Leading environmental groups and regulators have come to realize that the power of the market can be harnessed and channeled toward the achievement of environmental goals, through an economic incentives approach to regulation. Forward-looking businessmen have come to appreciate the fact that cost-effective regulation can make them more competitive in the global marketplace than regulations which impose higher-than-necessary control costs.

As the world community becomes increasingly conscious of both the need to tighten environmental controls and the local economic perils associated with tighter controls in a highly competitive global marketplace, we can now summarize what we know about this promising approach to pollution control that may be especially relevant to current circumstances. This chapter draws upon economic theory and actual experience to provide a brief overview of some of the major lessons we have learned about one particular economic incentive approach -marketable emission permits- which has now been applied in the United States in a number of different settings.

T. Sterner (ed.), Economic Policies for Sustainable Development, 20–45.

1 INTRODUCTION

Beginning in 1975 burgeoning costs associated with the rigidities inherent in its traditional predominantly legal approach to controlling air pollution, led the U. S. Environmental Protection Agency (EPA) to begin experimenting with an economic incentive approach now known as the **Emissions Trading Program**, a limited version of a system of marketable emission permits. Since that time the marketable emission permit concept has been applied to several new areas of environmental policy and is currently being proposed for several more.

Support for the use of this market approach to environmental control has clearly grown in the United States, as reflected in the favorable treatment it has received both in the popular business (Main, 1988) and environmental (Stavins, 1989) press. Some public interest environmental organizations have even adopted economic incentive approaches as a core part of their strategy for protecting the environment.[1] It is also being adopted in Poland and is under active consideration by both the OECD and the United Nations Conference on Trade and Development as a strategy for controlling global warming.

The intellectual foundation for this policy is provided by the economic concept known as the marketable emission permit. Our knowledge about this particular form of control has grown rapidly in the two decades in which it has received serious analytical attention. Not only have the theoretical models become more focused and the empirical work more detailed, but we have now had over a decade of experience with a limited, but operational, version of this approach. It seems a propitious time to stand back and to organize what we have learned about this practical and promising approach to pollution control.

In this chapter I draw upon economic theory, empirical studies, and actual experience with implementing the various versions of marketable emission permit programs to provide a brief overview of some of the major lessons we have learned about this approach (Tietenberg, 1980; 1985; Dudek and Palmisano, 1988; Hahn and Hester, 1989). Some of the proposed applications will also be discussed. Extracting the lessons we have learned is helpful not only in exploring the relation between economic analysis and policy, but also in providing some idea of the problems and prospects faced by others having an interest in pursuing this approach.

2 THE POLICY CONTEXT

2.1 The Traditional Approach

Stripped to its bare essentials, the U.S. approach to pollution control relies upon a **command-and-control** approach to controlling pollution. Ambient standards, which establish the highest allowable concentration of the pollutant in the ambient air or water for each conventional pollutant, represent the targets of this approach. To reach these targets emission or effluent standards (legal discharge ceilings) are

---

[1] See the various issues in Volume XX of the *EDF Letter,* a report to members of the Environmental Defense Fund.

imposed on a large number of specific discharge points such as stacks, vents, outfalls or storage tanks. Following a survey of the technological options of control, the control authority selects a favored control technology and calculates the amount of discharge reduction achievable by that technology as the basis for setting the emission or effluent standard. Technologies yielding larger amounts of control (and, hence, supporting more stringent standards) are selected both for emitters in areas where it is very difficult to meet the ambient standard and for new emitters. The responsibility for defining and enforcing these standards is shared in legislatively specified ways between the national government and the various state governments.

2.2 Conventional Air Pollutants

In an attempt to inject more flexibility into the manner in which the objectives of the Clean Air Act were met during the last half of the 1970's, the U.S. EPA created what has now become known as the Emissions Trading Program. The program attempts to facilitate compliance by allowing sources a much wider range of choice in how they satisfy their legal pollution control responsibilities than possible in the command-and-control approach. Any source choosing to reduce emissions at any discharge point more than required by its emission standard can apply to the control authority for certification of the excess control as an "emission reduction credit" (ERC). Defined in terms of a specific amount of a particular pollutant, the certified emissions reduction credit can be used to satisfy emission standards at other (presumably more expensive to control) discharge points controlled by the creating source or it can be sold to other sources. By making these credits transferable, the EPA has allowed sources to find the cheapest means of satisfying their requirements, even if the cheapest means are under the control of another firm. The ERC is the currency used in emissions trading, while the offset, bubble, emissions banking and netting policies govern how this currency can be stored and spent (Federal Register, 1986).

The **offset policy** requires major new or expanding sources in "nonattainment" areas (those areas with air quality worse than the ambient standards) to secure sufficient offsetting emission reductions (through the acquisition of ERC's) from existing firms that the air is cleaner after their entry or expansion than before. Offsets are also required for major modifications in areas which have attained the standards if the modifications jeopardize attainment. Prior to this policy no new firms were allowed to enter nonattainment areas on the grounds they would interfere with attaining the ambient standards. By introducing the offset policy EPA allowed economic growth to continue while insuring progress toward attainment.

The **bubble policy** receives its unusual name from the fact that it treats multiple emission points controlled by existing emitters (as opposed to those expanding or entering an area for the first time) as if they were enclosed in a bubble. Under this policy only the total emissions of each pollutant leaving the bubble are regulated. While the total leaving the bubble must not be larger than the total permitted by adding up all the corresponding emission standards within the bubble (and in some cases must be 20% lower), emitters are free to control some discharge points less than dictated by the corresponding emission standard as long as sufficient compensating ERC's are obtained from other discharge points within the bubble. In essence sources are free to choose the mix of control among the discharge points as long as the overall emission reduction requirements are satisfied. Multi-plant bubbles are allowed, opening the possibility for trading ERC's among very different kinds of emitters.

Netting allows modifying or expanding sources (but not new sources) to escape from the need to meet the requirements of the rather stringent new source review process (including the need to acquire offsets) so long as any net increase in emissions (counting any ERC's earned elsewhere in the plant) is below an established threshold. Insofar as it allows firms to escape particular regulatory requirements by using ERC's to remain under the threshold which triggers applicability, netting is more properly considered regulatory relief than regulatory reform.

Emissions Banking allows firms to store certified ERC's for subsequent use in the offset, bubble or netting programs or for sale to others.

2.3 Lead in Gasoline

The marketable permit concept has since been applied in a number of new areas, demonstrating its versatility. In the month prior to the issuance of new, more stringent regulations on lead in gasoline, EPA announced the results of a cost/benefit analysis of their expected impact. The analysis concluded that the proposed .01 grams per leaded gallon (gplg) standard would result in $36 billion (1983) in benefits (from reduced adverse health effects) at an estimated cost to the refining industry of $2.6 billion; the regulation was unquestionably justified on efficiency grounds.

A main concern of EPA in issuing these regulations was the rigidity of the intermediate deadlines used to implement the phasedown. While some refiners could meet early deadlines with ease, others could do so only at a significant increase in cost. Recognizing that meeting the goal did not require every refiner to meet every deadline, EPA initiated the lead banking program to provide additional flexibility in meeting the regulations.

While not formally a part of the emissions trading program discussed above, the lead banking program does have some design similarities to it. Under this program, refiners reducing lead more than required by the applicable standard in each quarter of the year could bank the credits for use or sale in some subsequent quarter. Banked credits were fully transferable among refiners.

The lead banking program, though plagued by less-than-perfect implementation procedures, eased the transition to the new, more stringent regulatory regime (Nussbaum, 1992). Refiners had an incentive to respond quickly because reductions in lead undertaken prior to the deadlines became valuable under this new program. Acquiring these credits made it possible for other refiners to comply with the deadlines, even in the face of equipment failures or Acts of God; fighting the deadlines in court, the traditional response, was unnecessary. Designed purely as a means of facilitating the transition to this new regime, the lead banking program ended as scheduled on December 31, 1987.

2.4 Ozone-Depleting Chemicals

The ozone shield in the stratosphere protects humans from harmful ultraviolet radiation. Current evidence suggests that this shield is being depleted by man-made chemicals such as chlorofluorocarbons and halogens and the resulting increase in ultraviolet rays raises the incidence of both skin cancer and damage to eyesight. These gases have also been implicated in the greenhouse effect as discussed in the next section.

Responding to this threat, 24 nations signed the Montreal Protocol during September, 1988. According to this agreement signatory nations have to restrict their production and consumption of the chief responsible gases to 50% of 1986 levels by June 30, 1998. Marketable permit systems provide one way of accomplishing that goal.

On August 12, 1988 the U.S. Environmental Protection Agency committed itself to this route by issuing regulations implementing a marketable permit system to achieve the targeted reductions.[2] According to these regulations all major U.S. producers and consumers of the controlled substances were allocated baseline allowances based on 1986 levels. Each producer and consumer is allowed 100 % of this baseline allowance for each year before July 1, 1993, 80% between July 1, 1993 and June 30, 1998 and 50 % of the baseline allowance after June 30, 1998. These allowances are transferable within producer and consumer categories and production allowances can be transferred across international borders to producers in other signatory nations provided that the transaction is approved by the EPA and results in the appropriate changes in the buyer and seller production allowances in their respective countries. Production allowances can be augmented by demonstrating the safe destruction of an equivalent amount of controlled substances by approved means, but so far no means have been approved.

Though transfers of the production allowances are allowed, even across international borders, they are constrained rather severely. The regulations allow any producer to increase his production allowance by any means (including transfer of a portion of another producer's allowance) by a maximum of 10% of his apportionment before 1998 and 15% of his apportionment after that date.

Though the EPA clearly chose a grandfathered approach to allocating the production allowances, they were clearly uneasy about this choice. The possibility of ultimately replacing this approach with an auction market has been proposed. If instituted the revenue from these auctions would go into the general Treasury (53 *Federal Register* 30598, August 12, 1988). Since the demand for these allowances is quite inelastic, supply restrictions increase revenue. By allocating allowances to the seven major domestic producers of CFC's and halons, the EPA was concerned that its regulation would result in sizable windfall profits (estimated to be in the billions of dollars) for those producers. Furthermore the EPA was concerned that the existence of these windfalls could create an economic incentive for producers to delay the introduction of chemical substitutes which could have adverse environmental consequences.

Confronted with scientific evidence that the reduction in CFC use mandated by the Montreal Protocol might not be sufficiently stringent, concerned about the excess profits to which the allowance holders would be entitled and seeking new sources of revenue to counteract a growing budget deficit, the U.S. Congress imposed

---

[2] 53 *Federal Register* 30598 (August 12, 1988). The final rules governing transfer of import and production allowances are in 54 *Federal Register* 6376 (February 9, 1989).

a special tax on ozone-depleting chemicals. Which are CFC-11, CFC-12, CFC-113, CFC-114, CFC-115, Halon-1211 and Halon-2402 as described in 103 Stat 2365. The amount of the tax per pound of the chemical sold or used is equal to a base tax multiplied by an "ozone-depleting factor" specific to each chemical. These factors range from a low of 0.8 for CFC-113 to 10.0 for Halon-1301. The base tax rates are scheduled to rise from $1.37 in 1991 to $2.65 in 1994 and will rise 45 cents each year after that.

2.5 Point-Nonpoint Water Pollution

Virtually all water pollution control policy in the United States has been focused on point sources-large, identifiable polluters emitting effluents from specific discharge points. As the controls on point sources have been tightened, nonpoint sources (such as the overflow from urban storm sewers or the runoff from farms) become responsible for an increasingly larger share of the remaining pollution. Currently nonpoint sources are responsible for the largest proportion of the remaining problem.

More attention has been focused on nonpoint sources recently because the marginal cost of controlling them is now considerably lower than the marginal cost of securing further reductions from point sources. One result of this attention has been the introduction of an option to trade waste reduction permits between point and nonpoint sources for bodies of water where further control is required.

One example of this approach is occurring in the Lake Dillon Watershed, a primary source of water for Denver, Colorado. (Northwest Colorado Council of Government, 1984). Changing land uses and development have produced near-eutrophic algae in the lake, despite the fact that all wastewater treatment plants currently employ advanced wastewater treatment for phosphorous removal. Even with zero phosphorous discharge from treatment plants in the future, nonpoint phosphorous sources from growth areas would make the lake eutrophic.

As part of a management plan for the lake all waste treatment plants would continue to apply advanced waste water treatment, and state-of-the-art nonpoint source controls would be applied by local governments to all new development projects in the basin. An effluent trading system was developed to accommodate expected source growth beyond 1990 by encouraging reductions for nonpoint sources which existed prior to 1984 and therefore were not subject to the new regulations. Authorized by the State Commission the trading rules require a 2:1 ratio to account for uncertainties in the process. One pound of waste reduction credit is certified for each two pounds of phosphorous eliminated from pre-existing nonpoint sources. It is expected that this approach will keep phosphorous loading at 1982 levels while accommodating expected source growth. It allows local governments to control phosphorous in the most cost-effective manner without being limited only to further reductions in point sources.

As the political forces are gearing up for the periodic reauthorization of the Clean Water Act, marketable permits are being discussed in three different contexts[3].

---

[3] Telephone conversation with Dr William O'Neill, U.S. Environmental Protection Agency, June 7, 1991.

First, significant interest in generalizing and expanding the point-nonpoint trading approach as illustrated by the Dillon Reservoir has materialized. Second, the use of transferable development rights as a means of protecting wetlands is being discussed. Finally, the possibility for trading responsibilities for pretreating waste entering into publicly owned sewage treatment plants is also being explored. At this stage it is impossible to know which, if any, of these ideas will find their way into the revised law.

2.6 Acid Rain

A version of the emissions trading concept has also been incorporated into the U.S. approach for achieving further reductions in those electric utility emissions contributing to acid rain. This title was included in the Clean Air Act Amendments of 1990 (which became law on November 15, 1990, as described in 104 Statparagraph 2584). Analyses of the application of the emissions trading concept to acid rain have been described in Atkinson (1983), Ranfer and Feldman (1984), Oates and McGartland (1985), Feldman and Ranfer (1987), and Tietenberg (1989a). Under this innovative approach allowances to emit sulfur oxides are allocated to older plants; the number of allowances will be restricted to assure a reduction of 10 million tons in emissions from 1980 levels. These allowances are defined for a specific calendar year, but unused allowances can be carried forward into the next year. They are transferable among the affected sources. Any plants reducing emissions more than required by the allowances could transfer the unused allowances to other plants. Emissions may not legally exceed the levels permitted by the allowances (allocated plus acquired). The act even anticipates the possibility of interpollutant trading between sulfur and nitrogen oxides by asking for a study of its feasibility.[4]

Adopting the tradeable allowance approach resulted from the Congressional belief that the acid rain reduction goals could be met at a much lower cost than would otherwise be possible. Utilities that could afford to reduce their emissions relatively cheaply would do so, selling or leasing any excess reduction to those for whom further reductions would be much more expensive. Both the plants and their customers could be made better off by the allowance transfer. The allowances would flow to their best use, minimizing the overall cost of control in the process, while holding constant the legislatively mandated total emission reduction.

3 LESSONS FROM THEORY

Theory can help us understand the characteristics of these economic approaches in the most favorable circumstances for their use and assist in the process of designing the instruments for maximum effectiveness. The lessons will be summarized in a number of points.

1. Assuming all participants are cost-minimizers, a "well-defined" emissions trading market could cost-effectively allocate the control responsibility for meeting a

---

[4] 104 Stat 1591.

predefined pollution target among the various pollution sources despite incomplete information on the control possibilities by the regulatory authorities.

The intuition behind this theorem is not difficult to grasp. Cost-minimizing firms seek to minimize the sum of permit costs and control costs. Minimization will occur when the marginal cost of control is set equal to the permit price. Since all sources will be setting their marginal control costs equal to the same price, a permit market will equalize marginal control costs across all discharge points, precisely the condition required for cost-effectiveness. It should be noted that while the allocation is cost-effective, it is not necessarily efficient. It would only be efficient if the predetermined target happened to coincide with the efficient amount of pollution. Nothing guarantees this outcome. In essence sources needing extra emission reduction either as a precondition to entering an area or to meet emissions standards can purchase marketable emission permits from sources with the lowest marginal costs of control.

Though derived in the rarified world of theory, the practical importance of this theorem should not be underestimated. Marketable emission permits offer a unique opportunity for regulators to solve a fundamental dilemma. Control authorities usually want to allocate the responsibility for control cost-effectively, but they rarely have the information required to achieve this objective. Marketable emission permits create a system of incentives in which those who have the best knowledge about control opportunities, the environmental managers for the industries, are encouraged to use that knowledge to achieve environmental objectives at minimum cost. Emission charges would sustain a cost effective allocation of the control responsibility for meeting a predefined pollution target only if the control authority knew the correct level of the charge to impose or was willing to engage in an iterative trial-and-error process over time to find the correct level. The permit market does not face this problem because the price level is established by the market, not the control authority, once the correct number of permits is determined. The correct number of permits is dictated by the pollution target (Tietenberg, 1988). Information barriers do not preclude effective regulation.

2. Marketable permits encourage more technological progress in pollution control than the command-and-control system. Milliman and Price (1989).

Traditional command and control policies usually base standards on technologies known to the regulators. Meeting those standards can be accomplished by simply adopting the identified technology. Adopters have little incentive to search for superior technologies.

With marketable permits, adopters not only have an incentive to search for new technologies which reduce the cost of compliance of meeting the mandated standard, they have an incentive to search for technologies which can reduce emissions more than required by the standard. Selling the emission reduction credits (or unused allowances) produces revenue which can be used to finance the new technologies. Grandfathered permits provide fewer incentives for technological progress than either emissions charges or auctioned permits.

3. What constitutes a "well-defined" transferable permit system depends crucially on the attributes of the pollutant being controlled (Montgomery, 1972; Palmer et al, 1980; Tietenberg, 1985).

To be consistent with a cost-effective allocation of the control responsibility, the permits would have to be defined in different ways for different types of pollutants. Three differentiating characteristics have been identified in the literature so far. Two of these are relatively straight-forward. Permits designed to control pollutants which are uniformly mixed in the atmosphere (such as volatile organic compounds, one type of precursor for ozone formation) can be defined simply in terms of a rate of emissions flow per unit time. Permits sharing this design characteristic are called **emission permits**. Permits to control stock pollutants (such as heavy metals) which build up in the environment over time are defined in terms of cumulative emissions, rather than an emissions flow. These are typically called **cumulative emission permits**. The former regulates pollutant flow, while the latter regulates the accumulated stock .

Permit design is somewhat more difficult when the pollution target being pursued is defined in terms of concentrations measured at a number of specific receptor locations (such as sulfur oxides or particulates). In this case it is necessary for the cost-effective permit design to take into account the **location** of the emissions (including injection height) as well as the **amount** of emissions. As long as the control authorities can define for each emitter a vector of transfer coefficients, which translates the effect of a unit increase of emissions by that emitter into an increase in concentration at each of the receptors, receptor-specific permits can be defined which will allocate the responsibility cost-effectively. The permit design which is consistent with cost-effectiveness in this context is called an **ambient permit**.

Unfortunately while the design of the ambient permit is not very complicated, (each permit allows the holder to degrade the concentration level at the corresponding receptor by one unit) implementing the markets within which these permits would be traded is rather complicated. In particular for each unit of planned emissions an emitter would have to acquire separate permits for each affected receptor. When the number of receptors is large, the result is a rather complicated market.

4. As long as markets are competitive and transactions costs are low, the trading benchmark in an emissions trading approach does not affect the ultimate cost-effective allocation of control responsibility. When markets are noncompetitive or transactions costs are high, however, the final allocation of control responsibility is affected. (Hahn, 1984; Tietenberg, 1985; Misiolek and Elder, 1989).

Once the control authority has decided how much pollution of each type will be allowed, it must then decide how to allocate the permits among the sources. In theory permits can either be auctioned off, with the sources purchasing them from the control authority at the market-clearing price, or allocated among existing sources free-of-charge based on some regulatory distribution rule. This latter approach favors older sources over newer sources, and is known as "grandfathering". The theorem suggests that either approach will ultimately result in a cost-effective allocation of the control responsibility among the various polluters as long as they are all price-takers, transactions costs are low, and the permits are freely transferable. Even when the permits are randomly distributed without cost among existing sources, the after-market in which firms can sell excess permits and purchase additional ones corrects any problems with the initial allocation. This is a significant finding because it implies that under the right conditions the control authority can use this initial allocation to pursue distributional goals without interfering with cost-effectiveness.

When firms are price-setters rather than price-takers, however, cost effectiveness will only be achieved if the control authority initially allocates the permits so a cost-effective allocation would be achieved even in the absence of any trading. (Implementing this particular allocation would, of course, require regulators to have complete information on control costs for all sources, an unlikely prospect). In this special case cost-effectiveness would be achieved even in the presence of one or more price-setting firms because no trading would take place, eliminating the possibility of exploiting any market power. For all other initial permit distributions an active market would exist, offering the opportunity for price-setting behavior. The larger the deviation of the initial allocation of permits to a single price-setting source from its cost-effective allocation, the larger the deviation of ultimate control costs from the least-cost allocation. When the price-setting source is initially allocated too many permits, it can inflict higher control costs on others by withholding some permits from the market. When the price-setting source is initially allocated too few permits, however, it necessarily bears a higher control cost as the means of reducing demand (and, hence, prices) for the permits.

Similar problems exist when transactions costs are high. High transactions costs preclude or reduce trading by diminishing the gains from trade. When the costs of consummating the transaction exceed the potential gains, the incentive to participate in the market is lost.

4 LESSONS FROM EMPIRICAL RESEARCH

5. A vast majority, though not all, of the relevant empirical studies have found the control costs to be substantially higher with the regulatory command-and-control system than the least cost means of allocating the control responsibility.

While theory tells us unambiguously that the command-and-control system will not be cost-effective except by coincidence, it cannot tell us the magnitude of the excess costs. The empirical work cited in Table 1 adds the important information that the excess costs are typically very large. This is an important finding because it provides the motivation for introducing a reform program; the potential social gains (in terms of reduced control cost) from breaking away from the status quo are sufficient to justify the trouble. Although the estimates of the excess costs attributable to a command and control presented in Table 1 overstate the cost savings that would be achieved by even a completely unrestricted permit market (a point discussed in more detail below), the general conclusion that the potential cost savings from adopting economic incentive approaches are large seems accurate even after correcting for overstatement.

A similar expectation motivated the recent inclusion of transferable sulfur oxide allowances in the acid rain portion of the Clean air Act Amendments of 1990. The evidence suggests that the cost advantage of using this approach instead of simply imposing the emission standards could be considerable. The Congressional Budget Office, for example, has estimated that the per ton cost of achieving a 10 million ton reduction of sulfur oxides would be reduced from $360 per ton under the traditional approach to $327 per ton using transferable allowances (Congressional Budget Office, 1986). Another study, examining the cost savings that could be achieved within a single state (Illinois) concluded that the cost of control would be approximately one-third lower if transferable allowances were introduced (Feldman and Ranfer, 1987). The third and most recent study makes it clear that even a severely restricted A market would yield substantial savings, which have been estimated to be very large even if trades were limited to discharge points within the same utility (ICF Resources Inc., 1989).

6. Only a "grandfathered" transferable permit system would guarantee that sources would be no worse off than under the command-and-control system. The financial outlays associated with acquiring ERCs in an auction market would be sufficiently large that sources would typically have lower financial burdens with the traditional command-and-control approach than with this particular economic incentive approach. The summary of the evidence is described in Tietenberg (1985) while for detail of the individual studies the reader is referred to the following literature: Atkinson and Tietenberg (1982) Atkinson and Tietenberg (1984), Hahn (1984), Harrison (1983) Krupnick (1986), Lyon (1982), Palmer et al. (1980), Roach et al. (1981), Seskin (1983) and Shapiro and Warhit (1983).

From the point of view of the source required to control its emissions, two components of financial burden are significant: (1) control costs and (2) expenditures on permits. While only the former represent real resource costs to society as a whole (the latter are merely transferred from one group in society to another), to the source both represent a financial burden. The empirical evidence suggests that when an auction market is used to distribute permits, the permit expenditures would frequently be larger in magnitude than the control costs; the sources would spend more on permits than they would on the control equipment. Under the traditional command-and-control system firms make no financial outlays to the government. Although control costs are necessarily higher with the command-and-control system than with a marketable permit system, they are not so high as to outweigh the additional financial outlays required in an auction market permit system. For this reason existing sources could be expected to vehemently oppose distributing permits by an auction market despite its social appeal, unless the revenue derived is used in a manner which is approved by the sources and the sources with which it competes are required to absorb similar expenses.

In the absence of either a politically popular way to use the revenue or assurances that competitors will face similar financial burdens, this political opposition could be substantially reduced by distributing the permits free-of-charge to existing sources on the basis of a grandfathering rule. Under grandfathering, sources have only to purchase any additional permits they may need over and above the initial allocation (as opposed to purchasing all permits in an auction market). Grandfathering is *de facto* the approach taken in the U. S. emissions trading program.

Table 1. Empirical Studies of Air Pollution Control

Study	Pollutants Covered	Geographic Area	CAC Benchmark	Cost Ratio CAC to Least Cost
Atkinson and Lewis	Particulates	St. Louis	SIP regulations	6.0[a]
Roach et al.	Sulfur dioxide	Four corners in Utah, Col., Ariz. & N Mex	SIP regulations	4.25
Hahn and Noll	Sulfates	Los Angeles	California emission standards	1.07
Krupnick	Nitrogen dioxide	Baltimore	Proposed RACT regulations	5.96[b]
Seskin et al.	Nitrogen dioxide	Chicago	Proposed RACT regulations	14.4[b]
McGartland	Particulates	Baltimore	SIP regulations	4.18
Spofford	Sulfur Dioxide	Lower Delaware Valley	Uniform percentage regulations	1.78
	Particulates	Lower Delaware Valley	Uniform percentage regulations	22.0
Harrison	Airport noise	United States	Mandatory retrofit	1.72[c]
Maloney and Yandle	Hydrocarbons	All domestic DuPont plants	Uniform percentage reduction	4.15[d]
Palmer et. al.	Nonaerosol CFC emissions	United States	Proposed emission standards	1.96

CAC = command and control, the traditional regulatory approach, SIP = state implementation plan, RACT = reasonably available control technologies, a set of standards imposed on existing sources in nonattainment areas.

[a] Based on a 40 $\mu g/m^3$ at worst receptor.

[b] Based on a short-term, one-hour average of 250 $\mu g/m^3$

[c] Because it is a benefit-cost study instead of a cost-effectiveness study, the Harrison comparison of the command-and-control approach with the least-cost allocation involves different benefit levels. Benefit levels for the least-cost allocation are only 82 percent of those for the CAC allocation. To make cost estimates more comparable, as a first approximation, the least-cost allocation was divided by 0.82 and the resulting number was compared with the command-and-control cost.

[d] Based on 85 percent reduction of emissions from all sources.

Grandfathering has its disadvantages. Although reserving some permits for new firms is possible, this option is rarely exercised in practice. As a result, under the free distribution scheme new firms typically have to purchase all permits, while existing firms get an initial allocation free. Thus the free distribution system imposes a bias against new sources in the sense that their financial burden is greater than that of an otherwise identical existing source, even if the two sources install exactly the same emission control devices. This new source bias could retard the introduction of new facilities and new technologies by reducing the cost advantage of building new facilities which embody the latest innovations.

7. While it is clear from theory that larger trading areas offer the opportunities for larger potential cost savings in an emissions trading program, some empirical work suggests that substantial savings can be achieved in emissions trading even when the trading areas are rather small.

Sometimes political considerations mandate a trading area which is smaller than the ideal design. The question of whether large trading areas are essential for the effective use of this policy is therefore of some relevance. The amount of cost savings achieved by any permit market would be a function of the size of the area within which the permits may be traded. In general the larger the trading area the larger the potential cost savings because a wider set of cost reduction opportunities becomes available. The empirical question is how sensitive the cost estimates are to the size of the areas.

One study of utilities found that even allowing a plant to trade among discharge points within that plant could save from 30 to 60% of the costs of complying with new sulfur oxide reduction regulations, compared to a situation where no trading whatsoever was permitted (ICF Resources Inc., 1989). Expanding the trading possibilities to other utilities within the same state permitted a further reduction of 20%, while allowing interstate trading permitted another 15% reduction in costs. If this study is replicated in other circumstances, it would appear that even small trading areas offer the opportunity for significant cost reduction. As indicated below, the fact that so many emissions trades have actually taken place within the same plant or among contiguous plants provide some confirmation for this result.

8. Although only a few studies (de Lucia, 1974; Hahn, 1984; Maloney and Yandle, 1984, for individual studies, and Tietenberg, 1985, for review) of the empirical impact of market power on emissions trading have been accomplished, their results are consistent with a finding that market power does not seem to have a large effect on regional control costs in most realistic situations.

Under favorable circumstances for the exploitation of market power, the available evidence suggests that while price manipulation in auction permit markets could have a rather large impact on regional financial burden, it would under normal circumstances have a rather small effect on control costs. Estimates typically suggest that control costs would rise by less than 1% if market power was exercised by one or more firms.

The effects of market power depend on whether the permits are distributed by auction or grandfathering. In an auction market the price-setting source reduces its financial burden by purchasing fewer permits than otherwise in order to drive the price down. To compensate for the fewer number of permits purchased, the price-setting source must spend more on controlling its own pollution, limiting the gains from price manipulation.

It should not be surprising that price manipulation could have rather dramatic effects on regional financial burden in an auction market, since the cost of **all** permits is affected, not merely those purchased by the price-setting source. The perhaps more surprising result is that control costs are quite insensitive to price-setting behavior. This is due to the fact that the only control cost change is the net difference between the new larger control burden borne by the price searcher and the correspondingly smaller burden borne by the sources having larger-than-normal allocations of permits. Only the costs of the marginal units are affected.

Within the class of grandfathered distribution rules, some rules create a larger potential for strategic price behavior than others. In general the larger the divergence between the number of permits received by the price-searching source and the cost-effective number of permits, the larger the potential for market power. When allocated an excess of permits by the control authority, price-searching firms can exercise power on the selling side of the market, and when allocated too few permits, they can exercise power on the buying side of the market.

According to the existing studies it takes a rather considerable divergence from the cost-effective allocation of permits to produce much difference in regional control costs. Since most realistic rules used to distribute permits are estimated to affect control costs to such a small degree, the deviations from the least cost allocation caused by market power pale in comparison to the much larger potential cost reductions achievable by implementing a marketable emissions permit system. Strategic price behavior is not the only potential source of market power problems. Firms could conceivably use permit markets to drive competitors out of busines (Misiolek and Elder, 1989). This problem is relatively rare and can be dealt with on a case-by-case basis, should it arise (Tietenberg, 1985).

5 LESSONS FROM IMPLEMENTATION

Although comprehensive data on the effects of the program do not exist because substantial proportions of it are administered by local areas and no one collects information in a systematic way, some of the major aspects of the experience are clear.

9. The existing emissions trading program is not even close to the marketable permit approach envisioned in economic theory. It complements the traditional regulatory approach, rather than replaces it.

Rather than a market with well-defined prices the current emissions trading process involves negotiated trades between sources individually supervised and approved by regulatory agencies on a case-by-case basis. When judged from the perspective "Did it improve upon the system that it preceded" the answer is certainly "yes!" Judged by whether it has achieved full cost-effectiveness, the answer is "no!".

The program has unquestionably and substantially reduced the costs of complying with the requirements of the Clean Air Act. Most estimates place the accumulated capital savings for all components of the program at over $10 billion. This does not include the recurring savings in operating cost.

On the other hand the program has not produced the magnitude of cost savings that was anticipated by most proponents at its inception. Part of this failure to fulfill expectations can be explained as the result of unrealistically inflated expectations. More restrictive regulatory decisions than expected and higher than expected transaction costs also bear some responsibility.

The models used to calculate the potential cost savings were not (and are not) completely adequate guides to reality. The cost functions in these models are invariably *ex ante* long-run cost functions. They implicitly assume that the modeled plant can be built from scratch and can incorporate the best technology. In practice, of course, many existing sources cannot retrofit these technologies and therefore their *ex post* control options are much more limited than implied by the models.

The models also assume all trades are multilateral and are simultaneously consummated, whereas actual trades are usually bilateral and sequential. The distinction is important for nonuniformly mixed pollutants because bilateral trades frequently are constrained by concerns about decreasing air quality at the site of the acquiring source. With multilateral trades the concerns would frequently be allayed by compensating reductions coming from other near-by sources. In essence the models implicitly assume an idealized market process, which is only remotely approximated by actual transactions. Atkinson and Tietenberg (1991) concluded that the amount of potential cost savings sacrificed in bilateral, sequential trading of nonuniformly mixed pollutants is quite large.

In addition some non-negligible proportion of the expected cost savings recorded by the models is attributable to the substantially larger amounts of emissions allowed by the modeled permit equilibrium (Atkinson and Tietenberg, 1987). For nonuniformly mixed pollutants, for example, the cost estimates imply that the control authority is allowed to arrange the control responsibility in any fashion that satisfies the ambient air quality standards. In essence the models allocate more uncontrolled emissions to sources with tall stacks because those emissions can be exported. Exported emissions avoid control costs without affecting the readings at the local monitors. That portion of the cost savings estimated by the models in Table 1 which is due to allowing increased emissions is not acceptable to regulators. Some recent work has suggested that the benefits received from the additional emission control required by the command and control approach may be justified by the net benefits received (Oates et al., 1988). The regulatory refusal to allow emission increases may not have been such a bad idea. Not all of the cost savings, of course, are due to the abilitity to increase emissions. The remaining portion of the savings, which is due to taking advantage of opportunities to control a given level of emissions at a lower cost, is still substantial and can be captured by a well-designed permit system which does not allow emissions to increase beyond the command-and-control benchmark as calculated by Atkinson and Tietenberg (1987).

Certain types of trades, assumed permissible by the models, are prohibited by the actual trading rules. New sources for example are not allowed to satisfy the New Source Performance Standards (which imply a particular control technology) by choosing some less stringent control option and making up the difference with acquired emission reduction credits; they must install the degree of technological control necessary to meet the standard. Typically this is the same technology used by EPA to define the standard in the first place.

A lot of uncertainty is associated with emission reduction credit transactions since they depend so heavily on administrative action. All trades must be approved by the control authorities. If the authorities are not cooperative or at least consistent, the value of the created emission reduction credits could be diminished or even destroyed.

For nonuniformly mixed pollutants, trades between geographically separated sources will only be approved after a significant amount of dispersion modeling has been accomplished by the applicants. Not only is this modelling expensive, it frequently ends up raising questions which ultimately lead to the transaction being denied. Few trades requiring this modelling have been consummated.

Trading activity has also been inhibited by the paucity of emission banks. The U.S. system allows states to establish emission banks, but does not require them to do so. As of 1986 only seven of the fifty states had established these banks. For sources in the rest of the states the act of creating emission credits is undervalued because the credits cannot be legally held for future use. The supply of emission reduction credits is hence less than would be estimated by the models.

10. Transferable permits have facilitated compliance with the pollution control acts by making compliance cheaper and easier. They have increased the possible means for compliance and sources have responded.

Somewhere between 7000 and 12000 trading transactions have been consummated. Each of these transactions was voluntary and for the participants represented an improvement over the traditional regulatory approach. Several of these transactions involved the introduction of innovative control technologies.

Transferable permits seem to have worked particularly well for trades involving uniformly mixed pollutants and for trades of nonuniformly mixed pollutants involving contiguous discharge points.

It is not surprising that most consummated trades have been internal (where the buyer and seller are either part of the same corporation or share a common corporate parent) rather than external. Not only are the uncertainties associated with inter-firm transfers avoided, but most internal trades involve contiguous facilities which are not required to supply dispersion model results. The fact that so many trades have taken place between contiguous discharge points serves as confirmation that substantial savings can be achieved even if the geographic boundaries of the trading area are quite restricted.

It is also not surprising that the plurality of consummated trades involve volatile organic compounds, which are uniformly mixed pollutants. Since dispersion modelling is not required for uniformly mixed pollutants even when the trading sources are somewhat distant from one another, trades involving these pollutants are cheaper to consummate. Additionally trades involving uniformly mixed pollutants need not worry about local air quality deterioration since the location of the emissions is not a matter of policy consequence.

11. Transferable permits have encouraged technological progress in pollution control. Although generally the degree of progress has been modest, it has been more dramatic in areas where emission reductions have been sufficiently stringent as to restrict the availability of emission reduction credits created by more traditional means (Tietenberg, 1985: Dudek and Palmisano, 1988).

Theory would lead us to expect more technological progress with emissions trading than with a command-and-control policy because it changes the incentives so drastically. Under a command-and-control approach technological changes discovered by the control authority typically lead to more stringent standards (and higher costs) for the sources. Sources have little incentive to innovate and a good deal of incentive to hide innovations from the control authority. With emissions trading, on the other hand, innovations allowing excess reductions create saleable emission reduction credits.

The evidence suggests that the expectations based on this theory have been borne out, but to a limited degree in the operating program. The most prominent example of technological change has been the substitution of water-based solvents for solvents containing volatile organic compounds. Though somewhat more expensive, this substitution made economic sense once the program was introduced.

It should probably not be surprising that the number of new innovations stimulated by the program is rather small. As long as cheaper ways of creating credits within existing processes are available, it would be unreasonable to expect large investments in new technologies with unproven reliabilities. On the other hand as the degree of control rises and the supply of readily available credits dries up, the demand for new technologies would be expected to rise as well. This expectation seems to be borne out in those areas where unusually low air quality or stringent regulatory rules have served to limit the available credits as described by Dudek and Palmisano (1989) for the experience in California.

6 CONCLUSION

Our experience with economic incentive programs has demonstrated that they have had, and can continue to have, a positive role in environmental policy in the future. I would submit the issue is no longer **whether** they have a role to play, but rather **what kind** of role they should play. The available experience with operating versions of these programs allows us to draw some specific conclusions which facilitate defining the boundaries for the optimal use of economic incentive approaches in general and for distinguishing the emissions trading and emission charges approaches in particular.

First: emissions trading integrates particularly smoothly into any policy structure which is based either directly (through emission standards) or indirectly (through mandated technology or input limitations) on enforceable regulations.

In this case emission limitations embedded in the operating licenses can serve as the trading benchmark if grandfathering is adopted. Implementing the system in this way is politically easy because no polluting source is worse off by its introduction. Any source that chooses not to engage in trading is controlled by exactly the same regulations that would have applied if transferable permits had not been adopted. On the other hand since all trades are voluntary any source that chooses to trade will be unambiguously better off by being offered the opportunity to trade.

Second: emissions trading is probably not equally applicable to large and small pollution sources.

It appears that much of the trading activity in the United States has involved large corporations. The transactions costs are sufficiently high that only large trades can absorb them without jeopardizing the gains from trade.

Third: emissions trading seems to work especially well for uniformly mixed pollutants.

No diffusion modelling is necessary and regulators do not have to worry about trades creating "hot spots" or localized areas of high pollution concentration. Trades can be on a 1:1 basis. This is one of the characteristics which has led to the current high level of interest in exploring the use of marketable permits to control greenhouse gases, which can be treated as uniformly mixed gases.

Fourth: because transferable permits allow the issue of who will pay for the control to be separated from who will install the control, it introduces an additional degree of flexibility into the regulatory system.

This flexibility is particularly important in nonattainment areas since marginal control costs are so high. Sources which would not normally be controlled because they could not afford to implement the controls without going out of business, can be controlled with emissions trading. The revenue derived from the sale of emission reduction credits can be used to finance the controls, effectively preventing bankruptcy.

Fifth: because it is quantity based, emissions trading also offers a unique possibility for leasing.

Leasing is particularly valuable when the temporal pattern of emissions varies across sources. When a firm plans to shut down one plant in the near future and to build a new one, leasing credits is a vastly superior alternative to the temporary installation of equipment in old plant which would be useless when the plant is retired. The useful life of this temporary control would be wastefully short.

Finally: emissions trading can improve on command and control even when used on a very limited scale.

Regulators can respond to initiatives from those being regulated on a case by case basis. It is not necessary to establish a well-functioning market before the system can be effectively used. We live in an age when the call for tighter environmental controls intensifies with each new discovery of yet another injury modern society is inflicting on the planet. But resistance to additional controls is also growing with the recognition that compliance with each new set of controls is more expensive than the last. While economic incentive approaches to environmental control offer no panacea, they frequently do offer a practical way to achieve environmental goals more flexibly and at lower cost than more traditional regulatory approaches. That is a compelling virtue and one which is worthy of our continuing pursuit.

REFERENCES

Ackerman, Bruce A. and Richard B. Stewart. 1988. "Reforming Environmental Law: The Democratic Case for Market Incentives", *Columbia Journal of Environmental Law* vol. 13, no. 2 (no month listed): 171-199.

Anderson, Robert J. Jr., Robert O. Reid and Eugene P. Seskin. 1979. An Analysis of Alternative Policies for Attaining and Maintaining a Short-Term NO 2 Standard, a report to the Council on Environmental Quality, prepared by MATHTECH, Inc.

Atkinson, Scott E. 1983. "Marketable Pollution Permits and Acid Rain Externalities", *Canadian Journal of Economics* vol. 16, no. 4 (November): 704-722.

Atkinson, Scott E. and Donald H. Lewis. 1974. "A Cost-Effectiveness Analysis of Alternative Air Quality Control Strategies", *Journal of Environmental Economics and Management* vol. 1, no. 3 (November): 237-250.

Atkinson, Scott E. and T. H. Tietenberg. 1982. "The Empirical Properties of Two Classes of Designs for Transferable Discharge Permit Markets", *Journal of Environmental Economics and Management* vol. 9, no. 2 (June): 101-121.

Atkinson, Scott E. and T. H. Tietenberg. 1984. "Approaches for Reaching Ambient Standards in Non-Attainment Areas: Financial Burden and Efficiency Considerations", *Land Economics* vol. 60, no. 2. (May): 148-159.

Atkinson, S. E. and T.H. Tietenberg. 1987. "Economic Implications of Emission Trading Rules for Local and Regional Pollutants", *Canadian Journal of Economics* vol. 20, no.2 (May): 370-186.

Atkinson, S. E. and T. H. Tietenberg. 1991. "Market Failure in Incentive-Based Regulation: The Case of Emissions Trading", *Journal of Environmental Economics and Management*, vol. 21, no. 1 (July): 17-31.

Baumol, William J. and Wallace E. Oates. 1975. *The Theory of Environmental Policy*, Prentice Hall, Englewood Cliffs, N. J. .

Bohm, Peter. 1988. *Economic Instruments for Reducing CFC Emissions*, Copenhagen: Nordisk Ministerrad.

Collinge, R. A. and W. E. Oates. 1982. "Efficiency in Pollution-Control in the Short and Long Runs: A System of Rental Emission Permits", *Canadian Journal of Economics* vol. 15, no. 2 (May): 346-354.

Congressional Budget Office. 1986. *Curbing Acid Rain: Cost, Budget, and Coal-Market Effects*, U.S. Government Printing Office, Washington, DC.

Dales, John H. 1986. *Pollution, Property & Prices* : University of Toronto Press, Toronto.

David, M., W. Eheart, E. Joeres, and E. David. 1980. "Marketable Permits for the Control of Phosphorus Effluent into Lake Michigan", *Water Resources Research* vol. 16, no. 2 (April): 263-270.

del Calvo y Gonzales, Jorge A. 1981. "Markets in Air: Problems and Prospects of Controlled Trading", *Harvard Environmental Law Review* vol. 5: 377-430.

Downing, Paul and William E. Watson. 1975. "Cost-Effective Enforcement of Environmental Standards", *Journal of the Air Pollution Control Association* vol. 25, no. 7 (July): 705-710.

deLucia, Russell J. 1974. *An Evaluation of Marketable Effluent Permit Systems*, Report no. EPA-600/5-74-030 to the U.S. Environmental Protection Agency (September).

Downing, Paul and William E. Watson. 1975. "Cost-Effective Enforcement of Environmental Standards", *Journal of the Air Pollution Control Association* vol. 25, no. 7 (July): 705-710.

Dudek, Daniel J. and John Palmisano. 1988. "Emissions Trading: Why is this Thoroughbred Hobbled", *Columbia Journal of Environmental Law* vol. 13, no. 2 (no month listed): 217-256.

Dudek, D. J. and A. LeBlanc. 1990. "Offsetting New CO_2 Emissions: A Rational First Step", *Contemporary Policy Issues* vol. 8, no. 3 (July): 29-42.

Endres, A. 1986. "Charges, Permits and Pollutant Interactions", *Eastern Economic Journal* vol. 12, no. 3 (July-Sept.): 327-336.

51 Federal Register. 1986. "Emissions Trading Policy Statements" (December 4): 43829.

Feldman, Stephen L. and Robert K. Raufer. 1987. *Emissions Trading and Acid Rain Implementing a Market Approach to Pollution Control*, Rowman & Littlefield, Totowa, NJ.

Foster, J. David. 1978. "The Size and Price of Emission Offsets", paper presented at the 71st Air Pollution Control Association annual meeting (June).

Gollop, Frank M. and Mark J. Roberts. 1985. "Cost-minimizing Regulation of Sulfur Emissions: Regional Gains in Electric Power", *Review of Economics and Statistics* vol. 67, no. 1 (February): 81-90.

Hahn, Robert W. 1983. "Designing Markets in Transferable Property Rights: A Practitioner's Guide", in Erhard F. Joeres and Martin H. David, eds., *Buying a Better Environment: Cost-Effective Regulation Through Permit Trading,* University of Wisconsin Press: 83-97, Madison, Wis.

Hahn, Robert W. 1984. "Market Power and Transferable Property Rights", *Quarterly Journal of Economics* vol. 99 (Nov): 753-765.

Hahn, Robert W. and Roger G. Noll. 1982. "Designing a Market for Tradeable Emission Permits", in Wesley A. Magat, ed., *Reform of Environmental Regulation,* Ballinger: 119-146, Cambridge, Mass.

Hahn, Robert W. and Roger G. Noll. 1982. "Barriers to Implementing Tradable Air Pollution Permits: Problems of Regulatory Interactions", *Yale Journal of Regulation,* vol. 1, no. 1: 63-91

Hahn, Robert W. 1986. "Trade-offs in Designing Markets With Multiple Objectives", *Journal of Environmental Economics and Management* vol. 13, no. 1 (March): 1-12.

Hahn, Robert W. and Gordon L. Hester. 1989. "Where Did All the Markets Go? An Analysis of EPA's Emission Trading Program", *Yale Journal of Regulation* vol 6, no. 1 (Winter): 109-153.

Hahn, Robert W. 1989. "Economic Prescriptions for Environmental Problems: How the Patient Followed the Doctor's Orders", *The Journal of Economic Perspectives* vol. 3, no. 2 (Spring): 95-114.

Hahn, R. W. and G. L. Hester. 1989. "Marketable Permits: Lessons from Theory and Practice", *Ecology Law Quarterly,* vol 16: 361-406.

Harford, Jon D. 1978. "Firm Behavior Under Imperfectly Enforceable Pollution Standards and Taxes", *Journal of Environmental Economics and Management* vol. 5, no. 1 (March): 26-43.

Harrington, Winston. 1981. *The Regulatory Approach to Air Quality Management* (Washington, D.C.: Resources for the Future).

Harrison, David, Jr. 1983. "Case Study 1: The Regulation of Aircraft Noise", in Thomas C. Schelling, ed., *Incentives for Environmental Protection,* MIT Press: 41-143, Cambridge, Mass.

Howe, Charles W. and Dwight R. Lee. 1983. "Priority Pollution Rights: Adapting Pollution Control to a Variable Environment", *Land Economics* vol. 59, no. 2 (May): 141-149.

ICF Resources, Inc. 1989. "Economic, Environmental, and Coal Market Impacts of SO_2 Emissions Trading Under Alternative Acid Rain Control Proposals" a report prepared for the Regulatory Innovations Staff, USEPA (March).

Kneese, Allen V. and F. Lee Brown. 1981. *The Southwest Under Stress: National Resource Development Issues in a Regional Setting,* Johns Hopkins University Press for Resources for the Future, Inc., Baltimore, Md.

Kolstad, C. D. "Empirical Properties of Economic Incentives and Command-and-Control Regulations for Air Pollution Control", *Land Economics* vol. 62 no. 3 (August): 250-268.

Kostow, Lloyd P. and John F. Kowalcyzk. 1983. "A Practical Emission Trading Program", *Journal of the Air Pollution Control Association* vol. 33, no. 10 (October): 982-984.

Krupnick, Alan J. 1986. "Costs of Alternative Policies for the Control of Nitrogen Dioxide in Baltimore", *Journal of Environmental Economics and Management*, vol. 13, no. 2. (June): 189-197.

Krupnick, Alan J., Wallace E. Oates, and Eric Van de Verg. 1983. "On Marketable Air Pollution Permits: The Case for a System of Pollution Offsets", *Journal of Environmental Economics and Management* vol. 10, no. 3 (September): 233-247.

Levin, Michael H. 1982. "Getting There: Implementing the 'Bubble' Policy", in Eugene Bardarch and Robert A. Kagan, eds., *Social Regulation: Strategies for Reform,* ICS Press, San Francisco, Calif.

Levin, Michael H. 1985. "Statutes and Stopping Points: Building a Better Bubble at E.P.A.", *Regulation* vol. 9, no. 3 (March/April): 33-42.

Linder, Stephen H. and Mark E. McBride. 1984. "Enforcement Costs and Regulatory Reform: The Agency and Firm Response", *Journal of Environmental Economics and Management* vol. 11, no. 4 (December): 327-346.

Liroff, Richard A. 1980. *Air Pollution Offsets: Trading, Selling and Banking,* Conservation Foundation, Washington, D.C.

Liroff, Richard A. 1986. *Reforming Air Pollution Regulation: The Toil and Trouble of EPA's Bubble*, Conservation Foundation, Washington D.C.

Lyon, Randolph M. 1982. "Auctions and Alternative Procedures for Allocating Pollution Rights", *Land Economics* vol. 58, no. 1 (February): 16-32.

Maloney, Michael T. and Bruce Yandle. 1984. "Estimation of the Cost of Air Pollution Control Regulation", *Journal of Environmental Economics and Management* vol. 11, no. 3 (November): 244-263.

Maloney, Michael and Gordon L. Brady. 1988. "Capital Turnover and Marketable Property Rights", *The Journal of Law and Economics* vol. 31 (April): 203-226.

Main, Jeremy. 1988. "Here Comes the Big Cleanup", *Fortune,* (21 November): 102.

McGartland, Albert Mark. 1984. "Marketable Permit Systems for Air Pollution Control: An Empirical Study" (unpublished Ph.D. dissertation, University of Maryland).

McGartland, Albert Mark, and Wallace E. Oates. 1985. "Marketable Permits for the Prevention of Environmental Deterioration", *Journal of Environmental Economics and Management* vol. 12, no. 3 (September): 207-228.

Meidinger, Errol E. 1985. "On Explaining the Development of 'Emissions Trading' in U. S. Air Pollution Regulation", *Law and Policy* vol. 7, no. 4 (October): 447-480.

Milliman, Scott R. and Raymond Prince. 1989. "Firm Incentives to Promote Technological Change in Pollution Control", *Journal of Environmental Economics and Management*, vol. 17, no. 3 (November): 247-265.

Misiolek, Walter S. and Harold W. Elder. 1989. "Exclusionary Manipulation of Markets for Pollution Rights", *Journal of Environmental Economics and Management* vol. 16, no. 2 (March): 156-166.

Montgomery, W. David. 1972. "Markets in Licences and Efficient Pollution Control Programs", *Journal of Economic Theory* vol. 5, no. 3 (1972): 395-418.

National Commission on Air Quality. 1981. *To Breathe Clean Air* (Washington, D.C.: U.S. Government Printing Office).

Noll, R. G. 1982. "Implementing Marketable Emissions Permits", *American Economics Review* vol. 72, no. 2 (May): 120-124.

Northwest Colorado Council of Governments. 1984. "Point Sources-Nonpoint Sources Trading in the Lake Dillon Watershed" an unpublished final report (September).

Nussbaum, B. (1992). "Phasing Down Lead in Gasoline in the U.S.: Mandates, Incentives, Trading and Banking" in *OECD, Climate Change: Designing a Iradeable Permit System*, OECD 21-34, Paris.

Oates, W. E., and A. M. McGartland. 1985. "Marketable Pollution Permits and Acid Rain Externalities: A Comment and Some Further Evidence", *Canadian Journal of Economics* vol. 18, no. 3 (August): 668-675.

Oates, Wallace E., Paul R. Portney, and Albert M. McGartland. 1988. "The Net Benefits of Incentive-Based Regulation: The Case of Environmental Standard Setting in the Real World", *Resources for the Future Working Paper* (December).

O'Neil, William B. 1980. "Pollution Permits and Markets for Water Quality", (unpublished Ph.D. dissertation, the University of Wisconsin-Madison).

O'Neil, William B. 1983. "Transferable Discharge Permit Trading Under Varying Stream Conditions: A Simulation of Multiperiod Permit Market Performances on the Fox River, Wisconsin", *Water Resources Research* vol. 19, no. 3 (June): 608-612.

Oppenheimer, Joe A. and Clifford Russell. 1983. "A Tempest in a Teapot: The Analysis and Evaluation of Environmental Groups Trading in Markets for Pollution Permits", in Erhard F. Joeres and Martin H. David, eds., *Buying a Better Environment: Cost-Effective Regulation Through Permit Trading,* University of Wisconsin Press, Madison, Wis.

Palmer, Adele R., William E. Mooz, Timothy H. Quinn, and Kathleen A. Wolf. 1980. *Economic Implications of Regulating Chlorofluorocarbon Emissions from Nonaerosol Applications*, Report #R-2524-EPA prepared for the U.S. Environmental Protection Agency by the Rand Corporation (June).

Raufer, Roger K. and Stephen L. Feldman, 1984. "Emissions Trading and What it May Mean for Acid Deposition", *Public Utilities Fortnightly* vol 114, no. 4 (August 16): 17-25.

Roach Fred, Charles Kolstad, Allen V. Kneese, Richard Tobin, and Michael Williams. 1981. "Alternative Air Quality Policy Options in the Four Corners Region", *Southwestern Review* vol. 1, no. 2 (Summer): 29-58.

Roberts, M. W. 1983. "A Remedy for the Victims of Pollution Permit Markets", *Yale Law Journal* vol. 92, no. 6 (May): 1022-1040.

Roumasset, James A. and Kirk R. Smith. 1987. "Environmental Policy and Public Health: Regulating Air Pollution with Exposure Trading", *Working Paper of the Environment and Policy Institute,* East-West Center Honolulu, Hawaii 96848.

Russell, Clifford S. 1981. "Controlled Trading of Pollution Permits", *Environmental Science and Technology* vol. 15, no. 1 (January): 24-28.

Ryan, Donald R. 1981. "Transferable Discharge Permits and the Control of Stationary Source Air Pollution: A Survey and Synthesis: Comment", *Land Economics* vol. 57, no. 4 (November): 639-641.

Seskin, Eugene P., Robert J. Anderson, Jr., and Robert O. Reid. 1983. "An Empirical Analysis of Economic Strategies for Controlling Air Pollution", *Journal of Environmental Economics and Management* vol. 10, no. 2 (June): 112-124.

Shapiro, M. and E. Warhit. 1983. "Marketable Permits: The Case of Chlorofluorocarbons", *Natural Resource Journal* vol. 23, no. 3 (July): 577-591.

Spofford, Walter O., Jr. 1984. "Efficiency Properties of Alternative Source Control Policies for Meeting Ambient Air Quality Standards: An Empirical Application to the Lower Delaware Valley". Discussion paper D-118 Resources for the Future (November), Washington D.C.

Stavins, Robert N. et. al. 1988. "Project 88: Harnessing Market Forces to Protect Our Environment", unpublished manuscript sponsored by Senators Timothy E. Wirth and John Heinz (October).

Stavins, Robert. N. 1989. "Harnessing Market Forces to Protect the Environment", *Environment* vol. 31, no. 1 (January/February): 4-7,28-35.

Stewart, Richard B. 1988. "Controlling Environmental Risks through Economic Incentives", *Columbia Journal of Environmental Law* vol. 13, no. 2 (no month listed): 153-169.

Teller, Azriel. 1970. "Air Pollution Abatement: Economic Rationality and Reality", in Roger Revelle and Hans Landsberg, eds. *America's Changing Environment* Beacon Press, Boston.

Tietenberg, T. H. 1974. "The Design of Property Rights for Air Pollution Control", *Public Policy* vol. 27, no. 3 (Summer): 275-292.

Tietenberg, T. H. 1980. "Transferable Discharge Permits and the Control of Stationary Source Air Pollution: A Survey and Synthesis", *Land Economics* vol. 56, no. 4 (November): 391-416.

Tietenberg, T. H. 1985. *Emissions Trading: An Exercise in Reforming Pollution Policy*, Resources for the Future, Washington, D.C.

Tietenberg, T. H. 1986. "Uncommon Sense: The Program to Reform Pollution Control Policy", in Leonard W. Weiss, and Michael W. Klass eds., *Regulatory Reform: What Actually Happened*, Little Brown and Company: 269-303, Boston.

Tietenberg, T. H. 1989a. "Acid Rain Reduction Credits" *Challenge* Vol. 32. no. 2 (March/April): 25-29.

Tietenberg, T. H. 1989b. "Marketable Permits in the U.S.: A Decade of Experience" in Karl W. Roskamp, ed. *Public Finance and the Performance of Enterprises*, Wayne State University Press, Detroit, MI.

Tietenberg, T. H. 1992. *Environmental and Natural Resource Economics*, 3rd ed. New York: Harper Collins Publishers, Scott, Foresman and Company, Glenview, Illinois.

U.S. General Accounting Office. 1979. *Improvements Needed in Controlling Major Air Pollution Sources* (Report CED-78-165).

U.S. General Accounting Office. 1986. *EPA Program to Assist Leaded-Gasoline Producers Needs Prompt Improvement*, (Report CED-86-182).

Vivian, W. 1981. "An Updated Tabulation of Offset Cases" cited in National Commission Air Quality, *To Breathe Clean Air,* U.S. Government Printing Office, Washington, D.C.

Vivian, W. and W. Hall. 1979. "An Empirical Examination of U.S. Market Trading in Air Pollution Offsets", Institute of Public Policy Studies, University of Michigan.

Yaron, Dan. 1979. "A Model for the Analysis of Seasonal Aspects of Water Quality Control", *Journal of Environmental Economics and Management* vol. 6, no. 2 (June): 140-151.

CHAPTER 3

Environmental Taxes: A cautious start in Sweden

by

Thomas Sterner and Marianne Löwgren*

Abstract

This chapter provides a survey of Swedish environmental policies concentrating on emissions to the atmosphere and to water as well as solid wastes. In particular we review the Swedish experiences of environmental tax reform, energy policies and deposit refund schemes. Environmental regulation in Sweden has many traits in common with the US and in many instances it has, indeed used the US as a model. When it comes to choice of policy instruments, however, Sweden has not started to use tradeable emission permits, at least not yet. Instead taxes have been given a quite prominent role particularly in connection with the recent tax reform and we try briefly to discuss some of the possible reasons for this difference, and the lessons that can be learnt on the usefulness of taxes as an environmental policy tool.

*Thanks for useful comments from Gunnar Köhlin and Milford Aguilar.

T. Sterner (ed.), Economic Policies for Sustainable Development, 46–67.

1 INTRODUCTION

As we saw in Chapter 2, the sheer costs of "Command and Control" (CAC) policies more or less forced the introduction, in the US, of economic instruments such as tradeable emission permits. In Europe the general development of policies concerning environmental regulation has been quite similar, although in general it started a little later. Similar command and control regulations were set up and in many cases US legislation was used as a model. The initial use of subsidies also had its similarities but the tradeable emission permits have basically not been copied (see Chapter 5 for a major new exception) in Europe.

When searching for reasons one may note that the general policy context is different in Europe. In most European countries the role of the state, either directly in economic activity or indirectly through economic planning is somewhat greater, increasing the potential for state action. On the other hand, we also find that the relative size of the largest companies (as a share of say GDP) is often larger in Europe than in the US making them relatively more influential. The combination of these two factors - mutual dependency between powerful monopolies and an interventionist state - have given the process of environmental control another, perhaps more informal or negotiating character that may have reduced the perceived need for tradeable permits. For a permit trading program to work well, we have seen that we ideally need many large polluters emitting the same or similar pollutants in a particular area. This is probably somewhat less common, at least in a small European country such as Sweden. This is not to say though, that TEPs could not be used. Their extensive use has indeed recently been suggested for nitrogen and phosphorus. Another relevant difference due to the smaller size of European countries is that a large share of their environmental problems are caused abroad while a similarly large share of their own pollution is exported. This reduces the scope and rationale for purely domestic policies (except the policy of building higher chimneys!).

On the other hand public resistance to state involvement appears smaller, particularly in the Nordic countries, than in the US. Thus it is quite symptomatic that environmental taxation has been perceived as a somewhat more acceptable policy measure. In spite of this, however, environmental taxation still plays a subordinate role in most European countries. Majone (1990), among others, claims, that the choice between policy instruments is less dependent on their formal properties than on the political and administrative structure in which they operate. Different perspectives are held by experts, who may recommend solutions to environmental problems from purely technical and economic points of view, and policy makers, who are forced to take into consideration additional limitations that are imposed by the actual context. To put it bluntly, vested interests and institutional structures, rather than abstract theory are the factors that shape policy. However, a combination of growing interest in the environment and the deregulation trends of the 1980s is likely to pave the road for an extended use of economic instruments in policy-making.

The theoretical rationale for environmental taxation has, of course, quite a long history in economics: we could begin with Ricardo's enthusiasm for taxation of rents on land but the most pertinent concept in the context of the environment, strictu sensu, is the Pigouvian tax. Pigou intended the tax to correct for the external cost caused by a certain product or activity. More recently there has been some discussion about a wider concept of green taxation which takes into account the need not only to correct for externalities but also to minimize the inevitable excess burden generated by any form of taxation, see for instance Sandmo (1975). From the theory of optimal taxation we know about a number of criteria which should characterize a good candidate for taxation: inelasticity of demand, negligible (or at least not strongly regressive) effects on income distribution and so forth. We know that present forms of taxation are heavily flawed and thus a partial substitution of excise, income or other taxes for environmental taxes could, in some cases, be beneficial not only for the environment but also to reduce the excess burden of present forms of taxation.

2 ECONOMIC INSTRUMENTS IN THE NORDIC COUNTRIES

We noted above that at an initial stage of environmental pollution control both Sweden, other West European countries and the U.S. relied mainly on command and control. Over time the CAC-strategies have been supplemented with economic instruments: taxes, charges, deposit-refund systems and various kinds of producer responsibilities for clean-up costs. Several such instruments and incentives have run for two decades or even more[1] - an OECD-survey reports a 1987 total of 85 economic instruments in six Western European countries (OECD, 1989). Most applications in the 1970s and 1980s have concerned waste disposal or emissions to water rather than to air. Presumably the latter have appeared more difficult to measure or monitor, or perhaps they may have been considered as regional rather than local and national problems. But now that these issues are being approached, taxes and charges are highlighted as means to limit gaseous emissions.

The Nordic countries have many similarities in their use of economic incentives for environmental protection as regards the types of incentives used, and their both financial and distributive role as policy instruments. Table 1 shows the main economic instruments (excluding subsidies and enforcement incentives). From the marginal cost perspective taxes and charges are identical when intended to internalize environmental costs. In practice, the distinction lies in the fact that taxes are regular revenues to the state treasury, while the inflow of charges and fees are explicitly destined to eliminate negative consequences of little pollution. For example, Swedish battery charges are intended to cover the costs of collection and safe disposal of used batteries, and some charges on fossil fuels finance the liming of acid lakes and the development of better incineration technologies.

Product taxes, some of which are differentiated (e.g. for leaded/unleaded gasoline), are the most widely used economic instruments related to air pollution control. Purely effluent-related fees have been rather sparse so far, but as monitoring technology improves such measures will probably replace some of the present product charges, for instance the ones now applied to control the impacts caused by fossil fuels. The Nordic countries all have differentiated taxes to lower the turn-over of non-reusable package materials and deposit-refund systems to recycle beverage packages. The deposit-refund concept also covers car hulks in Sweden and Norway.

---

[1] The first experiments with charges for water date back to the Ruhr in the 1930s.

A preventive approach is taken through the use of administrative charges for chemicals and pesticides, that are used in agricultural and forestry programs. In Sweden fee calculations are area-related in order to favor the use of low-dose products. Product charges and brand registration fees are mainly designed to cover the administration and monitoring costs for the regulating body, the National Chemicals Inspectorate.

Table 1 Economic instruments in the Nordic countries 1/1 1991.

PRODUCTS	SWEDEN	NORWAY	DENMARK	FINLAND
Fossil energy (PT)	All fossil	All except gas/coal	All except gas	Transport fuels only
Carbon (PT)	All fossil	Except coal		All fossil
Sulphur PT/EC	All fossil	Oil only		
Aircraft	PT on NOx	EC on Noise		
CFC	AC	PT/DR	PC	
Car hulks	DR	DR		
Batteries	PC	PT		
Lamps			PT	
Food containers	PT/DR	PT/DR	PT/DR	PT/DR
Lubricating oils		PT		PC
Solid waste			PT	
Fertilizers	PC	PC		PC
Pesticides	PC/AC	PC/AT	AC	AC

Sources: Nord 1991:27, OECD.
PT/PC Product Tax/Charge. EC Effluent Charge, AC/T Administrative Charge/Tax and DR Deposit-refund.

User fees are levied for the treatment of wastewater and solid wastes. Municipalities still operate the majority of treatment facilities on a non-discriminatory and non-profit basis, except in Denmark, where waste minimization is being encouraged through the price mechanism. In Sweden local authorities have again been given greater jurisdiction over policies for waste collection and are now allowed to set fees in order to get an incentive effect and not just to cover costs. Some municipalities, for example Varberg (South of Gothenburg), have started to charge households per kilo of trash instead of a fixed fee per year for waste collection. According to preliminary results the waste collected has been cut in half (supposedly the rest is now composted locally. Lets hope it's not just dumped somewhere).

3 THE DEVELOPMENT OF SWEDISH ENVIRONMENTAL POLICIES

It is tempting, in this chapter on Sweden, to focus on the use of environmental taxation because of the contrast provided with the US experience. This should not obscure the fact that environmental policies in both countries are very much more complex than "permits versus taxes". In fact there are many similarities between the regulatory structures in the two countries. One fundamental difference, though, should be kept in mind: Swedish environmental legislation aims at *emission* control while *ambient* quality control is the key feature of the U.S. protection strategy. This, of course, has a significant impact on the eligibility of policy instruments. For example, in Sweden there is no equivalent to the American "Nonattainment Areas", in which new additions to total pollution are banned even with best available technology. Incidently, this may be another reason why Sweden (and most European countries) lack the trade in emission permits that characterize the US system[2].

Sweden is one of the countries in Europe where there has been quite an early and vivid interest in environmental issues. As a result of popular awareness, environmental policies, including economic instruments, were implemented relatively early. One reason for environmental interest in Sweden probably is the fact that the country industrialized rather late. It is sparsely populated; despite urbanization the traditions and the culture of the former agrarian society are still part of public awareness. Free access to the countryside (woods, lakes, beaches, etc) is a public right, even on private land, and hiking, camping, hunting, angling and other outdoor activities are very much part of the national life-style.

In spite of its low population density, (nineteen inhabitants per square kilometer) and vast tracts of fairly untouched nature, Sweden was also hit early by major environmental problems related to acid rain. The reason for this is that Sweden happens to have an extremely sensitive ecology with respect to acidification, see Kuylenstierna & Chadwick (1989). This has implied, that the consequences of acidification became visible to researchers, anglers, foresters and others much earlier than in other countries of Europe. While damage abroad from acidifying combustion emissions appeared speculative to the British or Germans, it was much more credible to the Scandinavians who saw their lakes dying.

In a historical perspective, though, it is still reasonable to say that environmental concern is, in Sweden as in other countries, a recent phenomenon. In the first half of this century it was practically synonymous with nature conservation. The Swedish Society for Nature Conservation was founded in 1909, the same year the first national park was established. Not until industrialization and urbanization had started to make its mark in the post-war period did the need for more systematic environmental legislation appear. Statens Naturvårdsverk, the Swedish Environmental Protection Agency was set up in 1967 together with the basic legal framework, codified in the Environmental Protection Act of 1969, complemented by a law on

---

[2] We have already noted other possible explanations in the introduction. It is also difficult for affected parties to bring a polluter to court and the courts very rarely assess indemnities. Taking the State to court, as in the US, is not part of everyday life either.

hazardous substances in 1973. During the late 1980s quite a number of new laws came into force in order to supplement the Act of 1969. 1986 saw the introduction of new laws on Chemical Products and on Vehicle Exhausts. A preventive and comprehensive approach was demonstrated by the 1987 legislation on Planning and Building and on the use of Natural Resources, and in 1990 there was a new Waste Bill requiring detailed assessment of the quantities and characteristics of all municipal wastes. Sorting of waste at the source is to be mandatory from 1994 in order to implement recycling and minimize the harm to the environment.

The Environmental Protection Act is mainly concerned with industrial and municipal emissions. As mentioned above, the initial approach was a regulatory one, based on a licensing system that requires all new plants or projects to have prior approval according to a number of environmental criteria. Virtually all new sources are required to use the "best available" appropriate technology that can be "afforded" by a typical enterprise in that particular branch of industry. Furthermore, plants are to be located in a way that "minimizes" negative environmental effects without incurring "unreasonable" costs. These licenses are issued by regional or national authorities, depending on how serious the pollution is, or even, in some cases, by the Government. At this level of generality the framework is fairly similar to that in the US, but the mode of implementation differs considerably. The characteristic feature of the Swedish policy style was (and is) the search for consensus between regulating authorities and their "counterparts" in business. The approved emissions are determined in a negotiation process, and this strategy also includes the ambition and the potential of tightening given permits as new technologies evolve.

This is not the place to make a general, comparative analysis of legal and judicial systems, but enterprises in Sweden seem to have had a fairly relaxed legal system within which to operate, by comparison with the US and many European countries, see for instance Smith & Kromarek (1989). The authorities, always look for a trade-off between environmental and economic goals. The effects of enforcement incentives are highly dependent upon the vigor of implementation. The Swedish environment protection charge, enacted in 1981, is a weak instrument, not intended to affect behavior, but to ensure that there will be no profits from breaking environmental protection laws. Few cases have been brought to court, because it must be proven, that the polluter actually made a profit from violating the rules. The amount charged is supposed to eliminate the profits gained from non-compliance which is a rather moderate sanction. Self-monitoring is (as in the US) the usual method of checking for routine compliance and violations are hard to prove, given all the difficulties involved in the techniques for the gathering of information.

4 TAX REFORM: THE ENVIRONMENT AS A NEW SOURCE OF TAXATION

Sweden is known to be a country of high taxes and particularly in the late 1980's we must have been regarded with a mixture of admiration and incredulous horror as marginal taxes on income approached, and surpassed the 90% level. There were several factors behind these record rates: firstly the sheer size of the public sector including welfare-related income transfers as a share of GDP, secondly the preference given to direct income taxation (as opposed to indirect taxes) and, thirdly, the progressivity of the tax schedule.

In part this tax regime was the accidental product of progressivity and inflation. Due to inflation nominal incomes rose and ordinary workers came into the income - and hence tax - brackets originally intended for the very high income earners. For a decade or two this process gave the politicians ever increasing sums of money for new "reforms" with which they could boost their popularity. As time passed the tax system was "reformed" by adding more and more taxes, new rules and, when the effects became blatantly unacceptable, exceptions or loop-holes - until in fact many of the wealthiest actually paid little or no taxes since they were essentially evadable through complicated (deductible) financial operations.

Although most of these loop-holes were an issue for the wealthy few, who can manipulate their portfolios, there was at least one important area of everyday - and environmental - concern in which a very large share of the population could "benefit", and that was gasoline taxation. In the 1980´s gasoline used to carry a relatively high tax (although far from the highest in Europe - see Chapter 16). Expenses for driving to work were however income deductible according to the "logic" of that time: since they were necessary in order to earn your income. Combining this deductibility, (roughly 9 billion SEK were deducted from aggregate taxable income each year in the late 80-ies, which is almost half the yearly sales of gasoline in the country (1 USD = roughly 8 SEK in 1993)), with the high marginal taxes, obviously made gasoline appear pretty cheap to many drivers which explains the low price sensitivity of gasoline demand in Sweden.

In 1991 the tax system was radically reformed with a view to reducing marginal taxes on higher incomes and of creating transparency, simplicity and minimum distortions. Income taxes were cut to 30% for most wage-earners and a maximum of 50% for high incomes (actually this is still quite an underestimate since social security fees are levied on the total wage bill in addition to personal taxes. At the same time excise taxes on certain luxuries were abolished and the capital taxes were simplified and made more uniform. This was all financed by a somewhat higher uniform level of VAT, which was applied to a broader tax base than earlier. Additional financing was gained through reduced deductibility from personal income and through higher taxes on a number of environmentally related products, the most important of which are in various ways related to energy, such as the carbon dioxide tax.

The need for a major tax reform appears to have created an opportunity for a swift introduction of relatively higher environmental taxes than would otherwise have been possible. A summary of current tax revenues is shown in Table 2. Note that the definition of "environmental taxes" can be quite problematic: since such taxes are likely, at present, to be more acceptable to the public than other taxes, there is an incentive for politicians to rename other taxes. For instance, if energy taxes are simply renamed, it is hard to see this as an environmental reform. Partly this can be said of the 1991 reform, since the former energy taxes were cut in half as a (partial) compensation for the new CO_2 and other environmental taxes. We take the approach here that all taxes levied on environmentally hazardous products can be seen as "environmental taxes" even if that was not their original purpose. Gasoline taxes are clearly an example, but sometimes it may be hard to tell. Taxes on tobacco clearly do have an environmental effect but it might not be wholly correct to describe them as purely environmental. The same goes for the pure energy tax - at least when applied to hydro power[3]! We will, however, be liberal in the sense of including all taxes that have some reasonable relationship to important environmental issues. We have, however, not included liquor taxes although some would argue that the consumption of wine and alcohol does cause some very important externalities.

The sum total of all taxes that are environmental according to this definition (excluding VAT) is around 50 Billion SEK. Out of this total, tobacco accounts for 7 BSEK and the overwhelming part of the rest is related to energy use, including transport vehicles and thereby mainly concerns emissions to the air. Other environmental taxes only add up to a few hundred million SEK. Thus environmental taxes correspond to roughly 6% of total tax revenue (5% of spending). Expressed as a share of central government taxes they actually account for more than 15% (but less than 10% of spending). The difference is due to the budget deficit. Taxes raise 325 Billion but spending is 520! The truth of the matter is actually more complicated since some taxes are directly or indirectly deductible. All the excise taxes are basically deductible from corporate profits and, as already mentioned, private individuals can still, in many cases, deduct the costs of driving to work. Furthermore many companies give their employees company cars (which can be attractive when marginal taxes are high - even if the recipients are now taxed for such "payments in kind"). This often implies that the driver does not pay the gasoline himself and so the incentive effect is reduced. The company does of course have to pay the gasoline taxes but then these costs are deductible against corporate profit tax.

---

[3] This is a tax on old power stations motivated by the desire to capture some of the windfall they experience due to rising electricity prices. It has no environmental motivation.

Table 2 The budgetary impact of environmental taxes 1992/3 (Forecast)

Total Public sector; Revenue	Billion SEK 880
Central government: Taxes Income taxes Social security VAT Other excise taxes etc ***Whereof Environmental***	 325 38 68 116 70 ***roughly 50:***
Gasoline	20.6
Energy	13.3
Sulphur	0.5
Nuclear	0.13
Hydro	(0.97)
Vehicle tax	4.0
Kilometer tax (diesel)	3.1
Sales tax new vehicles	1.3
Charge on NOx	0 (1.1 refunded)
Beverage containers[a)]	0.15
Fertilizer/Pesticides	0.15
Batteries	0.02
Other administrative environmental charges	0.1
Tobacco	7.0
(Wine and alcohol)	(9.2)

a) Abolished May 1993

5 POLICIES FOR AIR POLLUTION CONTROL

5.1 Background

The 1969 Environmental Protection Act introduced limitations to emissions of polluting substances into air, soil and water. The Act was accompanied by subsidies to industry 1971-75 for the installation of pollution control devices. This enabled existing plants to achieve air (and water) emission limits corresponding to the BAT-requirements, mandatory for new plants. Further, charges (combined with regulations on quality standards) on oil products appeared in 1976 for the purpose of lowering the sulphur content in oil used for heating. The revenues were destined to finance measures against acidification, mainly the liming of lakes (see also Section 6). The national policy mix set up to control sulphur emissions has been partly successful. During the 1980s Swedish sulphur emissions decreased 60 per cent. However, this is not enough to protect flora and fauna in Sweden: emissions of acidifying gases from the European continent have only decreased 20 percent and deposition still grossly exceed loads that are ecologically tolerable. The national abatement of nitrous oxides has proved to be even more complicated. More than half of the NO_X are generated by traffic, and decreases achieved through technical improvements during the 1980s have now been outweighed by growth in the volume of traffic. Other main nitrogen contributions come from incineration and agriculture. Neither Sweden nor other European countries are likely to reach the emission targets agreed upon within the framework of the Geneva Convention (the ECE Convention).

5.2 Energy and carbon taxes

Current policies directed to industry mostly rely on the negotiation of concessions and the main area of policy attention for airborne emissions is now directed to transport and energy. The main taxes are, as already mentioned, the energy tax, which was halved in 1991, and the new carbon tax together with a number of special taxes on sulphur, lead, old cars, purchase of new cars, different qualities of diesel. These were again reformed in 1993 and current taxes are shown in Table 3. Table 4 gives some additional detail for different types of fuel and provides a comparison with 1990 and 1991 levels.

Table 3 Main Environmental taxes in Sweden, January 1993

Fertilizers	0.6 SEK/kg N 1.2 SEK/kg P
Pesticide	8 SEK/kg active ingredient
Beverage containers[a] Returnable Disposable	 0.08 SEK a piece 0.1-0.25 (depends on size)
Batteries Alkaline/mercury oxide Nickel/Cadmium Lead batteries	 23 SEK/Kg 25 SEK/kg 40 SEK a piece
Energy related taxes VAT General energy tax Carbon dioxide Sulphur in fuels Gasoline tax Leaded gasoline NO_X in large scale combustion plants	 25% (except air traffic) Differentiated -see below 0.25 SEK/kg 0.08 SEK/kg for industry 30 SEK/kg. (27 SEK/m3 for each 0.1% S in oil) 3.14 SEK/l but only 0.8 SEK for motor alcohol 0.51 SEK/l extra 40 SEK/Kg (refunded in prop to energy produced)
Domestic air traffic NO_X and Hydrocarbons CO_2	 12 SEK/kg 1 SEK/kg
Electricity Nuclear power Hydro (>1.5MW) **General energy tax** (No CO_2 tax on electricity)	 0.002 SEK/kWh + 0.02 funded for waste 0.01-2 SEK/kWh (by age) Industry: 0 SEK/kWh Heating etc. 0.063 N Sweden 0.035 Others =.085 SEK/kWh
Vehicle Tax Yearly Sales tax	Yearly tax by weight. Sales tax differentiated by environm. characteristics
Kilometer Tax	Proportional to weight, distance etc. for diesel vehicles.To be replaced.
Other taxes...	Tobacco, waste. Deposit refund car hulks...

a) Abolished May 1993.

Table 4 General energy and CO_2 taxes[1] for selected fuels[2] 1993; (and 1990/91)

	Unit	Energy tax 1993	Carbon tax 1993	Total tax 1993	*Tax 91*	*Tax 90*
		Ind / other	Ind / other	Ind / other	*Ind/other*	*Ind/other*
Oil[3]	m^3	0 / 540[4]	230 / 920	230 / 1460	*1260*	*1078*
Coal[3]	tons	0 / 230	200 / 800	200 / 1030	*850*	*460*
Nat gas	1000 m^3	0 / 175	170 / 680	170 / 855	*710*	*350*
LPG	tons	0 / 105	240 / 960	240 / 1065	*855*	*210*
Electr	MWh	0/35-63-85	0	0 / 35 -85	*50 / 72*	*70 / 92*

1. NB that VAT and other environmental taxes on nuclear power, gasoline etc are additional.
2. Peat, waste and bio-fuels pay no carbondioxide or general energy tax.
3. Sulphur taxes are also additional, depending on the sulphur content, see Table 3.
4. Energy taxes are also differentiated by environmental quality. For diesel they range from 90 for class 1, 290 for II to 540 for class III. For gasoline the carbon tax is 0.74 SEK/l and for aviation fuel 1 SEK/l.

The tax reform of 1991 implied higher taxation on energy which was heavily resented by industry. Obviously companies do enjoy a similar tax deductibility as private individuals, since energy and other goods they buy is deductible from corporate profit tax. Moreover the energy-intensive companies had special preferential rules that maximized their total energy taxes to 1.7 per cent of sales. Still the new system of taxation was heavily criticized by industry. Their main argument was, that they were paying more taxes than their competitors abroad. It was also criticized by the environmentalists because of the fact that the really major users were facing practically no marginal taxes on energy use (because of the ceiling of 1.7 per cent), and finally the fact that this was a tax concession was seen as a potential source of trouble with GATT rules on subsidizing domestic industry. Foreseeing the need for harmonization with EC legislation, the government appointed a committee to revise industrial taxation, see SOU 1991:90.

This led to a new energy tax reform from January 1993. The key elements of this reform were that industry (and horticulture) were exempted from all general energy taxation and furthermore 75% of carbon taxation. This cut was financed by increases for private consumers, particularly in the carbon tax which increased from 250 to 320 SEK/ton of CO_2 and the general tax on electricity (an additional 13 SEK/MWh)[4]. Table 4 shows that these changes do indeed imply a very different level of taxation for industry compared to households or other commercial users for oil, coal, gas and electricity. The last two columns show, by way of comparison, the tax levels for 1990 and 1991. In both of these years industry and other users basically paid the same tax (with the exception of a small difference for electricity and also the

[4] There were some additional changes concerning the differentiation of diesel fuels. There are also some transitional rules maximizing total carbon taxes for industry.

"ceiling" on energy taxes). As the reader will notice these taxes were indeed raised quite substantially in 1991. The reform of 1993, however, brings industrial tax levels back down to a much lower level than before the reform of 91 (except for LPG), while other consumers get a further increase in tax levels.

The prime motivation for this was obviously to safeguard the competitiveness of Swedish industry. When criticized for reducing environmental taxation the official standpoint was, that the general energy tax was *not* environmental but purely fiscal. As a fiscal tax there was no reason to tax intermediary inputs. (If, however, one sees these energy taxes as Pigouvian taxes correcting for a number of environmental effects of energy production and consumption - as we do - then the conclusion would logically have been different). As for the carbon tax, atmospheric warming (which it is supposed to address) is a global environmental problem about which Swedish incentives alone can accomplish nothing. In fact, it was argued, higher energy taxation in Sweden will just cause a relocation of industry to other countries and thus there will be no aggregate effect at all. Sometimes it was even suggested that the new countries where industry chooses to locate will most likely have less stringent environmental rules and incentive structures so that the overall environmental effect might even be negative. This argument may in principle be correct, and the Swedish carbon tax is high by international standards, but on the other hand relocation depends on many factors and increased taxes may also speed up increases in every efficiency that can turn out to be a competitive advantage. Finally, if no country takes the lead international progress is bound to be slow.

It might seem curious to some readers that there is both a carbon tax and a general energy tax in addition to more specific taxes on sulphur, lead etc. For a number of reasons the energy tax was not abolished completely in favor of a carbon tax. Basically the most important of these concern hydroelectricity and nuclear power, which would have been strongly favored by such a change. For hydro, existing power stations would have experienced a "windfall gain" perceived as unfair (they are already taxed to compensate for the gains they have experienced due to the rise in electricity prices). On the other hand the number of potential new hydro stations is very limited, so the incentive effect on supply would be quite small. As for nuclear industry, we have a specific parliamentary decision to phase out nuclear power after the useful life of the present reactors. Although we have yet to see this actually happen, this is officially the current state of affairs. This phase-out would logically require the support of some form of tax or price policy to limit demand and to encourage alternative supplies. Although no such policy is being directly pursued, the keeping of at least some form of general energy tax should perhaps be interpreted as a reflection of the fact that every form of energy production including, in particular, nuclear power, has some negative externalities[5].

---

[5] The politics of energy are however always intricate and many politicians still see energy saving and energy self-sufficiency as important goals. This seems to be the reason why peat is exempt from both energy and carbon taxes. Although renewable it is not clear if it really does renew in a relevant time span and from an environmental point of view it has many other disadvantages. The rationale for preferential tax treatment would thus not seem strong, but it is *domestic!*

5.3 Other energy and transport related taxes

As we could see in Table 2, the single largest environmental tax revenue is from gasoline which is subject not only to the carbon tax but also a specific gasoline tax of 3.14 SEK/l unleaded and an additional 0.51 SEK/l for leaded gasoline. Leaded fuel has now been reduced to less than half of total gasoline consumption. After the latest increases Sweden has among the highest gasoline taxes in the world. For diesel, however, the tax levels have traditionally been much lower, the difference being made up by a mileage tax on diesel vehicles. The advantage of this tax from an environmental viewpoint was, that it could be differentiated by type and weight of the vehicle[6]. In fact this system could have been developed to better reflect actual emissions. For the sake of harmonization with the EC this tax is, however, now to be phased out and replaced by higher taxes on diesel fuel. It is a positive step that the tax on different qualities of diesel is now being heavily differentiated (see Table 4 note 4), but while such differentiation can catch the effect of variations in sulphur or aromatics it can obviously not catch differences in the exhaust vector that depend on the motor or the vehicle. This is for instance often the case with NO_X emissions.

In addition there are annual vehicle taxes that vary by type and weight of the vehicle and also a sales tax on new vehicles that is differentiated by environmental characteristics. Thus cars that meet the more stringent California requirements (class 1) will be subsidized, while the cars in class 3 that only meet the minimum legal requirements will be taxed. One of the main differences between classes 1 and 3 is the NO_X emissions per km and thus it would seem that this tax addresses one of the deficiencies mentioned above. Note, however, that since this is a tax on the vehicle it does not account for the distance driven, and once the vehicle is bought there is no tax to internalize the *marginal* emissions of NO_X.

One of the problems of taxing NO_X is precisely the fact that emissions do not depend in any simple way on fuel characteristics (compare the case of SO_X which always comes from the sulphur content of the fuel - thus the latter has simply been subject to a uniform tax of 30 SEK/Kg). Although typical emission profiles are available for various vehicle types, exact emissions vary quite a lot depending on maintenance, temperature, speed and a number of other factors.

Direct measuring of NO_X is quite complicated and thus expensive, at least on a small scale. In January 1992 a charge was levied on large combustion plants that is based on actually measured emissions. This applies to some 200 units >10MW. If, however, only these plants had been taxed, smaller (and generally less efficient from both an energy and a NO_X viewpoint) plants would have been seen to benefit. Consequently a charge instead of a tax was used. The proceeds of the charge are simply refunded to the same group of plants but in proportion to the amount of energy produced so that no net taxation of this group is involved.

Domestic air transport has, by way of contrast, been subjected to a pure tax on both NO_X and hydrocarbons (12 SEK/kg in addition to the 1 SEK/kg carbon tax). Lack of space precludes a more detailed treatment of all the transport related environmental policies followed in the country. Naturally traffic regulation and

---

[6] Typical tax rates were 0.2-3 SEK/km for passenger cars but 0.53-69 SEK/Km for 16 ton lorries and somewhat less for busses of the same weight.

planning as well as the financing and provision of public transport do have major impacts that ought to be considered in this context. Furthermore, local municipalities such as Stockholm or Gothenburg have been given increased rights to regulate traffic and may even be introducing road pricing or similar (more environmentally based) fees in the future.

6 POLICIES FOR WATER POLLUTION CONTROL

In Sweden the funding of public works has a long tradition. Municipal subsidy programs started in the mid-forties with the combined purpose of creating jobs for men returning from the army and improving health and sanitation by the provision of clean drinking water and wastewater treatment in urban areas. The post-war Swedish program for public water pipes and sewers was switched to the exclusive financing of wastewater treatment plants in order to ameliorate the introduction of emission licensing, according to the 1969 Environment Protection Act. The aim of that program was to connect 90 per cent of the urban population to 'satisfactory' treatment facilities by 1972, and 100 per cent by 1975. 50 per cent of construction costs were granted for approved technologies, except during the economic recession 1971-73, when 75 per cent were granted in areas with high unemployment. 'Satisfactory' was defined as the removal of 90 per cent of phosphorus and BOD, preferably by tertiary treatment (chemical precipitation) technologies. This goal was reached in the late 1970s, and the grant program ceased in 1980. By international standards Sweden has reached an unusually high level of wastewater treatment: 90 per cent of the urban population (which means over 80 per cent of the total population) is served by tertiary treatment and most of the remaining 10 per cent has secondary treatment. The wastewater from rural households and farms are subject to regulations from local Health and Environment Protection Boards.

In addition to the municipal program the Swedish government supported private company pollution control 1969-75. The state covered a maximum of 50 per cent of costs for the provision of technical equipment to reduce emissions into air and water, mostly by end-of-pipe technologies. Of course the existence of these subsidies facilitated the fulfillment of emission control goals for old plants. It is difficult to separate the share of environmental protection investment from ordinary business renewals and reinvestments, but even during the clean-up period 1969-75 the total Swedish industrial investment for water protection was estimated to no more than 5 per cent of gross industrial investment annually (Löwgren, 1988). This is similar to the American figure for the same period, without any federal or state grants to private pollution control investment. Notably, despite the lack of subsidization more than 80 per cent of the U.S. industry achieved the target of Best-Practical-Technology compliance by 1977 (Yeager, 1991).

Looking at municipal wastewater pollution control we can find some similarities between the early Swedish and U.S. policies. The U.S. federal grant program originally provided capital to share the construction costs of municipal wastewater treatment facilities. Environmental ambitions rose during the 1960s, and the stated objectives of the 1972 Clean Water Act were to make waters everywhere clean enough for fishing and swimming by 1983, and to obtain "zero discharges" by 1985. The means were discharge permits, technology-based standards and construction grants, but evidently this was not enough: in 1981, thirty-seven states reported that pollution from non-point sources would prevent them from attaining the national objectives. The Reagan administration decentralized responsibilities to state and local governments and the Water Quality Act of 1987 called for a phasing out of federal construction grants.

We find, that the municipal wastewater treatment grant programs in the two countries both were technology-based, although in different ways. The U.S. grant program simply aimed at implementing secondary wastewater treatment in urban areas. The 1987 act has a mix of effluent standards and ecological considerations, and to maintain or improve surface water quality there is a strong emphasis on multi-year management plans to control polluted run-off from farms, streets, construction sites and other non-point sources. The Swedish program was designed to stimulate BAT-solutions by relating the amount of state funding for municipal wastewater treatment to the degree of phosphorus and BOD removal. This seemed to have a strong incentive effect: chemical precipitation technology (tertiary treatment) was implemented in almost all urban areas, even the very small ones. However, treatment plants were not built everywhere. Instead, networks of sewers were constructed around the cities to transport the wastewater from suburbs within a radius of 30-40 kilometers, or even more, to centrally located treatment plants (Löwgren, 1988).

We should, however, see the "success" of the Swedish subsidization scheme in a more critical fashion: cheap on-site treatment methods, suitable for small urban areas, e.g. the growing of energy crops, were overlooked, and instead uniform large-scale and energy-consuming technologies were applied. Here it might be appropriate to make a distinction between efficiency and effectiveness. Efficiency is a more limited technical ratio between input and output while effectiveness should be seen in relation to general goals. Hence, if we accept tertiary treatment as the given Best-Technology solution, centralization was an efficient policy. Investment costs per population equivalent are lower for large plants, and so are of course wages, administration and monitoring costs. At low energy prices these economies-of-scale for wastewater treatment counterbalance the costs of transportation for polluted water and sludge.

From a broader effectiveness perspective, however, the idea of sending human wastes from fringe areas into the center of our urban areas seems somewhat peculiar. Maybe the flow in our sewers ought to be reversed! There are, in fact, growing concerns about the appropriateness of the present system of water and wastewater management, for economic and ecological reasons. It is hardly consistent with the management concepts of the 1990s, including recycling of matter and resource recovery. Some municipalities question the idea of using large amounts of highly purified drinking water simply for waste transportation, and maintenance costs are rising as leakages from the aging wastewater pipes pollute groundwaters. In this respect general subsidization was not a cost-effective incentive. Surprisingly, neither U.S. nor Swedish policy-makers have really utilized effluent fees as disincentives for wastewater discharges. For industries, such policies ought to be a feasible alternative to regulations. For households, however, flat rates might still be appropriate and it may be more instrumental to price the supply of clean water more heavily according to quantity used. This also offers a means to cut leakages from agricultural irrigation.

Swedish legislators took a step to reduce the non-point leakage of nitrogen and phosphorus by imposing a product charge on fertilizers in 1984 (see Tables 2-3). The tax, however, only means a price increase of roughly 10 per cent and this has not had a very significant impact on the quantities used by farmers. Earlier the attention to non-point source impacts had already been directed towards acidification caused by transboundary transports. The program for liming of acid lakes started in 1976, and it will unfortunately be necessary to continue with it for quite a long time. Swedish emissions of SO_2 have decreased considerably over the last decade (this is however not so for nitrogen emissions, see final section. 75-90 per cent of acid rain depositions in Sweden now originate from other parts of Europe, but the implementation of the 1985 Helsinki agreements within the ECE-Convention proceeds slowly (SNV, 1991).

Inland soils and waters can only be partly protected by national rules, but our surrounding "global commons" are even more vulnerable. The public and political apprehension of water quality as a matter of proper technical management shifted during the 1980s through alarming reports on marine eutrophication. A peak of public attention was reached in 1988, when many seals in the Baltic and the North Sea died from an epizootic disease. Some scientists and media put all the blame on environmental pollution and called for fundamental societal changes (Löwgren, 1991). This event helped the new Green party to attract enough votes to enter Parliament in the elections -which is relatively difficult because of a 4 per cent barrier to entry. The Greens were outvoted in the next (1991) elections, and the death of the seals turned out to be due to a complicated interaction of many contributing factors.

Nevertheless marine pollution abatement entered a new phase (see Hjorth, 1992), and the long-lasting work of international cooperation, particularly within the HELCOM (The Helsinki Commission on the Protection of the Marine Environment of the Baltic Sea Area) was intensified by the creation of a Task Force group. One result was that some large Swedish coastal wastewater treatment plants now invest in facilities for nitrogen removal to reduce marine eutrophication. This has stirred a new discussion on cost-effective abatement policies: many of our neighbour cities on the Southeast side of the Baltic still lack the most basic wastewater treatment while the marginal costs of additional nutrient removal is considerably higher in Sweden. Thus it is easy for Swedish emitters to argue that it would be wiser for us to invest money in the new Baltic states or in Poland.

7 ECONOMIC INCENTIVES FOR THE CONTROL OF SOLID WASTES AND CHEMICALS

Wastes create multi-dimensional environmental problems. Sometimes it is as simple as a matter of space, sometimes safety and sanitary risks are urgent, and occasionally concerns about the use of natural resources have been raised. Household wastes, and the main part of the industrial wastes, are bulky, but basically not very harmful. In the 1990s suitable landfill sites are becoming rare in many countries, and the common hierarchy of strategies to deal with this problem is "Reduction, Re-use and Recycling or Recovery". For some materials recycling offers the greatest environmental benefit. In other cases different recovery methods, such as energy recovery through clean incineration, is a viable management option. Presently 50 per cent of Swedish household wastes are incinerated in about twenty plants, generating heat, while most of the industrial wastes are still buried in landfill sites. Even if we (with the exception of a few major urban areas) do not have too much difficulty in finding space enough to deposit wastes, there are at least two important reasons for Sweden to develop her waste policies: one is an ambition to be a leading country in the environment policy field. Furthermore European integration requires harmonization in various ways with spatially less fortunate partners .

After considerable resistance from parts of the industrial and political establishment in Sweden, the Minister of the Environment has recently (February 1993) passed a Bill on comprehensive recycling. Inspired by German policies it requires a fundamental integration of resource management aspects into raw material extraction, production, distribution and destruction. The evaluation of the most environmentally appropriate options requires detailed knowledge about all stages of the material transformation, for instance through Life-Cycle Analyses. Let us consider one example: it is clear that the production of aluminium for beverage cans is a very energy-consuming process, which motivates the recycling of cans. For products made of cheap raw materials, like plastics, paper, glass bottles and cans, however, recycling might be questioned, at least when long lorry transports are required. Consequently, as far as we regard the growth of energy taxation as an internalization of externalities from fossil fuels (see Section 4), some firmly established beliefs in the general appropriateness of recycling might need reconsideration. It is however hard to generalize because economies-of-scale in the recycling and recovery industry is crucial for the viability of such programs. On the other hand environmentalists stress the educational effects of the established programs: the recycling behavior among the public has created good habits, that can be transferred to new areas. The full implementation of the Recycling Bill, mentioned above, will take a lot more of that!

The 1970s saw some rather unsuccessful attempts to separate a variety of garbage fractions by means of large-scale technologies, borrowed from extraction industries. The present strategy is one of source separation at the household and factory level. 90 per cent of Swedish municipalities (covering 97 per cent of the population) have permanent systems for the separation of paper, glass and batteries. 30 - 50 per cent of glass packages and 60 per cent of paper and board are recycled, but the markets for such materials are fluctuating and dependent on state intervention. In 1992 the municipalities were legally entitled to differentiate user charges to stimulate recycling, recovery or other environmentally sound waste management practices. The Recycling Bill presented objectives for the recycling of glass, aluminum, steel, cardboard, PET-bottles and other plastics, to be reached within five years. The objectives range between a recycling rate of 65 - 90 per cent, and for most materials they are within reach. One problem now under public debate is PET-bottles[7] and plastics, where government and the industrial lobby have not yet agreed

[7] The case of the PET bottles provides some interesting insights into how complicated the design of environmental policies can be. First government said they would definitely require recycling and thereby forced the big breweries to invest in very expensive washing equipment. The small breweries could not afford this technology and the government is now squeezed between the option of forcing the latter into bankruptcy or betraying the big breweries who will have invested in vain if recycling is not made absolutely mandatory.

on a strategy. The recycling of PET-bottles was delayed, due to technical and economic obstacles, and industry claims that clean incineration of plastics is a preferable option. Other significant volumes of wastes that need future attention are used car tires, discarded household appliances, for example refrigerators and freezers (including risks for CFC-emissions), and electronic scrap.

Glass bottles for soft drinks and liquor have been recycled since the days when it was simply commercially profitable. The deposit-refund programs of the early 1970s were created to reduce littering. Aluminum can recycling was introduced in 1983, since an eighty per cent rate of recycling was a prerequisite for allowing the aluminum cans in the first place. These programs are run by the beverage industry. Consumers are offered a refund of 0.5 - 4.0 SEK per package returned. In 1990, 95 - 98% of returnable beer and soft drink bottles were returned, and so were 80 per cent of liquor bottles and 83 per cent of the aluminum cans. These figures are high by international standards (SOU 1991:76). For various reasons, Swedish consumers have continued to buy enough beer and soft-drinks in returnable bottles to keep the deposit-refund system going, despite producers' and distributors' preferences for non-returnable packages. The tax differentiation (see Table 3) may have played some role, but despite this, a change in the total composition of package materials has occurred since the mid-60s. In terms of fixed prices the total value of packages has doubled since 1965. Glass and metals have kept their shares of the packaging material market since 1965, while paper and board have increased somewhat, wood has decreased slightly, and plastics have multiplied five times (SOU 1991:76). These changes are part of the general restructuring of trade, including increasing mass distribution and self-service.

The deposit-refund system for car hulks was developed in 1976 in order to eliminate abandoned vehicles. Part of the price paid for a new car is a deposit (at present SEK 850). When the used car is returned to an authorized dealer the owner gets an amount that is adjusted with respect to inflation, (SEK 1500). The recycling of scrap metals from cars is not a very profitable business at present metal prices, but the systems works, thanks to state involvement. In 1987 and 1988 the sales tax on new cars meeting 1989 emission standards was reduced by a sum corresponding to the extra cost of a catalytic converter. This "negative product tax" (cf. Section 5) was abolished when catalysts became mandatory in 1989 models. Around the turn of the century about 250 000 cars equipped with catalysts are expected to be ready for materials recycling, and their small contents of very precious metals are likely to be commercially recoverable.

The handling of hazardous substances that are dangerous for human health and environment is rarely subject to voluntary compliance, and the charges for heavy metals (see Table 3) may appear strange. Batteries containing mercury and cadmium were charged in 1987, lead batteries in 1991 and the tax differential between leaded and unleaded gasoline was introduced 1986. The background is, that despite the regulation of the main point-source emissions of metals in industry - for mercury also the dentist trade - soil and water concentrations remained alarmingly high in many areas. Batteries can hardly be banned, but the charges are intended to finance the collection of used batteries. The recovery of mercury from batteries has not succeeded in Sweden because of threats to workers' health in the reprocessing plant. Presently used batteries are stored at the central Swedish plant for the management of toxic wastes, SAKAB, and the construction of a final repository for used mercury, similar to that for highly active nuclear wastes, is under discussion. During the last few years new types of batteries with a low content of mercury have partly substituted the old harmful alkaline type. Experts claim, however, that the existence of charges has not contributed significantly to the development of new technologies. Rather, the combination of compulsory product information and regulations deserves the credits.

It is not possible for us to make close comparisons between Swedish and U.S. waste policies within the scope of this chapter, but we would like to make one observation. In both countries the management of household wastes traditionally has been handled at the local level while hazardous wastes is a matter of national/federal concern. There is, however, little correspondence between the assignments of economic responsibilities for old sins. America's 1980 Superfund legislation is a far-reaching tool to deal with the problem of abandoned hazardous waste sites. In order to finance clean-up or removal, a "feedstock" charge was introduced to create necessary intermediary funds. Charges are levied on petroleum, base chemicals and derivatives. In the end the costs fall on companies (and their insurers), according to strict retroactive liability rules. Over 1200 Superfund sites have now been identified by the EPA. Present actors, whether or not they maintain careful hazardous waste management, are forced to pay for clean-up programs caused by polluting activities in the past. Critics claim, that the incentive effects of such enforcement liabilities are low, because the feedstock charges are too low to influence the choice and the amounts of chemicals presently used. Sweden, like most European countries, holds the view, that cleaning up should be a public responsibility, financed by tax-payers. However, only a few sites have yet been restored in Sweden.

8 CONCLUSION

The increased Swedish use of environmental taxes and charges may perhaps be seen as an effort to implement the Polluter-Pays-Principle (PPP) of not admitting pollution "for free", (OECD, 1975). In theory full social costs should be internalized in the price of a commodity. But taxes and charges have not really been developed as means to reach environmental quality objectives; rather, the levels are decided according to general financial and political considerations (notably the need to finance the fiscal reform). We think it is fair to say, that taxes, charges and other economic incentives have played a rather modest role in the shaping of environment policies, at least until the mid-80s, possibly with the exception of the refunding of beverage containers and car hulks. Other, more recent, examples can be found in the energy and fossil fuel area, including sulphur and lead.

Subsidization as an economic instrument for pollution control was used until the period of economic growth ceased and government spending had to be cut. Obviously, the Swedish water protection program was successful as regards goal achievement, while the American was not. But of course it is easier to control municipal and industrial effluents than to manage the ecosystem of a river or a lake, and both countries learned, that point-source discharges are not the single determinant of water quality. Often non-point sources are more important, although in general the more-or-less steady flow of pollutants from municipal sewer systems and industrial processes may have greater impacts locally. The trivial lesson is, that a simple and undimensional goal is easier to achieve than a more complex one. Numerous harmful substances are irregularly discharged through agricultural and silvicultural run-offs, storm-sewer systems, leakages from waste dumps and mine tailings, airborne transports, and only a small part is yet under control.

An important area for future research is the comparative successes and failures of different policy instruments in different countries. We can obviously not provide a definitive answer within the present framework, but the Swedish experience shows that environmental taxes can provide a powerfull tool for environmental policy. By way of examples we choose some areas within which Sweden has actually committed itself to international agreements: Sulphur, Nitrogen and Carbon dioxide. As for Sulphur emissions, they have fallen considerably from 240 000 tons per year 1980 and are forecasted to around 80 000 1995 in which case the 65% reduction goal would be achieved (SOU 1989:83). Taxes on Sulphur have of course played a role, although we do not know how important, in this reduction. As for NO_x, however, the 30% reduction by 1995 seems far off indeed since there has been little reduction so far and the policy instruments applied must thus be considered insufficient. As for carbon dioxide the goal is to avoid further increases and this might possibly be achieved given recent increases in oil and particularly gasoline taxation. The net result depends on so many factors including the development of income, the phasing out of nuclear fuels, reduced taxes on industrial energy, international oil markets etc that a forecast is rather pointless. Naturally the adaptation of Swedish regulations to the EC as well as the development of the latter, will be an important determinant in the future.

REFERENCES

Hjorth, R. 1992. *Building International Institutions for Environmental Protection.* Linköping: Linköping Studies in Arts and Science 81. Diss.

Kuylenstierna, J. C. I. and M.J. Chadwick. 1989. "The relative sensitivity of ecosystems in Europe to indirect effects of acidic depositions", in *Regional Acidification Models*, ed. J. Kämäri, S.A. Norton & R.F. Wright, Springer Verlag, Berlin.

Löwgren, M. 1988. *Dynamics of Water Pollution Control. A Regional Evaluation.* Linköping: Linköping Studies in Arts and Science 26. Diss.

Löwgren, M. 1991. *Environmental Issues in Sweden 1973-1989:* Science and Policy. *Environmental Management* vol. 15, no.5, pp. 613-622.

Majone, G. (ed). 1990. *Deregulation or Re-regulation? Regulatory Reform in Europe and the United States*, Printer Publishers, London.

Nord 1991:27. *Ekonomiska styrmedel i miljöpolitiken i Norden - en kartläggning av nuvarande användning*. Köpenhamn: Nordiska Rådet.

OECD, 1989. *Economic Instruments for Environmental Protection.* Paris: OECD.

OECD, 1975. *Polluter-Pays-Principle, Definition Analysis Implementation.* Paris:

Sandmo, A. 1975. "Optimal Taxation in the Presence of Externalities", *Swedish Journal of Economics* pp 86-98.

Smith, T. and P. Kromarek. 1989. *Understanding U.S. and European Environmental Law, A Practitioner's Guide.* Graham & Trotman, London.

SNV 1991. *Acidification and Liming of Swedish Waters.* Monitor 12. Naturvårdsverket, Solna

SOU 1990:85. "Översyn av skatten på dryckesförpackningar". Delbetänkande av förpackningsutredningen. Stockholm: Allmänna Förlaget.

SOU 1991:76. "Miljön och förpackningarna". Slutbetänkande från förpackningsutredningen. Miljödepartementet. Allmänna Förlaget, Stockholm. SOU 1991:90 "Konkurrensneutral energibeskattning", (Competition-neutral taxation). Allmänna Förlaget (In Swedish), Stockholm.

Yeager, P.C. 1991. *The limits of law. The public regulation of private pollution.* Cambridge University Press, Cambridge.

CHAPTER 4

Environmental Policies in the Former Soviet Union*

by

Ann-Mari Sätre Åhlander

Abstract

This paper highlights the difficulties involved in implementing changes in environmental policy in the former Soviet Union. By using Soviet data we show that environmental disruption is considerable but that official attention to environmental problems has increased. Accordingly, we have seen many administrative and legal changes. However, as long as the legal system does not function, respect for laws and regulations remains arbitrary. Similarly, the so-called "economic incentives" that have been introduced are not likely to be effective until the whole economy is built on the basis of economic incentives.

* Work on this article started before the demise of the USSR and we have kept the terms "Soviet" etc since it is actually the old Soviet system that is analyzed. Thanks to 'Tomasz Żylicz, Thomas Sterner and an anonymous referee for valuable comments.

T. Sterner (ed.), Economic Policies for Sustainable Development, 68–81.

1 INTRODUCTION

The Soviet Union was never a mass-consumption society and has therefore not "suffered" from some of the drawbacks of Western life-style such as disposable packing, massive use of private automobiles, plastic articles and bleached paper. Instead, neglect and inefficiency appear to have been the main causes of environmental degradation. Alarming reports show that environmental disruption is considerable. From various places there are reports of high frequencies of lung diseases, intestinal and skin diseases and increased infant mortality. The press is also prompt to report incidents of fish kills, oil and chemical spills, leaks of radioactivity and outbreaks of food poisoning. In addition, forest depletion and extraction of natural resources have implied environmental problems on a large scale. Likewise, gigantic projects, conceived to take advantage of real or imaginary "economies of scale" have had serious consequences for the environment and people living there. Soviet readers regularly encounter reports of cover-ups, incompetence and negligence in environmental affairs.

According to the State Committee for Environmental Protection, Goskompriroda, the ecological situation is unsatisfactory in an area the size of Western Europe (Doklad, 1990). In a considerably smaller territory but still larger than Scandinavia, conditions are characterized as so severe that irreversible changes in nature have taken place.

In general, it is the Stalinist strategy of development that bears much of the responsibility for the present environmental situation. In the strive for rapid industrial expansion, the leadership pursued an extractionist policy concerning natural resources. As the focus on the annual plan implied a short-sighted policy, there was little room for environmental consideration. With massive industrial conglomerates based on the exploitation of local resources, this strategy also resulted in the concentration of several types of ecological stress in the same region. With high population density in these industrial areas, high levels of pollution affect a large proportion of the Soviet population.

According to Yablokov (1990), some 80 percent of all diseases relate, directly or indirectly, to environmental factors. Only 23 percent of Soviet children under the age of seven have been determined as "practically healthy", no more than 20 percent of younger school-children are judged to be "absolutely" healthy, while the corresponding figure for older school-children is 14 percent. Studies indicate that the prevalence of nervous disorders, allergies and illnesses of the intestinal tract among children increased from eight percent in the 1970s to 20 percent in 1989. Especially alarming figures on public health come from the industrial regions of the Urals, from southern Siberia, from the Aral Sea basin and from parts of the Ukraine.

Besides the general increase in illness, environmental pollution has also given rise to previously unknown diseases. In 1986, in the Ukrainian city of Chernovtsy, 200 children began to loose all or most of their hair (Yablokov, 1990 see also Mikhalisko et al, 1988). Medical tests failed to identify the causes of the disease. In 1988-89 similar cases of balding were registered in Zaporozhe in the Ukraine, in Zlatoust in the Urals, in Moscow and in Biisk in Siberia, see also chapter 7.

2 THE ENVIRONMENTAL SITUATION IN GENERAL

Some official statistics on various aspects of resource management and on emissions of waste and pollutants have been available since the mid-1970s. For example, the statistical yearbook *Narodnoe khozyaistvo SSSR* has published data on emissions since the early 1980s. Recently, however, the availability of such data has become both richer and more detailed. Three major documents have been issued in an attempt to make up for previous decades of neglect. One report was released in 1989, by Goskompriroda, Doklad (1990), together with a special volume of environmental statistics, Okhrana. (1990). The third, which is the most policy-oriented, is a report compiled by Aleksei Yablokov (1990), Boris Yeltsin's adviser on environmental affairs.

Many problems of definition and reliability arise in connection with data of this kind, see Altshuler et al (1990). Definitions are vague and the purpose has often been more political than scientific. Although this changed to some extent as a result of *glasnost*, many practical problems remain to be solved. The tradition of using vague definitions which could be interpreted to fit political purposes is not easily changed. A lack of time series data makes adequate analysis very difficult. The most immediate problem, however, is simply getting practical access to the data that is theoretically available. Environmental research has been conducted by 1,065 institutions under the auspices of seventy different ministries (Peterson, 1990), which means that data will not always be comparable, as each institution has its own methodology for collecting, compiling and interpreting environmental data.

We may note that with respect to water pollution, all of the three documents mentioned above agree that the situation has deteriorated. But when it comes to air pollution, the former two contradict Yablokov's pessimistic account, arguing that there has actually been an improvement, in spite of an increased use of natural resources. Who is right is hard to determine. According to a state official[1] at Goskompriroda, one important aim of Soviet energy policy is that the planned conversion from oil- and coal-fired power plants to nuclear power plants will reduce air pollution. However, by expanding nuclear power at the expense of oil and coal, one source of certain pollution is substituted by increased risks of serious accidents and pollution.

In the Goskompriroda report the ecological situation is described as unsatisfactory in 290 regions that cover 16 percent of Soviet territory with about one fifth of the Soviet population (60 million) in 1988. (This figure does not include territory affected by the Chernobyl accident). Using a system of environmental mapping, this area has been subdivided into three categories (Doklad, 1990).

The first category, "slightly affected areas" are principally affected by one single form of environmental degradation and natural resource exhaustion. In this category are waters that have been affected by pollution or exhaustion, such as the Azov Lake, the Black Sea, the White Sea, part of the Caspian Sea, Lake Onega and Ladoga. Agricultural lands account for a large proportion of this category in which overgrazing, intensive cultivation and deforestation from logging operations have led to changes in the chemical composition of the soil, wind erosion, desertification, and

---

[1] Sergei Kutukov, Goskompriroda, personal interview, Moscow, March 15, 1991.

compacting of the topsoil. These forces have been significant enough to cause a noticeable decline in the productivity of the land. Other characteristic examples of this category are disruption from mining operations, and degradation and overcutting of forests. About ten percent of the former Soviet territory falls into this category, located chiefly in northern Kazakhstan and the Black Earth region.

The second category refers to areas with intermediate damage. In these areas degradation has proceeded so far that even under favorable circumstances the local environment will take decades, maybe even centuries, to recover. In some of these areas, such as the Aral Sea region, the threat to human health is serious. This category, covering about three percent of the total territory, includes many lakes and rivers that have been turned into sewers, but also parts of the Black Earth region and Moldavia that have suffered massive damage from overcultivation and overapplication of agrochemicals.

The third category, that of "seriously affected areas" is characterized by environmental degradation to or beyond the point of irreversible change. Heavy industrial concentrations together with major mining operations account for the bulk of this category, which covers 3.3 percent of Soviet territory; an area larger than Scandinavia. Areas that are particularly affected include the Donbass in the Ukraine, the Kuzbass in Siberia and the eastern Urals, together with many other densely populated centers.

3 OFFICIAL RECOGNITION

After long neglect, environmental issues suddenly caught the attention of the central planners in the early 1970s. The immediate cause was an impending crisis in public health (Gustafson, 1980). Cholera had for instance broken out in southern river basins. At the same time, demand for clean water in the South was rapidly rising as a consequence of the spread of irrigated agriculture.

Accordingly, a heavily funded environmental program aimed chiefly at preserving clean water was established. Annual investments in water quality and waste treatment were raised abruptly, and in 1970-73, detailed water legislation for each of the union republics came into effect. In the 11th Five Year Plan (1976-1980) a section on nature and environmental protection was incorporated into the national economic plan, and a special division for the environment, with subdivisions for air and water quality was established within Gosplan, the State Planning Committee. In short, attempts were made to incorporate the environment into most parts of the government structure. However, a single administrative body for overall environmental management was not established until 1988.

In addition to the primary aim of preventing immediate threats to public health, the environmental program aimed at protecting natural resources for future economic use. A water charge for the industrial use of water was introduced in 1982 (DeBardeleben, 1983).

Gidromet, the State Committee for Hydrometeorology and Environmental Control, was established in 1978. Special environmental subdivisions were also created within the State Committee for Science and Technology and Goskomstat, the Statistical Administration. The Commission for Environmental Protection and Rational Use of Natural Resources under the Presidium of the USSR Council of

Ministers was set up in 1981. In the beginning of 1988, the increasing alarm that marked the ecological debate led to the creation of a single central authority, Goskompriroda, the State Committee for Environmental Protection. Thus, the responsibility for the use and protection of water resources was transferred from Minvodkhoz, the Ministry for Melioration and Water Resources, to Goskompriroda.

The increased official attention to environmental problems in the early 1970s is also reflected in a number of resolutions in the period 1972-78. The Soviet Union has further enacted a comprehensive set of laws and regulations which set air quality standards, require approved filters before factories are permitted to operate and prohibit various damaging practices. Apart from the law on protection of the atmosphere (1980), the Soviet Union has also adopted national laws for public health (1970), a subsoil legislation (1975), and legislations on forest utilization (1977) and protection of wildlife (1980).

Waste treatment and water-recycling programs as well as targets for the provision of pollution control equipment have been assigned to ministries along with material resources for their fulfillment. The authorities have also attempted to control the ministerial preference for concentrating investment in heavily populated, long-established industrial areas. There was, for instance, a list of 34 towns in the Russian republic where construction of new or expansion of existing enterprises was forbidden (Dyker, 1983). Limits for the maximum permissible concentration have been established for more than 500 air pollutants by the Ministry of Health. In 1988 the level of air pollution was checked in 537 cities with a population over 100,000 by the Ministry of Health and Gidromet (Okhrana, 1990, p. 32). In 1990, a new type of organization was set up. The "environmental business organization" with the right to deal with foreign companies, and to represent other Soviet enterprises who want to do so. According to Kutukov (personal interview), Soviet enterprises export natural resources, waste and in some cases even technology, and with the hard currency they get they buy environmental equipment.

In January 1988 a resolution on *perestroika* of the environmental protection in the Soviet Union was adopted ("O korrenoi perestroike....1988). The program was an important cornerstone of official environmental policy for the period 1991-2005, at least for Russia. It is not clear how relevant it was for the other republics. Three items which are directly connected with the increased role of economic tools and economic incentives can be identified (Doklad, 1990).

1. The use of cost-benefit analysis in environmental decision-making.
2. The introduction of pollution charges and payments for the use of natural resources.
3. The adoption of self-financing systems for environmental protection measures at the national and regional levels.

The general principles for using cost-benefit analysis in environmental decision-making were worked out by Gosplan, together with the Academy of Sciences and the State Committee for Construction in the form of a Handbook (*Vremennaya Tipovaya Metodika*) for valuation of environmental measures (Vremennaya...,1986). This focused on how natural resource evaluations could be used to provide a basis for choosing environmental protection measures and to determine the order in which measures should be carried out. It also provided a method for valuation of damage of environmental pollution.

Proposals for the other two items were worked out in a new version of the Handbook which was released in Moscow in 1987 (Gofman et al, 1987). These reflected the changes in Soviet economic policies concerning the governing of the enterprise towards more independence and more reliance on economic incentives. The Handbook from 1987 also contains suggestions on how these proposals could be implemented such as premia for fulfillment of environmental protection measures. Another proposal was that enterprises pay money into special environmental funds at different levels of the economy to finance environmental protection measures. In the autumn of 1989 a resolution stating that ecological experts must be consulted before any decisions on large-scale production are made was adopted (Byullentin, 1990).

Thus, we see considerable administrative and legal changes. But laws and resolutions do not automatically achieve anything. While production plans generally are accompanied by the allocation of resources required to fulfill them, regulations are not. If the necessary inputs and technical equipment are not provided, even enterprises actually motivated to comply might not be able to do so.

4 COST-BENEFIT ANALYSIS IN DECISION-MAKING

4.1 Criteria for measures

A special decree on the use of cost-benefit analysis in environmental decision-making was adopted in 1983 and later revised to be better coordinated with the *perestroika*. The Handbook states that certain measures are needed to satisfy basic quality requirements of the environment. These are expressed as norms in physical units and are determined to protect health and conserve nature.

The Handbook emphasizes that all social revenues and costs should be taken into account. A measure is conventionally defined as socially efficient if its social gain exceeds its social cost. According to the Handbook the central planner is to choose the measure which maximizes the social net revenue per year, provided that the given norm is achieved. However, in the Soviet context, measures may be considered even if they are socially unprofitable for political reasons. This is evident from the statement of the Handbook that if costs exceed benefits, these should be chosen so that the loss is minimized.

The practice of using cost-benefit analysis for environmental problems in the Soviet Union differs from that of conventional theory in a number of ways. One basic difference concerns the estimation of benefits. The principle of valuing benefits of environmental improvements in accordance with the marginal willingness to pay, which is used in conventional theory, is rejected on the grounds that it gives too much roughness and subjectivity to evaluation.

Instead, such evaluations are based on estimations of only those economic consequences which can be measured "objectively". For instance, benefits from reducing health risks would be estimated from saved costs for medical care and value of the additional labour from those who do not become ill. It is emphasized that such evaluations would just include one part of the benefit of measures, but that they correspond to conventional methods of estimation of GNP, productivity and other economic parameters which are used in most countries. Moreover, cost-benefit analysis is mainly seen as an instrument for fixing the minimum level of national expenditures on environmental protection.

It is emphasized that the method of evaluation differs depending on the aim. The method outlined above would be used for decisions on lower levels. For instance, it would be used to evaluate the effect of sewage facilities at a certain plant. But it would not be used when it is important to evaluate the total social effects of a large-scale health project. In such a case the desired level of health security becomes the aim of the project and the problem is how to achieve this aim with minimum costs.

4.2 Pollution charges and natural resource use

The Handbook further states that prices should be set so as to make it profitable for the enterprise to undertake measures which are socially beneficial. The enterprise itself decides when measures are needed, although it obtains directives from superior authorities by way of norms for the maximum emission of pollutants. To make it profitable for the enterprise to fulfill its norm, the Handbook suggests that it obtain premiums that are added to profits. In the traditional system, while plan targets generally are accompanied by plans for supplies, norms and regulations are not. Thus if the required materials are unobtainable, it is not possible to comply with norms. Therefore, there is a general habit of breaking rules.

The financial revenue (*khozraschetnyi rezultat*) of the enterprise of taking a certain measure is equal to the increase in revenue, or the decrease in costs of production. Costs for capital investments would not be included since these do not generally affect the enterprise. In effect this means that the state would pay for investment in water purification, filters, etc., while the enterprise pays for running costs. Compliance with norms is secured if the premiums for compliance plus the pollution charges avoided exceed operating costs.

For activities which are financed out of the state budget, shadow prices should be used. However, if the enterprise is governed by the principle of self-accountability, matters become different, as the enterprise does not face shadow prices, but prices which are set on the basis of normative costs of production (defined as the average cost of production, over a five-year period).

5 PAYMENTS FOR NATURAL RESOURCES AND POLLUTION CHARGES

Payments for utilization of natural resources such as land, water, forests and minerals were to be introduced in 1991, (O korrenoi perestroike..., 1988, Gofman 1988). The stated functions of such payments are:

1. To provide an economic incentive for the efficient use and protection of natural resources

2. To provide an instrument for controlling the market price of products of extracting industries

3. To provide financial revenue for budgets at various levels of the economy

4. To remove differences in costs of production in extracting industries which are due to differences in natural conditions

Apart from payments for the use of natural resources, in 1991, pollution charges were to be introduced in all branches of the Soviet economy. In 1989 and 1990, Goskompriroda carried out experiments with pollution charges and payments for the use of natural resources. In about 50 cities in RSFSR, the Ukraine and in Tadzhikistan, the method that had been worked out by Gofman and his colleagues was to be used, (Kutukov 1991, personal interview).

Pollution charges were to be established for all principal pollutants emitted; air and water and for solid waste. One rate would be levied on ordinary, permissible emissions. Another on pollution in excess of the norm, ("O korrenoi perestroike... 1988; Gofman, 1988; Doklad, 1990). In the experiments carried out in Moscow, it was five times higher. However, if they had not bothered to apply for permission to pollute, which they can get free at Moskompriroda, they would be liable to pay twice the charge, (Personal interview, Moskompriroda, Moscow, March 11, 1991). The more severe the violation, the higher the charge would be. The pollution charge would not be levied on the actual amount of pollution. It would be equal to the quantity regulated by the pollution norm. This norm would be determined on the basis of knowledge about the technology used at the plant and by statistics on previous emissions from the plant. This implies that the polluter must prove that the actual amount of discharge is lower than the norm in order to decrease the charge to be paid. For instance, it would have to improve environmental equipment at the plant and install systems for measuring pollution.

Pollution charges would be set in the Five Year Plan and would include calculations of yearly reductions in emissions. The size of the charge to be paid would be calculated taking three factors into account: physical quantity, toxicity and geographical dispersion, in much the same way as in Estonia. See chapter 7 for a detailed description of a very similar, and equally complex, tax construction. The charge would be paid out of profits except for emissions above the norm or accidental emissions which would be paid from the income of the workers (*khozraschetnyi dokhod kollektiva*) see Doklad (1990).

6 REGIONAL ENVIRONMENTAL FUNDS

In order to ensure that means for environmental protection are available, special funds would be created at the regional and national levels (Doklad, 1990). The assets of these funds would mainly be derived from enterprises in the form of pollution charges, rental payments for the use of natural resources, penalties for breaking environmental laws and payments for the use of environmental funds. The point here is that payments would not just as before go into the state budget, but would be paid mainly into regional funds from which regional environmental programs would be financed. In the Moscow fund in 1990, ten percent was to go into the republican fund of RSFSR, two percent to an insurance fund for accidents and emergencies and five percent to a fund for premia to enterprises and environmental inspectors, (O provedenii ekonomicheskogo eksperimenta... (1990, appendix, p. 2.).

The intention was also that environmental protection activities should be financially accountable, just like any other industrial activity. The regional environmental funds would be used to cover the difference between the industrial enterprise's own assets for financing environmental measures and current costs. As a first step, the funds would be used to subsidize the above-mentioned activities at individual plants. It was also suggested that the funds should be used for premiums to enterprises that fulfill their environmental obligations and to workers at organizations for environmental control (Gofman et al, 1987).

Gofman (1988) proposes that these environmental funds be transformed into environmental banks in the future. The bank would be used to finance measures of environmental conservation and have the same sources of income (charges etc.) as the funds as well as having the right to issue special environmental bonds. By adjusting the price-ratio between rental payments for the use of natural resources and payments for conserving them, the bank would dispose of an economic device for controlling the use of natural resources. This would be a major policy instrument for development.

The idea of creating regional funds for financing environmental measures is not new, see Gofman (1977). However, in the 1970s it received little response from state officials. By 1988, Estonia was the only republic where such a fund had been set up, see chapter 7. In Latvia, Kazakhstan and Georgia, environmental funds were created shortly thereafter by the republican Goskomprirodas. By 1990, regional funds had been created in every economic region in the Soviet Union. The intention was that the republics themselves were to decide on the use of the funds (Ozipov, 1988, personal interview). A central environmental fund was also established to be financed by five percent of all regional fund money. This fund is mainly used to finance unexpected tasks, such as cleaning up of the environment after accidents, (O korrenoi perestroike..., 1988).

The internalization of all activities under a single administrative head in each region is a precondition for more effective monitoring and exercise of ownership rights over resources. From this point of view it matters less whether the funds come from pollution charges or from the budget. However, this is provided that the regional bodies have the power to enforce the right over resources and that they can obtain the physical resources required to carry out their programs.

6.1 Environmental funds at the enterprise

Another type of fund proposed would be specific for each enterprise. In this case, the enterprise itself would finance its own environmental measures out of its own profits, assets or by means of credits. The Handbook suggests that environmental funds be created at enterprises which are heavy polluters. The fund would work like a bank account in a special "bank" for environmental preservation and would be used to finance environmental measures at the enterprise.

One advantage of enterprise specific funds is that the money stays within the enterprise although its use is restricted. Furthermore, if the assets of the fund are not enough to cover the necessary expenditures, the Handbook suggests that means could be borrowed from the "environmental bank", up to a certain limit. Moreover, if this is reached, the enterprise would be obliged to use its "Material Incentive Fund", which has a strong incentive effect since it is used as a form of bonus payment. Moreover, it is proposed that funds which have not been used during the year can be saved for later years. This was not generally the case for existing funds for "economic incentives" at a Soviet enterprise.

7 THE EFFECTIVENESS OF ECONOMIC INCENTIVES

In the traditional Soviet system, an official ambition to reduce environmental pollution would have led to the introduction of a plan indicator or a norm for reduction of emissions. The problem is that its fulfillment might imply a reduction of production, at least in the short run. This is presumably why there has not been any sign of such a change in major plan indicators.

As noted above, the Handbook states that it should be profitable for the enterprise to take measures which are socially beneficial. Thus the first requirement is that enterprises are interested in increasing profits. The law on state enterprises from 1988 did indeed set the stage for such a change in the role of the enterprise. The intention was that the enterprise become more independent from its "superiors" and to a great extent be guided by economic incentives. At the least, this would require that net profits were left in the enterprise to the benefit of its staff, and not confiscated by the state (see also Chapter 5, section 1).

7.1 The incentive effect of charges

The introduction of charges for the use of water and other resources is an important change from the earlier ideological "principle of free use of natural resources". Soviet resource economists have long persisted in the view that charges are compatible with Marxist theory if they are based on the labour expenditure necessary to restore a particular resource to its original state. They argued that the charge should be equal to the differential rent, without discussing the consequences on resource use and it is not clear what incentive enterprises have to maximize the differential rent if this is then confiscated.

The Handbook's proposal implies that the enterprise pays two kinds of payments for pollution. The pollution charge would be paid to the regional fund while payments in the form of deductions from profits (which are also a form of pollution charge) would be made to the enterprise fund. The primary aim of these payments is that the enterprise itself should finance all its production costs. Payments for the use of natural resources and pollution charges are natural in the light of the law on state enterprises.

The effectiveness of a charge, however, depends on whether it is paid out of money that has an alternative use to the enterprise. Most payments for the use of natural resources that existed in the Soviet Union were paid from the "profits" of the enterprise. However, they were paid from the 70 percent of the profits which went to taxes without affecting the fixed 30 percent share of profits left in the enterprise! As it does not matter to the enterprise if the money it pays is called taxes or pollution payments, such payments cannot provide the enterprise with any economic incentive whatsoever to save on its use of resources. The payment ought of course to come from profits which the enterprise could otherwise have used at its will.

7.2 The nature of budget constraints

One intention behind the new enterprise law is to increase the dependence of enterprises on economic incentives. In Kornai's (1980) terminology this means a general attempt to change from "soft" to "hard" budget constraints. However, no budget constraints will have any incentive effect unless the enterprises can obtain the technical equipment and other physical resources needed for reducing emissions. Profits do not provide an incentive as long as they require materials that have not been allocated by the central authorities in the first place and that are not available due to general shortage.

Thus, the creation of environmental funds at the enterprise is not likely to have much effect in itself. The vast environmental problems to be solved require firstly a thorough restructuring of the economy with the introduction of a consistent market economy alongside a strengthening of environmental policies. Secondly, it is clear that massive international assistance with technology and finance are needed.

8 PROSPECTS FOR THE FUTURE

The Soviet strategy for development designed by Stalin in the first Five Year Plan created a managerial system which permitted and even promoted waste and destruction of natural resources. In effect, the institutions which were once created to effectively impose the central priorities, developed their own objectives and resisted any change jeopardizing their interests. As the currently most available natural resources become exhausted, a continuation of the extractionist policy requires heavier and heavier investments. The Stalinist priority on growth has become embedded in institutions which impede attempts by central decision-makers to change the strategy for development. The longer this was to continue, the greater the problems became.

Further deterioration of the environmental situation in former Soviet republics might strengthen environmental movements, and to cope with this authorities might again resort to tighter repression. In particular, they might find it necessary to place restrictions on *glasnost* as to information about the environmental situation and to avoid opposition and protests in the most heavily affected areas (for instance Chernobyl). On the other hand, a policy of increasing priority for environmental protection would probably also be blocked by influential groups who stand to lose from such a reallocation of resources. With the economy falling apart, an effective policy of this kind is even more unlikely.

Reform in the Soviet context was a rather difficult concept. Although the leadership legislated far-reaching reforms, it was often the case that nothing really changed. Two apparent examples of this are the attempts to reform under Krushchev after Stalin's death in the late 1950s, and the so-called Kosygin reform which was started in 1965. The Gorbachevian reforms seem also to have been hit by a similar fate.

Now that the Soviet Union has ceased to exist, the prospects for the environment will have to be analyzed for each republic separately, (see Chapters 6-7).

The political and economic policies to be followed in the various republics are still an open issue, but a number of points are at least slightly promising in this rather black picture. Firstly, market economy and private ownership has become generally accepted. Secondly, more resources to institutions for environmental protection have already resulted in control and measurement. Improved information on the state of the environment has at least improved the statistics on which future decisions must be based. Improved statistics together with democracy and freedom of speech are the first necessary steps towards an improved environmental situation. Similarly, improved methods for evaluating damages to the environment should contribute to improving the allocation of resources.

The so-called "economic incentives" are, however, not likely to be effective until the whole economy is built on the basis of economic incentives.

REFERENCES

Altshuler, Igor I. and Yuri N. Golubchikov. 1990. "Ecological Semi-glasnost: On the Publication of the first Three Official Documents on the State of the Environment in the USSR" *Environmental Policy Review. vol. 3, no 2.*

Byullentin No. 1 1990. *O deyatelnosti Goskomprirody SSSR v 1989 godu.* Goskompriroda i Press-Tsentr Bsesoyuznoe Obshchestvo "Znanie", Moskva.

DeBardeleben J. 1983. "Marxism-Leninism and economic policy: Natural resource pricing in the USSR and the GDR", *Soviet Studies*, pp. 36-52.

Doklad 1990. Sostoyanie prirodnoi sredy v SSSR v 1988 godu. Goskompriroda, Moskva: Lesnaya Promyshlennost.

Dyker D. 1983. *The process of investment in the Soviet Union.* Cambridge University Press,Cambridge.

Gofman K. N. 1977. *Ekonomicheskaya otsenka prirodnykh resursov v usloviiakh sotsialisticheskoi ekonomiki.* Moscow: Nauka.

Gofman, K. N. et. al. 1987. *Tipovaya metodika opredeleniya ekonomicheskoi effektivnosti stimulirovaniya osushchestvleniya prirodookhrannykh meropriyatii i ekonomicheskoi otsenki ushcherba ot zagrizneniya okruzhayushchei sredy.* proekt, Moskva.

Gofman, K. N. 1988. "Khozyastvennyi mekhanizm prirodopolzovanyia: puti perestroiki", *Ekonomika i Matematicheskie metody*, vol. 24, no. 3, pp. 389-399.

Gustafson, T. 1980. "Environmental Policy under Breznev: Do the Soviets really mean business" ed. Kelly, *Soviet politics in the Brezhnev era*, New York.

Kornai, J. 1980. *Economics of Shortage.* North-Holland, Amsterdam.

Mcintyre, R. and J. Thornton. 1978. "On the environmental efficiency of economic systems", *Soviet Studies*, vol. 30, no 2, pp. 173-192.

Mikhailisko, M. and Tovstink. 1988. "Questions about semiconductor plants and thallium poisoning in Chernovtsy", *Radio Liberty Research*, November 24, pp. 1-5.

Narkhoz (various years) *Narodnoe Khozyaistvo SSSR* (Statistical Yearbook), Moscow: Finansy i Statistika.

Nove, Alec. 1982. *The Soviet Economic System*. George Allen & Unwin, London.

Okhrana okruzhayushchei sredy i ratsionalnoe ispolzovanie prirodnykh resursov v SSSR 1990, Finansy i statistika, Moscow.

O korrenoi perestroike dela okhrany prirody v strane 1988. Tsentralnyi Komitet KPSS I Sovet Ministrov SSSR, postanovlenie, 7 yanvariya 1988 godu, no. 32. Moscow: Kreml.

O provedenii ekonomicheskogo eksperimenta po sovershenstvovaniyu khozyaistvennogo mekhanizma prirodopolzovaniya V.g. Moskve, 1990. Reshenie 14 aprelya 1990 g., no. 840, Moskovskii Gorodskoi Sovet Narodnykh Deputatov Inspolnitelnyi Komitet.

Peterson, D. J. 1990. "The State of the Environment: An Overview", *Report on the USSR*, February 23.

SSSR v tsifrakh v 1987 godu, 1988. Moscow: Finansy i statistika.

SSSR v tsifrakh v 1988 godu, 1989. Moscow: Finansy i statistika.

Sätre, Åhlander, A-M. 1989: "Miljöproblemen i Sovjet", *Världspolitikens Dagsfrågor 8.*

Sätre, Åhlander, A-M. 1993. *The Effect of the Soviet Shortage Economy on the Environment and the Use of Natural Resources, Department of Economics, Stockholm University, Doctoral Dissertation.*

Vremennaya tipovaya metodika opredeleniya ekonomicheskoi effektivnosti stimulirovaniya osushchestvleniya prirodookhrannykh meropriyatii i otsenki ekonomicheskogo ushcherba prichinyaemogo narodnomu khozyaistvu zagryazneniem okruzhayushchei sredy. 1986. Gosplan, Gosstroi i Prezidium Akademii Nauk. Moskva: Ekonomika.

Yablokov, A. 1990. "The Current State of the Soviet Environment", *Environmental Policy Review*, vol. 4, no. 1.

Ziegler, Charles E. 1980. "Soviet environmental policy and Soviet central planning", *Soviet Studies*, vol. 32, no.1, pp. 124-134.

Ziegler, Charles E. 1982. "Centrally-planned economies and environmental information: a rejoinder", *Soviet Studies*, vol. 34, no. 2 pp. 296-299.

Ziegler, Charles E. 1987. *Environmental Policy in the USSR*, University of Massachussetts Press, Amherst.

CHAPTER 5

Environmental Policy Reform in Poland

by

Tomasz Żylicz*

Abstract

The chapter identifies the causes of poor environmental performance in the former Centrally Planned Economies including Poland. Their excessive resource use had its roots both in the general inefficiency of the non-market allocation mechanism, and in inappropriate environmental policies. While it can be expected that the introduction of market logic will gradually eliminate one source of problems, a proper choice of policy priorities and instruments poses a challenge. A number of instruments can be applied to implement priority programmes. Permit markets have several distinct characteristic features which make them a promising environmental, sectoral, and regional policy tool. They combine effectiveness with flexibility, and are likely to assist policy makers in Poland and elsewhere in Central and Eastern Europe to efficiently address their economic restructuring and social concerns. In Poland, emission charges (in use since the early 1980's) have already become very substantial, they rank among the highest in the world, and it is unlikely that the government will be able to raise them further within the next couple of years. Thus, in order to approximate least-cost solutions, other economic instruments, and, most importantly, permit markets should be applied.

The argument is developed in 10 sections. The troublesome heritage is discussed in section (1). In section (2) Poland's domestic environmental priorities are described. The next five sections deal with various problems of environmental policy design. Its relation to the general economic reform (3), and to its political requirements (4) are addressed first. These are then followed by a broad outline of economic instruments (5), a discussion of the Polluter Pays and User Pays Principles (6), and an explanation why the policy design should be kept simple and transparent (7). The next sections describe how various policy principles and options have been actually implemented in Poland since the 1989 (8), and what are the political and social constraints of this process (9). The last section (10) offers some conclusions, which suggest that - while there are hardly any major symptoms of environmental improvement yet - Poland has taken a small step towards a sustainable economy.

* This chapter was prepared while the author was Valfrid Paulsson Guest Professor at the Beijer International Institute of Ecological Economics (The Royal Swedish Academy of Sciences, Stockholm).

T. Sterner (ed.), Economic Policies for Sustainable Development, 82–112.

1 THE HERITAGE

It is well documented that Centrally Planned Economies (CPE) used to exert a significantly greater pressure on their environmental resources than comparable market economies. For instance, there is a clear distinction between the European Communities (EC) and the CPEs in Central and Eastern Europe (CEE) with respect to the energy and resource intensities of their domestic products. The intensities tend to decline when material welfare increases in either group (Krawczyk 1991). However, even the wealthiest CPEs (German Democratic Republic, Hungary and Czechoslovakia) had in general higher intensities than the least wealthy EC states (Portugal, Greece and Ireland). This suggests that the two groups of economies - Poland being a typical example of a European CPE (see Table 1) - did not follow the same pattern of development. For data availability reasons, the table does not include the former Soviet republics. See, however, Chapter 6, which shows a similar pattern in Estonia, Latvia and Lithuania. Even though the central planning mechanism has been abandoned in Europe, the problems remain, and they should be taken into account when designing clean-up and recovery policies.

Table 1

ECONOMIC PRESSURE ON THE ENVIRONMENT IN THE LATE 1980's

		Poland	**CEE-6**	**EC-12**
1	GDP per capita, $1000/person	3.5	4.8	10.1
2	Energy intensity of GDP, TOE/$1000	0.98	0.77	0.23
3	Energy intensity of GDP, TOQE/$1000	0.59	0.56	0.21
4	Water intensity of GDP, m^3/$1000	134	153	82
5	Pollution intensity of GDP:			
6	- solid waste, tonnes/$	1.4	1.0	0.4
7	- wastewater, m^3/$1000	38	83	24
8	- gases, kg/$1000	45	51	24
	- dust, kg/$1000	13	13	1

CEE-6 = Bulgaria, Czechoslovakia, GDR, Hungary, Poland, and Rumania. **EC-12** = European Community. **TOE** = tonne of oil equivalent. **TOQE** = tonne of "oil quality" equivalent: identical with TOE for oil and gas; 2 TOE of coal are assumed to be 1 TOQE; 1 TOE of hydro- and nuclear electricity is assumed to be 3 TOQE.

Source: Author's estimates based on Krawczyk (1991) and Olszewski et al. (1987).

A recent study carried out at Warsaw University (Krawczyk 1991) - using some of the most up-to-date econometric techniques - confirms that not the level of industrial development, but rather the economic system adhered to, is crucial in explaining differences in environmental performance among the European countries. Atmospheric emissions provide a literally visible proof of the environmental protection failure in CPEs. But this could only partially be attributed to an ill-designed environmental policy as it primarily resulted from running inefficient economies. General inefficiency of a non-market allocation results in an excessive (relative to the output) use of any resource. This is accompanied by several additional factors which lead to an excessive use of the natural resources in particular.

A bias towards heavy industry and the resulting under-representation of the service sector are perhaps the most important single causes for the continuing pressure on natural resources in the (former) CPEs. The position of heavy industries has its historical roots and proved to be stable despite modernization efforts. The interest groups connected to these industries still exercise some power, and contribute to the inertia of the economy they are part of, because of the weakness of democratic institutions that could effectively represent social preferences. The dominance of heavy industries is coupled with weakness of environmental enforcement inherited from the past.

Furthermore, there were in the CEE some additional misconceptions on environmental policy itself. For instance, in the 1980's, in Poland the policy was (*de facto*, but sometimes even *de iure*) almost totally left to hardly existing market forces supposed to achieve the protection through a system of financial incentives. Similarly in the Soviet Union most of the conceptual effort in the 1980's was directed towards designing a system of fees rather than direct controls, monitoring and enforcement. See Chapter 4. Unfortunately, many CEE economists advocate emission charges rather than alternative tools, overlooking the fact that even in the highly developed market economies environmental management has not been left to uncontrolled market forces (OECD, 1989). The excessive pollution is then linked to an inappropriate level of taxes or fines, and thus the attention of policy-makers is distracted from the real issues. It should be clearly acknowledged that in the system where all essential inputs were allocated administratively and the firms were operating under so-called soft budget constraints (Kornai, 1986), there was no need to pay much attention to price stimuli.

The pure effect of policy failure - as opposed to the effects of general system inefficiency - becomes evident when comparing lines 2-7 and 8 in table 1. In general, the European non-market economies required roughly 2-3 times more inputs to produce a given effect, and this explains much of the difference in their environmental performance.[1] In particular, the hard-to-abate gaseous emissions resulting from fuel combustion (line 7) can be explained in terms of excessive energy use which is typically 2-3 times higher than in the West (lines 2 and 3).

Energy intensities of GDP are either directly or indirectly attributable to system inefficiency. CEE countries - especially Czechoslovakia and Poland have used a fuel mix of a much inferior quality than the European average. Taking into account quality differentials, the energy efficiency gap is smaller, but still exists and represents a direct effect of system inefficiency (line 3). Given their inability to compete in international markets, CPEs have had to rely on domestic resources as much as physically possible. Hence their inability to upgrade the fuel mix can be viewed as an indirect effect of the system inefficiency (accounted for in line 2). In

---

[1] The figures in Table 1 are based on various studies (both Eastern and Western) of the CPEs carried out in the late 1980's. According to more recent findings, the dollar GDP figures for Poland and CEE-6 (although not the energy and resource statistics) might have been overestimated. This only makes the distinction between the two groups of economies even more evident.

sum, the excessive gaseous emissions in CPEs result (either directly or indirectly) from general system inefficiency, and to a limited extent could have been mitigated *via* better environmental protection practices.

On the contrary, the particulate matter emissions (line 8) offer a sharp contrast to this pattern. Here the gap between CPEs and market economies is enormous and cannot be explained in terms of inefficiency. Simultaneously the abatement techniques are less costly and have been known (and practiced - also in CEE) for decades. Thus it was only inability or reluctance to enforce the abatement that allowed CEE industries to become "dirty" in the most literal sense too. A portion of "excessive" particulate matter emissions can be attributed to the fuel mix of inferior quality of fuel used, but the environmental performance gap is certainly much wider than that.

The comparison of lines 7 and 8 in Table 1 thus illustrates a major difference between environmental performance of the European CPEs and market economies. The latter did not do a perfect job with respect to sulphur dioxide abatement and even less so with respect to nitrogen oxides throughout the 1980's. Consequently the contrast between both groups of countries is not so apparent as in the case of particulate matter emissions. By no means could the latter be explained in terms of (excessively) consumed energy. Only because of firm environmental policies, can the developed market economies now enjoy low levels of particulate matter (dust) emissions which indeed are fairly easy to abate. Despite moderate abatement costs and moderate level of technological sophistication, CEE economies have failed to solve their dust emission problem clearly because of the lack of adequate policy measures.

2 NATIONAL ENVIRONMENTAL PRIORITIES

The emerging market structures in Poland and elsewhere in CEE are likely - at least in the long run - to stimulate more environmentally sound developments there. In this case, environmental goals have been fully compatible with the goals of the general economic reform implemented in Poland since January 1, 1990. However, firm yet flexible government policies are needed in order to make this happen. A consistent environmental policy is an absolute must. In particular it has to determine a set of short- medium- and long-term priorities, and a rational mix of market-oriented tools and direct controls, since both these instruments have their merits and should be relied on in certain circumstances.

Setting priorities is a delicate issue, as it implies not only inclusions in, but also exclusions from the collection of objectives to be addressed. This is why several time horizons should be adopted: whatever cannot be accomplished in the short run ought to be taken care of later, but within a specified time frame. Otherwise, the policy may become either unrealistic if it tries to integrate too many "justified" goals, or it may lack social support if the public is disappointed with too many painful exclusions.

In 1990, the government of Poland outlined a program (Ministry, 1990a) attempting to reconcile the long-term considerations with short-term requirements and constraints. The program objective is to restore the environment after years of abuse and neglect and to put the country on a sustainable path of development within the next 30 years. In a shorter time frame of 7-10 years it will attempt to adapt Poland's institutions and environmental requirements to those existing in Western European countries which initiated significant abatement efforts in the late 1960's. During the initial, 3-5 year phase, a program is being implemented to eliminate extreme hazards caused by existing sources of environmental disruption.

In the short-run, the activities supported by the program concentrate on eliminating extreme hazards for human health and to saving that portion of the country's natural heritage which has not been irreversibly lost. The Ministry of Environment (MoE) prepared twelve action programmes which were related to water, air, solid waste, nature protection, and food.

With respect to water, a priority has been given to the supply of safe potable water in urban agglomerations and to the Baltic Sea coastal zone clean-up. To achieve this goal, the main effort is first directed to investing in those sewage treatment plants which protect tributaries of the Vistula and Oder Rivers, as well as the Baltic coastal zone. Additional improvement will result from introducing a new river-basin management system, and from relating user charges directly to the water resources management budgets.

For many years to come coal will be the main fuel in Poland. Air protection is fundamentally linked to improving energy efficiency programmes, and to the coal-washing project which will not only reduce emissions, but also increase electricity production in existing plants. Similar effects are expected from introducing clean coal technologies like fluidized bed combustion. They combine higher combustion efficiency - which implies economic yields - with decreased emissions of sulphur dioxide, nitrogen oxides, and particulate matter. In addition to energy efficiency programmes, end-of-pipe technologies are necessary too - especially with respect to particulate matter emissions where a radical improvement is needed first. Upper Silesia in Southern Poland as well as more than 20 other areas of ecological hazard, receive priority. 27 such areas were officially delineated in 1983 covering 10% of the country's area and 1/3 of its population. Greater control over low stacks, which plague most of Poland's towns, must be exerted too. Here improvement will require the substitution of dispersed, inefficient coal-fired household stoves with district heating systems.

Neutralization and commercial utilization of industrial wastes - many of them being toxic - serves as another example of an activity which reconciles ecology with business. First pilot treatment and reduction systems for toxic and hazardous waste are being installed. Within a few years, all sources of substances that directly pose a threat to human health should be eliminated. A comprehensive program for municipal waste was drafted under the World Bank loan in 1992.

Reforestation of watershed areas and regions affected by severe ecological damages in Southern Poland continues. In Northern and Eastern Poland, protection of areas and habitats of particular ecological significance is strengthened by expanding the network of national parks among other things.

This overview of short-term priorities would be incomplete without the program of safe food which has two dimensions. First, unspoiled ecosystems in Northeastern Poland will be protected to promote a number of benefits, one of these being organic farming which is capable of supplying safe, high quality goods both for domestic and foreign markets. Second, food production in highly degraded regions - most importantly, Silesia - will be eliminated. Significant allotment of funds has been budgeted to implement a change in use of these lands from food production to non-food crops.

It is not the purpose of this chapter to discuss the viability of this program in great detail. On the one hand, some of its objectives or target dates will probably be missed as the implementation has turned out to be more difficult than expected. On the other hand, the central and regional authorities who implement it have been under constant pressure from environmental groups and other interested parties who consider the program to be too selective. What is important, however, is that it prioritized investment projects, and offered practical guidance for the authorities on how to spend public funds earmarked for environmental protection. The basic construction of the program is correct as it distinguishes between what is desirable and feasible; it offers some visible improvement in the short run, and sets more strategic goals for the entire next generation.

Cost estimates to put Poland on a sustainable path have reached the incredible sum of US$ 260 billion (more or less triple current GDP) to be spent on all the necessary changes in its economy, including (but not confined to) environmental protection investment. It is difficult to realistically expect that the economy can bear such a burden even in a 30-year perspective. If, however, market forces can be effectively "harnessed", necessary investment expenditures may turn out to be much lower. The next sections of this chapter will address in more detail how Poland's environmental priorities can be or are implemented.

3 COMBINING ECONOMIC AND ENVIRONMENTAL REFORMS

In their struggle for a friendlier, safer environment the CEE countries like Poland have to overcome two barriers: general system inefficiency and inadequate policy principles. Economic reforms hopefully continued by the new governments will remove the first obstacle. Given all the recent developments in the region, it is unlikely that a sudden come-back of the *ancien regime* would threaten the future of economic and political reforms. Nevertheless preventing social disturbances or dealing with their effects may postpone achieving efficiency goals of the reform and make environmental improvements slower.

Quite commonly in CEE, the failure of environmental policies has been linked so far to an inadequate level of charges and to the lack of markets. Thus there is a natural temptation to conclude that with the advent of a market economy some "optimally calculated charges" will - at last! - start to work.[2] This feeling is occasionally reinforced by Western authors (e.g. Sand (1987), Anderson *et al.* (1990)) who uncritically refer to East-European financial instruments in environmental protection.

---

[2] It is worth noting that a prominent Estonian expert sees this the other way around. Reporting on the progress of the Estonian fee system, he observes that "due to the collapse of the centrally planned economy, many issues related to the use of natural resources and environmental protection have become <u>more</u> (emphasis added - T.Ż.) complicated" (see Chapter 7). While indeed market economies in general require more sophisticated control instruments than centrally planned ones, I do not think any fee system could have effectively worked under the former regime. Likewise its effectiveness in the transition period will be substantially constrained.

The rationale for emission charges stems from the fact that in a world of full information and perfect competiton the same socially desirable environmental effect can be achieved both through setting emission quotas and a per unit charge. If the marginal costs of abatement and the marginal benefits from it are known, then the point where they meet defines the socially optimal level of emissions. This level minimizes the sum of environmental damages and protective activities. Environmental policy-makers can reach that level by simply not allowing emissions to be higher than optimal. Under standard microeconomic assumptions the same effect can be achieved through establishing a charge (corresponding to the level of the marginal abatement costs and marginal benefits) - called a Pigouvian tax - per unit of emission released into the environment.

The equivalence of both solutions is only a formal one. In the real world the superiority of one system over the other is contingent upon specific assumptions (Weitzman, 1974). For all practical purposes (Adar & Griffin, 1976), there is a strong, *a priori* preference for the first, i.e. quantity-based approach. Unfortunately, neither the seminar paper of Weitzman, nor the subsequent discussions have ever been referred to in the East-European and Soviet literature on emission charges, which represent the price-based approach.

There is a way to reconcile the need for firm, quantity-based regulations with the flexibility of market response. The method required is through marketable permits and it conforms perfectly with Herman Daly's (1984) well-known principle of separating scale and allocation decisions in environmental policy.[3] To regulate the environment means to decide to what extent a given resource - say, the carrying capacity of the atmosphere or an aquifer - should be used, and what portion of the resource should be allocated to any of its potential users. Only the second problem is suitable for market regulation. When it comes to the question of scale the market obviously fails as a guide, and the solution should be arrived at by means of a public debate and, perhaps, an administrative standard. This theoretical background and an enormous cost-reducing potential make marketable permits a preferred instrument of environmental policy in many applications.

It should be stressed that the quantity-based approach is not just a more understandable and acceptable option for those exposed to non-market mechanisms. It is not that the preference for marketable permits may result from CEE managers' familiarity with physical rather than financial targets (Levin, 1989). Also it is not just a preferred tool in an economy with soft budget constraints. This is an instrument which combines the certainty and effectiveness of a standard with the flexibility of a market incentive. Its viability was first demonstrated in a developed market economy, but - contrary to charges and fines - it may well work also in a poorly developed institutional context even though here its cost-saving potential can not be fully utilized.

Despite the fact that marketable permits theoretically make a preferred instrument, their applicability is limited. The constraints originate from technological and/or institutional problems (Żylicz, 1993) and leave certain areas exempt from any

---

[3] Also David Pearce (1987) argues for the need for external (with respect to the market) constraints on the use of environment. However, it has to be admitted that Herman Daly's separation principle is far from universally accepted by economists.

form of market control. But this certainly affects charges and fines as well. The awareness of the fact that quantity control in certain spheres is compatible with the general market mechanism is far from universal in CEE economies.

4 SECTORAL AND REGIONAL *VERSUS* FINANCIAL APPROACH

Striking the balance between sectoral and/or regional *versus* financial (macroeconomic) approaches is, perhaps, the major challenge environmental and industrial policies have to face. On the one hand, any discretionalism has to be avoided, in order to achieve the necessary psychological breakthrough in the attitudes of industrial managers in the former CPEs, who are used to the excessive paternalism of state administration. Since the very beginning of the present reforms, they have been seeking individual or sectoral subsidies, exemptions, tariff protection, etc. To yield to such pressures would lead to the instant decay of the emerging market system in CEE. On the other hand, the over-reliance on financial measures - in the absence of well established market structures and entrepreneurial behaviour - has led (at least in Poland) to an economic collapse much deeper than initially expected, and, perhaps, deeper than absolutely unavoidable.

Is there any way to reconcile the need for sectorally and regionally customized policies with the necessity to stick to firm financial rigor? Obviously, the answer cannot simply point at the positive OECD experience, since these countries have combined discretionary measures with functioning of well established markets. Eastern European economies do not operate under the same circumstances.

There is, however, a possibility to gradually integrate market choices into sectoral and regional physical plans. The option is provided by marketable permits which can be applied both at regional and sectoral levels. Successful examples of regional implementation of these instruments are provided by numerous "bubbles" found to be the only practical and cost-effective way to meet ambient standards in many non-attainment areas in the United States. The textbook example of a successful sectoral program is phasing-out lead additives in American refineries. Finally, combined sectoral/regional effects were observed in cases where industry-specific pollutants (like e.g. volatile organic compounds released from laundries) were tackled on a municipal basis.

So far, practical implementation of marketable permits has been almost entirely confined to the United States. Despite their obvious advantages, environmental policy in Europe has largely ignored this option. Very complex legal and administrative traditions in many Western European countries can be identified as the main obstacle to introducing marketable permits there.

In their transition to a "greener" economy, the Central and Eastern European societies and governments are offered assistance by the best Western European and North American experts. Environmental policies for former CPEs have become a part of general environmental policy studies (Howe, 1991). They have also become a separate target of some analyses (Żylicz, 1990, 1991), (Dudek, Stewart, and Wiener, 1992). Post-communist Europe is thus given a chance to learn from the Western experience and to avoid some of its mistakes. One study of economic instruments concludes with a statement whose optimism is, however, somewhat premature:

> *Market-based environmental policies are an ideal tool for nations nurturing new market-based economies. Employing market-based approaches to environmental policy from* *the outset* [emphasis added] *can avoid some of the costly mistakes made in the U.S., and propel Eastern Europe into the forefront of environmental protection.* (Dudek, Stewart, and Wiener 1992).

The assumption about "the outset" is far from obvious. Although it is true that environmental reforms in CEE ought to be comprehensive, this does not mean that their architects may start from scratch. The countries of the region have had extensive legislative systems which cannot be ignored without putting at risk environmental objectives (at least in the short run).

Nevertheless, the need to reform environmental institutions is quite obvious in CEE. It is thus both desirable and probable that the post-communist economies will replicate the American experience with market-oriented instruments sooner than the rest of the continent.

The need to base post-communist economic policies on firm, system solutions while the new system itself is *in statu nascendi*, and certain discretionary measures are unavoidable is the major challenge these policies have to confront. A careful balance between the necessary state intervention and a general system development is therefore of paramount importance.

There should be identified (and implemented) a number of policy steps to provide a "critical mass" so that environmental and economic reforms get the necessary momentum to proceed. Otherwise, environmental interventionism could be an obstacle to a successful therapy of the economic system. It is possible, however to design a set of instruments which serve the purpose of improving environmental policy and supporting the market logic simultaneously, which is a prerequisite for sustainable development. Economic instruments have a particularly important role to play in this context.

It is commonly expected that the return to market logic will cause economic actors to be much more sensitive to price signals. At the same time they will be forced to seek every opportunity for cost reduction by way of energy and material efficiency comparable to levels in Western Europe, thus curbing a fundamental source of pressure on the environment and its resources. Achieving market flexibility and efficiency will not solve the problem automatically. Moreover, as a recent World Bank (1991) study for Poland shows, the short-run structural adjustments of a post-communist economy may, in fact, increase rather than decrease pressure on the environment. This paradox can be explained in terms of lack of abatement equipment in the existing light industries, whose output is most likely to rapidly expand in response to market stimuli, before environmental authorities have even an opportunity to react. This clearly points at the necessity of an extremely careful design of environmental policies matching the pace of macroeconomic ones.

It is the standard wish (and expectation) of environmentalists that economic actors allow ecological considerations the same standing in their calculations as profit. This means that each kilogram of emissions and each tree should be priced in such a way that firms only emit pollutants or disturb nature when socially optimal. This unfortunately is unrealistic as a policy option, and it is important to make the public and decision makers in CEE aware that in none of the market economies are firms regulated through the use of this type of signal. Perhaps in the future economists will be able to accurately enough value nature to allow environmental management to rely just on fees. So far the usefulness of fees for the use of nature has been as a means of raising funds for environmental management and less as a stimulus to reduce pressure on the environment. Hence it is necessary to employ other tools for setting limits on use of the environment.

5 OUTLINE OF ECONOMIC INSTRUMENTS

The establishment of competitive markets will unleash tendencies to save on costs. This in turn will reduce energy and material intensities of production, thus attacking the main single cause of environmental disruption. This same tendency, however, will also create incentives to save on environmental protection costs, thereby calling on the need for environmental authorities to be particularly effective in enforcement programmes. Following the example of the developed market economies, the post-communist ones should make use of market-oriented instruments. Simultaneously, governments should implement direct regulation wherever necessary and where commonly applied worldwide.

Economic instruments include, first of all, charges and marketable permits. These are supplemented by subsidies (grants, tax allowances, soft-loans etc.); budget-neutral instruments (e.g. tax differentiation and deposits on harmful products); and finally, non-compliance fees. Adhering to the following four policy principles while applying economic instruments is likely to enhance the chance for success:

(i) Seeking economic efficiency through "harnessing" market forces in order to minimize the total cost of policy implementation;
(ii) Setting limits so that the overall scale of use of the environment is not exceeded despite economic agents' willingness to pay a non-compliance fee or other form of financial reimbursement;
(iii) Regionalism understood as adapting environmental requirements to regional circumstances and giving local authorities the freedom to choose instruments including the right to use effluent charges as a way of (co)financing local environmental programmes;
(iv) Polluter Pays Principle (PPP) understood as the polluter's responsibility for carrying out all the expenditures necessary to comply with environmental regulations in order to free the authorities from excessive responsibility for the implementation of abatement programmes.

Economic instruments perform a number of useful functions. The most important task of these instruments is to minimize overall costs of environmental protection through an efficient differentiation of control requirements. The agents with the lowest abatement costs should be given the most stringent requirements. In practice, only marketable permits can perform this role in an environmentally safe way. Theoretically, the same goal can be achieved by setting effluent charges at sufficiently high (i.e. Pigouvian) levels, however, in practice this is unusual due to political and methodological obstacles. Another function performed by economic instruments is to raise funds to be spent on environmental management needs. Charge systems throughout the world serve this purpose, and their implementation in the post-communist economies is expected to do the same. Charges, as well as other economic instruments, may also create incentives for environmental conservation and improvement, but this - for the time being - is their secondary role.

According to the PPP - as interpreted by the OECD countries - the polluter is financially responsible for meeting the standards set by the respective environmental authority. The OECD countries, however, acknowledge the need to bypass this principle under special circumstances, especially if the polluter is to pay for the backlog of neglect for which it may not have been fully responsible. Moreover, PPP is considered not to be violated if the polluters are financially supported through funds collected from charges. Here the role of the charges is to raise funds which can be used by environmental authorities to share the costs of the most urgent projects.

Effluent charges should be made available for the regional or local authorities responsible for regulating the effluent. On the other hand, product charges (e.g. a surcharge on fuel prices) do not have to be decentralized, and can be used to raise environmental funds at the national level.

In particular, charges in many CEE countries are and will be used in water resources management (for water intake and sewage discharge), in waste management (for disposal and storage), in air quality management (for emissions), in the protection of living resources, and in the protection against noise and radioactivity. The rates should meet the budgets devoted to the respective sectors of environmental protection or resource management. These budgets should be self-financing with the possibility of receiving moderate support from the general budget of the national or local governments - especially during the next few years when the backlog is enormous.

Extractive activities should be subject to licensing procedures and charges whose rates may vary with the quality of the deposit. The charge should be paid into the national budget (on behalf of the owner, i.e. the state) or to a fund dedicated to the development of the extractive sector. When the competitive markets for geological services and mining activities have developed, the charge should be substituted by a concession fee arrived at through a bidding procedure. This will ensure that the budget receives the full rent due. To ensure that the geological/mining sector operates smoothly, exploration and documentation activities should be carried out continuously. Up to now this sector in Poland and elsewhere in CEE has been sponsored by the state which should continue until the market fully develops for geological services.

Forest resources - which for the most part in CEE are under state administration - are also an element of national wealth which can raise revenues (in the form of a rent) for the budget. At the same time, given that the forestry sector is adversely affected by environmentally disruptive economic activities, the governments should provide this sector with subsidies. These subsidies can also support the development of new forest lands. The entitlements of these subsidies should be established by law.

The scope of subsidies for environmental protection, paid from public funds, should be retained and even broadened during the period of eliminating the backlog.

The subsidies may be continued in the form of direct grants from the national or local budgets for environmental investment. Tasks pertaining to the creation of a (minimum) municipal infrastructure (e.g. facilities providing water supplies, or basic sewage and solid waste treatment), which is the responsibility of the municipality, should be financially secured in the local budgets. In municipalities with low revenues, this share should be guaranteed by means of allocations from the national budgets. This approach would be comparable to that of meeting the basic needs of education, health care and public safety. Subsidies for water resource management budgets - now widespread - should be gradually eliminated so that in the near future each river basin would be self-financed through increased user fees. Subsidies (to a limited extent) for industrial environmental protection programmes should also be employed as a part of the governments' programmes to restructure the economy.

A portion of the subsidies for environmental projects may take the form of tax allowances. Their performance - wherever applied - should be analyzed in order to work out detailed guidelines for an efficient use of these budgetary means. Also soft-loans for environmental projects can be offered. To this end, governments may wish to consider a possibility for allotting budgetary funds to be channelled through (selected) commercial banks in the form of reduced interest rates, extended grace periods, etc. for environmental protection loans. Alternatively, such loans can be offered through extra-budgetary "environmental funds", which are operating in some countries. Of course, the departure from purely commercial terms requires a source of financing (e.g. from pollution charges and/or non-compliance fees as in Poland).

Budget-neutral instruments can be introduced to provide incentives for speeding up pro-ecological changes in the economy and society. Deposits on commodities, chemical compounds or containers that are not environmentally friendly serve as examples here. The environmental lobbies can also plea for tax and tariff differentiation to penalize manufacturers and users of environmentally harmful products, regardless of whether the difference stays in the general budget or gets earmarked for environmental projects.

Non-compliance fees based on fixed (perhaps even high) rates contradict the principle stating that a predetermined overall scale of use of the environment must not be exceeded in exchange for a fine. For this reason, non-compliance fees, which have existed e.g. in Poland, can be accepted only as a means of discouraging accidental, one-time spillovers. With respect to the polluters being consistently in non-compliance, other enforcement measures should be applied.

6 "POLLUTERS PAY" AND "USER PAYS" PRINCIPLES

In some OECD countries, whenever strict responsibility of a given polluter is hard to enforce, an alternative *Polluters Pay Principle* (note the plural) is applied. The direct relationship between environmental stress and payment is relaxed by requiring a whole group of polluters collectively to pay, but considering the alternative of charging the general taxpayer, the modified principle offers a compromise. In Poland, the Polluters Pay Principle is implemented through the National Fund for Environmental Protection and Water Resources Management (National Fund) and 49 Regional Funds for Environmental Protection and Water Resources Management (Regional Funds). In 1989 the National Fund was separated from the state budget and established as a legal entity reporting to a Board appointed by the Minister of Environment. In contrast, Regional Funds are a portion of the state budget managed by respective regional administrators. The revenues of the National Fund and Regional Funds come from emission charges and non-compliance fees. These are collected by regional authorities according to rates set by the Council of the Ministers on an annual basis. The current division of funding (which is determined by the Environmental Protection Act amended in 1989) leaves slightly more than 50% of these funds at the regional level. Despite the recession, the funds are now annually collecting and spending at least 20 times more in real terms than in 1990. They channel more than 40% of Poland's environmental expenditures, the rest being financed mostly from polluters' own sources.

It is not the intention of the Polish government to further increase the overall real level of the total intake of charges for environmental policy purposes.[4] The efficient - "Pigouvian" - level, as understood by policy theorists (i.e. equal to the marginal cost of abatement needed to meet policy objectives), is in Poland 7-8 times higher than the current one in the case of e.g. sulphur dioxide. Although still higher than typical charged rates, average abatement costs are several times lower than marginal ones. The current level of rates thus serves as a means to raise revenues rather than a means to create incentives for reduction in pollution (as almost anywhere else in the world). It is simply aimed at raising funds to secure an adequate public share in financing protection and recovery. This share should be kept within reasonable limits.

It is assumed that the (direct) polluters' share will grow - in accord with the original PPP - as a result of keeping the absolute amount of public funds more or less stable in real terms, and expanding private and municipal spending throughout the 1990's.

The expected stabilization of emission charges has to be distinguished from the necessary flexibility and freedom in setting user charges for environment-related services (tap water supply, sewage treatment, waste collection, etc.). These are not to be controlled by state authorities, perhaps not even by local ones. In the process of privatization (or, at least, marketization) of such services, their prices may go up as a result of removing municipal subsidies which have been applied as a common practice up until now.

To the extent that privatized plants can typically achieve higher economic efficiency than state-owned ones, the privatization process (which is a cornerstone of the economic reform) is welcomed by most environmentalists in Poland. Also MoE endorses privatization of abatement-related activities in its official documents. Whenever municipal authorities enquire about sources of financing for sewage treatment, waste disposal etc, the MoE encourages them to adopt the User Pays Principle. Not only does this approach identify a source of finance to smoothly run such facilities, but also to attract private investors thus solving the question of capital

---

[4] The current charge rates are not low any more. The SO_2 rate was roughly US$80 per tonne of emission in 1992. This is higher than almost anywhere in the world. However, it is still lower than the marginal costs of, say, 30% reduction estimated at almost US$ 600 per ton of SO_2 abated. The Swedish tax of 30 SEK/kg corresponds, however, to about 4000 USD per ton of SO_2 and is thus an example of a real Pigouvian tax, see Chapter 3.

and management. As a result, parts of municipal water and/or sewage infrastructure have already been privatized in several towns (e.g. in Gdansk). Also private firms are beginning to operate in waste collection systems (e.g. in Warsaw). It is too early to judge whether these changes indeed do improve the quality of the services, or decrease their costs.

Both the user and emission charges provide an important source of environmental project financing in Poland. Emission charges and their "recycling" method through the National and Regional Funds make a visible contribution to the environmental recovery process and are a crucial part of the financial mechanism. Operation of such funds should be encouraged throughout CEE.

7 MAKING THE RULES OF THE GAME CLEAR

Economic restructuring implies a massive investment process expected to take place within the next 30 years or so. This effort requires not only the mobilization of resources domestically, but also internationally. For foreign investors, the most striking feature of the environmental management in CEE is the disparity between strict regulation and lax enforcement. With its 32 $\mu g/m^3$ ambient standard for sulphur dioxide (mean annual concentration), Poland exceeds the EC, Switzerland, and the USA! Obviously, nobody takes such a standard seriously. Poland is not an exception among the CEE countries, and its SO_2 standard is not an isolated case.

Plans for adopting the EC standards - first in former Czech Republic, Hungary, Poland and Slovakia, then probably in the rest of the region - indicate the likely evolution of environmental policy in CEE. The expected harmonization of standards offers a valuable reference point for both national and foreign investors. However, a number of problems are to be sorted out in order to determine when and how these (reasonable) standards will be enforced.

Pollution control policy provides an apt illustration of the place of economic instruments. First of all, it is necessary to clearly state that national ambient standards (e.g. concentrations of toxic substances in the air, water quality classification, soil contamination limits) are binding on government bodies at the regional or other levels legally responsible for environmental regulation. Achievement of standards - within the framework of timetables set in conjunction with government agencies (e.g. Ministries of the Environment, regional administrators) and formalized in parliamentary resolutions or some other high-level acts - is the responsibility of the government body specifically in charge of environmental permitting. Individual firms in turn are responsible for preparing timetables, laying out their abatement programmes and submitting them to the appropriate authorities. These sub-timetables are an important means for meeting ambient standards regionally.

Neither regional nor municipal government authorities are necessarily responsible for current ambient conditions which are beyond their control as a result of interregional or international flows of pollutants. It is the responsibility of the national government (e.g. through parliamentary action on proposals prepared by the Ministries of the Environment) to incorporate into the regional timetables constraints on interregional "exports" of pollutants. These constraints can also follow from a given country's international obligations.

Within the framework of the above-mentioned constraints, in an effective environmental management system, the agency empowered to issue emissions permits should have full flexibility to plan and implement pollution control policies. In particular, the agency, based on its informational, technical, and staff capabilities, may choose one or more of the following four methods. *First*, it can demonstrate attainment of national ambient standards by way of compliance by individual sources with their respective emission standards as established by national authorities. Currently there are emission standards for a limited number of pollutant and source types in the CEE countries. In Poland, for instance, there have been air-emission standards for SO_2, NO_x and particulate matter for major sources of combustion (since 1990), and wastewater concentration standards for major sources (since 1992). *Second*, it can by administrative action implement stricter emissions or discharge limits for individual sources which are not exchangeable for charges or fines. *Third*, it can regulate the use of the environment by means of a system of charges and fines similar to the one in use currently in Poland (as well as in many other countries). *Fourth*, it can institute permit markets in which individual users trade all or part of their rights to emit or discharge to other users of the same water- or air-basin, subject to the approval of the relevant permitting authority.

The approach proposed here rests on two postulates. First, it should be stated clearly and decidedly that environmental protection cannot rely on a system of charges and fines as the sole stimulus for required activities. Second, it is necessary to create possibilities for entities responsible for implementing these activities to generate funds for this purpose. In the case of firms, which are the main target group of environmental protection requirements, this is made possible by the abandonment of administrative price control. In the case of national and local governments, which are co-responsible for implementation of environmental policy, this is made possible by allocating the ability to raise funds at precisely the level where governmental responsibility for a given portion of this policy rests. Alternately, establishing the level of subsidies for environmental protection derived from general tax revenues represents a decision to be politically determined taking into account both actual progress in achieving policy objectives and the state's international obligations in this area.

8 IMPLEMENTATION OF ENVIRONMENTAL POLICY REFORMS

As outlined above, Poland's environmental policy reform is implemented simultaneously with massive economic restructuring. Are there any signs of how "free markets" contribute to environmental improvements? Unfortunately, the potential for increased profits may come at the expense of environmental quality too. For instance, one of the first effects of relaxing the straight-jacket that hampered the spirit of entrepreneurship in Poland was the private importation of hazardous wastes (disguised as "raw materials") from Western European countries. It was a lack of adequate, enforceable regulation which invited these sorts of abuses. Incidents like this have forced the government to design effective policy tools as quickly as possible. They are however not necessarily efficient. The total ban on import of wastes - including non-toxic wastes - introduced by Parliament is a controversial measure and it has been contested by the paper and pulp sector (which uses recycled paper as an input), as well as other manufacturers.

In 1990, 18 million tonnes of illegal waste import were attempted; only 60 thousand tonnes succeeded in reaching the country according to the Chief Environmental Inspector's records (presumably there are instances of "successful" undiscovered smuggling too). The same numbers for 1991 are: 3.7 million tonnes attempted *versus* 0 deposited (and discovered).

On the other hand, the first months of the new economic order triggered a recession which caused emissions of most pollutants to decrease. The emergence of markets has therefore been a mixed blessing from the environmentalists' point of view, and it will take more time before more permanent environmental benefits resulting from the market-led restructuring of the economy can be observed.

Apart from the indirect changes resulting from economic restructuring, radical change in environmental policy itself has also been found necessary. Despite some misleading features, Poland's environmental protection in the 1980's was not one of command-and-control. In principle, firms were required to comply with certain emission limits. A common (and legal) practice, however, was to let them pollute above the set standard in exchange for paying a fine based on a multiple of the effluent charge. Thus, the system resembled a market with unlimited access to the environment, treating it as if its resources were limitless. Even though the charges and fines were not prohibitively high, they were much higher than in most developed market economies. It was thus due to poor enforcement - unavoidable in a shortage economy with a prevailing state-owned sector - that this system was doomed to failure.

After 1989, the government attempted to solve the enforcement problem by making more courageous use of administrative instruments, including forced shut-downs[5] and restructuring the fine system so that most cases of non-compliance trigger an administrative action (non-compliance fees should only be used in the case of accidental spillovers). This, however, turned out to be more difficult than expected, and non-compliance fees are still collected in some "chronic" cases too. As indicated in previous sections, an effective alternative to a shut-down would be a marketable permit option, However, because of the insufficiency of the existing legal framework, exercises of that kind can be done on an "experimental basis" only. See Dudek, Kulczyński and Żylicz (1992) for a description and assessment of Poland's first emissions trading project in Chorzów (Southern Poland). Another project in Police (North-Western Poland) is also under way.

It should be stressed once again, that Poland has become a country with fairly high pollution charges. In 1990, charge and non-compliance fee rates were decoupled from the official annual inflation index (computed with a time lag) thus allowing the government to flexibly determine the revenues of environmental funds. The first significant rate increases - to restore the real value of these funds - were effective in July, 1990. Additional significant increases were made effective in January, 1991.

---

[5] In 1990, roughly 100 heavy industrial polluters were forced to shut down either completely or in part (i.e. being allowed to continue their less polluting operations). In 1991, from the "Top 80" polluters list alone, the number of plants actually closed (either completely or in part) is 18; 1 plant should have been closed, but still operates; an additional 5 were given shut-down schedules.

The next change became effective in January, 1992. Supplemented with a new system of more frequent charge collection they changed the operation of environmental funds dramatically. These funds, in turn, should be viewed as a key element of environmental management in the period of recovery.

As a result of these steps, in 1991, environmental investment expenditures in Poland reached US$1.3 billion. Of this sum, US$840 million were spent on the environment *sensu stricto*, i.e. excluding water retention and water supply systems[6]. The remainder of the analysis is confined to this narrow definition of environmental protection.

The 1991 expenditure in real terms was roughly 50% higher than in 1990 (the previous most successful year). Its percentage share in the country's national income grew from 1.1% to 1.6% according to the statistical methodology applied in previous years (*Material Product System*, MPS, constant 1984 prices). It turns out, however, that prices for environmental protection goods and services grew at a slower pace than the overall inflation index. Thus, if evaluated at current prices, the percentage share increased only from 0.9% to 1.3%. Finally, Poland's Gross Domestic Product (according to the *System of National Accounts*, SNA, methodology) is larger than its earlier estimates. Taking this into consideration, it can be concluded that the environmental investment expenditure grew from 0.7% of GDP in 1990 to 1.1% of GDP in 1991. Thus, for the first time ever, Poland reached a relative level of environmental investment effort commensurate with what is spent per unit of GDP in the OECD countries.

This increase in expenditures was achieved despite eliminating - as economically inefficient - major tax allowances (which were a remnant of the old system) for environmental investors. 1990 was the first year Polish enterprises faced hard budget constraints. Simultaneously, it was the last year of income tax allowances for enterprises which undertake environmental investments. It is thus obvious that 1990 was the only year ever for those allowances to work. Large numbers of allowances were granted by tax authorities. Occasionally, MoE was consulted whether an investment complied with the definition of an "environmental project". Since the Tax Law was vague on that issue, all modernization projects - which typically somewhat improve environmental performance of the plant - could have been considered for the allowance. On the other hand, too liberal an interpretation of the Law would have resulted in a collapse of the State Budget. And so its actual application had to be a compromise. The Economics Department at MoE developed an interpretation of the law referring to two criteria; *technology* and *impact*. The former was satisfied if the restructuring project in question introduced an environmentally sound technology whose acquisition or development was of interest to Poland; the latter took into account the population affected by its effects. Despite the fact that many projects were deprived of a potential subsidy, this narrow interpretation was never challenged. Interestingly, the elimination of these tax

[6] Many environmentalists would insist that water retention and water supply is more a part of the environmental problem than of its solution. It is, therefore, better to exclude these from the analysis. All figures quoted are the author's estimates based on the reports from the Central Statistical Office in Warsaw, checked against the data collected by various departments of the Ministry of Environment.

allowances in 1991 turned out to be more than compensated for by the activities of environmental funds.

The recent incremental expenditures correspond thus to the rapid increase in pollution charges and non-compliance fees which are recirculated through the National Fund, and its 49 regional counterparts. The estimated breakdown of finance for the overall investment of US$840 million was in 1991 as follows:

-State budget (grants)	5%,
-National Fund (grants + soft loans)	15%,
-Regional environmental funds (grants)	25%,
-Enterprises (polluters' own resources + commercial loans)	30%,
-Municipalities (municipal budgets + commercial loans)	20%,
-Foreign assistance (grants + development loans)	5%.

It should be noted that 95% of the expenditure was financed from various domestic sources.

It is too early to observe any spectacular effects of the newly implemented policies. The government has not succeeded in restoring the environment yet. Nevertheless, it would be inappropriate to claim that its new policies have been fruitless even during this take-off period.

Despite the economic recession, environmental expenditures increased in real terms, and even increased their share of GDP (Table 2). This indicates that the policy became more effective. There are significant reductions of pollution loads discharged into the environment (Table 5-7). The fact that they are deeper than the GDP decline, indicates that they not only reflect lower production, but also "active" adjustments to the government policy. In particular, one can observe a dramatic increase in emphasis on air pollution abatement (Table 3). However, despite the recent growth in expenditures, the incremental abatement capacity fluctuates widely (Table 4) as a result of substantial time lags and a growing emphasis on process-integrated rather than "end-of-pipe" solutions, but also as a result of possible departures from cost-effectiveness. The latter point reinforces the need for developing and applying least-cost strategies.

Last, but not least, one should note the steady progress in extending protection over Poland's natural heritage (Table 8). This trend can be illustrated by the expanding network of national parks and many other forms of protection. Also symptomatic for a better care for the country's living resources is a drastic change in timber production patterns: 1990 was the first year after the World War II that harvests in Polish forests were down-sized to the sustainable level.

ENVIRONMENTAL PROTECTION IN POLAND: STATISTICAL TABLES 1988-91

Table 2 Environmental investment expenditures (public and private)

	1988*	1989*	1990	1991
Million US$ ('91 dollars)	540	510	580	840
As percent of GDP at current prices	.6	.5	.7	1.1

* For 1988-89 - rough estimates

Table 3 Percentage breakdown of total environmental investment expenditures

	1988	1989	1990	1991
Total*	100	100	100	100
Water	64	62	48	45
Air	18	18	31	40
Solid waste	19	20	21	15

* The total includes also expenditures on nature conservation, anti-noise measures, etc, which account for less than 1%

Table 4 Environmental protection equipment (annual increments)

	1988	1989	1990	1991
Wastewater treatment plants completed	263	280	299	287
Capacity added, 1000 m^3/day	658	1117	1002	348
Air protection: abatement capacity added				
Particulate matter, 1000 tonnes/year	1261	144	436	248
Gaseous pollutants, 1000 tonnes/year	7	6	45	14

Table 5 Air pollution from registered stationary sources (Million tonnes)

	1988	1989	1990	1991
Particulate matter	1.6	1.5	1.2	.9
SO_2	2.8	2.8	2.2	2.0
NO_x	.8	.8	.6	.6

Table 6 Municipal and industrial wastewater requiring treatment (Billion tonnes)

	1988	1989	1990	1991
Total	4.5	4.4	4.1	3.8
Treated	2.8	2.9	2.8	2.6
Treated as percent of the total	62	66	68	70

Table 7 Industrial and municipal waste

	1988	1989	1990	1991
Landfills recultivated, hectares	364	288	346	416
New industrial waste generated, 1,000,000 tonnes	186	171	144	128
Industrial waste treated/recycled, 1,000,000 tonnes	117	108	90	71
Municipal solid waste, 1,000,000 m^3	46	46	43	41[a]

[a] The number does not include households served by small privately owned waste collection companies.

Table 8 Nature protection and forestry

	1988	1989	1990	1991
Roundwood production, 1,000,000 m^3	22.7	21.3	17.6	17.0
Number of national parks	14	15	17	17
National park area, 1000 hectares	127	141	166	177

Source: Author's estimates based on Ochrona *(1989-1992)*.

The 1992 expenditures grew in real terms, as a result of the 1991 increases in pollution charge rates. However, pollution charges in Poland have already become very high, and the economy approaches the limits of what it can spend on the environment from its domestic resources. The conclusions are, therefore, twofold. First of all, the time has come to scrutinize environmental expenditures carefully, and apply various innovative instruments (in addition to charges and fees) in order to obtain maximum physical effects per dollar spent. Moreover, any additional spending - especially that on projects with mainly transboundary or global impacts - would require some form of international cooperation.

The contribution of the state budget, as well as that of foreign assistance programmes will remain marginal. Poland's state budget claims roughly 30% of the country's GDP, and its share is expected to further decrease. The G-24 assistance to Poland (supported by the 24 industrialized countries and coordinated by the EC) has probably reached its peak now, and the focus will gradually move to other post-communist countries. These countries are creating institutions (to a large extent modelled after the Polish pattern) to absorb such an assistance. So far Poland has managed to consume by far the largest proportion of bilaterally pledged funds.

Debt-for-environment swaps are a different story. They provide a source of assistance which will last potentially longer - up to 18 years, i.e. the time horizon of the agreement with the Paris Club. In 1991 Poland achieved 50% reduction of its outstanding official foreign debt. Simultaneously the Club decided that an additional 10% may be swapped in a series of bilateral and voluntary agreements with each of the 17 creditor countries. The Polish government used this opportunity to launch a large scale debt-for-environment swap initiative. The initiative envisages supporting in particular those projects which have transboundary and global significance. If all the creditors approved the 10% clause, then Poland would additionally gain over $3 billion to be spent on the environment over 18 years. The time profile of debt service is not uniform, and the 10% would correspond to $120 million *per annum* in 1991-93, and up to $400 million around the year 2000, when the peak payments are due. However, not all the creditors are ready even to discuss the initiative.

Recently Poland's Minister of Finance established *EcoFund*, a foundation to administer whatever resources will become available as a result of debt-for-environment swaps. For the time being, EcoFund's resources are modest; they come from the U.S. commitment ($6.5 million *per annum* for the first three years). Also France committed a portion of its 10%.[7] Switzerland agreed to join the EcoFund in 1995. Some other creditors indicate their interest as well, but it may take time to convince skeptics that EcoFund will be an efficient, reliable, and professionally run facility. However, even under the most optimistic scenario - with all creditors contributing - EcoFund would never account for more than, say, 15% of Poland's environmental investment expenditures. One can expect that the debt-for-environment swap will gradually extend and substitute other forms of foreign assistance. Nevertheless these external sources will always contribute only a fraction of what is spent from various domestic funds.

Thus there will be no ecological miracle in Poland. But there were no ecological miracles anywhere else in the world. In all regions which succeeded in

---

[7] Initially only 1% of the annual payments due.

recovering from ecological catastrophes - like London, Pittsburgh or the Ruhr Basin - the success was achieved gradually, as a result of lengthy investment programmes. Their effects became visible only after years of steady investing.

9 THE POLITICS OF ENVIRONMENTAL POLICY REFORM

The transition from an environmentally disruptive to an efficient, "green", economy has been the aim of many reform-minded people in Poland. There is no doubt that the unsound environmental policies of the old system had to be abandoned. But there is also too much faith put in the benign environmental impacts of the market economy. A lot of confusion, has arisen regarding the characteristic features of the system to be built.

In the case of general economic reform, there is a more or less well-identified minimal set of institutions to be established. These institutions characterize every developed market economy and serve as a reference point for the reformers (i.e. the government). As far as other sectors are concerned, the international experience has been much more diversified. It would be difficult to find some non-trivial "common institutional denominator" in any of the fields such as education, culture, medical care, urban policy, or environmental management. See Żylicz, (1991). Thus, the design of new environmental policies had to be controversial.

Obviously any regulatory reform meets resistance from the reformed institutions. This resistance coupled with confusion about the proper reference point for policy reform make recent Polish environmental developments an interesting case in the post-communist history of East European economies.

A number of actors, both individual and institutional, are active in Poland's environmental arena. The configuration is far from the simple dichotomy of environmentalists *versus* developers. The weakness of both groups results in a much more diversified pattern of conflict.

It would be unfair to completely disregard the importance of the environmental lobby. Occasionally they file complaints, organize on-site events, give embarrassing media interviews - yet without any serious effect due to low overall social awareness about environmental problems. The most complete summary of the views of Polish environmentalists is included in the *Protocol of the Round-Table* of the early 1989. (See also Bochniarz & Bolan, 1990). There are two items of interest in this context, which proved to be lasting issues despite the changes in the political dialogue. First is the preference for regional decentralization of environmental authority (starting with water basin management agencies). Second is the separation of the National Fund from the MoE which was implemented in 1989.

As for the "developers", or entrepreneurs in general, there are very few involved in environmental debates in Poland. In 1990, a number of regional administrators - acting on behalf of suburban coal-fired greenhouse owners - filed complaints about the excessive level of emission charges. Apart from that, industry has stayed rather quiet except for complaints regarding its financial predicament.

The greenhouse owners' complaints, however, unexpectedly culminated at the Supreme Constitutional Court in 1991, in a case against the Government of Poland. The Court has found it unconstitutional to regionally differentiate pollution charges. The judgment only relates to air emission charges (i.e. the ones that were actually challenged by the greenhouse owners) but it is just a matter of time until others will be challenged too unless the government is successful in its appeal. Even though cases heard by the Constitutional Court require a one stage procedure, the government could and actually did request that the case be resolved at a plenary session of the Court (so far it was heard only by a specially appointed team of judges). In case of failure, this ruling would seriously undermine any further efforts aimed at establishing a rational system of economic instruments for environmental protection in Poland.

The MoE should be identified as the architect and promoter of the reform, despite its heterogeneity (see Box 1 for a review of activities aimed at improving the country's environmental management). While the institutional make-up was already designed at the time of the Round-Table, promotion of the concepts of efficiency and the rational use of market mechanisms is a later addition. Here the MoE had to confront a plethora of amateur economists from the Parliament, NGOs, academia, and various parts of the government, who strongly advocated for Pigouvian taxation (though the term itself was not referred to explicitly).[8] Most of the discussants asserted that market economies rely on price incentives when managing environmental quality. This view has been so widespread that the MoE decided to publish (and distribute free of charge) a Polish translation of the OECD (1989) report which is proof to the contrary. Several other translations of that sort were carried out or are under way in order to correct the false image of Western environmental policies.

An attempt to experiment with Pigouvian taxation would be dangerous. It would clearly be impossible to raise emission charges to their efficient levels, as most enterprises would have been eliminated from the market. Under these circumstances, to claim that incentive charging is a prerequisite for environmental protection would be equivalent to admitting that the protection is premature. Indeed, it looks as if some proponents of "solving" the problem through price mechanisms - at least subconsciously - were expecting such a bottom line.[9]

There is also a common belief held in Poland that environmental protection does not require expenditures, provided that the polluters are given the "right" price incentives. As a result, people resist the idea of bearing the burden of abatement. Meanwhile, the communists are expected to pay for the clean-up of "the mess for which they are responsible". Nobody is outspoken against environmental protection. However, when it comes to money, even moderate proposals meet with resistance. In 1990, the MoE tried to introduce a fuel charge averaging 4% (*ad valorem*) earmarked for environmental protection on top of existing excise taxes, which are (in the case of petrol) in the order of 100%. The charge on liquid fuels, natural gas, and lignites can raise as much as US$300 million per year (hard coal should be added to

---

[8] The ruling of the Constitutional Court reflects the intellectual disarray of the Polish academic community which has not been able to provide the Court with sufficient expertise related to the rationale for using pollution charges. The extensive interpretation of the charge system which accompanied the decision is extremely weak in terms of professional argument (when judged against the literature and current academic discussions). This explains why MoE puts so much effort in disseminating the knowledge of contemporary environmental and resource economics; see Box 1.

[9] This was a typical opinion voiced by the Minister of Industry in 1990, some Ministry of Finance officials, and many others.

the list above as soon as its price is fully freed from state subsidies). A certain degree of rate differentiation was also suggested so as to account for different qualities of fuels (e.g. 8% for leaded vs. 2% for unleaded petrol, and so on). The proposal met with almost unanimous opposition. The official opinion of "Solidarity" was typical. It read: "While the union is for environmental protection, it will not approve any such burden laid on the impoverished society". Later in 1991, the charge was again on the political agenda, this time at the initiative of small groups of "green" members of Parliament.

The resistance to introducing product charges which are thought of as a source of revenues for the National Fund is inconsistent with the widespread expectation that 100% of the emission charges and non-compliance fees should be retained at the regional level. As long as it is also expected that some funding from a central fund is indispensable (e.g. for projects involving several regions) the only way to reconcile the two propositions - without totally ignoring the PPP by charging the general taxpayer - is to accept the idea of product charges. These charges (levied on environmentally harmful goods), which cannot be convincingly claimed by any single regional administration, make a natural source of centrally managed revenues. Therefore, MoE has proposed that emission charges be fully decentralized as soon as product charges are established to make up for the resulting "losses" by the National Fund. Such charges are resisted on several grounds. The reluctance to accept an additional burden was already identified, but more sophisticated arguments can also be made.

There is an active group of lawyers that is working on drafts of environmental protection legislation (e.g. the general Environmental Protection Act, and "sectoral" laws on water, forestry, waste, inspection, etc.). The lawyers are encouraged by the conceptual vacuum left by the communists apparently opening up the possibility of building new legislation from scratch. As a result, they tend to disregard practical experience, and create concepts that appeal to their own sense of beauty and clarity. The idea of a product charge apparently does not fit into this ideal framework, as "no earmarked taxes should exist".

Applying an aesthetic argument, some lawyers also objected to a number of ideas to make state environmental inspection viable at a regional level, despite the fact that such solutions are applied worldwide. It was not until mid-1991 that the new state inspection act was finally approved by Parliament after months of arguing against the idea of "ecological police" with powers to control the environmental performance of state and municipal authorities too. Controversies like these make it difficult to design a rational level of regionalism, as the grievances of municipal self-governments are strong. Here, again, an ideological argument - to grant municipalities almost unconstrained power to control the environmental resources (including the commons) that fall within their territory - is applied despite obvious world experiences which justify state intervention in municipal authority regarding environmental matters.

In brief, the current environmental reform includes most of the relevant opinions of the "environmental opposition" of the 1980's. As a result, there are no clear alternatives (with the one possible exception for Pigouvian taxes) to the proposals the government - and, in particular, MoE - has advocated. In short, these offer an array of direct regulations supplemented with marketable permits, and a revenue-raising mechanism to support environmental abatement projects where PPP cannot be fully enforced. Nevertheless, the reforms progress slowly because a large number of peripheral issues and loosely-involved actors have entered the political arena and clouded the issue. These problems can be considered as manifestations of either society's reluctance to pay the costs of environmental protection, or as attempts by various professional groups to implement something monumental without questioning the economic efficiency and administrative viability of their proposals.

It was interesting to observe in 1991 an informal "upgrading" of the position of MoE at the government forum. When in mid-1991, Poland's Prime Minister officially launched the initiative to coordinate debt swaps offered by the Paris Club within the framework of an EcoFund, it was the effect of a major intra-governmental debate. The idea of the EcoFund won a competition with all the other debt-for-something swaps proposed by respective Ministers of Industry, Agriculture, Health, Construction, Privatization, Transport, Communication, and so on.

This "greening" of the government would not have been possible without the support of the Ministry of Finance which later incorporated debt-for-environment negotiations into its strategy towards debt rescheduling. On the other hand, however, the swaps accomplished have provided an argument for those within the Ministry of Finance who would like to save on budgetary environmental expenditures, as the environment "seems to be better off" (compared to other sectors) anyway. Overall, the environment is indeed relatively better off, although not because its status has been elevated within the government,[10] but - paradoxically - because it has become somewhat independent of the government's budget. The existence of earmarked pollution charges and environmental funds proved to be the most important factor of environmental management in Poland since 1991.

10 SUMMARY AND CONCLUSIONS

The heritage of the former CPEs, including Poland, can be summarized in a series of statistical indicators showing that the resource and pollution intensities of Gross Domestic Product were roughly twice or three times as high as in the West. General inefficiency of a non-market allocation resulted in an excessive (relative to the output) use of resources. But there were also additional factors which led to an excessive use of the natural resources in particular: most importantly, a bias towards heavy industry, and furthermore misconceptions in environmental policy itself.

The policy misconceptions were basically threefold: Firstly too little rather than too much reliance on direct regulations, secondly existence of strict regulations not really meant to be enforced, and finally inappropriate use of economic instruments - that is waiting until Pigouvian taxes start to stimulate the proper behaviour.

The instability of the political environment is a crucial factor contributing to this troublesome heritage. IMF-consulted structural adjustment policies are socially controversial, and people in CEE are anxious to see rapid changes in their welfare, which is obviously unrealistic. Adding thorny privatization issues, one can see that environmental policy makers have to operate within a very turbulent and explosive political environment. They simply have to move fast in order to match the pace of macroeconomic policy reforms.

---

[10] This relatively high status enjoyed in 1991 has however not turned out to be stable.

There is a need for firm, non-discretionary, market-oriented, solutions in environmental policy. This is caused by the fact that the main constraint to the transition process in CEE is the psychological one. A "critical mass" for the market reforms has to be created to convince people that they have to respond to market stimuli rather than seek government support and rescue whenever they have a problem. Scarcity of administrative skills is another reason to avoid excessive interventionism.

But, on the other hand, administrative solutions are unavoidable in CEE because inherited sectoral and regional problems really do require discretionary measures, markets are weak, and finally direct environmental regulations have been proven effective in the OECD countries.

Marketable pollution permits (and harvest quota, concession rights, etc.) is the option which deserves the most serious consideration as a solution to this dilemma. Marketable permits are:

* theoretically sound, as they conform with Herman Daly´s principle of separating allocation and scale decisions (the former can be best handled by markets; the latter typically require some exogenous regulation);
* they are good substitutes for Pigouvian taxes;
* they can combine sectoral or regional considerations (that is - an administrative discretionalism, or quantity-based approach) with the flexibility of market response;
* lastly, there are some pilot projects under way in the region.

The Polluter Pays Principle is difficult to implement, because of:

* historical contamination problems (mainly for industries) - the polluter does not exist any more;
* and because of equity reasons (mainly for municipalities).

However, rather than charging the general taxpayer, the Polluters Pay Principle (note the plural form) can be implemented through "environmental funds". These in Poland took the form of the National Fund and its 49 regional counterparts operating in 49 administrative regions. They charge polluters in general and then recirculate money according to environmental policy priorities.

Emission charges in Poland are high by OECD standards, but still below Pigouvian (i.e. efficient) levels; efficiency (or, strictly speaking, cost-effectiveness) is expected to be achieved through marketable permits rather than elevating pollution charges to their Pigouvian levels. Existing emission charges play an indispensable revenue raising role, as environmental funds are independent from the state budget. The importance of this cannot be explained on efficiency grounds only. These funds make the environmental protection relatively independent - both financially and politically - from the extremely turbulent political environment.

The general strategy towards environmental policy reform adopted by Poland's Ministry of Environment has been as follows:

* *First*, generate the "demand" for environmental protection through ecological education, the new legal framework for enforcement and through public

environmental funds.

* *Second*, build domestic capacity (i.e. the "supply" of environmental management skills) by creating centres of professional excellence and halting (eventually reverting) brain-drain.
* *Third*, create lobbies for environmental improvement and regulatory reform. Such lobbies include: environmental research teams, bureaucrats in environmental agencies (within the government or outside its regular structures), and environmental businesses (in consulting, engineering and manufacturing).
* *Fourth*, "harness" scarce international assistance sources to support institutional capacity building. This is why, for instance, Poland's debt-for-environment swap has been designed so as to establish a highly professional, and somewhat independent, agency - the EcoFund - to administer the swapped funds rather than simply have them spent.

We can now see the first, modest results of this strategy:

* the 1991 environmental investment expenditures exceeded $800 million, i.e. 1% of GDP (roughly quadrupling the 1980 levels); it should be noted that 95% of this expenditure was financed from domestic sources, with public environmental funds providing 40% of the total;
* centres for professional excellence are developed (EcoFund was established in mid 1992);
* "constituency for efficiency" is gradually promoted among political elites and researchers as a result of a massive educational effort focusing on the proper use of economic instruments.

Our final recommendations can be grouped under two headings. First, further research needs, then institutional strategy.

10.1 Environmental and resource economics multidisciplinary research priorities.

* Promote professionalism in related disciplines (especially in economics). Do not rely on amateurs, as their recommendations can easily harm the reputation of environmental lobbies.
* Encourage multidisciplinary projects involving best expertise from related disciplines; if a particular skill is missing in the country, then look for a partner from abroad.
* Develop thorough understanding of merits and applicability of alternative economic instruments (charges, marketable permits, tax differentiation, deposit-refund systems, bonds, etc.)

10.2 Institutional capacity building.

* Create environmental lobbies in a systematic way by enhancing "immunity" of environmental agencies from political pressures, generating significant public environmental expenditure preferably through recirculating pollution charges and finally developing ties between research teams and environmental

agencies to let them support each other.

* Develop the human resource base for environmental management, that is solve the brain-drain problem, use external assistance to enhance professionalism in domestic environmental institutions, do not just spend the money on hardware and foreign consulting services.

A comprehensive assessment of the initial period of the Polish environmental policy reform is not possible at this stage. Nevertheless the discussion carried out in this chapter points at the following final conclusions. (1) Moderate progress has been achieved with respect to creating a conceptual framework for the regulatory reform. (2) Minimal environmental adjustment symptoms (to be attributed to the emerging market system) have been observed in the economy. (3) The new position of the state *vis à vis* economic agents has resulted in a more courageous approach to environmental non-compliance which led to a number of forced shut-downs. (4) The environmental expenditures have kept growing despite the widespread economic crisis. (5) Environment has become an issue at various government fora.

Box 1 ENVIRONMENTAL DEVELOPMENTS IN POLAND 1989 - MID 1992

In **March 1989**, "The Round Table" talks between the communist establishment and the Solidarity-led opposition took place. The resulting semi-free parliamentary elections in June 1989 triggered the collapse of central planning throughout Central and Eastern Europe. The post-communist economies started to reform their institutions.

● **April 1989**. (1) The National Fund for Environmental Protection and Water Resources Management (the National Fund) is established as a public agency responsible for a fixed proportion of emission charges and non-compliance fees. The charges and fees earmarked for environmental protection projects have existed for a long time, but were administered through central and regional state budgets. The National Fund may choose whatever spending method (e.g. subsidy, soft-loan, equity share in a joint-venture) it deems appropriate for a given project. (2) Charge and fee rates are pegged to official annual (*ex post*) inflation index.

● **October 1989**. Work on environmental policy reform is launched by the Ministry of Environment. Marketable pollution permits are among the new instruments to be introduced.

● **May 1990**. Charge and fee rates are decoupled from the official inflation index (as a result of the April 1989 law, because of hyperinflation, the 1990 environmental fund revenues were slashed in real terms). From now on the Council of Ministers sets the rates on an annual basis (or more frequently if requested by the Minister of Environment) taking into account expected (*ex ante*) inflation, and other considerations as well.

● **June 1990**. (1) First significant charge and fee increase effective July 1990. (2) Polish division of the European Association of Environmental and Resource Economists (EAERE) is formed at an academic meeting hosted by the Minister of Environment.

● **September 1990**. Environmental policy document is finally drafted. An extensive appendix on the application of economic instruments is prepared and distributed in Polish and English.

● **November 1990**. Environmental policy document is approved by the Council of Ministers. Sustainable development and widespread use of market-oriented instruments for environmental and resource management become elements of the official government program.

● **December 1990**. (1) Second significant charge and fee increase effective January 1991. (2) Environmental investment expenditures are no longer tax deductible (most of the corporate income tax exemption titles discontinued). The government argues that the increased pollution charges, which (unlike non-compliance fees) subtract from taxable income, are a more appropriate budgetary contribution to environmental investment expenditures. (3) Polish translation of the 1989 OECD report on *Economic Instruments for Environmental Protection*) is published and widely distributed.

● **January 1991**. A commercial Environmental Protection Bank Inc. is established in Warsaw. Its major shareholder, the National Fund, offers subsidies to interest rates for priority projects.

● **March 1991**. (1) Minister of Environment circulates *Memorandum on Redirecting Debt Service for Environmental Recovery Purposes* identifying investment areas of transboundary and global importance. (2) Marketable pollution permits project for the city of Chorzów is launched by the Ministry of Environment, local authorities, and the Environmental Defense Fund (New York). (3) Geological concession and royalty fees are established as an instrument of non-renewable resource policy.

● **May 1991**. (1) Parliament approves the November '90 environmental policy document. (2) New *Environmental Protection Act* is drafted. Its Article 45 reads: "The terms of a pollution permit for a plant can be transferred to another plant, either entirely or in part, subject to the approval of the authority who issued the original permit". When passed, the Act will justify simple marketable permit schemes.

● **June 1991**. Poland's Debt-for-Environment swap initiative is officially launched by the Prime Minister. The initiative is based on the Paris Club April '91 decision (on reduction and rescheduling of the Polish debt).

● **July 1991**. In the absence of a fully adequate legal framework for transferring pollution permits, the Minister of Environment lets local authorities proceed with the Chorzów project "on an experimental basis".

● **September 1991**. *Forestry Act* is passed. The Act establishes tax and subsidy rules supporting sustainable uses of forests and marginal agricultural land.

● **October 1991**. *Nature Conservation Act* is passed. The Act justifies admission fees and other decentralized revenues to benefit national parks.

● **November 1991**. Regulations on the collection and distribution of geological fees are issued by the Council of Ministers. A fixed proportion of the fees transferred to the National Fund is to be spent on geological exploration and environmental protection projects in mining sector.

● **December 1991**. (1) The pollution charge system - with higher rates in the most polluted and congested regions - is challenged as "unconstitutional". The government appeals. (2) Third significant charge and fee increase effective January 1992.

● **January 1992**. Chorzów project brings the first (very modest) physical improvement in one of the most polluted neighbourhoods.

● **April 1992**. The Minister of Finance establishes *EcoFund* as a foundation to administer debt-for-environment swap funds. The foundation will start its operations administering the funds committed by the U.S., France, and possibly other creditors.

● **May 1992**. In a letter to The World Bank, the Minister of Environment explains the policy of linking emission regulations to ambient quality targets and standards, and endorses the use of marketable permits to make the compliance cheaper.

● **June 1992**. Ministry of Environment, National Fund, and Environmental Protection Bank contribute to the Third Annual EAERE Conference held in Kraków.

REFERENCES

Adar, Z. and J. M. Griffin. 1976. "Uncertainty and Choice in Pollution Control Instruments", *Journal of Environmental Economics and Management*, vol. III, pp 178-188.

Anderson, R. C., L. A. Hofman, and M. Rusin. 1990. "The Use of Economic Incentive Mechanisms in Environmental Management", *Research Paper* #051, American Petroleum Institute.

Bochniarz, Z. and R. Bolan eds. 1990. *Designing Institutions for Sustainable Development: A New Challenge for Poland*, Białystok: Białystok Technical University.

Daly, H. E. 1984. "Alternative Strategies for Integrating Economics and Ecology", in: A-M Jansson (ed.), *Integration of Economy and Ecology. An Outlook for the Eighties*, Proceedings from the Wallenberg Symposia, Stockholm, pp 19-29.

Dudek, D. J., R. B. Stewart and J. B. Wiener. 1992. "Environmental Policy for Eastern Europe": Technology-Based versus Market-Based Approaches, *Columbia Journal of Environmental Law*.

Dudek, D. J., Z. Kulczyński and T. Żylicz. 1992. "Implementing Tradeable Pollution Rights in Poland", paper presented at the Third Annual Conference of the European Association of Environmental and Resource Economists, Cracow.

Howe, C. W. 1991. "Lessons from the U.S. Experience for the Single European Market and Eastern Europe", *Mimeo*. Agricultural University, Wageningen.

Kornai, J. 1986. "The Soft Budget Constraint", *Kyklos*, vol. 39, pp 3-30.

Krawczyk, R. 1991. "Wzrost gospodarczy a środowisko - wzajemne zależności", unpublished Ph.D. thesis, Economics Department, Warsaw University. [Economic growth *versus* environment - mutual relationships].

Levin, M. H. 1989. "An Environmental Manifesto for Poland", *Wall Street Journal*, October 24.

Ministry of Environment. 1990a. *National Ecological Policy*, *Mimeo*. Ministry of Environment, Warsaw.

Ministry of Environment. 1990b. *National Environmental Policy - Outline of Economic Instruments*, *Mimeo*. Ministry of Environment, Warsaw.

Ochrona Środowiska. 1989-1992. Central Statistical Office, Warsaw [Poland's Environmental Statistical Yearbook].

OECD. 1989. *Economic Instruments for Environmental Protection*, OECD, Paris.

Olszewski, D. W. Bielański and M. Kamińska. 1987. "Economic pressure on the environment in the European CMEA countries". Statistical tables, *EKO²* *Series*, no. 8716, Warsaw University.

Pearce, D. W. 1987. "Foundations of an Ecological Economics", *Ecological Modelling*, vol. 38, pp 9-18.

Sand, P. H. 1987. "Air Pollution in Europe": International Policy Responses, *Environment*, vol. 29, no.10, pp 16-20 & 28-29.

Weitzman, M. 1974. "Prices vs. Quantities", *Review of Economic Studies*, vol. XLI, pp 447-491.

World Bank. 1992. *Poland. Environmental Strategy,* Report no. 9808-POL, Washington DC.

Żylicz, T. 1990. "Environmental Policies for Former Centrally Planned Economies", paper presented at the First Annual Conference of the European Association of Environmental and Resource Economists, Venice.

Żylicz, T. 1991. "Environmental Reform in Poland: Theories Meet Reality", *European Environment*, vol. 1, part 1, pp 16-18.

Żylicz, T. 1993. "Improving Environment through Permit Trading: The Limits to Market Approach", Beijer Discussion Papers no. 23, The Royal Swedish Academy of Sciences, Stockholm.

CHAPTER 6

Environment and Energy in the Baltic Countries*

by

Jürgen Salay**

Abstract

This chapter discusses the challenges for environmental policy in the Baltic countries; Estonia, Latvia and Lithuania. The first part describes their major pollution problems, focusing on water and air and changes in Baltic environmental protection that have occurred since independence. The second part considers their energy use and its negative impact on the environment and the economy because of low efficiency and high dependence on imported fossil fuels. It concludes that energy conservation will be an important policy instrument for the Baltic countries in order to reduce pollution and cut energy costs.

* Parts of this chapter are reproduced, with permission, from the author's article (with J. Fenhann, K. Jaanimägi and L. Kristoferson) "Energy and Environment in the Baltic States" in the Annual Review of Energy and the Environment, vol. 18, 1993, by Annual Reviews Inc.

** Thanks are due to Tomasz Żylicz and Katarina Katz for comments.

T. Sterner (ed.), Economic Policies for Sustainable Development, 113–131.

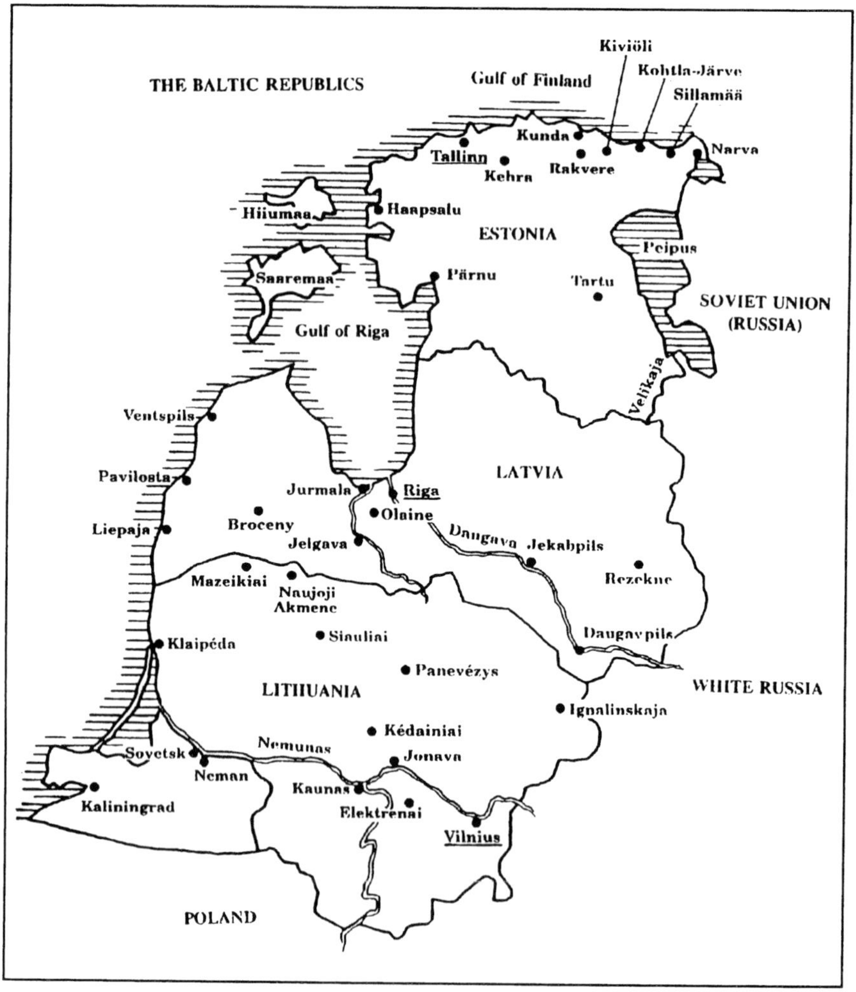

1 INTRODUCTION

With the rebirth of Estonia, Latvia, and Lithuania three new members have joined the East European group of former centrally planned economies (CPEs) striving towards democracy and market economy. As newly independent states the Baltic countries are challenged to recreate national political and economic structures that were destroyed or distorted during the Soviet regime. One area that was particularly neglected in the USSR was environmental protection. More than 40 years of heavy industrialization has resulted in environmental problems like polluted air and water that now must be addressed by the Baltic governments.

Like in other East European countries dependent on fossil fuels, a major source of pollution in the Baltic countries is the production and use of energy. A general lack of cleaning facilities in industry and power plants combined with low energy efficiencies aggravates the pollution load from energy use. Fossil fuels imported from Russia are the most important energy sources. A principal problem for the Baltic states is how to solve their energy situation without increasing the burden on the environment. The Baltic countries' heavy dependence on imported energy also has serious economic implications. As small economies without the financial means to buy oil and other fuels on the world market, the Baltic states are extremely vulnerable to disturbances in energy supply from the former Soviet Union.

Although pollution has decreased since 1990 as a result of falling industrial production and energy use, there is an obvious risk that the long-term development of industry and transport will conflict with environmental considerations. At the same time, the Baltic governments' short-term objective of securing energy supplies must be weighed against long-term goals of increased reliance on indigenous energy sources and energy conservation. This chapter highlights the dilemma the Baltic and other governments in the former Soviet Union encounter in their struggle to protect the environment during political and economic transition. It provides an overview of the environmental situation in Estonia, Latvia and Lithuania with a particular focus on energy use and its effects on the environment.

Table 1, Area and Population of the Baltic States in 1989

	Estonia	Latvia	Lithuania
Area (km^2)	45100	63700	65200
Population (1000s)	1583	2687	3723
Pop. density (per km^2)	35	42	57
Share of titular nationality (in %)	62	52	80
Share of minorities (in %)			
Russians	30	34	9
Other East Slavic	5	8	2
Poles			7

Source: Brian Van Arkadie & Mats Karlsson, (1992).

2 THE ENVIRONMENTAL SITUATION

Most environmental problems in Estonia, Latvia and Lithuania are similar to those of other industrialized economies. However, some features typical of former centrally planned economies (CPEs) make the situation of the Baltic states different from that of countries in Western Europe and North America. Water, raw materials and energy were free or underpriced. Consequently, industrial production in the Baltic states had, and to a large extent still has, a high intensity of raw material and energy use, which made it exceedingly polluting. Treatment of waste water and air pollution is based on rudimentary technology and is far from sufficient. Despite a fairly well-developed system of environmental inspection in the Soviet Union, little was done to reduce emissions from industry and other polluters. Since enterprises were subordinated to central ministries, it was often difficult to determine who should be held responsible for violation of environmental laws and regulations. Until independence in 1991, local and republican authorities in Estonia, Latvia and Lithuania had very limited influence on economic activity within their territory.

The state of the environment in Estonia, Latvia and Lithuania is comparable to that of countries in Eastern Europe, although an overall assessment probably concludes that the situation is less acute in the Baltic countries. With the possible exception of northeastern Estonia (see Chapter 7), they do not suffer from the type of complex and serious regional environmental problems that have been recognized in Saxony, Northern Bohemia and Upper Silesia in East Central Europe. Some areas in the Baltic states still hold wildlife that has disappeared in most of Western Europe and Scandinavia. At the same time, it is evident that the Baltic states face several environmental problems that call for immediate action.

2.1 Water pollution

Water pollution in rivers, lakes and the Baltic Sea is probably the most acute environmental problem in the Baltic states. There are three major sources of polluted water: insufficiently treated sewage from towns and municipalities, industrial sewage and agriculture. According to official statistics for 1989, Estonia discharged 517 million m^3 of used water in need of treatment. Latvia discharged 367 million m^3 and Lithuania 450 million m^3. In Estonia, about half of the water in need of treatment was "standardly" treated (that is, discharged after legally required treatment, still with a high concentration of pollutants, although lower than permissible levels according to Soviet criteria at that time). In Latvia this share was only 30 % in the same year, and in Lithuania it was even smaller - 25 %. The remaining part of the waste water in the three republics was insufficiently treated, or discharged without any treatment (see Table 2).

Existing sewage treatment capacity is far from satisfactory. In 1991, several Baltic towns had no sewage treatment facilities at all. Moreover, most of the available sewage treatment plants are equipped only with mechanical and biological treatment. Biological-chemical treatment is only available in a few cases, which means that nutrients cannot be handled. Some industries, like food-processing or metallurgy, have their own treatment plants where waste water requires special treatment. However, most enterprises channel their sewage directly to the municipal treatment plants, despite the fact that these plants lack appropriate equipment to treat industrial sewage.

Construction of new treatment plants has been slow. Equipment has to be imported. More sophisticated technology, for instance for chemical treatment, can only be bought for convertible currency. Funds for hard-currency imports are still very scarce. Another problem is the maintenance of existing treatment plants. Lack of money means that equipment is not maintained properly. Spare parts are difficult to get. Inadequate training of the staff also causes low efficiency of operation.

Table 2, Sewage Discharge (million cubic meters, 1989)

	Estonia	Latvia	Lithuania
Total discharge of which:	517 (100%)	367 (100%)	450 (100%)
a) standardly treated:	271 (52%)	110 (30%)	114 (25%)
b) partially treated:	192 (37%)	257* (70%)	124 (28%)
c) untreated:	54 (10%)		211 (47%)

*) b+c

Sources: Environment '89, Apkartejas (1990), Gamtunauda (1990).

In Estonia, the rivers belonging to the catchment area of the Gulf of Finland in the northern part of the country are the worst affected by water pollution. Groundwater quality is unstable in several settlements. In the north-east the level of groundwater has sunk as a result of the oil-shale mining. About 350 million m^3 water are pumped out of the mines each year. Another serious problem in this area is contaminated water leaking from stored ash at the thermal power plants in Narva. As a result of polluted seawater and unfavorable changes in the natural algae communities, the spawning and living conditions for many fish species have deteriorated along the Estonian part of the Baltic coast.

In Latvia, the Lielupe River Basin is considered to be the most polluted area. The Lielupe River flows into the Gulf of Riga which in turn is one of the most polluted parts of the Baltic Sea. The major reason for the bad state of the Gulf of Riga is sewage from Riga, the capital of Latvia, with almost one million inhabitants. In 1989, Riga pumped 90% of its waste water (almost 160 million m^3) untreated into the Gulf. That was 61% of the total amount of untreated sewage in Latvia that year. Municipal sewage is the most significant source of pollution in inland and coastal waters in Latvia. Hardly any Latvian town has sufficient capacity to handle its waste water.

Lithuania has the lowest standard of sewage treatment of the Baltic states. In 1989, the two largest towns, Kaunas and Vilnius, accounted for 177 million m^3 or about 40% of the total amount of waste water in need of treatment in the country. In 1991, Kaunas did not have any treatment facilities at all, and in Vilnius the sewage was only mechanically treated. The Nemunas river, which is a border river to the Kaliningrad region (administered by Russia) and flows into the Curonian Bay, is among the most polluted waters in the Baltic countries. According to official estimates, 85% of the Curonian Bay and 45% of the Baltic Sea coastal area in Lithuania are heavily polluted. Apart from municipal waste water, contamination of wells around large agricultural production complexes has become a growing problem in the last ten years.

2.2 Air pollution

Per capita emissions of several pollutants in the Baltic states are comparable to those in other East European countries and typically higher than in Western Europe. Emissions of sulphur dioxide (SO_2) from the Baltic countries are on the same order of magnitude as those from Scandinavian countries, but per capita emissions are several times higher in Estonia and at least 50% higher in Lithuania. (Table 3) In 1989, East Germany was the only country in Europe to have a higher per capita emission of sulphur dioxide than Estonia. The reason why Estonia stands out in an international comparison is its burning of oil-shale in thermal power plants. See Chapter 7.

Per capita emissions of nitrogen oxides from the Baltic countries are in the same range as from most other European countries. Estonia has one of the highest per capita emissions in Europe; about 40% higher than in Scandinavian countries, (Table 3). About half of total Estonian nitrogen emissions was estimated to come from mobile sources in 1989. In Latvia the share was about 70%, and in Lithuania 50-60%.

Table 3, Emissions of Sulphur Dioxide (as S) and Nitrogen Oxides (as NO_2) in 1989

	Sulphur Dioxide		Nitrogen Oxides	
	Total (ktons)	Per Capita (kg)	Total (ktons)	Per Capita (kg)
Estonia	134	85	106	67
Latvia	36	13	78	29
Lithuania	108	29	167	45
East Germany	2621	158	705	42
Poland	1955	52	1480	39
Czechoslovakia	1282	82	1122	72
Sweden	87	10	384	45
Denmark	96	19	252	49

Emission data for the Baltic countries calculated by the author based on fuel consumption from Fennhann (1992) and Latvian Ministry of Energy (1993), and emission factors from Tähtinen and Nurste (1992). Emission data for other countries officially submitted to the monitoring group of the European monitoring and Evaluation Programme (EMEP) which was started in 1977 and is carried out under the UN Economic Commision for Europe's Convention on Long Range Transboundary Air Pollution. Population data from Table 1 and Rocznik Statystyczny (1992).

Air pollution in the Baltic states has decreased markedly after 1989 because of falling industrial production and energy use. But while emissions from power plants and other stationary sources are likely to stay below 1989 levels in the next few years[1], the nitrogen contribution from cars and other mobile sources will probably increase.

The effects of air pollution are apparent both at the regional and local level. Sulphur and nitrogen emissions contribute to acidification of soils and lakes in Northern Europe and are widely believed to be a major cause of increasing forest damage in Eastern Europe. Latvia has the highest degree of forest damage among the Baltic countries and one of the highest in Europe. In 1991, more than a third of Latvian forests showed at least 25% defoliation. Local air pollution by particulates and other emissions is particularly severe in the heavily industrialized northeastern region of Estonia, and around certain industrial complexes in Latvia and Lithuania like the Lithuanian refinery in Mazeikiai.

2.3 Other problems

There are virtually no processing plants for industrial residuals or waste in the Baltic countries. Only a minor share of the industrial waste is recycled and returned into production, most being dumped together with household waste at unchecked storage sites. For example, in Estonia in the 1980s, oil-shale processing for chemical products produced more than 1.6 million tons of slag and sludge annually, and the power stations in Narva generated more than 8 million tons of ash each year. There are about 400 dumping sites in Estonia covering a total area of 550 hectares where 2.5 million tons of household waste and more than 10 million tons of industrial waste are deposited each year. Hazardous waste, like toxic chemicals or radioactive substances, are with few exceptions stored at places inadequately protected from leakage. The three Baltic countries are planning to build combustion plants for hazardous and toxic wastes. Preliminary contacts have been taken with foreign enterprises specialized in this field, but the financing of such projects has yet to be arranged.

Pollution from Soviet military activities in Estonia, Latvia and Lithuania is an issue of growing concern of the Baltic governments. Soil and groundwater contamination from fuels and weapons as well as radioactive pollution have been discovered in former military bases. For example, in December 1989, more than 100 tons of airplane fuel leaked out from a Soviet army airport in western Estonia, 32 tons of which contaminated the river Pärnu. Similar accidents have also been reported from other Soviet military bases in Latvia and Lithuania.

3 ENVIRONMENTAL POLICY

Concern about the environment was a pivotal force behind the independence movement in Estonia, Latvia and Lithuania in the late 1980s and early 1990s. After public protests several construction projects were terminated in the three republics. For example, phosporite mining activities were canceled in Estonia, construction on a nuclear reactor was stopped in Lithuania and a dam project on the Daugava river

---

[1] So far, air pollution in the Baltic states has fallen because of the drastic drop in economic activity. In order to secure future reductions of emissions, industries and power plants must switch fuels or install adequate cleaning equipment.

was terminated in Latvia. One of the objectives in the Baltic peoples' struggle for independence was to get control of the natural resources in their countries. For many Estonians, Latvians, and Lithuanians, large industrial complexes and power plants became negative symbols of Soviet domination in their republics. The centrally designed industrial policy was perceived as an arbitrary exploitation of their domestic resources. In the elections to the Baltic Parliaments in the beginning of 1990, the environment was one of the most debated issues. As a result, environmental interest groups were well represented in all three parliaments after the elections.

In the 1980s, the development of environmental policy in the Baltic republics more or less moved along the same lines as in the USSR. In 1988, a Soviet state committee for environmental protection, Goskompriroda, was founded (see Chapter 4). Simultaneously, corresponding committees were created in the different republics. In 1989 and 1990, Goskompriroda supervised the preparation of an environmental protection programme for the USSR. The programme was expected to be adopted in 1991 but was never implemented because of the disintregation of the USSR.

Despite the failed attempt by Goskompriroda to improve Soviet environmental protection, Estonia, Latvia and Lithuania continued to reform their systems of environmental management and pursued their own policy independently of the USSR. In many respects the Baltic states are now implementing ideas of environmental control similar to those discussed earlier at the central level in the former Soviet Union. National systems of taxes on the use of natural resources and charges for emissions of various polluting substances were introduced in Estonia (see Chapter 7) and Latvia in 1991. In Lithuania a similar system was introduced later the same year.

The organization of nature protection and environmental control has been significantly changed in all three republics. The republican environmental protection committees (republican "Goskomprirodas") created in 1988 in Estonia, Latvia and Lithuania were reorganized in different stages in 1989 and 1990. The result of these changes was the creation of a Ministry of Environment in Estonia, an Environmental Protection Committee in Latvia and an Environmental Protection Department in Lithuania.

Estonia has chosen an administrative model comparable with that of many European countries. The Ministry of Environment, which started its work in the spring of 1990, is responsible for the overall organization of environmental protection and use of natural resources. It prepares economic regulations and laws. The ministry also conducts environmental inspection through 19 local departments. These departments are administrated by the local governments and are also responsible for issuing licenses for use of natural resources and setting permissible limits for emissions of various pollutants.

In Latvia and Lithuania the approach to environmental management is somewhat different. The Latvian Environmental Protection Committee and the Lithuanian Environmental Protection Department have the same functions as their Estonian counterpart. The organization of nature protection and environmental control also follows the Estonian pattern, with basically the same division of responsibilities between central and local levels. However, the Latvian Committee and The Lithuanian Department are subordinate directly to Parliament, independent of the government and consequently has greater formal authority than a ministry. This system is intended to give environmental protection precedence over other questions by forcing the government to consider the environmental impact of various proposals it submits to the Parliament for approval. If the government proposes a project or regulation that is not acceptable to the Committee or the Department they have the right to block it.

The model adopted in Latvia and Lithuania may prove difficult to realize. Before independence in August 1991, there was a general consensus on environmental policy among Latvian and Lithuanian politicians, partly because the need to show a united front in the negotiations with the Soviet Union about the control of natural resources on their territories. Having gained full control over their territories, there is an obvious risk that the Latvian and Lithuanian governments will find it difficult to work with an independent environmental protection agency outside their influence. Conflicts between economic and environmental priorities are likely to arise, which may force the government to demand that the veto right of the environmental protection agency should be overruled. If this happens, the Committee or Department will lose much of its credibility, which in turn may have a negative influence on the enforcement of environmental control in Latvia and Lithuania. In 1991, there were indications that the Lithuanian Environmental Protection Department had difficulties in cooperating with the government. The government was creating its own structure of environmental experts to assist it in negotiations with the Department and in contacts with the Parliament.

Estonia, Latvia and Lithuania have a strong interest in international agreements and cooperation in the field of environmental protection. They have joined several such initiatives, mainly with the Scandinavian countries and Finland. The latter countries have well-developed environmental protection systems but are worried about air and water pollution from the Baltic states and other parts of the former USSR close to the Baltic Sea. Assistance to Estonia, Latvia and Lithuania is given in a wide number of areas. A substantial part of it is focused on the improvement of sewage-treatment facilities. Other areas of cooperation are nuclear safety (in Lithuania), waste management and air pollution abatement, as well as training of environmental protection staff.

The basis for much of the work on water protection in the Baltic states is the Convention on the Protection of the Marine Environment of the Baltic Sea Area, also called the Helsinki Convention. The convention has been signed by all the bordering states of the Baltic Sea. According to an agreement from 1988 (which later was joined by the Baltic states), the countries in the catchment area of the Baltic Sea have committed themselves to reduce their total discharge of most pollutants by up to 50% by 1995.[2] The convention also affects air pollution, since part of the emissions in the Baltic region are deposited in the Baltic Sea. In 1990 the signatory parties to the Helsinki Convention agreed to prepare a joint action plan with the aim of improving the ecological situation of the Baltic Sea. The idea was to concentrate efforts to about twenty so-called "hot spots," mainly in Poland, the Baltic countries, and Russia, where discharge of polluted water is particularly serious. Total costs of installing the necessary treatment capacity in these spots are estimated at more than $15 billion. According to the outline of the plan, new sewage treatment facilities are to be financed with the help of the richer countries in the region, as well as through loans

---

[2] The total annual discharge of nitrogen and phosphorus to the Baltic Sea from Estonia, Latvia and Lithuania is estimated at about 25,000 tons and 2,400 tons, respectively.

from the World Bank, the European Bank for Reconstruction and Development, and the Nordic Investment Bank.[3]

Another important multilateral agreement that is likely to affect the Baltic countries is the International Convention on Transboundary Air Pollution, which calls for the reduction of SO_2 emissions by 30% of 1980 levels by 1993. This convention was signed by the USSR, but it is unclear if it should be considered to be binding for its European successor states, including the Baltic countries.[4] Similarly, it is not clear if the Estonian government is obliged to follow an agreement between the USSR and Finland in 1989 to reduce SO_2 emissions by 50% by 1995 in the areas near Finland, including Estonia. Although emissions are expected to have fallen in 1991 and 1992 due to the drop in industrial and energy production in the Baltic countries, further reductions are needed and international pressure may force their governments to take action in the next few years. Unlike the Helsinki Convention, there is no multilateral plan for joint financing of air pollution abatement in the Baltic region. The situation is particularly difficult for Estonia because of the dominating role of its power plants in regional air pollution. Equipping the two power plants in Narva with modern desulphurisation technology is estimated to cost up to $1 billion.

4 ENERGY USE

With the exception of oil-shale, which is exploited in Estonia, the Baltic states have limited domestic energy resources. Latvia and Lithuania have hydro-power resources, but most of the potential has already been exploited. Lithuania has a small amount of oil. About 1 million ton per year is estimated to be recoverable. The oil is of high quality and is expected to be used for the production of lubricants rather than for fuel purposes. Peat has traditionally been used as fuel in all three republics, and is still being exploited in Estonia and Latvia. Wood for heating is mainly used in the countryside. Wood consumption is likely to have increased since 1990 because of increasing energy prices and unreliable supplies of other fuels.

The Baltic states satisfy their energy demand almost exclusively through fossil fuels. In Estonia, oil accounted for 41% of primary energy consumption in 1990, oil-shale 35% and natural gas 13%, while coal, peat, wood and other fuels contributed 12%. The same year, 50% of primary energy use in Lithuania was oil, 33% natural gas, 5% coal, while nuclear and hydro-power contributed 8%, and the rest was made up by other sources. In Latvia, 36% of primary energy consumption was oil in 1991, 29% natural gas, 22% was covered by hydro-power and imported electricity, 6% by coal, and peat and wood contributed 7%, (Table 4).

---

[3] In the beginning of 1993, hardly any of the needed money for the action plan had been announced. Economic slowdown in Western Europe, and the high risk of lending to the former USSR, have made the financing of large multinational projects in the Baltic region increasingly difficult.

[4] Since the Baltic countries claim that they were occupied by the USSR (and, in fact, never were officially recognized as part of the USSR by the US government and several other countries) their status in many international treaties signed by the USSR is not clear.

Primary energy consumption grew steadily until the end of the 1980s in all three countries. For example, in Lithuania the use of primary energy increased from about 230 petajoules (PJ) in 1965 to some 650 PJ in 1988. In 1985 total and per capita primary energy consumption was 321 PJ and 210 gigajoules (GJ), respectively, in Estonia; 335 PJ and 124 GJ in Latvia; and 618 PJ and 167 GJ in Lithuania. By 1990 total consumption had decreased to 306 PJ and per capita consumption to 193 GJ in Estonia; and to 604 PJ and 162 PJ in Lithuania. In Latvia primary energy consumption had fallen to 257 PJ in 1991, and per capita consumption was down to 96 GJ.

Estonia's per capita use of primary energy in 1990 was close to the Soviet average and higher than in most West European countries. Lithuania's per capita use was comparable to that of France or Western Germany, while Latvia's was lower than per capita levels of most other European countries.

Unfortunately, data are scarce on final energy consumption in the Baltic countries. According to available data for Latvia in 1991, industry accounted for 27% of final energy use, residential and service for 29%, transport for 18%, agriculture for 13%, and other users for 13%. This final demand pattern reflects a structure of energy use typical for former CPEs. Calculated on a per capita basis, energy use for industrial and agricultural production is larger than in most developed market economies and consumption for freight is about the same, while consumption for homes, services and travel is smaller than in western countries.

Table 4, Primary Energy Consumption According to Sources (in percent)

	Estonia[1] 1990	Latvia 1991	Lithuania[1] 1990
Total (PJ) Per capita (GJ)	306 193	257 96	604 162
Oil	41	36	50
Natural gas	13	29	33
Coal	2	6	5
Primary electricity[2]	-	22[3]	8[4]
Oil-shale	35	-	-
Peat, wood, other	10	7	4

1) Excluding exported electricity
2) Multiplied by a factor of 3 to convert in to primary energy
3) Hydro-power and imported electricity (mainly produced by oil-shale and nuclear power)
4) Nuclear power and hydro-power.
Sources: Fenhann (1992), Energy Balance for Latvia, (1993).

Electricity production in the Baltic states increased by 19% from 43.6 TWh in 1985 to 52.1 TWh in 1990, while total gross consumption increased by 9% from

33.5 Twh to 36.9 TWh in the same period. Their total electricity output in 1990 was about 14 TWh more than gross consumption (including grid losses and auxiliary consumption) in the three states, which means that they had a significant amount of over-capacity. Lithuania is the largest producer of electricity of the three Baltic states. In 1990 it produced 28.4 TWh, of which about 40% was exported. Estonia's electricity production was 17.2 TWh in 1990. About half of this production was exported. By contrast, Latvia was a net importer of electricity.

Table 5, Final Electricity Consumption (excluding own needs of power plants and grid losses)

	Estonia 1985	Estonia 1990	Latvia 1985	Latvia 1990	Lithuania 1985	Lithuania 1990
Total (TWh)	6.6	7.1	7.9	8.6	11.7	12.8
Per capita (MWh)	4.2	4.5	2.9	3.2	3.2	3.4

Sources: See Table 4

In 1990, final electricity consumption in Estonia and Latvia was 7.1 and 8.6 TWh, respectively, and in Lithuania 12.8 TWh. Per capita consumption was 4.5 MWh in Estonia, which was well above the per capita level in Latvia 3.2 MWh and Lithuania 3.4 MWh. Per capita electricity consumption in the Baltic countries is comparable with that of the East European countries but typically lower than that of developed market economies, (Table 5).

Although no exact figures are available, rough estimates suggest that energy intensity (energy used per output) in the Baltic countries is up to three times higher than in developed market economies. There are several reasons why energy intensities are higher in the Baltic countries and other former CPEs than in developed market economies. An important explanation for the high energy per output ratio is the rigidity of the centrally planned system, which impeded any initiatives to rationalize energy use on the enterprise level. The main concern for Soviet energy planners was to ensure that there was enough supply of fuels and electricity and that the energy distribution system worked. Energy was allocated to users according to annual and five-year plans, which essentially were the results of complex negotiations about fuel and electricity quotas between enterprises and their supervising ministries. In this system there were few, if any, incentives for enterprises to rationalize their energy use. Rather than save energy, they would typically try to maximize the quotas they were allocated. Another important reason has been subsidized energy prices, in particular prices paid by households for electricity and heat, which has contributed to high energy intensities in all sectors of the economy.

Moreover, there was a bias toward heavy and energy-intensive industry, rather than manufacturing of consumer goods, in the former CPEs. At the same time, the service sector was much less developed than in market economies. Industry and agriculture account for a larger share of final energy consumption in the Baltic countries than in developed market economies. The share of heavy industry in industrial output is also larger in the Baltic countries than western countries. In

Estonia, the oil-shale mining and processing industries consumes roughly half of all industrial energy use. In Lithuania, chemical, petrochemical, and building materials industries accounted for 84% of final energy use in industry and 24% of the country's total final energy consumption in the end of the 1980s. These industries are not only very energy-intensive per se, but they also seem to have higher energy per output ratios than similar branches in developed market economies.

The potential for energy conservation in the Baltic countries may be as large as 50%. Substantial energy losses occur virtually in all sectors of the economy and in all steps from production to distribution and final consumption. Since district heating is well developed in the three countries, it is an obvious target for energy conservation. Lithuanian energy researchers estimate that at least 50% of the heat consumption in Lithuania could be saved by upgrading district heat systems and retrofitting buildings. The reasons for the high level of heat consumption lie both in distribution and consumption. The losses in networks are very high because of leaking pipes and inefficient substations. For example, heat losses in Estonia are estimated at about 30%. Heat use in Estonian multi-family buildings is estimated at 210-260 kWh/m^2. In Sweden, a country with a similar climate, the average heat consumption for dwellings is 120-160 kWh/m^2. As a rule, consumers have no heat consumption regulators or thermostats, and residential consumers have no meters. Buildings are poorly insulated. Heat losses in industrial, agricultural, and commercial buildings are high. There are also substantial potentials for energy conservation in industrial processes.[5]

While inefficient energy use in the Baltic states is a structural problem that will have to be addressed over a longer period of time, there are also more acute energy problems that must be solved. Estonia, Latvia and Lithuania are extremely dependent on fuel imports from Russia and other parts of the former USSR. Before 1991, the energy system in the Baltic states was almost completely under Soviet control. In 1991 Estonia, Latvia and Lithuania created their own energy ministries or equivalent governmental agencies. The ambition is to establish energy agencies that work more or less in the same way as their counterparts in western countries, that is formulating national policies and implementing regulating measures. The Baltic governments are, however, still far from this goal. In 1991 and 1992, the main occupation of the Baltic energy administrations was to supervise the production and distribution of electricity and heat, as well to secure the supply of fuels to the republics. Deliveries of Russian oil and natural gas to the Baltic countries fell drastically in 1991. In 1992, repeated fuel shortages periodically paralysed transport and heat production in the three countries. Since Estonia, Latvia and Lithuania have not yet developed any sizeable export incomes in convertible currencies, their abilities to buy fuels from other markets are very limited. With their weak position on the world market they will (at least for a transitional period of years) have to establish

[5] A survey of six energy-intensive industrial enterprises in Estonia carried out by Swedish consultants in 1991 showed that some 10-30% of industrial energy consumption could be saved by improving the efficiency of processes like space heating, cooling processes, air compression, as well as improving general operation and maintenance routines. Such measures would not require any substantial capital investments. The energy use could be reduced even more with modern technology.

trade agreements with Russia and other parts of the former union in order to guarantee essential deliveries of oil, natural gas and coal.[6]

The Baltic governments are painfully aware of the acute supply situation and are thinking of various ways to address it. Most enterprises and households are still dependent on the state distribution system for the supply of fuels. To address the many problems related to the energy crisis, national energy plans are being elaborated in all three countries. The main objectives of the Estonian, Latvian, and Lithuanian plans are the same; to reduce the dependence on oil imports from Russia, to develop domestic resources, to stimulate energy efficiency through pricing policies and conservation programs, and to eventually reduce air pollution according to international agreements.

5 ON THE ROAD TOWARDS IMPROVEMENT

Politicians and governmental officials in the Baltic states are well aware of the environmental problems in their countries. There is a wide consensus in the Baltic states on the need to improve environmental protection. They have a clear picture of what has to be done to stop the ecological degradation. In the past few years there has been a lively debate in the Baltic governments, parliaments and among the general public on the means and measures to achieve an improvement of the situation. However, to really improve the environment in Estonia, Latvia and Lithuania, some key issues must be tackled. The energy situation is perhaps the most important of these problems.

A highly energy-intensive industrial structure, low efficiency of energy consumption and extensive use of dirty fossil fuels contribute to an unnecessarily heavy environmental burden in the Baltic states. Although less energy is used (and wasted) due to supply disturbances and falling economic activity since 1991, energy production will continue to be the most serious source of air pollution in the Baltic countries throughout the 1990s. This is especially evident in the case of Estonia. Thanks to its domestic resources of oil-shale, Estonia can cover its own electricity demand and part of its heat production itself. But the environmental price paid for this energy supply is extremely high. As mentioned earlier, the northeastern part of Estonia where oil-shale is mined is the most polluted area in the Baltic states. The water balance of this area is seriously threatened by the expansion of pits and mines for oil-shale. An even more acute problem is air pollution from the thermal power plants. Adequate cleaning equipment is lacking. The power plants producing electricity are based on old technology and some of their units need to be replaced. The quality of the oil-shale is decreasing, making it more expensive to maintain electricity production. Moreover, mining costs are increasing each year.

In order to rationalize the oil-shale industry and satisfy international requirements on emission reductions, the Estonian government has decided to gradually decrease its output of electricity (see Chapter 7). The restructuring of the

---

[6] Although the prices of Russian oil and natural gas were getting closer to world market prices in 1993, opportunities of barter trade with Russia still made its oil and gas more attractive than imports from the world market. Moreover, adequate pipelines and port facilities for oil and gas deliveries from the West and pipelines are lacking.

oil-shale industry in Estonia will, however, be a difficult and expensive undertaking. The oil-shale provides the single base for energy and petrochemical industries in the country as well as 15% of industrial employment. Most of the workers engaged in oil-shale production are Russians. Thus, to the technical and economic problems of restructuring there is also an added problem of social and ethnic dimensions.

Another example of the conflict between economic, energy and environmental interests is the Lithuanian nuclear power plant in Ignalina. It provides Lithuania with about half of its electricity supply. Electricity from the power plant is also exported to neighboring countries like Latvia, Belorussia and Russia (the Kaliningrad area). Consequently, both the Lithuanian government and its nearest neighbors are interested in maintaining production at Ignalina. But since the reactors at the plant are of the same type as those at Chernobyl and far from satisfactory with regard to their security systems, they will not be internationally acceptable without reconstruction.[7]

Hardly surprising, the Ignalina plant has been the subject of considerable political interest both in and outside Lithuania. When the Soviet government blocked oil and gas supplies to Lithuania in 1990, the Lithuanian government responded by threatening to close Ignalina and stop electricity deliveries to Belorussia and the Kaliningrad area.

Ignalina has also been much debated in Lithuania. Environmental protest against Ignalina in the 1980s played an important role in the Lithuanian independence movement's struggle against communists and the central authorities in Moscow. The stopped construction of a third reactor in 1987 was seen by many as a step towards the ultimate goal of closing the whole plant. Ignalina was also regarded by some as a national security risk because virtually all of its personnel are Russians. But when the non-communist Lithuanian government entered office in 1990, it became clear that there were strong interests within the government to maintain the electricity production at Ignalina. The Ministry of Energy has advocated a completion of the third reactor, possibly with Western technology, to replace the first reactor (which is considered more of a safety risk than the second).[8] By contrast, the Lithuanian Environmental Protection Department has stated its opposition to Ignalina. It claims that the plant is inadequately secured against crustal movements in the ground and that it is located in the catchment basin of the country's main artesian aquifer. The Environmental Protection Department also points out that the power plant gets its

---

[7] Ignalina has two Soviet RMBK reactors with a capacity of 1500 MW each. They were scaled down to 1250 MW after the Chernobyl-accident in 1986. Environmental protest at the end of the 1980s stopped the construction of a third reactor, while plans for a fourth were canceled. Concerns about the Ignalina plant have been raised from neighboring countries, most notably Sweden, which was seriously affected by radioactive deposition from the Chernobyl accident. On the initiative of the so-called G7 group in July 1992, Ignalina and other East European nuclear stations are being examined in order to prepare an international assistance program for improving their safety.

[8] A report to the Ministry of Energy in 1992 suggests that construction costs could be covered by electricity exports. This presupposes a market for electricity exports in the late 1990s. However, existing supply in Lithuania's neighboring countries easily exceeded demand in 1993.

cooling water from a nearby lake where the water temperature has increased and destroyed most of the cold-water fauna.

By improving energy efficiency in the Baltic economies energy supply constrains can be eased and pollution from energy use reduced. The most important economic instrument for reducing energy waste is pricing. While prices of energy carriers and other products were adjusted from time to time in the CPEs, there was little change in energy prices relative to other prices. Since the Baltic countries became independent, energy prices for industrial and residential consumers have been increased several times, both in absolute terms and in relation to other prices. With drastically increasing fuel costs, electricity- and heat-distribution companies need to cover their expenses. At the same time it is difficult for the Baltic governments to abolish all subsidies on household energy prices because of already decreasing real incomes.

It is important to understand that the decline in energy consumption since 1990 is largely a result of contracting production and lack of fuel supply, rather than an effect of increasing energy prices or improved energy conservation. It will be difficult to assess the true impact of higher energy prices before the supply situation has been normalized. Experience from Poland, where most energy prices have been adjusted to West European levels since 1989 and where there have been few energy supply shortages (with the exception of imported gas from Russia) since 1992, shows that private consumers have started to reduce their electricity and fuel consumption, while there have been mixed reactions from state enterprises.

To adjust prices on energy carriers is not only a possible way of reducing consumption, it is also essential to cover the costs of energy producers and distributors so they can finance efficiency improvements in their own systems. But even if electricity and heat supply run as normal, drastically increased energy prices will not necessarily result in increased revenues for utilities and district heat companies in former CPEs. Customers can simply chose to refuse paying their bills. For example, in 1991 and 1992 an increasing number of Polish households and enterprises delayed their payments or did not pay at all.[9] Although the main concern of Baltic energy users in the beginning of 1993 was still unreliable fuel supply, there are signs that payment problems similar to those experienced in Poland have began to occur.

To overcome technical, legal, and economic barriers, the Baltic countries need competent specialists and managers. There is a shortage of competent specialists in the fields of power engineering, heat engineering and construction. While many managers of state enterprises were highly skillful in securing supplies in the old system of centrally planned resource allocation, few of them have the experience and training necessary for managing a modern company. Local government officials, building managers, and engineers also need training in economic management. It is

---

[9] In the electric power sector this kind of behavior created a vicious circle of unpaid debts. Distribution companies that were not being paid by their customers lagged behind with their payments to the transmission company. Power plants did not receive money from the transmission company in time and ended up delaying their obligations to coal mines. Closing the circle, some mines did not pay for the electricity they got from the distribution companies.

crucial that such training focus on the energy-using sectors and on those persons who are in an economic and institutional position to implement energy-efficient measures, not only on experts in energy production and distribution.

Environmental control will be easier to enforce when enterprises and other polluters of the environment become responsible for their economic decisions. If an enterprise is forced to cover its expenses including pollution costs, it is more likely to take some action to reduce its pollution. It is also important to enhance the role of environmental inspection. Revised laws on environmental protection, taxes for the use of natural resources and higher charges for pollution are being introduced in all three republics. Awareness and concern about the environment is well-developed among the population. But even with broad political support it will not be easy to implement new environmental policies. With urgent economic problems and minimal financial resources, the Baltic governments will have to make decisions that may conflict with environmental priorities. It will be difficult to close down old and polluting industrial plants, or even reduce their output, if production is vital for other sectors of the economy. Governments also fear the effects of unemployment. Conflicts of this kind are already retarding the progress of environmental protection and will continue to do so in the near future.

Air and water pollution does not stop at borders. The effects from polluting emissions can be felt far away from their original sources. Regional cooperation will be essential for improving the energy and environmental situation of the Baltic states. There is much to gain from coordination of such policies between Estonia, Latvia, and Lithuania. Collaboration is especially important in order to make the best use of available energy infrastructure such as pipelines, ports, power systems, and storage and refining facilities. Cooperation between the Baltic states and neighboring countries like Russia, Poland, Finland, and the Scandinavian countries is also critical. Because of the latter countries' experience in energy conservation and environmental protection, there is a large potential for technical and educational interaction in these areas. To improve energy conservation, the focus should be on identifying low-cost measures; in particular in the residential sector. Local demonstration projects can provide concrete examples of how energy efficiency can be implemented.

While considerable bilateral and multilateral assistance to Estonia, Latvia, and Lithuania has occurred since 1991, it is still to early to assess its actual effects. It is important that help offered to the Baltic states is sustained over a long period of time, and that it is in accordance with these states' own priorities. If carefully implemented, such support should help Estonia, Latvia, and Lithuania to bring slow but steady progress in environmental protection and energy management in the next five to ten years.

REFERENCES

Apkartejas vides aizsardziba un dabas resursu racionala izmantisana Latvija (Latvian Environmental Statistics), 1990. Latvian Environmental Protection Committee, Riga.

Barabaner, N. I. and I. Z. Kaganovich. 1990. "Ecological and Economical Aspects of Resource Development in Oil Shale Power Engineering in Estonia", in *Energy trends: Integrated Europe - Decentralized USSR*, Conference Proceedings, October 21-24, 1990, Tallinn, pp. 132-137.

Calculated Budgets for Acidifying Components in Europe, 1985, 1987, 1988, 1989, 1990, and 1991. 1992. EMEP/MCS-W Report No. 1, The Norwegian Meteorological Institute.

Energy Balance for Latvia. 1993. Latvian Ministry of Energy.

Energy in Estonia, Latvia, and Lithuania. 1991. Ministries of Energy in Estonia, Latvia, and Lithuania.

Environment '89. 1990. Estonian Nature Management Scientific Centre, Tallinn.

Fenhann, J. 1992. Energy and Environment in Estonia, Latvia and Lithuania, Risö National Laboratory, Roskilde.

Gamtunauda ir gamtosauga Lietuvoje. 1989. (Lithuanian environmental statistics 1989). 1990. Lithuanian Environmental Protection Department, Vilnius.

Hedlund, R. and M. Widengren. 1990. "Miljöteknik i Baltikum samt Leningrad- och Kaliningradområdena (Environmental Technology in the Baltic republics, and the Kaliningrad and Leningrad areas)", *Rapport Sovjetunionen 9003,* Sveriges Tekniska Attachéer, Stockholm.

Informacija apie atmosferos oro tersima Lietuvoje 1989 metas (Data on air pollution in Lithuania 1989). 1990. Lithuanian Statistical Committee, Vilnius.

National Plan for the Protection of the Baltic Sea of the Republic of Estonia. 1991. Estonian Ministry of Environment, Tallinn.

National Report of Estonia to UNCED. 1992. Ministry of the Environment, Tallinn.

National Report of Latvia to UNCED. 1992. Environmental Protection Committee, Riga.

National Report of Lithuania to UNCED. 1992. Environmental Protection Department, Vilnius.

Olsson, I. and P-Å Strandsäter. 1991. 2Proposals for improvement of the energy efficiency in some Estonian companies", paper presented at the seminar "Eastern Europe and Energy Efficiency - A Business Opportunity", Stockholm.

Punning, J. 1991. "The Conditions of the Estonian Environment" (Unpublished paper), Institute of Ecology and Marine research, Estonian Academy of Sciences, Tallinn.

Pädam, S. 1990. "Energy and environment in Estonia - an introduction", Report 1990:R14, Swedish National Energy Board, Stockholm.

Rocznik Statystyczny 1992. Central Statistical Office of Poland.

Salay, J. 1991. *Östeuropas miljö. Problem och framtidsutsikter* (Eastern Europe's Environment. Problems and Future Perspectives), Naturia, Stockholm.

Salay, J., J. Fenhann, K. Jaanimägi and L. Kristoferson. 1993. "Energy and Environment in the Baltic States", in *Annual Review of Energy and the Environment*, 1993.

Sandström, P. 1991. *Baltiskt dilemma* (Baltic Dilemma), SNS, Stockholm.

Some Facts about the Lithuanian Power System. Undated. Lithuanian Ministry of Energy.

Tähtinen, M. and H. Nurste. 1992. *Energy Use and Emission Scenarios to the year 2000 for Estonia*, Technical Research Center of Finland.

Van Arkadie, B. and M. Karlsson. 1992. *Economic Survey of the Baltic States*, Pinter Publishers, London.

CHAPTER 7

Economic Instruments in Estonian Environmental Policy

by

Tiit Kallaste*

Abstract

This chapter provides a brief overview of environmental policy in Estonia. The problems of more efficient exploitation of natural resources and environmental improvement through the use of economic instruments are discussed. The extremely sophisticated transition from a command economy to a market-oriented system complicates the implementation of economic instruments. The devaluation of the former Soviet Union monetary unit - rouble - which was still the officially Estonian currency in June 1992, accelerated throughout this period making the economic instruments (based on the rouble price level of 1989/1990) purely symbolic. The chapter tries to give a brief survey of the main principles for the imposition of payments for using land, water, mineral and organic resources, which were worked out in the late eighties. Special attention is devoted to the Estonian Environmental Fund and to the new system of environmental pollution control. Some basic aspects concerning the implementation of emission taxes and non-compliance fees for air pollution control are described in more detail. Some preliminary results for air pollution control in Tallinn are also presented.

*Comments from T. Żylicz, T Sterner and an anonymous referee are gratefully acknowledged.

T. Sterner (ed.), Economic Policies for Sustainable Development, 132–147.

1 INTRODUCTION

Intensive use of local natural resources, especially oil shale and phosphate resources, under central planning has significantly damaged the natural environment in North- and North-East Estonia. All components of the environment have been seriously deteriorated by pollution here including human health. Health status in the most polluted areas in North-East Estonia is significantly lower compared to other areas. To control the situation some market-oriented environmental policy instruments for economic management were introduced in Estonia in 1991.

Estonia was one of the most advanced republics in the former Soviet Union in environmental protection activities, research and development. The first nature protection regulations were enacted already in the 1920s. In many areas such as the creation of an Estonian Environmental Fund, the Green Movement, economic control of pollution, and ecological-environmental research, Estonia took a leading position. But due to the collapse of the centrally planned economy, many issues related to the use of natural resources and environmental protection have become more complicated. Estonia has reached the situation, where it is coming closer and closer to the principles of market economy but still has only just started building up the appropriate economic and administrative mechanisms. In many cases the new system of regulations is quite weak and economic regulations and legislative acts from the previous socialist period still continue to exist.

Today various changes are taking place in the economic structure, in natural resource accounting and in the introduction of environmentally benign technologies. The final aim is the conservation of resources and a decrease in pollution levels. By now future strategies in research and development have been formulated. One of the most efficient tools seems to be the system of payments for the use of natural resources and taxes for pollution of air, water and waste disposal. The new taxation system is not fully based on market principles, nor on economic theory. It relies mostly on "expert judgment".

Preliminary results for 1991 show great differences in the revenues and efficiency in different spheres of implementation of economic instruments. The result is that air pollution taxes have no significant impact on the behaviour of polluting enterprises. In the case of waste water and solid waste disposal, however, economic mechanisms have had considerable effect.

2 AN OVERVIEW OF THE ENVIRONMENTAL SITUATION

Large-scale, intensive use of natural resources and insufficient levels of waste treatment have decreased the quality of the environment throughout Estonia. In many urban as well as rural areas ecological conflicts have occurred as a result of rapid industrial growth. In some areas acid rains have been registered (pH 4 and less). At the same time alkaline rains due to the high limestone content in oil shale, which is burned in power plants, occur in the north-eastern part of Estonia; pH values in some cases reach more than 8. Many Estonian towns, e.g., Tartu, Kuressaare and Tapa, do not yet have sewage treatment plants.

2.1 The most severely affected areas

The most severely affected areas are found in the North-East around Narva, Kohtla-Järve and Kunda. Emissions in this area also cause concern from the point of view of transboundary pollution, particularly with respect to waste water and sulphur dioxide.

The total share of emissions from North-East Estonian enterprises is more than 78% of all pollutants emitted into air from stationary sources, including roughly 92% of solid particular matters and 74% of sulphur dioxide (Environment '90). There are significant amounts of various noxious emissions from phosphate mining and mineral fertilizer production in Maardu, just on the border of Tallinn, and its new residential area Lasnamäe. Sillamäe has experienced increased radiation levels in recent years. One can quite easily conclude that the main problems are connected with mining and processing of one of our most important natural resources - oil shale. The top priority pollution problems are the huge emissions of SO_2 and flue ash from the oil shale based power plants near Narva.

Oil shale mining as well as its use in power stations and chemical industries give rise to many of the serious pollution effects mentioned above. This is closely related to the colonial attitudes towards local natural resources by the former Soviet "all-union ministries" of coal mining, chemical and petro-chemical industries. The extensive character of oil-shale mining allowed the output to grow to almost 31 million tons per year in 1980. Today oil-shale is mined in six mines and four open-cast pits around Kohtla-Järve and as far as the Eastern border with Russia in the county of East-Virumaa. Yearly output has now been decreased to 22.5 million tons (1991) of which 11.1 Mtons in mines and 11.4 in quarries. Losses account for as much as 21% on average (Environment' 90).

Alkaline flue ash from the electrical filters of two oil- shale power plants, located nearby Narva, is transported to the ash-fields, which cover more than 2,000 ha of land. These 160 million tons of ash, containing heavy metals, radioactive elements and other extremely noxious compounds pose a constant threat to the local population and nature. A similar source of danger to nature and human health are ash-hills of semicoking residue. Large quantities of organic and inorganic compounds, oil, etc. are leaching to the surface as well as into the ground water. The rivers passing through the oil-shale mining or treatment area are as a rule heavily polluted by phenols, oil, and all kinds of waste from chemical and petro-chemical industry. This type of description could unfortunately be continued on many more pages. The extremely polluted living environment in these areas has significant impacts on human health. Many physical factors of the environment like noise, vibration, electromagnetic fields, radioactivity or high contents of nitrates and heavy metals in food imply major risks to human health. Various functional, immunological and biochemical changes take place in the organism of local inhabitants.

Comparative health studies have been undertaken by the Institute of Preventive Medicine in several industrial and relatively unpolluted living districts in Tallinn as well as in Narva, Rakvere and Kohtla-Järve. Long-term tests and examinations indicate noticeable disturbances both in child and adult health. In the oil shale region, as well as in the chemical industry and power engineering regions, the frequency of respiratory diseases has increased 1.2 - 1.5 times, discomfort 4 times, chronic respiratory diseases 1.5 times, cardio-vascular diseases 1.9 times and emergency aid is needed 1.2 times more often than in the non-polluted control area (Etlin, 1990). The concentration of heavy metals - Hg, Pb, Cd and Cu in humans has risen relatively fast in northern Estonia (Viitak et al., 1990).

Significant health symptoms showed up in the spring of 1989 in Sillamäe with alopecia (hairs loss) among children as the most alarming indicator. Children in the Northeast often suffer from dystrophy of the nails and pathological diseases such as skin, neuro-psychical, digestion tract and inner secretion system pathologies. Symptoms of rickets, numerous abnormal consistencies of the cell structure of the blood and several other disorders of the organism are frequent (Environment' 89).

In conclusion this area is the worst affected and at the decision-making level this means that preference in pollution abatement measures must be given to this area.

2.2 Some explanations

There are a number of principal causes pertaining to the old Soviet system which explain the relatively high levels of environmental pollution in Estonia:

* There was never any direct responsibility nor serious interest in preserving nature or using natural resources efficiently from the centrally planned and controlled industry, agriculture, transport, etc. Actually, no authorities were responsible for the damage to nature;
* the domination of the so-called economic-branch approach over regional management has caused many environmental conflicts;
* direct economic and administrative regulations for more efficient use of natural resources have been extremely ineffective until recently;
* for many years there were no significant incentives for investments in environmentally benign technologies or waste purification equipment.

2.3 Nature conservation

Although there was no chance of implementing a cost efficient use of natural resources or restrictions on environmental pollution, there were two areas in which some progress was traditionally possible: classical nature protection and monitoring the level of pollution. This somehow worked like a compensation mechanism for those worrying about nature. Intensive research has been carried out in many nature reserves of international importance, e.g. Matsalu, Viidumäe, Lahemaa, the West-Estonian Biosphere Reserve, Lahemaa nature reserve etc. More than forty institutions deal with nature conservation and environmental protection research in their every-day work. The subjects cover a wide spectrum of topics.

One example is the Scientific Nature Management Information Centre where on the basis of the Geographical Information System-(GIS), a base map of Estonia has been elaborated. These maps are related to thematic map layers reflecting the distribution of natural resources and sources of pollution. Data bases of the most important natural resources of the republic have been compiled. Today GIS is used for several purposes including the design and implementation of economic instruments for environmental improvement.

Thanks to a long tradition of classical nature conservation, to the enthusiastic work of many people and institutions against the colonial exploitation of natural resources and pollution by the command economy (since the Soviet invasion in 1939), Estonia had some advantages. The work needed to design environmental protection regulations did not have to start from scratch.

3 THE IMPLEMENTATION OF ECONOMIC INSTRUMENTS

In spite of being the smallest republic in the huge territory of the former Soviet Union, Estonia was the first to implement non-compliance fees for polluting natural water bodies and payments for the use of fresh-water. This has enabled our environment protection agencies to gain some experience during recent years. The first step towards the taxation of the environment was the foundation of the Estonian Fund for Nature Protection and Rational Use of Natural Resources in 1983. Fines for the pollution of water resources paid by polluting enterprises, agricultural farms, army units, etc were its major source of revenue. In recent years the fund has collected revenues of more than one million roubles per year.

The total sum paid for causing harm to nature was 952,200 roubles in 1988, including 25,000 roubles for violating fishing and hunting regulations and about 22,000 roubles for deficient forest management. In 1989 the total sum paid to the Fund reached 1,233,000 roubles (inc. debts for 1988). Payments in 1990 were over 3,7 Million roubles (Environment' 90). This is quite a considerable sum of money for one year. It may for example be compared to the capital investments financed from the state budget. According to the five-year plan of 1986-1990 total environmental investments reached more than 125 million roubles.

The most remarkable principle of this Fund was that for the first time ever more than 90% of the revenues remained in Estonia instead of being syphoned off by the all-Union government. This gave the Estonian authorities a chance to use the money at their own discretion. No similar fund was ever established in the whole former Soviet Union. The Fund could be used for compensating the damage caused by pollution at the regional level, for investments in environmental technology, projects, research and development projects, training, grants, international cooperation, etc.

The next step in the field of economic pollution control started with the establishment of principles for setting prices for natural resources like oil shale, peat, mineral building materials and water resources in 1985/1986. This was followed by the imposition of taxes on water pollution, air pollution and solid waste deposition.

3.1 The Estonian Environmental Fund

In 1990 the previous fund was reorganized into the Estonian Environmental Fund (hereafter - Fund), which is a republican organization with the rights of a legal person. It has been founded to collect revenues and use them for supplementary financing of environmental improvement. The Fund is divided into the centralized fund, local county or municipal funds and special, so-called earmarked funds.
Revenues of the Fund come from:

1) emission taxes;
2) payments for compensating the damage to natural resources;

3) fines applied when exploitation of natural resources exceeds norms:
4) fines for violating environmental protection laws;
5) donations for special purposes;
6) grants from state and local budgets;
7) profit from entrepreneurship and other income.

The assets of the Fund are used for:

1) environmental protection programs;
2) environmental monitoring systems;
3) comprehensive accounting of natural resources;
4) training of personnel in ecology, environmental protection technology, etc.;
5) scholarships and prizes etc.;
6) international cooperation incl. fulfillment of international agreements;
7) research and development;
8) catastrophe-relief;
9) development of environmental entrepreneurship;
10) special premia for high level employees and specialists or environmentally benign enterprises.

The Fund is attached to the Estonian Ministry of Environment; local funds to the local county or municipal environmental protection boards. The activities of the Fund are run by the Council of the Fund, the composition of which is fixed by the Estonian Government following a proposal from the Ministry of Environment. Local (county or municipal) funds have the right to use the Fund's revenues at their own will.

The total revenues to the Estonian Environmental Fund amounted to 59.7 million roubles in 1991. In comparison with the revenues of the year 1990 - 3.7 million roubles it is considerably more. Emission taxes of 54.2 million roubles accounted for the major part - 91% of the Fund's revenues. Until 1991 the main source of finance for environmental investments was the state budget but in the future a significant part of the overall investments is expected to come from the Fund.

3.2 The Choice of economic instruments

The most important result expected from the use of these economic instruments is the gradual shift in production and consumption in a more environmentally efficient direction, which will form a basis for sustainable development in Estonia. As distinct from international practice e.g. in some Nordic countries, Finland, Sweden, Norway, the money from pollution taxation is earmarked for environmental improvement purposes.

According to OECD classification economic instruments can be classified (Nicolaisen and Hoeller, 1990) into:

* charge systems,
* subsidies,
* deposit-refund systems,

* market creation such as tradeable emission permits
* enforcement incentives, i.e. non-compliance fees, performance bonds.

From this list of economic instruments only **market creation** is not used in Estonia. Some other economic instruments are partly combined with regulatory instruments, like payments for the use of fresh water and disposal of waste water and wastes (**user charge**). They have been in use in Estonia for several decades already. **Subsidies** and **deposit-refund** systems have been used in combination with regulatory instruments for a long time. **Deposit-refund** systems are used for glassbottles and jars but presently (1993) the system is in crisis and needs reorganization. An interesting proposal for a deposit-refund system for flue ash from electric filters of oil-shale power plants has been discussed but was finally abandoned. **Subsidies** have been in use for larger environmentally oriented investments. Indirect subsidies for the use of fresh water and disposal of waste water by households could also be mentioned. Polluting enterprises pay significantly more for water compared to households thereby subsidizing the latter. **Emission charges** and some elements of **enforcement incentives** are the latest additions to the arsenal for combating pollution control in Estonia. Fines for violating fishing or hunting regulations and for some types of water pollution have however been used for a long time.

Beginning in January 1991, the government has introduced taxation on the use of natural resources (Decree, 1990), as well as compensation charges, emission taxes for atmospheric pollution, waste disposal and the use of water and mineral resources. They can be classified into:

* <u>resource payments</u> for use, use of water, mineral and organic resources, oil shale, peat, etc.;
* <u>compensation charges</u> for changing the type of land use (in towns and settlements, rural areas, forested areas);
* <u>charges</u>, emission charges (taxes), which include charges for regular emissions of wastes (waste water, gaseous emission and solid waste disposal), based on health standards;
* <u>non-compliance fees</u>, fines for emissions exceeding the official limits;
* <u>non-compliance fees</u>, fines for accidental emission of wastes.

Payments for use of natural resources and compensation charges are paid into the local or state budget; emission taxes and non-compliance fees into the local county or municipal funds. The local environmental protection boards take care of the revenues of the local fund.

Payments for the use of natural resources like oil shale, peat, mineral building materials and water resources are paid both to state and local county budgets. For example, 80% of the payments for oil shale and water resources are paid to state and 20% to the local budget (for peat and mineral building materials, 30% and 70% respectively).

There is also a system of differentiated compensation charges for changing the planning zones of agricultural, forestry and urban land use.

In each case local authorities have the right to submit their proposals for tax rates, time schedule, and the further use of the funds. They are given the right to increase or decrease the norms established by the government by 20%, according to local environmental or economic conditions.

Regular emission taxes and payments for the use of fixed amounts of natural resources are imposed by executive bodies of the local governments on the basis of special entrepreneurship contracts. All polluters are supposed to pay the previously confirmed regular emission tax not later than in the middle of every three month period. In certain cases, taxes may be applied gradually as a kind of subsidy or tax allowance. Actually it depends on the willingness of the enterprise to start implementing the less polluting technology or installing the required purification equipment or waste treatment. The limit for the eligibility to the subsidy is that at least 25% of emissions have to be reduced by the enterprise itself. Another way is for the enterprises to get the environmental improvement investments partially refunded from the Fund.

3.3 Setting the tax-levels

First the total sum of taxes (and compensation charges) needed for the whole country is decided on the basis of expenditures needed for pollution abatement. It is not assessed on the basis of damage caused by emission of pollutants. In fact this total is in no way deduced from cost-efficiency analysis or based on market principles but simply ad hoc. In the next step four basic criteria are used when allocating this total to various areas and actually setting emission charges and non-compliance fees:

1) The total amount of money to be used for the pollution abatement measures. For example, in the case of air pollution a total was fixed at 5 million roubles per year (in 1989) and in the case of solid waste treatment - at 10 million roubles;
2) In waste-water control, the estimation of total expenditures for mechanical, chemical and biological purification up to the level set by health standards (maximum permissible concentrations);
3) Differentiation by type of pollution (air/water/solid waste) as well as by region. Local environmental protection boards have the right to set up a special list of most hazardous pollutants specifying the type of danger to local inhabitants or environment.
4) Ad hoc expert estimates to set the non-compliance fees, (as multiples of the ordinary charges) to be used when wastes exceed limits or in case of accidental emissions.

The rationale for these ad hoc measures was extreme urgency. As the reader will appreciate after the brief description of the environmental problems, Estonia faces as a result of 50 years of command economy, there was no time to lose in the introduction of the economic instruments. It was therefore considered better to implement approximate levels than to wait for theoretically more satisfying values.

In order to put recourse payments, compensation charges, emission taxes and non-compliance fees into force, the need for a smoothly functioning territorial system of environmental monitoring was obvious. Currently two kinds of data bases are in use covering: 1) the consumption of water and emission of waste water; 2) emissions of pollutants into the atmosphere. Both rely on the GIS approach mentioned above.

4 ECONOMIC INSTRUMENTS FOR AIR POLLUTION CONTROL

Taxes for air pollution will be applied for emissions from stationary sources of pollution (stacks, municipal boilers etc.). Regular emission taxes are imposed by executive bodies of the local governments, usually respective municipal or county environmental protection board, on the basis of the special entrepreneurship contracts. This implies that they are decided one year in advance.

There is as yet no system for taxing the transport sector in Estonia, but certain pilot projects have been started. The share of transports is calculated on the basis of fuel consumption and is estimated to be about 45% of total emissions into the air. A comparative emissions inventory study of Estonian and Finnish transport emissions has been undertaken to further investigate the role of motor vehicle pollution in Estonia (Mäkelä, 1990) and fuel tax proposals are now under discussion.

Current control of air pollution is mainly implemented through the following economic instruments:

Emission charges: Regular emission charges based on stack emissions containing up to about 50 pollutants, emissions of which must not violate the health standards - daily Maximum Permissible Concentration (MPC)s of pollutants (see Table 1).

Administrative charges are in use in annual technical inspection of transport vehicles' exhaust gases in respect of CO emissions as well as in the case of emission permits for polluting enterprises.

Enforcement incentives: non-compliance fees for exceeding the permit level for the pollution source as a multiple of the tax. The multiple applied depends on the toxicity of the pollutant: 5, 50 or 500 times higher than the regular tax for classes 3 or 4, 2 and 1 respectively. Similar non-compliance fees are also used in case of accidental emissions, disasters, explosions, etc.

Subsidies are provided in the form of tax allowances when the polluter starts investing in cleaner technology or end-of-pipe equipment. There is no standard procedure for subsidization. Each time tax allowances are designed, they are decided individually on the basis of expert assessments.

4.1 Calculating actual charges

The size of the emission tax[1] is, as mentioned, based on the health concept, ie. primarily on effects for the human organism. It is calculated from the following four factors:

- the volume of the emission;
- the toxicity of the pollutants emitted (see Table 1);
- the size of the polluted area;
- the type of land use in the area affected.

[1] Note that we call this an emission tax, but, since it takes account of the sensitivity of the areas affected it might be more appropriate to call it an ambient tax.

Table 1 Calculations of tax rates for some relevant pollutants (see Kallaste and Saare, 1991)

	MPC standards (mg/m^3)			Toxicity	Tax rate
Pollutant	20-min	24-hrs	Work-area	Class	P_i (rbl)
Sulphur dioxide (SO_2)	0.5	0.05	10.0	3	1.00
Nitrogen dioxide (NO_2)	0.085	0.04	2.0	2	2.50
Sulphuric acid (H_2SO_4)	0.3	0.1	1.0	2	2.24
Hydrogen sulphide (H_2S)	0.008	0.0008	10.0	2	7.91
Ammonia (NH_3)	0.2	0.04	20.0	4	0.79
Hydrogen fluoride (HF)	0.02	0.005	0.05	2	44.72
Formaldehyde (HCHO)	0.035	0.003	0.5	2	18.26
Oil-shale phenol	0.07	0.0007	0.5	3	37.80
Soot (C)	0.15	0.05	4.0	3	1.58
Cement dust	0.3	0.1	6.0	4	0.91
Particulates	0.5	0.15	6.0	3	0.75
Oil-shale flue ash	0.3	0.1	4.0	3	1.12
Petrol	5.0	1.5	100.0	4	0.06
Carbon monoxide (CO)	5.0	3.0	20.0	4	0.09
Phenol (C_6H_5OH)	0.01	0.003	0.3	2	23.57
Lead (Pb)	-	0.0003	0.01	1	408.25
Bens(a)pyren	-	0.000001	0.00015	1	57735.03

The emission tax T is calculated for each individual pollutant emitted. The total tax to be paid is the sum of the individual taxes for each specific pollutant. The total tax for each pollution source is calculated according to (1):

$$T = \sum z \; M_i * P_i * K_i \qquad (1)$$

where M_i is the actual emission of a pollutant i in tons per year; (i = 1..z).

P_i is the emission tax rate for a particular pollutant. It is proportional to the root-mean square of two extreme standards; working area and 24-hour standards for each pollutant (see 2). Sulphur dioxide is taken as a reference unit and given a value of 1 rbl.

$$P_i = A/(MPC_{i,24} * MPC_{i,w})^{1/2} \qquad (2)$$

where $MPC_{i,24}$ is the maximum permissible concentration of the i-th pollutant for 24-hour periods in the ambient air of settlements in mg/m^3.

$MPC_{i,w}$ is the maximum permissible concentration of the i-th pollutant in work areas in mg/m^3. Its value is significantly higher than MPC_{24hrs} or $MPC_{20\text{-}min}$ in general up to one order of magnitude.

The numerical value of the coefficient A is chosen as a so as to make the sulphur dioxide emission tax rate equal 1.

For sulphur dioxide $MPC_{24} = 0.05$ and $MPC_w = 10.0$ thus the value of scaling coefficient A equals to $(0.5)^{1/2} = 0.707$.

For example in the case of Formaldehyde (HCHO) the emission tax rate is 18.26 while for lead (Pb) it is 408.25 see (3)-(4).

$$P_{(HCHO)} = 0.707/(0.003 * 0.5)^{1/2} = 18.26 \qquad (3)$$

$$P_{(Pb)} = 0.707/(0.0003 * 0.01)^{1/2} = 408.25 \qquad (4)$$

The tax rates for the most common pollutants are summarized in table 1. Note, however, that in case of accidents etc, the tax rate is raised by a multiple 5,50 on 500 depending on the toxicity class (5 for classes 4 and 3, 50 for 2 and 500 for class 1).

Finally K_i in (1) is a coefficient calculated with the help of spatial analysis of the territories of various land-uses influenced by the stack emissions. Different land-uses are given different weights K_i depending on the potential impact of the pollutants. For example, open rural land carries a weight of 1, industrial areas carry a weight of 20 and recreation areas, which are the most sensitive, carry a weight of 50; Urban areas are given a weight of 20 if they have less than 50 thousand inhabitants, 25 for 50-200 thousand and 30 if there are more than 200 thousand inhabitants.

The territory influenced is estimated as a circle with radius = 80 * H where H is the height of the stack. The value K_i is finally given as a weighted average of the sensitivities (rural, urban, recreational etc) depending on their shares S_j in the area affected, see (5).

$$K_i = \Sigma_j S_j K_{ij} \qquad (5)$$

The value of coefficient K_i is fixed in the permit given to each enterprise on agreed yearly amounts of emission. The regular emission taxes are calculated every year which also provides an opportunity to revise parameters.

At present the emissions inventory data for the whole republic by enterprise is available in the computerized data bank of the Scientific Nature Management Information Centre. The pollution taxes have been calculated for emissions of about 50 pollutants in up to 500 enterprises throughout Estonia. More than 300 enterprises were actually charged in 1991.

5 PRELIMINARY RESULTS FOR AIR POLLUTION CONTROL IN TALLINN

The emission tax calculations for about 90 enterprises in Tallinn have been carried out and the respective entrepreneurship contracts signed for 1991. According to preliminary data the total of regular emission tax equals about 968,000 roubles per year (Kallaste, 1991). The main part of the revenue comes from the five to ten most polluting enterprises (see Table 2). The data about non-compliance fees were not available yet, but quite a sum is expected from that source too.

One can conclude that for further air pollution control, attention should be focused on a relatively small number of polluting enterprises. Among the "leading" polluters are three municipal heaters. Their emissions are relatively large, since they use sulphur-rich heavy oil and lack the necessary filter equipment.

There are also some polluters with comparatively small, but significantly more noxious emissions, e.g. the pharmaceutical plant and heavy machinery plant. These specific toxic pollutants are mostly emitted due to outdated technology requiring urgent retrofitting or new investments.

Table 2 Regular air pollution taxes for Tallinn, 1991 *)

Name of the enterprise	Total emission of pollutants per year (ton)	Tax to be paid (rouble)
Thermal power plant "Iru"	12609.0	313533.8
Heavy machinery plant	494.4	155261.7
Municipal heating enterprise A	5478.5	126103.7
Enterprise "Estonian Phosphorite"	3161.0	95342.2
Baltic Shipyard	525.5	34024.1
Enterprise"Silikaat"	1806.2	28174.6
Tallinn Metal Works	429.9	26118.9
Estonian Fish Treatment enterprise	148.8	20700.8
Municipal heating enterprise B	932.2	15063.0
Pharmaceutical Plant	75.4	11217.4
Total	25652	825540

* Source: Tallinn Environmental Protection Board.

6 CONCLUSION

During the fifty years of Soviet dominance there were no real possibilities for (economic) control over polluting sectors of the economy in Estonia, as they were extremely centralized by all-union ministries. 90% of all Estonian industries were controlled by the central government in Moscow. Republican authorities had very little influence over local production. As a result there was a permanent lack of money for environmentally oriented investments and accordingly environmental pollution reached critical levels in many places.

Up till today Estonia has signed international environmental agreements about restricting SO_2 and NO_x emissions and coastal water pollution. For that reason the investments to buy or build modern waste treatment equipment or low-waste technologies must be carried out very quickly. There is great urgency now, since earlier the main attention in industry was paid to maximum economic growth, as measured by net material product. Producers were not worried about the pollution of the environment or depletion of natural resources for which there were no economic incentives.

The neglect of the environment by the enterprises belonging to the all-union ministries was quite logical according to the principles of the whole economic system. In the Soviet economy natural resources did not have a price, they were assigned to the appropriate ministry free of charge. Hence for example, Estonian oil-shale deposits belonged to the all-union Ministry of Coal Mining in Moscow, which had its mining enterprises in North Eastern Estonia. Of course this ministry was responsible for maximizing output of oil-shale only. With no power for regional or local authorities, it was impossible to introduce the principles of comprehensive use of all natural resources found in the mining area. It is only thanks to the efforts and investments of the Estonian government and particularly of the previous Ministry of Forest and Nature Conservation that out of the total area, 9750 ha, spoiled by mining activities, 8130 ha have been recultivated, (whereof 6815 reforested and 100 for agriculture) according to Environment' 89.

One more aspect should be highlighted in this connection. Estonia produced the cheapest energy in the previous Soviet Union, based on oil-shale. Thereby her closest neighbours, Russia and Latvia, have saved approximately 5 billion roubles (Reinsalu, 1990). It is the damage to Estonian nature by this enormous "dirty" industry that has subsidized the Russian and Latvian access to "clean energy". They actually even bought electricity at a price below production cost! More than half the power generated was transmitted to our neighbours. Fixed (or commanded!) prices from the central ministry of energy have strongly shifted the proportions in the gross material product (GMP) of Estonia. Fuel and power only account for 8% of GMP, but 1/3 of fixed assets are in these sectors (Rajasalu, 1990). The new action plan for the energy sector foresees significant reduction in oil-shale mining and electricity production. High-level negotiations about the future energy policy in Estonia are now (1991) being held with Moscow.

Significant legal acts concerning economic and administrative regulations of environmental protection and the use of resources were passed in 1990. Some success has been gained in elaborating a system of economic instruments for limiting pollution and setting the price for the most important natural resources like oil shale, water, mineral building materials, peat, etc.

Tentative assessment of the results for the first year - 1991 - show that not all new economic instruments have provided the desired incentives for environmentally benign use of natural resources, cleaner technologies and sufficient level of waste treatment. The transition period from planned to market economy is still in its initial phase and there is still a lingering influence from the continued use of the old allocation mechanisms. Thus the economy is still partly characterized by soft budget constraints and centrally fixed prices in some important sectors, centrally planned and granted investments, etc.

It is obvious that under such conditions market instruments cannot work perfectly. In Estonia the new system of environmental tax policy follows a pragmatic approach combining some elements of economic instruments, resource pricing and direct regulations. The pollution tax rates, the rates of enforcement incentives, etc. are based mostly on experts' judgement not on economic analysis in its classical sense.

On the basis of the first results the conclusion can be drawn that pollution charges have been set too low to be a real incentive for polluters. In air pollution, charging of the polluters did not have much impact on economic behaviour of polluting enterprises. The revenue raising character of the tax thus dominated. Increasing inflation rates should obviously be taken into consideration when revising the new emission charge rates as well as the rates of payments for the use of natural resources. According to the results of 1991, the biggest revenues were collected in the sphere of water management.

The economic difficulties connected with the transition period from planned to market economy will probably make it hard to increase environmental investments. The Environmental Fund has also relatively limited resources. Lack of material and labour resources will obviously restrict many investments. For quick results it is obvious that Estonia's main hope is for subsidies and long-term loans from European and world institutions and also from neighbouring countries.

Environmental protection and control authorities probably overestimate the potential of new administrative regulations and economic instruments today. It is evident that due to the recent turmoil in political and economic life, there is considerable need for continuous revision and redesign of the economic instruments chosen.

Tallinn, December 1991.

REFERENCES

Bye, B., T. Bye, and L. Lorentsen. "Taxation of fossil fuels. The impacts on economic activity, energy markets and pollution". In: Nordic Workshop on integrated energy and Environmental modelling, Risö National Laboratory, February 1990. Ed. by K. Halsnaes, G.A. Mackenzie. Nord 1990:74.

Environment 89. 1990. Estonian Nature Management Scientific Information Centre.

Environment 90. 1991. Ministry of the Environment. Republic of Estonia.

Etlin, S. and L. Redko. 1990. "Effect of air pollution on the health in the oil-shale industry region Oil-shale, 7/2", pp.175-181. (in Russian).

Kallaste, T., ed. "Ecological-economic situation in Estonia. The viewpoint of scientists". 1990. Tallinn, The Estonian Academy of Sciences. (in Russian).

Kallaste, T. and L. Saare. 1991. "Control and assessment of the environmental pollution situation in Estonia". In: *Environment, Energy and Natural Resource Management in the Baltic Region* ed. Fenger e.t al. Nord:48 pp 385-395.

Kallaste, T. 1991. "The environmental problems in Estonia and some ways to solve them". Working Papers, no. 76. Research Institute of Northern Finland, University of Oulu.

Nicolaisen, J. and P. Hoeller. 1990." Economics and the environment: A survey of issues and policy options". OECD Working Papers no. 82.

Mäkelä, K. 1990. "Eestin tieliikenteen pakokaasupäästojen laskentajärjestelmä ELIISA. Tie- ja liikennelaboratorio. Tutkimusselostus Teknillinen Tutkimuskeskus, Tallinnan Teknillinen Korkeakoulu. Espoo.

Rajasalu, T. 1990. "Estonian economy and its development problems". reprint nr. 26. Estonian Academy of Sciences. Department of Humanities and Social Sciences. Institute of Economics. Tallinn.

Regulation of the Government of the Republic of Estonia from 20.11.1990, no 237. "On the regulations concerning the system of fines and payments of nature management" RT, 1990, Tallinn (in Estonian).

Reinsalu, E. 1990. "New principles of the Estonian energy policy". In: *Industry and Environment*. Tallinn, Kohtla-Järve. pp.12-15. (in Estonian).

Viitak, A., H. Kahn and H. Hödrejärv. 1990. "The human ecology:heavy metals in the blood and hair of the habitants of Estonia". In Kallaste 1990, (in Russian).

CHAPTER 8

Environmental Policies in Tanzania

by

Ammon V.Y. Mbelle*

Abstract

Awareness of the need to protect the environment is a recent phenomenon in many developing countries. The formulation of policies and the sensitization of the population on environmental issues is largely out of demonstration effects of actions in developed countries.
In their efforts to control environmental degradation, developing countries find themselves with a bitter reality, that of fostering economic growth at the expense of environmental conservation.

As one of the poorest countries in the world, Tanzania's economic growth is to a very great extent dependent on agricultural growth realized, ironically, through environmental destruction.

This chapter highlights the complexity of environmental issues in Tanzania and the limited options at hand largely due to the high cost of alternatives, which the country's own resources cannot meet. "Free" assistance of the international community is recommended.

* Many thanks to Thomas Sterner and an anonymous referee for comments and help.

T. Sterner (ed.), Economic Policies for Sustainable Development, 148–161.

1 INTRODUCTION: THE PROBLEM

As an agrarian economy, Tanzania's present and future depend on the preservation of her only major asset, agricultural land for her economic development and well-being of the people. It goes without saying that preservation of agricultural land or diversification of economic activities must feature high on the agenda.

In Tanzania, awareness of environmental degradation through human actions is quite high, being further facilitated by the advantage of a high literacy rate. Policies and actions have been formulated and are at various stages of being implemented - yet the threat to the environment even in urban areas is far from being arrested. Certainly, ignorance is not the issue. Why then do economic activities that are not beneficial to the environment continue?

This chapter attempts to answer the question as to whether economic growth in Tanzania is compatible with a limited and fragile environment. The methodology adopted is one of descriptive analysis of the issues. The chapter is divided into five sections including the introduction. Section two provides a general economic and ecological background while Section 3 examines the environmental problems. Section 4 discusses the policies being pursued in Tanzania in an effort to arrest environmental degradation. Concluding remarks is the subject of section five.

2 BACKGROUND: SOCIO-ECONOMIC AND ECOLOGICAL ISSUES IN TANZANIA

The United Republic of Tanzania consists of two sovereign states: Tanganyika (or mainland Tanzania) and Zanzibar, consisting of the islands of Zanzibar and Pemba. The merger was effected in 1964.

Mainland Tanzania covers an area of about 942,800 square kilometers of which 883,760 square kilometers (93.7%) are land area, while Zanzibar covers 240 square kilometers. The population is estimated at 22.5 million according to the most recent census (1988) with a growth rate of 2.8% per annum for mainland Tanzania and 3% per annum for Zanzibar. The population density is 25.6 people per square kilometer on the mainland and 260 people per square kilometer in the Isles.

Agriculture, carried out mainly by the peasantry, is the mainstay of the economy accounting for 46.2% of real GDP for the mainland (1990) and 49% for the Isles (1989). Over 80% of the population in both states lives on agricultural employment. About 75% of the country's foreign exchange earnings are derived from agriculture.

In terms of GDP, the mainland's GDP in 1990 prices was about US$ 2.1 billion (giving a per capita income of about US$ 86) while that of Zanzibar in 1989 was US$ 28.5 million or a per capita income of US$ 43.

For the past five years since the country adopted adjustment programmes (Economic Recovery Programme in 1986) GDP growth has averaged 4% per annum for the mainland and 2.3% per annum for the Isles. The high growth rate is mainly attributed to the growth of the agricultural sector in response to various incentive packages directed towards reviving agricultural production.

Domestic inflation has averaged 25% since 1986 with the current account deficit averaging 23% of GDP. The exchange rate has been adjusted drastically in the recent past from Tanzanian Shillings 32.7 per 1 US$ in 1986 to Shillings 360 per 1 US$ to date. (April 1993).

The terms of trade declined by about 7.9% between 1986 and 1990. The country's external debt stands at around US$ 5 billion, almost equal to ten years of export. Debt servicing accounted for 29.9% of the total current budget in 1989/90.

With regard to some social indicators, the literacy rate is over 90%, among the highest in the developing world, while life expectancy averages 53 years (1987) which compares well with 54 years as an average for other developing countries.

3 NATURAL RESOURCE ENDOWMENTS AND THE ENVIRONMENT

Tanzania is a vast country covering an area greater than the combined areas of her neighbours - Kenya, Malawi and Uganda. The country's ecology is diverse, ranging from areas with a pattern of bimodal rainfall, e.g. Zanzibar to the semi-arid central zone areas of the Dodoma region. In the sub-sections that follow, we highlight some of the issues related to natural resources and the environment. Appendix 1 gives more details of the different ecological zones of the country.

3.1 Land Use: Population, Farming, Livestock and Forests

Population density varies greatly from area to area with very high densities in areas like the Kilimanjaro region, Kagera, Rungwe etc. and sparsely populated regions like Lindi, Mtwara etc.

Tanzania has a high urban population estimated at 21% according to the 1988 population census. This percentage compares unfavourably with 13.8% in 1977 or 5.7% in 1967, the two previous census results. The rapid urbanization rate has resulted in the sprawling of "squatters", estimated to house between 60% and 70% of the urban population.

Land use in Tanzania is complex. On the basis of topography, climate and production conditions, 16 major zones and 40 sub-zones are identified by Mascarenhas and Ford (1987). In terms of climatic variations, 11 zones are identified.

Under Land Ordinance, Land in Tanzania is state property and is only leased to individuals or groups of individuals. Less than 20% of the arable land is currently under cultivation. 45,230 square kilometers (98.3%) of cultivatable land are rain-fed while 770 square kilometers (1.7%) are irrigated.

Livestock is an important activity in the economy accounting for about 10% of GDP. Tanzania has over 13 million cattle and over 10 million sheep and goats, the fourth largest ruminant population in Africa (World Bank, 1991).

About 43% of the total land area is forested. It is estimated that between 300,000 and 400,000 hectares of forest are cleared every year. 13.4% of the total area is protected in National Parks, reserves etc (compared to a world average of 4.0%) with plans in advanced stages to increase protected areas. Population pressure and the quest for agricultural land does, however, pose problems in some areas.

3.2 Energy and Water Resources

The main source of energy in Tanzania is wood from forests and other vegetation which accounts for about 90% of total energy consumption (1989) down from 91.4% in 1980, of which about 85% is consumed by households. The other sources of energy are oil fuel (8%), electricity (1.6%) and coal and others (0.4%). The dependence on wood fuel is quite high even in comparison with other developing countries, e.g. Zambia (58.3% in 1980).

Tanzania has abundant water resources with over 5 major rivers, 3 major lakes and the Indian Ocean. About 74% of the water supply is used in agriculture, 21% domestically and 5% in industry. The per capita consumption is 36 cubic meters per annum (compared to a world average of 660 cubic meters per annum).

4 ENVIRONMENTAL PROBLEMS IN TANZANIA

The rapid expansion of the urban population has brought severe pressures on the infrastructure as well as on the existing provisions for sound management of the urban environment, resulting in poor sanitation in most urban centers.

In particular, the urban sanitation system has been overwhelmed in the collection and disposal of solid waste and sewage. In many areas people lack safe drinking water.

The two problems above coupled with untreated disposal of industrial wastes (e.g. toxics from textile activities) have polluted surface as well as ground water in urban Tanzania. Water sources in close proximity to urban centers (e.g. lakes, the ocean and rivers) are generally used for disposal of almost all types of wastes.

The second set of urban environmental problems is air pollution though assessment of the extent of damage is limited technologically. The main sources of pollution include emissions from industries, motor vehicles, households which utilize fuelwood and the burning of wastes. Indoor levels of smoke due to firewood use in primitive stoves is a major health problem.

4.1 Environmental Problems in Rural Tanzania

As pointed out in Section 1, Tanzania's economy is agrarian. The environmental problems in rural Tanzania are primarily caused by land-livestocking. The major environmental problems are accelerated soil erosion, devegetation and drought with deforestation being the thorny issue.

According to Mascarenhas and Ford (ibid) (see also Chapter 11), the factors that are responsible for deforestation include:

1) Extension of farming land brought about by three factors: population pressure in many areas has brought pressure on arable land, thus necessitating migration or a move to marginal lands; abandonment of traditional farming methods which allowed longer periods of fallow for land to regenerate, and, thirdly the economic pressure to respond to agricultural incentives especially the multifold increase in producer prices of export crops in recent years, and

other government efforts towards increasing foreign exchange earnings for importation of essential production inputs and the liquidation of external debts.

The other demands for forest products include timber for construction purposes and the clearing of mangrove forests along the coastal areas, e.g. in Lindi region, Southern Tanzania, to give way to salt production ("salt farms") using the evaporation method. With no major industries to stimulate economic activities in the region, salt-making, is one of the most dependable sources of income, but unfortunately it poses a serious threat to the mangrove ecosystem.

2) Bioenergy bias: It has been estimated that (see URT, 1991a) the demand for fuel in Tanzania is about 2 cubic meters per person per annum (a total of 46 million cubic meters per annum). This demand exceeds the regeneration capacity by about 12 million cubic meters per annum.

The other sources of fuelwood demand are the economic activities of curing tobacco, (a very profitable export crop) and smoking of fish; the latter estimated to consume 4-5 kilograms of dry wood per kilogram of fresh fish.

The net result of all these activities is accelerated deforestation with desertification, depleted water sources and decreased rainfall as a consequence.

4.2 Soil Erosion and Drought

Additional causes of devegation include bad farming methods (see also (a) above), and overgrazing which leaves the top soil bare and prone to other agents of soil erosion. Devegetation (or land degradation) is a serious problem especially in the arid and semi-arid areas of central Tanzania with desertification affecting about 45% of the country, and threatening a further 35%.

Thus in a way, drought is a result of human activities especially brought about through deforestation or changes in land use. The drought-prone areas in Tanzania are the arid and semi-arid areas already mentioned, see particularly zones 2 and 3 of the Appendix.

To sum up, accelerated soil erosion is a result of various activities: deforestation, bad farming methods, devegetation etc. The persistence of these activities in the rural areas is a clear indication of short-sightedness and of the imperatives of survival that drive people towards current exploitation of the environment at the expense of the future, despite the bitter reality that environmental degradation is often irreversible and non-substitutable.

5 TANZANIA'S RESPONSE TO ENVIRONMENTAL DEGRADATION - DISCUSSION OF POLICIES

The background sections point out the fact that Tanzania's environmental problems are complex, many and of differing geographical dimensions. Further, the response to the awareness can be traced to less than a decade though certain initiatives started even before the 1972 "Stockholm Declaration" (on environmental protection). One of Tanzania's national goals is to control land degradation and protect other natural resources.

The response of the government to environmental challenges requires a sophisticated and multi-pronged approach varying from institutional measures to micro-projects. In the sub-sections that follow we examine the responses in general without a one-to-one problem-solution mapping though we recognize that each environmental degradation requires a specific policy instrument.

5.1 Institutional Responses

In this sub-section we review a number of the most important responses related to the institutional framework.

a) Education: Though not specifically addressed to environmental problems, Tanzania instituted universal primary education and adult education in the 1970s. The current high literacy rate (over 90%) has made it possible to sensitize the majority of Tanzanians to environmental issues through various campaigns employing the mass media and through literacy classes. Part of the on-going success in environmental protection is attributed to this high literacy rate. Indeed even donor support, e.g. by the Danish International Development Agency (DANIDA) to distribute booklets on environmental conservation found an easy audience.

b) Legal Institutions: Various laws have been enacted by the Tanzanian Parliament and by-laws adopted at the local community levels with the aim of protecting the environment. Some of these laws include: The Sites and Squatter upgrading (1972) to improve the living and working environment of the poor, the Town and Country Planning Ordinance, the Public Health (Sewerage and Drainage) Ordinance, the Water utilization (Control and Regulation) Act of 1974 amended as Act No. 10 of 1981, the Villages and Ujamaa Villages Act, 1972, Agricultural Policy 1983, the Forest Reserves Decree, The Wood-Cutting Decree, the Wild-life Policy (1984) and the Wild-life Conservation Act of 1974, the Protection from Radiation Act, 1983, the Mining Act (1979) etc.

   In addition, there are various village, district and regional by-laws restricting grazing in farm areas and afforested areas, tree-cutting, starting fires and by-laws instituting tree-planting each person in the village.

c) Creation of various Institutions to deal with specific environmental problems:

   (i) The National Environment Management Council for Mainland Tanzania as a national advisory board on environment (1983).

   (ii) Establishment of the Commission for Lands and Environment (COLE) in Zanzibar with the aim of land-use planning and effective sound environmental management.

(iii) Establishment of the Ministry of Environment (Ministry of Tourism, Natural Resources and Environment) to complement existing efforts (1990).

(iv) Establishment of a central board for research and investigation on water pollution.

(v) Establishment of a Ministry catering to women, (Ministry of Community Development, Womens´ Affairs and Children); the main participants in economic activities especially in the rural areas (agriculture). Special attention to such a disadvantaged group makes it easier to sensitize women on environmental issues.

d) Encouragement and involvement of Non-Governmental Organizations (NGOs) in environmental conservation. Over 40 Tanzanian and foreign NGOs of various sizes and coverages have been mobilized. Examples include the Tanzania Greenbelt Movement with environmental education, soil conservation and tree-planting as its main activities. The problems facing these NGOs are however numerous. They operate on an ad hoc basis, have limited knowledge of the local environment, and very limited resources, etc.

In addition, there exists a Journalist Environmental Association of Tanzania (JEAT) quite active in disseminating information, highlighting critical issues and exposing problem cases.

A private company, Industrial Projects Promotion (IPP) runs tree-planting competitions in Northern Tanzania. The problem with many of the tree-planting campaigns is that coverage is limited to areas surrounding homesteads and farms. In the central region, the drought conditions frustrate tree-planting campaigns.

e) Exemption of sales tax on electrical cookers to diversify to electricity as an alternative source of energy.

There are, however several problems with this: Firstly the majority of people live in the non-electrified rural areas, and use wood fuel. Secondly, deforestation is not mainly due to fuelwood purposes, see Chapter 11. Timber for construction and exportation is an equally important source of demand. Finally in the future there will be a lack of electricity. Probably this policy is more a support to the trade than to the environment.

f) Introduction of energy-saving charcoal stoves and other alternatives, for instance solar energy sources.

The main problem is limited resources to disseminate the technology and the inability of the majority of the population to afford the price of the stoves.

g) Agricultural extension services: These refer to efforts by the Ministry of Agriculture and Livestock Development to disseminate information to the farmers in modern agricultural farming methods.

The failure of these services to reach the majority of the peasants is mainly attributed to lack of resources.

5.2 Micro Projects for Environmental Conservation

This strategy has been adopted in view of the fact that environmental problems are diverse and localized, hence the need to have specific policies for specific areas. It is in such areas that NGOs are most active, with the participation of the local communities.

In view of limited central government resources, the government is encouraging people to participate in environmental conservation activities, e.g. tree-planting on a self-help basis.

5.3 International Cooperation

Tanzania actively seeks, participates and cooperates with the international community to preserve the global environment in general and the Tanzanian environment in particular.

International support is sought for two main reasons; namely, Tanzanian limited resources and the fact that some of the environmental problems transcend national boundaries.

It is in this spirit that the country participated in the June 1992 UN Conference on the Environment and Development.

5.4 Assessment of Tanzania's Ability in Controlling Environmental Degradation

The government of Tanzania is very serious about environmental protection despite being a late starter. Immediate future action plans include:

a) Adoption of a national environmental action plan.

b) Launching a major tropical forest resources management project.

c) Adopting new laws and regulations with regard to the ownership and use of land and other resources by 1994. It is clear that the farmers and other residents must be given title deeds to the natural resources on which they depend. Otherwise they will not have the proper motivation to protect them from degradation.

Despite these commitments, Tanzania has been facing some of the following problems:

1. Cultural ridigities: This refers mainly to livestock destocking. Cultural values attached to cattle, for instance by many tribes, such as the Maasai, Sukuma, etc. are likely to cause resistance to policies towards destocking.

2. Limited resources: For example to harness alternative sources of energy. The coal deposits in Kiwira, Southern Tanzania, for example, are many years behind the exploitation schedule due to inadequacy of resources - though of course once exploited, fears of air pollution, disposal of process water and acid rain may become a reality. The limited harnessing capacity also explains the failure to harness the country's hydro electric power resource potentials.

3. Laxity in enforcement: There are many laws in operation to conserve the environment but there are too many exceptions to the rules. A good example is the ban on the importation of motor vehicles over three years of use (a question of foreign exchange consumption through spares as well as the side benefit of limiting emissions of smoke). In reality, it is vehicles older than 3 years that form the bulk of motor vehicle imports, especially by private importers.

4. Limited support from the international community: so far international support has been rather on an ad hoc basis and on a micro scale. The impact is not likely to be felt widely.

5. Limited economic activities especially in the rural areas: agriculture, which is the mainstay, is a seasonal occupation. For the rest of the year, people resort to other income-generating activities which are environmentally disruptive, especially deforestation (charcoal burning, mining etc.).

6. Limited transportation facilities: the tracking of cattle for example from Northern and Central Tanzania to the east (Dar Es Salaam) and south has been criticized for environmental destruction along the path.

7. Limited technological capabilities: this refers to the possibility of checking degradation, e.g. through controlling the advance of arid zones and flood plains. This of course has a direct relationship with economic resources.

8. A narrow base for environmental taxation. Apart from the limited technological ability to be able to assess quantitatively the extent of environmental damage by each culprit, the enforcement of such a punitive or compensatory system of environmental taxation is difficult for various reasons. The foremost problem is that urban dwellers who benefit from environmentally sound conditions (such as improved sewage disposal systems) are relatively poor. Recently the government has introduced the cost-sharing or user fee concept extended to social services including garbage and sewage

disposal which in the past used to be freely provided by the government. The response of the beneficiaries has not been without grumbling.

Another possible taxation area is oil products, especially transport fuel. The experience of similar impositions in the past (though for the different purpose of raising government revenue) led to resentment as transport service operators passed these taxes directly to the final consumers. The government was forced to withdraw in many cases.

Secondly, when it comes to industrial concerns, the picture is even more disappointing. Having been barely in operation for decades, the industrial sector is in a very depressed state, hardly able to make ends meet - failing even to pay its workers their monthly wages. Environmental taxes would be uncollectible -that is why cheaper (and dangerous) methods of waste disposal are chosen in the very first place.

6 CONCLUSION

Tanzania is a poor developing country. Despite various good programmes to protect the environment, her ability to implement the programmes is limited by her very nature poverty. It is not an accident that the bulk of economic activities are environmentally degrading, given the country's limited flexibility in the areas of technical progress, possibilities for substitution as well as changing the consumption mix.

Like any other developing country Tanzania strives towards economic growth and the well-being of her citizens as a first step towards alleviation of poverty. However, (and sadly it seems), people think this can only be achieved through environmental degradation. The resources to deal with the immediate environmental problems resulting from these actions are very limited for a country which can hardly make ends meet without considerable external assistance.

Tanzania is cooperating very greatly through global efforts to conserve the environment, e.g. through afforestation to check global warming, an environmental degradation which Tanzania contributed very insignificantly to.

To a country which is debt-ridden, external resources to conserve the environment, (given that there are long lists of priorities like health, education etc.) can be released through alleviating the debt burden or through external financing which does not lead to debts ("free" assistance). The latter option seems all the more reasonable given that a different approach would tax the country unfairly, especially when it is cooperating to preserve the global environment.

Tanzania is now moving in the right direction explicitly incorporating environmental issues in the development programmes and various plans. The future challenge for Tanzania's survival (or demise) lies in environmental preservation and striking a balance between economic activities in the search for growth and development and environmental conservation.

Petrini (1991) summarizes the challenges in five aspects: management practices in farming, water resource management, deforestation and land degradation, overgrazing and bio-diversity. We believe these are the key areas to Tanzania's environmental problems. As shown in the Appendix the various regions of Tanzania are very diverse and their ecologies differ substantially. Some regions have an obvious potential for agriculture, others for wild-life and game.

In order to move towards a sustainable development the country needs a combination of external assistance and internal reform - not least of land ownership, in order to sustain the environment.

Appendix 1. Environmental characteristics of various zones[1]

1a Northern Coast, 35 000 km^2. Medium population density. Small scale rainfed cultivation; cashew, coconuts, cloves, roots and cereals. Sisal estates especially around Tanga and Korogwe. Softwood plantations. Fisheries.

The soils are generally poor. However, there is a potential for improvements in coconut and food crops; integration of crops and livestock; possible rehabilitation of sisal estates; fisheries development - tuna and other coastal species; forest plantation development.

1b Southern Coast, 30 000 km^2. Medium population density. Small-scale, locally dense rainfed cultivation; cashew, coconuts, cassava, cereals including rice and legumes. Softwood plantations and fisheries.

Low rainfall and labour constraint but cultivation could be improved through better cultivation and improved crop varieties; improvement of smallstock, extension and veterinary services and maybe forestry and fisheries development.

1c Islands, 3 000 km^2. High population density. Small-scale permanent rainfed cultivation of roots and cereals, cloves, coconuts and spices. Fisheries.

Main problems concern land tenure. Otherwise good prospects for improved clove and coconut varieties, rice cultivation, integration of crops and livestocks and finally fisheries.

2 Northern Arid Lands and Maasai Steppe 106 000 km^2. Low population density. Extensive nomadic grazing; game reserves.

Low rainfall but some scope for improving livestock production and marketing and possibly some potential for tourism.

3a Central Semi-Arid Lands 135 000 km^2. Medium population density. Extensive semi-nomadic grazing; smallscale cultivation of drought-tolerant roots, cereals, cotton, locally dense due to population pressure.

Low rainfall but possibilities for improving livestock production and marketing as well as improved crop varieties. Possible improved grazing of seasonal swamps.

3b South-eastern Semi-Arid Lands 74 000 km^2. Medium-low population density. Sparse small-scale rainfed cultivation and livestock; sorghum, cassava, cashew. Selous game reserve.

Low rainfall and tsetse infested. Poor potential.

4a Western Plateau 216 000 km^2. Low population density. Small-scale rainfed cultivation, locally dense due to population pressure; maize, cotton, tobacco. Sedentary and semi-nomadic grazing. Large areas of forest reserve (Miombo woodland). Lake fishing.

Poor soils and also tsetse infested but does have same prospects for improved livestock production; integration with agriculture; improved crop varieties, cultivation techniques, processing and marketing; development of lake fisheries; woodland management.

4b Southern Plateau 99 000 km^2. Low population density. Small-scale rainfed cultivation, locally dense. Maize. Few livestock. Lake fishing.

Tsetse infected but does have prospects through improvement of crop varieties, use of fertilizers and marketing. Introduction of livestock for draught and production.

---

[1] For each zone, we give area, density and current land use patterns. In the second paragraph, we give principal environmental problems and possible development potential if these problems are resolved. Source: Adapted from Ministry of Tourism, Natural Resources and Environment.

5a Southern Highlands 66 000 km². Medium population density. Small-scale rainfed cultivation, locally dense; wheat, maize, pyrethrum, temperate fruits; tea estates; sedentary grazing. Wattle and softwood plantation.

Cultivated area can be increased through improvement of crop varieties, fertilizers, integration of livestock; expansion of cash crops; woodlots/agroforestry.

5b South-western Highlands 22 000 km². Low population density. Small-scale rainfed cultivation; wheat, maize, millet, cassava. Limited sedentary grazing.

Droughty soils and a particularly long dry season. Also great distance to markets, however there may be some scope for improvement of crop varieties, cultivation and integration of livestock production.

5c Western Highlands 45 000 km². High population density. Small scale permanent cultivation; intercropped bananas, coffee with beans, maize, sweet potatoes.

At present tsetse infested, limits the extent of sedentary grazing. This problem is compounded by poor soils in some areas and resulting land pressure in others. However, there is a chance of developing improved crop varieties, cultivation techniques, use of fertilizers and integration of cattle, tea and woodlots/agroforestry.

6a Northern Highlands 19 000 km². High population density. Locally very intensive small-scale permanents cultivation; intercropped bananas, coffee, vegetables under shade trees. Milk production. Maize on lower slopes; wheat in dry (rainshadow) areas; sedentary, some nomadic grazing. Coffee estates. Game conservation.

Ecological conditions favourable, the main problem is land shortage. Possibly some coffee estates could be rehabilitated and perhaps some dairy sector development.

6b Isolated Granitic Mountains 13 000 km². High population density. Locally very dense, permanent small-scale cultivation. Coffee, tea, temperate fruit, maize, beans.

Land shortage again, except for Mahenge and Loliondo where communication and marketing infrastructure needs to be improved.

Alluvial Plains 23 000 km².: Kilombero. Medium population density. Sparse, small-scale permanent cultivation; sugar, rice on alluvial fans and higher ground not subject to flooding.

Flood hazards and tsetse as well as sleeping sickness. However, the area might be developed through improved water control; improved crop varieties. (Good potential for irrigation but very expensive flood control).

Rufiji. Medium population density. Small-scale semi-permanent cultivation including double-cropping and dry season cultivation after floods; rice, cotton, coconut, maize.

Flooding hazards but otherwise fair prospects through better water control. However, the building of the Stieglers Gorge dam may affect the water regime, bring prospects for irrigation but adversely affect prawn stocks).

Usangu. Medium population density. Small-scale mainly permanent cultivation around the south-east fringe; grazing in the central grassland and south-east with substantial immigration. Paddy, rice, maize, millet.

Water supply is limited for rice but fair prospects for the future through water control if storage dams turn out to be feasible.

Wami. Medium population density. Small-scale cultivation of maize, paddy, cotton and oilseeds. State-owned irrigated rice and sugar estate. Prospects, see Usangu.

REFERENCES

Christiansson, C. 1988. "Degradation and Rehabilitation of Agropastoral Land Perspectives on Environmental Change in Semi-arid Tanzania" *Ambio*, vol. 17, no. 2.

Danish International Development Agency (DANIDA). 1989. Environmental Profile of Tanzania.

Darkoh, M.B.K. 1982. "Desertification in Tanzania" *Geography* vol. 67, pp 331-420.

Mascarenhas, A. and B. Ford. 1987. "Resources and Sustainable Community Development: An agenda for Development Action in Tanzania". *Mimeo.*

Ngasongwa, J.A., P.K. Ndyetabula and C.C. Kajembe. 1990. "Environmental Effects of Agricultural Practices in Tanzania" Paper presented at a conference, Dodoma, 12-17 November.

Petrini, F. 1991. "Some Aspects of Natural Resource Economics in Tanzania Agriculture". Paper presented at the Economic Research Bureau Seminar, Dar Es Salaam.

United Republic of Tanzania. 1990. *Ministry of Tourism, Natural Resources and Environment Preparatory Report* for the UN June 1992 Conference on the Environment.

United Republic of Tanzania. 1991. *Economic Survey 1990*, Dar Es Salaam.

United Republic of Tanzania. 1991. *1988 Census Preliminary Report*, Dar Es Salaam.

World Bank. 1991. *Country Report Tanzania,* Washington.

World Resources Institutes. 1990. *World Resources,* New York.

CHAPTER 9

Energy, Forestry and Environment in Uruguay

by

Ruben Tansini*

Abstract

This paper explores fuel use in Uruguay as a result of energy policy for the last 25 years and consequences for forestry, given the increasing use of fuelwood. During the last 15 years, policy has focused on replacing imported petroleum by domestic energy sources. This was done through increases in taxes on petroleum products, and temporary tax reductions for projects aiming at substitution. The price and substitution elasticities of demand for various sources of industrial energy demand are estimated.

Wood and other biomass increased their share of total consumption from 22% in 1965 to 29% in 1989. Although wood consumption was not so high, given limited forested areas, the unbalanced growth of supply and demand of fuelwood could in the future lead to important ecological and economic damage. The increasing awareness of these problems motivated implementation of hydropower projects and of apparently successful forest legislation. The implemented mechanisms promoting afforestation (tax reduction, credits, external debt conversion, etc.) have turned out to be quite effective and the country can now look forward to a significant increase in forest area.

* Thanks to Thomas Sterner and an anonymous referee for useful comments.

T. Sterner (ed.), Economic Policies for Sustainable Development, 162–177.

1 ENERGY, FUELWOOD AND FORESTRY IN URUGUAY.

Energy consumption in Uruguay has been quite stable during the last decades, but we can still distinguish four periods. During the first, from 1965 to 1972 fuel consumption and GNP grew at a moderate rate (1.6% and 1.4%, respectively). Fuel consumption in tonnes of oil equivalent (TOE) in 1972 was 11% higher than in 1965. During the second period, 1972-1979 (with rising fuel prices), the growth in energy was again moderate (1.8%) in spite of higher GNP growth (4.3%).

The third period from 1980 to 1984 was characterized by economic recession, which explains most of the 15% reduction of fuel consumption (energy use fell at a annual rate of 4% and GNP at 3.8%). The last period, from 1985 to 1989, was one of economic recovery and redemocratization, characterized by significant growth rates (GNP grew at 3.8%, while energy consumption increased by 2.2% per year). At the end of the last period, energy consumption was at a level similar to 1973 and only 12% higher than 1965. Energy use per capita actually decreased by 5% during the period (see Figure 1).

Although petroleum products dominated the supply of energy over the entire period (see Table 1), their share decreased by 20% from 1973, while the shares of electricity and fuelwood increased. The share of fuelwood and biomass grew by almost 50% accounting for 29% of total energy consumption in 1989 compared to 22% in 1965. As we will analyze later, changing relative prices could be the reason for this reduction.

Table 1 Fuel consumption by source 1965-1989 (as % of total consumption)

Year	Fuelwood & Charcoal	Biomass	Petrol prod.	Mineral coal	Electri-city	Total Consumpt. Ktoe
1965	21.2	0.9	69.2	1.6	7.1	1718
1972	19.9	1.5	69.4	1.0	8.2	1913
1975	21.7	1.5	66.7	1.0	9.2	1882
1980	20.9	1.7	65.6	0.4	11.4	2105
1985	28.6	2.6	52.9	0.1	15.8	1763
1989	26.6	3.0	53.5	0.1	16.8	1919

Ktoe = Kilotons of Oil Equivalent.
Source: NBEU (The National Energy Board)

2 ENERGY CONSUMPTION AND ECONOMIC ACTIVITY.

The energy-GNP ratio decreased from 1973, especially between 1973-1979 when it fell 13%, and between 1985-89 (6%); it was 26% lower in 1989 than in 1973 (see Fig.1). This seems to indicate a more efficient use of energy, but it must be kept in mind that this measure is merely a preliminary indication of how energy may be related to economic activity, standard of living and stock of energy-using equipment. As Bhatia (1987) pointed out, "very important factors are lumped together in the energy-GNP ratio like changes in the mix of goods and services, changes in the energy intensity, changes in the composition of energy sources which provide more useful energy, etc..".

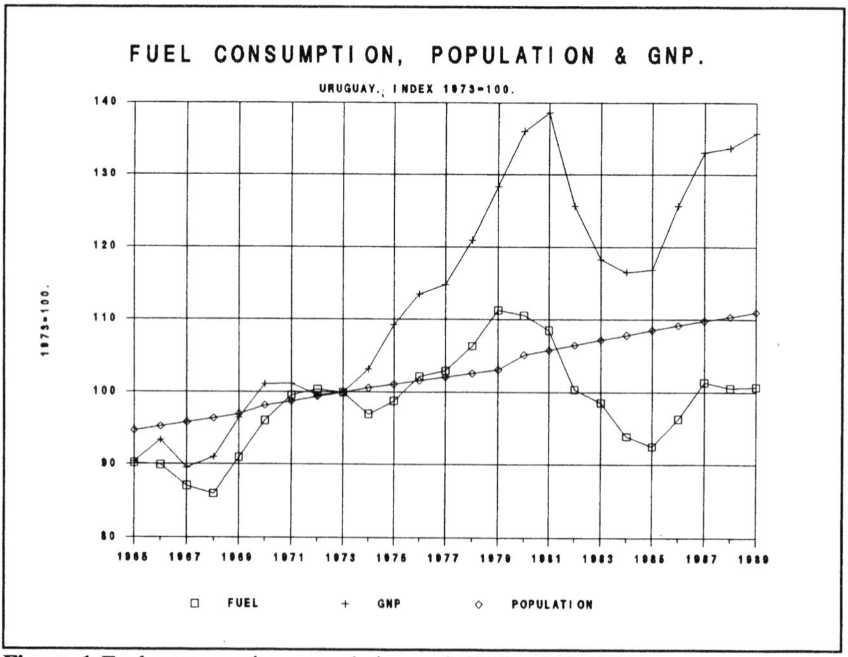

Figure 1 Fuel consumption, population and GNP, 1965-1989.

Another way to present the relationship between energy consumption and the economy is in terms of the simple energy-GNP growth elasticity, i.e., the ratio of annual energy consumption growth rate and GNP growth rate (see Table 2). This ratio has been lower after 1973 except for the period 1980-1984 when the decreasing rate of GNP was higher than that of fuels. On the whole, energy efficiency appears to have increased quite rapidly both for total and for industrial energy demand. During the entire period from 1965-1989, the energy-GNP elasticity was 0.27 and 0.43 for individual demand.

Table 2 Elasticity of energy demand to GNP and industrial output

	ENERGY (growth rate)	GNP (growth rate)	Simple output elasticity	Industry energy (growth rate)	Industry output (growth rate)	Simple output elasticity
1965-72	1.55	1.40	1.10	0.99	1.40	0.71
1973-79	1.80	4.25	0.42	3.52	5.14	0.68
1980-84	-3.97	-3.80	(1.05)	-5.80	-3.82	(1.52)
1985-89	2.15	3.81	0.56	4.74	4.39	1.08
1965-89	0.46	1.71	0.27	0.54	1.25	0.43

Source: NBEU & Central Bank.

3 ENERGY CONSUMPTION BY ECONOMIC SECTOR.

There has been a considerable stability in the distribution of energy consumption by sector. Residential and industry account for roughly 30% each, transport 25% and services and agriculture share the rest. The most important source of fuel supply for residential and service sectors was fuelwood and charcoal which represented about 50% of these sectors' consumption. Electricity shares increased sharply during the period from 11% to 27% while liquid gas increased from 3% in 1965 to 10% in 1989. The decline was concentrated to kerosene which fell from 26% to 7%.

Surprisingly, transport fuel consumption declined slowly at an annual rate of 0.15% between 1965-1989. Gasoline consumption fell by 15% in the same period in spite of the fact that the stock of cars increased on average by 14000 per year from 1985. In 1988 there were 280.000 cars and 50.000 trucks and buses.

Finally, both transport and agriculture (including fishing) had relatively constant shares. Both areas experienced a good deal of substitution of gasoline and kerosene for diesel. Diesel consumption represented 45% of total fuel consumption in 1965 but 65% in 1973 and 93% in 1989, while gasoline and kerosene decreased from 53% to 5%.

The industrial sector's consumption of organic fuels (fuelwood, biomass and charcoal) increased dramatically from 10% in 1965 to over 43% in 1989 (see Table 3). In fact the increase in the country's biomass consumption occurred mainly in the industrial sector: consumption by manufacturing increased 278% between 1965-1989. The biomass share of industrial fuel increased from 3% to 10% in 1989. At the same time the share of fuelwood and charcoal grew significantly from 7% to 33%. Electricity consumption also expanded, from 10% to 22%. The only fuels whose consumption was reduced were fuel oil and mineral coal. Fuel oil consumption was cut in half between 1973 and 1989. Reduction in mineral coal consumption (not shown in Table 1) was even more dramatic from several percent of total fuel consumption to practically nothing in 1989.

Table 3 Structure of fuel supply to the industrial sector (%)

Year	Fuelw. & Char-coal	Bio mass	Fuel oil	Diesel gasoil	Petrol	Electric ity	Total 1973 = 100
1965	7.2	3.1	81.7	1.5	1.0	10.2	93.6
1972	7.8	5.4	71.4	2.5	1.1	10.7	99.3
1975	9.4	4.9	70.4	1.1	0.7	12.3	107.4
1980	12.9	5.7	62.3	2.4	0.7	15.0	119.1
1985	29.7	10.0	35.9	2.0	0.2	21.2	88.5
1989	34.2	10.3	30.7	2.3	0.1	22.1	106.6

Source: NBEU

4 WOOD CONSUMPTION AND FORESTRY IN URUGUAY.

As a reaction to higher prices, soaring import bills and general uncertainty, the Uruguayan economy has turned increasingly to wood for fuel, particularly after 1973. This increasing consumption of fuelwood, added to the use of wood as a raw material, might cause serious environmental problems if the development of supply and demand for wood are not harmonized.

Uruguay is a country particularly well suited to agriculture. This sector has historically represented the main part of the country's GNP and an even greater share of its exports. Uruguay's territory is mainly covered by natural prairies and only 4% of its area (865.000 ha) was woodland in 1985, 75% of which was natural and 25% plantations. The plantations were often small units under 1 hectare (about 40%), originally intended to prevent erosion or as protection for livestock and for crops.

As we see in Table 4, an increasing share is used as fuel. The share of the furniture industry, which is closely related to building activity, decreased significantly from 1981. The increasing consumption of the paper industry prevented a more radical reduction in the share of wood used as raw material.

Table 4 Wood consumption: distribution by use

Year	Furniture industry %	Paper industry %	Fuelwood consumpt %	Extract. 1000M' Total	Extract. index 1973=100
1973	12.2	1.8	86.0	1522	100
1975	14.5	2.1	83.4	1750	115
1980	6.8	8.6	84.6	1564	103
1983	3.5	5.6	90.9	2357	155
1986	5.3	4.4	90.3	2668	175

Source: NBEU.

The consumption of fuelwood has been dominated historically by the residential sector which represented over 80% of total fuelwood consumption in the 1960s (see Table 5). For the last five years residential fuelwood consumption decreased by 15% mainly from 1987-1989, when relative prices reversed to favor oil and gas. As can be observed in Table 6, fuelwood prices have been fairly stable and increased at a lower rate than most other fuels, including electricity. Lately this situation has started to change. This is not unusual as the markets for wood are typically far from perfect. It is quite common to find "threshold effects" such that wood is first very cheap when it is perceived to be plentiful and then "suddenly" shortages evolve that send the price soaring, see further Chapter 12.

Table 5 Fuelwood consumption by economic sector

Year	Residential %	Services %	Industry %	Total Ktoe	Total 1973=100
1965	83.3	6.8	9.9	356	94
1972	82.3	6.9	10.9	373	99
1975	79.9	6.5	13.6	389	103
1980	75.0	6.2	18.9	424	113
1985	71.7	0.8	27.6	494	132
1989	61.7	0.7	37.6	489	130

Source: NBEU.

Table 6 Energy prices in the industrial sector (real price index, 1979=100).

Year	Fuel wood	Electricity	Fuel oil
1970	N.A.	129.9	28.2
1976	92.1	119.4	114.3
1980	118.7	99.0	114.9
1985	120.4	115.8	180.0
1988	114.3	120.1	132.8

Source: Central Bank of Uruguay.

The industrial sector increased its fuelwood demand dramatically since 1973 (see Table 5). From 1973 to 1979 fuelwood consumption increased by 70%, and by 149% between 1979 and 1989. Adding fuelwood consumption and wood as raw material, the share of the industrial sector in 1986 rose to 41% of total wood extraction in the country.

The increasing use of fuelwood by industry appears to have been determined by such factors as price and supply security since this fuel is clearly not the conventional choice. This process of substitution is neatly illustrated by the great number of boiler conversions that took place during the 1980s. In 1979 there were only 4 fuelwood boilers in the industrial sector, but in 1988 there were 119. Forty-five boilers were converted from oil to wood, while 74 new boilers were built for wood use.

In the industrial sector three branches (food, cement and paper industries) accounted for 75% of total fuelwood consumption by manufacturing in 1985. If we add textiles, beverages and tobacco industries they accounted for 93% consumption. It is striking to see the large wood consumption of the cement industry (5% of the total), in spite of an additional and growing use of other non-traditional fuels such as rice husks which currently represent up to 25% of fuel consumption in some kilns.

5 DEMAND FOR ENERGY IN THE INDUSTRIAL SECTOR.

We turn now to the substitutability of different fuels in the industrial sector. The extent to which interfuel substitution has taken place, and may still be possible can be evaluated by the examination of the own and cross-price elasticities of demand for individual fuels. The research reported below estimated those elasticities for the period 1976-1988. The three fuels considered are: liquid fuels/petroleum products, fuelwood & biomass and electricity (see Tansini, 1990).

Due to the large number of parameters to be estimated when the disaggregation of energy is considered in the cost function, a two level model was adopted (Fuss, 1977). At the aggregate level, the producer is assumed to chose the mix of capital (K), labour (L) and energy (E), which minimizes production cost for a given output level (Q). At the second stage, the price of energy is obtained from a unit cost function which, in turn, represents the cost minimizing behavior of the producer who seeks the optimal mix of electricity (El), fuelwood (W) and petroleum products (P) for a given energy level, see figures 2 and 3 for cost shares. The price of energy (P_E) is the link between the first and the second level. The demand for the factors of production is in both cases obtained by applying Shepard's lemma.

First a static single-stage translog model was estimated based on expenditure shares consistent with the two-stage model. The estimation was based on the well known non-homothetic translog expenditure share energy submodel and estimated by Seemingly Unrelated Regression (which is equivalent to Full Information Likelihood). The application of Shepard's lemma to the translog cost function yields the cost shares for each production factor:

$$(1) \quad S_i - \alpha_i + \sum_j \beta_{ij} lnP_j + \beta_{iQ} lnQ \qquad i,j - K,L,E.$$

The system of demand equations (2) was estimated with traditional homogeneity and symmetry restrictions imposed. The price of aggregate energy was obtained from a unit cost function which was also approximated by a second-order translog function, using in this case the prices of fuelwood & biomass (P_W), electricity (P_E) and of petroleum products (P_P):

$$(2) \quad \ln P_E - \lambda_z + \sum_t \lambda_t \ln P_t + 0.5 \sum_t \sum_s \delta_{ts} \ln P_t \ln P_s \qquad t,s - El,W,P$$

Applying Shepard's lemma gives each energy input's share in total energy cost. This system of equations (3) was also estimated with the traditional homogeneity and symmetry restrictions imposed. In both cases simple standard assumptions about normality of errors were made.

$$(3) \quad S_t - \lambda_t + \sum_s \delta_{ts} \ln P_s \qquad t,s - El,W,P$$

The data came from the annual survey of the National Directorate of Statistics of Uruguay (NDSU) and from the NBEU. The price series used in the expenditure share model were converted to a common unit, tons of oil equivalent (TOE). The share of capital was defined as the difference between value-added and labour costs. The labour price index used was the wage index for the manufacturing sector from NDSU and the index of imported equipment of the Central Bank of Uruguay was used for capital.

During the period 1976-1988, capital accounted for the largest cost share increasing from 59% to 68%. The labour cost share decreased from 34% to 25%. The energy cost share stayed rather constant, around 7%, during the whole period. The disaggregation of fuels shows that fuelwood & biomass increased steadily from 15% of energy cost in 1976 to 43% in 1988. The share of electricity also grew, at

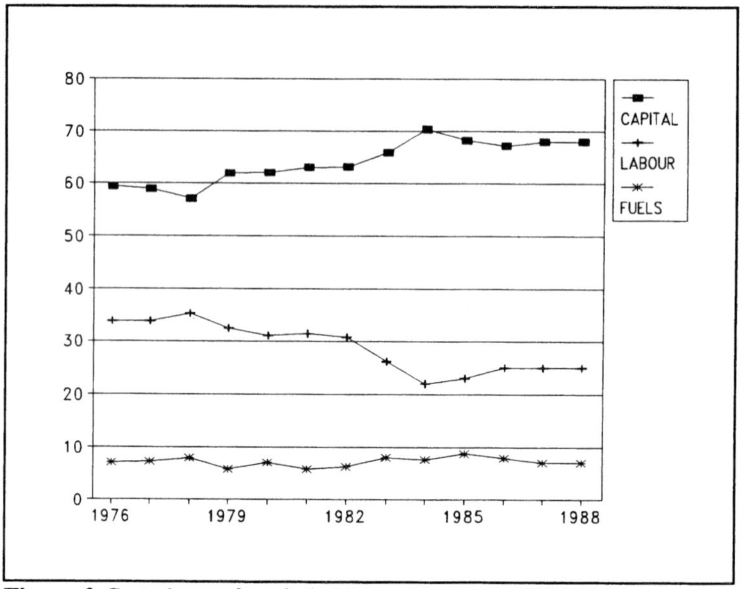

Figure 2 Cost share of capital, labour & energy. 1976-1988.

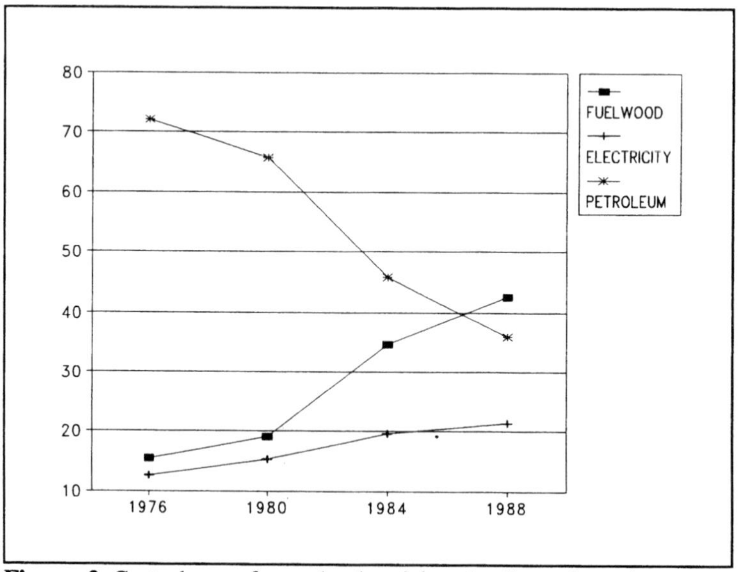

Figure 3 Cost share of wood, electricity & oil products in energy expenditures. 1976-1988.

a lower rate, from 13% to 21%, while the share of petroleum products decreased from 72% to 36% in 1988.

Table 7 presents the estimated average own and cross-price elasticities. Own price elasticities are negative, as expected and they are statistically significant. It can be seen that fuelwood-petroleum products and electricity-petroleum products are significant substitutes, while fuelwood and electricity are weak complements. The demand for petroleum products turned out to be the most price sensitive followed by the demand for fuelwood & biomass. The estimated parameters of the energy cost function were used to construct an energy price index for the following level of analysis.

Table 7 Cross and own price elasticities.

	Elect	Wood	Petrol
P_E	-0.4	-0.3	0.6
P_W	-0.1	-0.8	1.4
P_P	0.6	1.2	-1.3

The statistical fit of the system was acceptable and most of the coefficients significantly different from zero, and the hypothesis that the underlying production function was non-homothetic could not be rejected.

Table 8 displays the estimated average price elasticities for a constant output level. Own-price elasticities have negative signs as expected, however not significantly different from zero for labour. Most of the own and cross-price elasticities are less than one in absolute value, indicating limited adjustment to price changes. We note that the demand for energy is very price elastic with an elasticity above unity. With a rising relative price of energy this would explain the reduction in energy intensity. A similar case can be made for capital that the size of the elasticity estimated together with the relative prices does explain at least part of the increase in cost-shares. These effects are further reinforced by the sensitivity of the demand for energy and labour to the variation in capital prices. Looking at the cross-price elasticities we find that energy as a substitute for the other factors is quite sensitive to their price variations.

Table 8 Cross and price elasticities.

	K	L	E
P_K	-0.9	1.1	2.5
P_L	0.5	-0.6	0.7
P_E	0.3	0.2	-1.1

6 FORESTS: PRESENT SITUATION AND PERSPECTIVES.

Based on information from the National Energy Board of Uruguay (NBEU) and on Migues et al (1990), it is possible to analyze the supply and demand of wood in 1988. Migues et al (1990) was mainly intended for the evaluation of eucalyptus fuelwood demand of the industrial sector, but included other sectors and identified the contribution of the different types of trees to the supply of fuelwood in 1988.

The NBEU (1989) estimated that total fuelwood consumption in 1988 was about 1.735.000 tonnes equivalent of dry fuelwood estimated at 2700 kcal/kg which, in turn, represented about 468 KTOE. The difference with the reported total consumption of KTOE 487 reported by the NBEU is explained by the utilization of branches and by-products of trees that did not imply any direct damage to the forests.

Eucalyptus accounted for the highest share of consumption: 74% of total fuelwood consumption, while pine trees only accounted for 1%. Fuelwood from natural woods represented about 25% (see Table 9). Most of the "natural" forests' fuelwood (93%) was consumed by the residential sector (56% in urban residential and 37% in rural areas).

Table 9 Fuelwood consumption in 1988 by sector and origin: tonnes of fuelwood (at 2700 KCAL/KG)

Forest type	Urban resid.	Rural resid.	Industry	Commer-cial	Total
Natural %	246000 (46.8%)	159200 (33.8%)	0.0 (0.0%)	31000 (20.8%)	436200 (25.2%)
Pine tree %	17600 (3.3%)	2900 (0.6%)	0.0 (0.0%)	0.0 (0.0%)	20500 (1.2%)
Eucalyptus %	262300 (49.9%)	308900 (65.6%)	588250 (100%)	118000 (79.2%)	1277450 (73.6%)
Total %	525900 (100%)	471000 (100%)	588250 (100%)	149000 (100%)	1734150 (100%)
Total in TOE	142000	127000	159000	40200	468200

Source: NBEU.

Of the total consumption of eucalyptus fuelwood, the industrial sector took 46%, and commercial activities 9% (bakeries, restaurants, brick factories, etc.), 20.5% went to urban residential use and 24% to rural residential consumption. Of fuelwood consumption, 72% was concentrated around the capital, Montevideo, with 45% of the population. Natural forests accounted for 27% of this consumption and eucalyptus for 71%.

According to the estimate of the NBEU, the eucalyptus forest area increased by 4% or 4.300 hectares between 1985 and 1987, totaling roughly 25 millions m^3 of wood equivalent in 1987. The region which traditionally provides fuelwood to the capital, accounted for half of the newly forested area.

The NBEU also estimated the potential fuelwood supply from eucalyptus forests for 1988, based on the Average Annual Growth (AAG) of the country's forests with a reasonable exploitation of the woodland. They assumed that AAG would be 20 m^3/ha. by year, that the forests under 10 ha. are not exploited, to prevent environmental damage as a result of over-exploitation and that 33% of the area cut was replanted. The estimated production for 1988 was TEDF 1.010.000 contrasting with the utilization of TEDF 1.277.000 that year, which implies a deficit of TEDF 267.000, i.e. 26% of the potential supply. This deficit was equivalent to about 9.140 ha. of woodland or 30% of the eucalyptus forests over 10 ha. If the exploitation of half the forests under 10 ha. was allowed, the potential supply would increase to TEDF 1.277.000, eliminating the deficit estimated in the previous case. But it must be kept in mind that these forests under 10 ha. are generally either natural forests or plantations intended to prevent soil erosion.

Besides the use of wood as fuel, it is also in demand as a raw material. It was estimated by the Forestry Department of the Agronomic Faculty that the consumption of eucalyptus alone as raw material in 1988 was about 230.000 m^3. They estimated that about 90.000m^3 were intended for the paper industry, 150.000m^3 was exported and 80.000m^3 in demand by the furniture industry (Migues et al., 1990).

If the use of eucalyptus as raw material is added to the consumption of fuelwood in 1988, it is clear that it is not possible to avoid significant supply shortages in the near future, even if forests under 10 ha. are exploited. The amount intended for raw material would be equivalent to 16% of the wood cut in 1988, on the assumption that their growing-time is similar to that of trees intended as fuelwood, which probably is an optimistic assumption. If forests under 10 ha. are not exploited, the total deficit rises to 42% of total supply, but if 50% of the forests under 10 ha. are exploited the deficit is reduced to 39%. This deficit has been covered by import of wood from Paraguay and Brazil, mostly as raw material. NBEU was also aware of the damage caused by exploitation of natural woodlands and recommended that it be avoided.

Migues et al. (1990) also evaluated substitution possibilities for fuel oil in the manufacturing sector. Their analysis is based on a survey conducted in 1989 of the technical characteristics of boilers which could be converted to fuelwood. During 1988, fuel oil consumption of the industrial sector was 185.500 TOE, a third of industry's energy consumption and 80% of the country's consumption of fuel oil. They evaluated the substitution possibilities in three scenarios determined by different assumptions on price and technical restrictions for boiler conversions. The basic scenario assumed a fuelwood price of US$ 18 per ton (the average 1988 price, transport cost included). The pessimistic scenario was based on a price rise of 40% and the optimistic one on a decrease of 40%. In the basic scenario the substitution of fuel oil would be 12-15%, in the pessimistic scenario 5-10%, and finally in the optimistic scenario 17-18%. In the basic scenario this corresponds to roughly 10% of total fuelwood cut in 1988 (excluding forests under 10 ha.).

The state-owned electricity company is evaluating a wood-fired 100 MW. power plant to be operational before the year 2000, when hydropower capacity will reach its ceiling. This project was also analyzed by the Swedish consulting firm, Swedforest Consulting AB and three alternative fuel sources were evaluated: oil, coal and wood. Antman & Cian (1990) concluded that with certain prices fuelwood could be an adequate fuel and that eucalyptus would be more profitable than fuel oil, if capacity utilization was between 27% and 60%. The evaluation of wood vs. coal, on the contrary, is very sensitive to price relations. Estimated wood consumption would be about one million m^3, with a capacity utilization of 80%, which is equivalent to 50.000 hectares of forest (assuming a growth of 20 m^3/ha. by year). This new demand alone represents about half of the eucalyptus forests above 10 ha. in 1988. Thus to avoid future supply shortages, the only way to meet these requirements will be through new forest plantations.

Obviously the combination of raw material demand, industrial fuel conversion and new wood-fired power plants would pose a considerable threat to the sustainability of supplies. This has already caused some concern although little attention, if any, has been paid to the substantial environmental damage which could result from over-exploitation. The increasing consciousness has stimulated legislation and state intervention which clearly encourages afforestation, prevention of soil erosion and protection of indigenous forests, as well as increasing the supply of wood in the near future.

7 THE NEW FOREST LAW

In 1987, after two years of discussion, a new forest law was approved by Parliament (replacing the previous one from 1968). Its approval gained broad support from the various political parties. The most important aspects of the new legislation were that it anticipates tax reductions and financial facilities for afforestation to be provided by the government.

The present law is aimed at promoting so-called "artificial afforestation", in those areas not well-suited for agriculture, the conservation of soils, water, animals and indigenous vegetation. The legislation concerns three categories: 1) protective forests 2) production forests and 3) common forests. According to the law, the state should support protective and production forests as long as they are planted on "forest land". "Forest land" was defined as "that land which has no other permanent productive use or land declared of forest priority by the Forest Authority, for soil erosion considerations" (the priority area covers about 2.000.000 ha. of the country, ie. twice the total woodland area in 1988). Thus, the state restricts incentives to forestation to these priority areas, but allows forestation all over the country. The designation of land as forest priority should be based on soil conservation considerations. The legislation also mandates the afforestation of land seriously damaged by soil erosion and it forbids the exploitation of natural forests without authorization of the Forest Authority. Although soil degradation is not as serious as in other countries, it must be prevented before it becomes a serious or irreversible problem. FAO evaluation of soil degradation in Uruguay in 1983 reported that 7% of the territory was severely deteriorated, 28% was moderately deteriorated and 65% of the territory was lightly or not deteriorated by soil erosion.

The instruments included in the Forest Law are mainly tax exemptions, which in some cases can extend to 12 years. Another instrument is the so-called "Tax Reinvestment Mechanism" which is intended to encourage farmers to invest in afforestation of unproductive land. This mechanism allows a part of the investment in forest plantation to be tax deductible. Other important mechanisms are the implementation of special subsidies and credits for different stages of forest growth. The legislation also made legally possible the afforestation of a third person's land.

The National Forestry Plan aims for the afforestation of 420.000 ha.in 30 years, starting 1990. The first five-year goal is 100.000 ha. at an estimated cost of U$ 4 million. Of this, 47.000 ha. were intended to meet the annual deficit, 30.000 to face new demand as a consequence of boiler conversion, 6.500 for export and 15.000 for soil erosion prevention.

The forest legislation has shown encouraging results in its four years of application. The most important result is the forestry plan, which reasonably predicts future wood consumption and plans the growth of wood supply in accordance to it. During the 1970s and 1980s, the average new forest area was about 2.000 ha. per year and from 1989 has doubled every year until the present. In 1989 the afforested area was over 5.000 ha., in 1990 over 8.000 ha. and it is estimated to 20.000 ha. for 1991. There are other indications that show the growing interest in forestation such as the increase in projects submitted to the Forest Authority (114 projects in 1991 compared to 26 and 41, respectively, in 1989 and 1990). Furthermore some projects are financed through "Debt for Nature Swaps". In 1991, 23 projects were submitted of which 5 were for afforestation. The projected investment is US$ 70.000.000 allowing for the afforestation of 70.000 ha.

These projects, together with the fact that 35.000 ha. were afforested in the first two years of plan implementation, show that it should be possible to reach the goal of 100.000 ha. in five years. The forest law, together with these special mechanisms to reduce external debt and to promote direct investment thus appear relatively successful. The increasing interest in afforestation may be reinforced by the fact that the opportunity cost of land in Uruguay is lower than in the neighbouring countries (the Forest Authority estimated that the cost of forestation of eucalyptus tree was US$ 6.6 per m^3 under the assumption that land opportunity cost is 12%, rent of land included, while it was US$ 7.0 in Argentina and US$7.7 in Brazil).

8 CONCLUDING REMARKS

Like other oil-importing LDCs, Uruguay was badly hit by rising oil prices in the 1970s. The economy has responded by a combination of greater energy efficiency and substitution of oil by fuelwood. The energy-GNP ratio fell 26% from 1973 to 1989 and fuel consumption per capita decreased 9% in the same period. This trend is confirmed by the energy-output growth elasticity which was 0.27 for the economy as a whole for 1965-1989, and 0.43 for the industrial sector. In this sector the demand for energy has turned out to be quite sensitive to price variations

In this chapter we have seen how energy policy initially resulted in substantial increase in consumption of renewable fuels such as fuelwood. While the consumption share of petroleum products decreased from 68% in 1973 to 52.5% in 1989, the consumption of renewable fuels and electricity dramatically increased from 28% to 45%. Although the residential sector is the largest fuel-user, the substitution of fuels took place mainly in manufacturing, where the wood share increased from 12% in 1973 to 44% in 1989 and electricity from 11% to 22%.

The evaluation of the potential wood extraction from eucalyptus forests, under the assumption of sustainable forest management (avoiding deforestation and keeping regeneration capabilities unchanged) showed that the deficit in 1988 was 42% of total supply. This assumes that the exploitation of forests under 10 ha. is not allowed, otherwise the deficit is even worse if the exploitation of natural forests is avoided. This shows that the increasing consumption of wood, could lead to serious problems if there is no appropriate afforestation policy.

The main reason for the increasing fuelwood consumption in the industrial sector was the conversion of boilers. On the basis of a survey of the technical requirements and fuelwood prices in 1988, it was estimated that the potential substitution in manufacturing could be in the range of 12% and 15% of 1988 fuel oil consumption. This would represent about 10% of wood extraction from forests over 10 ha. which would further add to the existing deficit.

Current legislation enacted to remedy this deficit is, however. showing encouraging results in its first four years of implementation. 35.000 ha. have been afforested in the first two years and an additional 70.000 ha. is to be afforested through a debt-for-nature conversion. These results show that the planned 100.000 ha. of new forests in the first five years of the plan was a realistic goal. However, increasing wood consumption can still lead to bottle-necks in the future if the announced, and necessary, protection of natural forest areas is implemented.

Future energy requirements must be met by a combination of increased efficiency, higher price and improved forestry. Forest plantations should be the prime tool since they have the additional advantage of stopping soil erosion while natural forests need to be protected for recreation and biodiversity.

REFERENCES

Antmann, P. and G. Cian. 1989. "Proyecto de una Central Termoeléctrica con Caldera a Leña". *Revista de la Asociación de Ingenieros*, N.1.

Bathia, R. 1987. "Energy Demand Analysis in Developing Countries". *The Energy Journal*, vol. 8, Special LDC Issue.

Direccíon Nacional de Energía. *Estadísticas Anuales*. 1980-1989. Montevideo, Uruguay.

Direccíon Nacional de Energía. 1990. "Resultados Primarios de la Encuesta de Consumo de Energía Util en el Sector Residencial". Montevideo, Uruguay.

Direccíon Nacional de Energía. 1990. "Resultados Primarios de la Encuesta de Consumo de Leña en la Industría". Montevideo, Uruguay.

Fuss, M.A. 1977. "Demand for energy in Canadian manufacturing", *Journal of Econometrics,* vol. 5 no. 1.

Migues, C., M. Ibarburu and J. Montouliu. 1990. "Uso de la Leña como Combustible en la Industria". Fac. de Ingenieria, Universidad de la República, Uruguay.

Tansini, R. 1990. "Energy Demand in Uruguay", *Mimeo,* Dept. of Economics, Uruguay.

CHAPTER 10

Economics and Environment in Mexico

by

Marco Martinez and Thomas Sterner*

Abstract

This chapter starts with a discussion of Mexican environmental problems through history and then relates the current ecological crisis to the economic situation of the country. Special attention is given to Mexico City with its very particular set of environmental problems. The focus is mainly on air pollution from the transport and energy sectors but also on soil erosion, deforestation and several other causes for the poor air and water standards particularly in the capital. Finally recent legislation and other official efforts to remedy the situation are presented and discussed.

*The authors would like to thank Michael Walsh and Jorge Buzaglo for valuable comments.

T. Sterner (ed.), Economic Policies for Sustainable Development, 178–191.

1 INTRODUCTION

Mexico is often characterized as a country of contrasts, and although this may be a passing generalization it is true that this country possesses particularly stark contrasts be they scenic, geographical or cultural. It's true of the economic contrasts between the rich and the poor and there are also "ecological" contrasts: between the splendor of the countryside, the fertility of soil and diversity of nature on the one hand and the deforestation or the environmental squalor in parts of Mexico City on the other.

That environmental degradation and resource depletion are important factors is indicated by the estimates in Tongeren et al (1991) that the environmental adjusted net product is only 87% of conventional defined NDP or 77% of GDP. The (unaccounted) cost of natural resource depletion and environmental degradation would thus be at least 13% of NDP (this is said to be a conservative estimate). Another preliminary estimate of environmental costs in Mexico, Margulis (1992), ranks Mexican environmental problems according to the following order:

*	Diarrheal diseases (due to poor sanitation)	3.6 Billion USD
*	Health effects of air pollution in Mexico City	1.1 Billion USD
*	Excessive use of water due to underpricing	1.2 Billion USD
*	Soil erosion	1.0 Billion USD

Mexico is a country of very widely varying topography ranging from mountains of more than 5 600 meters to the coastal lowlands; from tropical rain forest in the South-East through temperate zones to desert in the North and North-West. At least some parts of the country, such as the central valley, are particularly fertile which is the reason they could support the population concentrations that were a precondition for such important civilizations as the Aztec.

With a little less than a quarter the size of the US, and 80 million inhabitants it is the third largest Latin American country after Brazil and Argentina. Its population density of around 500 per thousand ha is twice that of the US and high by Latin American standards (apart from the Caribbean) - again a reflection of agricultural fertility. Rising food imports, deforestation and massive migration from the countryside to the cities or to the US are, however, all signs that rising population is imposing a demographic stress.

The income level which is above the Latin American average, rose fast during the 1970s but has fallen during the 1980s. The economy is very dependent on primary commodities, in particular oil which accounts for a very large share of exports but also causes enormous ecological problems. Income is unevenly distributed with a fairly large rural population living on subsistence agriculture and heavy unemployment in the large cities. The expansion of relatively wealthy ranchers causes deforestation and pushes the subsistence farmers into marginal lands.

2 HISTORICAL BACKGROUND

2.1 Precolumbian society

Although the recent 500th anniversary of the Spanish "discovery" of America is a rather cruel cause for celebration one should remember that many of the so-called pre-Columbian cultures were not only violent but in some cases presumably ecologically unsound or "unsustainable" to use a perhaps anachronistic concept. According to Kandell (1990), the most likely explanation for the fall of powerful empires and cultures such as the Teotihuacana and the Maya (way before the arrival of the Spaniards) is in fact ecological mismanagement. Presumably the technologies known by these cultures could not support the concentration of population they brought together in order to achieve military (and architectonic!) objectives. The very size of the pyramids, built with slave labour, are witness to a good deal of disrespect for the working conditions of human labour and it is not unreasonable to assume that there may have been a similar disregard for nature. The great famine in 1450-55 which hit the heart of the Aztec empire is said to have been caused by heavy rain and floods that ruined crops (Meyer & Sherman, 1979), but increasing population pressure must surely have been a contributing factor.

Apart from the experience of one or two of these large, centralized cultures, however, there is also ample evidence of ecologically sound practices and of an agriculture that was well adapted to local circumstances. One of the obvious examples is the "Milpa" in which the maize is cultivated jointly with fruit, vegetables and beans. The fruit-trees and vegetables etc. provide soil-cover and other ecological benefits against soil erosion etc. whilst the beans, of course, are a source of fertilizing nitrogen to the soil. At the same time the combination of "tortilla con frijoles" - the basic diet of maize-bread with beans is a very efficient way of securing a fully satisfactory vegetarian protein diet.

2.2 The colonial period

Spanish rule also brought with it a mixed basket: there were some positive attempts at what we today would call "village development", undertaken often by the missionaries who introduced certain small-scale handcraft, petty industry or agricultural technologies that have proved beneficial. On the other hand there can be no doubt that in most areas, the Spanish victory not only meant a human calamity but also the onslaught of many new ecological problems. In the first half-century from 1518 to 1568 the indigenous population is estimated to have been reduced from around 25 million inhabitants to just a tenth: 2.5 million!

Some environmental problems were caused by ignorance. As outsiders the conquerors did not have the same knowledge of local ecology as that symbolized by the Milpa and brought with them production methods that did not always work. In the same way the Spaniards failed to understand the importance of the Aztec dikes that regulated the waters of the lake on which Mexico City stands. They destroyed them during battle and then never replaced them which led to periodic inundations of the whole city from the middle of the sixteenth century and on.

Mining was one important new source of environmental disturbance for a number of reasons. Two of its most serious effects were deforestation around the mines due to the need for fuel and the poisoning of streams and rivers due to the use of mercury in the separation of silver.

At a more general level the Mexican economy became developed in the usual colonial way, with a rich "comprador bourgeoisie" in the capital who lived off the mines and in some cases off large estates. The main thrust of the economy was raw-material production and exports: after silver and other metals came various agricultural products. Spanish economic policy was mercantilistic in the extreme and the sole purpose of the colonies was seen as enriching the "mother-country". The Spanish crown had a right to one fifth (the royal "quinto") of all proceeds from gold, silver, jewels and slaves sold. The colonies were only allowed to trade directly with Spain (not with each other or, God forbid!, with other countries). The Spaniards also kept a monopoly on all types of profitable inputs such as mercury, gunpowder, salt, pulque, tobacco. The colonists were even prohibited from growing vine or olives since this could threaten the export income of the powerful merchants in Sevilla!

Agriculture was redirected from the more sustainable practices of subsistence farming such as the "milpa" to a more conventional extractive production of export crops such as cacao, indigo, vanilla, henequen, wool and meat. Vast tracts were planted with the maguey cactus for the sake of the tiny parasite insects from which cochineal was extracted. Various foreign species such as sugarcane, wheat, citrus and so forth were imported. Forests were cleared not only for mining but also to give way for cattle ranching and for sheep to supply wool to the textile industry. Vast herds of both sheep and cattle destroyed indigenous agriculture in the central valleys of Mexico and Toluca and then roamed the lands particularly of the North. Just as large parts of Spain from the Pyrenees to the Mediterranean had been deforested (see Ramos-Oliveira, 1952) by the demands for meat and textiles, the same process accelerated in Mexico. Enormous areas (in some instances millions of hectares) were appropriated by successful colonists.

2.3 Independence and revolution

After independence (1821) followed a period of strife, both internal and external which lead to the loss of half the country which was incorporated into the US.

Towards the end of the last century there was a certain period of economic revival marked by fairly rapid industrialization under the rule of Porfirio Diaz which however degenerated into a dictatorship feeding yet another round of discontent and revolutionary civil war. During the so-called Porfirato, land was redistributed en masse from the Indian "ejidos" and poor peasants to rich hacendados. By 1910 more than half the best soil in Mexico was in the hands of a few hundred of such hacienda-owners. Again this was coupled to a further expansion of cattle ranching with its negative social and ecological effects. The second decade of this century saw one of the most prolonged and bloody civil wars of the whole continent. Out of a population of 15 million in 1910, it is estimated that up to around 2 million lost their lives. In spite of its high birthrate Mexico only had 14 million inhabitants in 1920!

The revolution, as it is generally called, left many losers but not so many victorious. Not only was the economy ruined but the very institutions of society: The church (already weakened after the reforms of the past century), the business class, the army and the political parties were all discredited or ousted. What remained was a rather instable coalition of "revolutionaries" who fought amongst themselves. Eventually a monolithic party, the PRI (The Party of the Institutionalized Revolution) became the sole party (not de jure but de facto) in Mexican politics. With radical rhetoric, corruption and a certain amount of repression they have continued up till this very day to cling to political power but are now rapidly losing it.

Economic power has furthermore been in very much the same hands as political power: In a highly politicized milieu the most important attribute for a businessman was to be like Carlos Fuentes figure Artemio Cruz, a former (phoney) revolutionary who uses his contacts with "revolutionary" politicians to get the necessary permits, licenses, subsidies and so forth to be able to act as a "front-man" for some American companies.

Officially the economic strategy that followed has been that of "import substitution" but in fact import-substitution has been somewhat caricatured in Mexico since the close contacts between economic and political power have led to exaggerated protection of many Mexican companies who have faced practically no competition and thus have not evolved much in the way of efficiency or competitiveness. As we can observe in the former socialist economies, inefficiency is a powerful cause for environmental degradation. When there is no incentive for companies to modernize technology or economize on natural resources, since they just pass the costs on to society, the environmental consequences will invariably be serious.

In the case of Mexico, waste with natural resources, labour and particularly with energy has been facilitated by their ample supply. This is particularly obvious in the case of petroleum products. Since Mexico is one of the major oil countries in the world, and since policy makers at various levels have treated it as a free good (see also Chapter 17) there has been an enormous waste of oil[1] - to the detriment not only of the economy but also of the air in the larger metropolitan areas. On a slightly smaller scale the same applies to forests, soil and many other natural resources (including man himself!).

Oil was discovered very early in Mexico and the first oil-boom occurred during the revolution: in fact some cynical historians claim the revolution was primarily a fight between rival (British and American) oil companies. While that is clearly exaggerated it is true that the oil companies were more or less forced to collaborate with the local leaders, whoever they were, just to be able to continue operations. Considering that Mexico was the World's second oil producer between 1918 and 1926 this was obviously big business and eventually conflicts over oil took a dramatic turn with the nationalization of all oil 1938 under president Lázaro Cárdenas. With Cárdenas the "revolution" was radicalized, land was redistributed (this time back to the ejidos) and some major foreign industries (oil, railways) were taken over by the state.

---

[1] For a strict neoclassical economist there is no "waste", just adaption to low prices. We, however, choose to use the term "waste" in a normative sense: It would have been better for the environment, for the sustainability of the resource and thus for the economy, if oil had been used more cautiously.

2.4 The petroleum economy

The nationalization of oil was a very radical step that had a dramatic impact on international relations between the oil companies and the various countries in which they operated, indeed for the structure of the whole international oil industry (see Sterner 1991a). In this context, we are however more interested in the way it shaped the Mexican economy. Obviously it led to an immediate embargo and although this was lifted as part of war-time diplomacy (to halt the expansion of German interests) there remained a good deal of animosity between Mexico and the major Western economies.

This, perhaps more than the current ideologies of the time, is one of the most important reasons for Mexico's relative isolation and the choice of the "import-substitution" strategy. Import substitution generally leads to protection and to pricing policies that are out of line with World market prices. In the case of Mexico this was compounded by the availability of cheap oil - which after the "anti-imperialist struggle" for nationalization was seen as every Mexican's birthright. The state oil company PEMEX formed after nationalization has suffered from all the traditional problems of state ownership. It has not only been charged with developing oil fields, refining and selling products of doing so but without charging any undue prices to the Mexican public and without selling the Mexican oil to the imperialists abroad; PEMEX has also been expected to build houses and hospitals for its employees and in fact to provide employment for as many as possible! With the passage of time PEMEX has become more and more infected by corruption and inefficiency. Its pricing policies have been determined not by commercial but by political considerations: Cheap kerosene was seen as favouring the poor, cheap gasoline would facilitate transports and cheap fuel-oil would speed up industrialization. Cheap fuel-oil would also make electricity cheaper and so forth. Instead cheap oil has mainly benefitted the motorists and caused a great deal of waste.

Throughout the post-war period Mexico was relatively prosperous with rapid growth but this culminated in the late 1960s with a fall in growth, balance of payment problems and a political crisis (culminating in the Tlaltelolco massacre just before the 1968 Olympics). The rise in price of oil at this very time appeared to save Mexico from its problems. Instead of restructuring the economy to face the basic problems of competitivity, a second oil-boom was inaugurated.One of the most important factors behind this development was foreign, particularly US, pressure to accept foreign loans to develop the oil sector. The US was anxious to develop a new source of oil that was less vulnerable than the middle East. The policy of not exporting oil was abandoned and instead a crash-program of oil investments was carried out which sent oil reserves soaring from 3 billion barrels in 1975 to almost 40 in 1980. Production of crude rose at an annual rate of around 20% and the oil share of GDP went from 3% in 1975 to 8% in 1982 (and the latter figure is a clear understatement due to the low domestic price of all petroleum products).

The environmental costs of this ruthless rate of expansion were enormous, not only in the southeastern oil-states where rivers, coast, wetlands and other large tracts of land have been devastated by poisonous spills of oil and oil-products and by the disruptive social effects of the influx of thousands of oil-workers into previously indigenous areas (see Toledo, 1983), but particularly in the off-shore sector. This was sadly but clearly illustrated by the Ixtoc blowout in the Gulf of Campeche which went on for almost a year before it could be stopped. The total amount of oil spilled into the sea was an incredible 3.1 million barrels - more than the Torry Canyon and Amoco Cadiz accidents combined and more 15 times the similar North Sea blowout of Bravo 14 that took 8 days to stop in 1977. Several other large spills and accidents have occurred including a natural gas explosion in Mexico City killing over fourteen hundred.

In addition the Mexican economy caught what economists call the "Dutch disease" which briefly implies that if you have one booming sector such as gold-mining or oil which is extremely profitable then this will lead to deindustrialization of the rest of the economy. The booming sector attracts all the best labour, capital and other resources thus pushing up wages and other prices; its exports are so successful that the need to devalue the currency or to stop domestic inflation are hidden. In the case of Mexico around 1980, imports soared, non-oil exports dwindled but few realized the severity of the crisis because oil covered the deficit. Thus non-oil industries and export-oriented agriculture, tourism and other sectors were badly hit by the overvalued currency and soaring inflation while the main beneficiaries were the energy-sector itself and closely related industries such as petrochemicals.

We can draw a straight line from the Dutch disease which disrupted the non-oil sectors of the economy, led to overvaluation of the currency and underestimation of the problems associated with the loans for development of oil-fields through the fall in oil prices and rise in international interest rates up to the debt crisis of the 1980s.

The physical expansion of the oil industry led to numerous local ecological disasters and the "petrolisacíon" of the economy (as it came to be called in Mexico) had serious indirect effects but, as shown in Sterner (1985 & 1989), the main ecological effect may well be that the availability of cheap oil encouraged the adoption of an enormously wasteful technology. When americans started to think of fuel efficiency, most of the old "gasguzzlers" seem to have been sold to Mexico where poor students could afford to drive them because the gasoline was almost free. And which entrepreneur would worry about insulating a steel furnace or cement kiln when there is no economic incentive to economize on energy? As we can see also in Chapter 17, it is a general tendency for the oil countries in the World to subsidize domestic consumption and it invariably leads to considerable waste. In the case of Mexico, the energy intensity of GDP in 1988 was 0.67 kg of oil equivalent per dollar compared to 0.44 for the US, 0.4 for W Germany or 0.26 for Japan.[2]

2.5 Nature conservancy and environmental considerations.

Although the main tendency of economic development has been unsustainable and ecologically unsound, there have been a number of conscious efforts at improving environmental conditions, starting, as usual, with nature conservancy. Already in 1878 president Sebastian Lerdo de Tejada expropriated the forest-zone called the "Desierto de los Leones" because of its proximity to the bustling capital. And in fact it still is a most popular breathing space for the inhabitants of Mexico City in spite

[2] But note that Poland had an energy intensity of 0.98, see Table 1 in Chapter 5.

of the fact that most of its trees are dying. Porfirio Diaz also created an "ecological reserve" in Hidalgo 1898 and under the presidency of Cárdenas (during the 1930s) a total of 40 national parks and 7 ecological reserves were set up.

On the administrative side an authority for the control of hunting, forestry and fishing was set up in 1918 and a National Board governing all the parks and reserves was set up in 1983. Efforts to deal with pollution of air and water are much more recent.

3 DEFORESTATION, POLLUTION AND ENVIRONMENT.

The total area of the country is about 200 MHa (million hectares) with a great variety of ecosystems that can be grouped into four main zones: the arid Northeast; the temperate center; the humid tropical zone in the Southeast and the dry tropical (North). 14% of the area is used for agriculture although only 9% really have adequate soils. More than half the national territory is used for extensive ranching and pasture although only 12% of the area can be considered naturally suitable for such uses (Toledo, 1990). Cattle farming additionally absorbs a third of all agricultural produce and 40% of the output from fisheries. Since the cattle is largely intended for export and does not help raise the protein intake of poor Mexicans, this causes a good deal of resentment.

Together with other causes such as agriculture, urbanization or infrastructure, the extension of ranching is causing the deforestation of at least 500 thousand hectares per year (according to official figures). The contribution of felling for firewood is only a minor factor in this context (see Grupo de Energéticos, 1989). According to Toledo (1990) and Cervantes et al (1984) the annual rate of deforestation is two to three times higher than officially recognized ie 1-1½ MHa. According to these sources forest cover decreased from 56 MHa to 40MHa during the 1970s alone and today they estimate that only between 5-10% of the original forests remain. One of the few tropical rainforest areas left - la Lacandona - in the very South is severely threatened.

Mexico is still very rich in biodiversity with 447 different species of mammals, 1051 bird species. 685 reptile species and 284 amphibians. At least 342 of these species are threatened by extinction of which 169 are unique to Mexico. Similarly 582 species of plants are listed as being in danger of extinction.

Water availability varies by region but contamination is an increasing problem throughout the country. At best, only 15% of municipal and industrial sewage waters are treated. Total discharge of organic material as measured by BOD (Biological oxygen demand) is 2.4 Mtons per year of which 64% comes from industry (principally chemical and sugar-refineries) while municipal wastes account for the remaining 36%.

Inefficient waste treatment has led to extensive pollution of the land, air, rivers and other biotypes of Mexico. The largest lake, Lago de Chapala is seriously threatened by the risk of pollution and of drying up since the rivers that feed into it have been diverted for various purposes and used for sewage disposal by both industries and agriculture. It was once estimated by Humboldt to measure 4 840 sq kms but is today reduced to just 800. Its average depth has gone from 11 to 7 meters.

The second lake in size (Pátzcuaro) has similarly gone from an average depth of 6 meters in 1940 to 2.7 in 1988. In 1981 public resistance stopped plans for a large nuclear research center along the shores of Lake Pátzcuaro.

Total solid wastes are estimated at 52 thousand tons per day from households and 370 thousand from industry. Of the municipal waste only 75% is actually collected which implies that 13 000 tons per day are left to the dogs and rats! Out of the waste that is collected only 16 thousand tons are deposited on controlled dumping sites. In the slums surrounding Mexico City several million residents lack adequate sanitary services. The dust from the remnants of the dried out lake where these people live, alongside the waste-dumps, infects the whole city.

In spite of all its oil and gas Mexico has not been spared from radioactive pollution. Around 1980 when Mexico seemed to be awash in oil-money the government launched an enormously oversized nuclear program which foresaw the building of 20 GW of nuclear capacity before the turn of the century (some 20 to 30 reactors) in spite of the fact that enormous quantities of natural gas were simply being flared to no use at the oil-fields. In fact the plans had to be scrapped when the money dried up and only one plant has been built, Laguna Verde 1 with a capacity of 654 MW which has been a complete scandal in terms of delays, cost-overruns and incidents. In fact it took about 25 years to build so that the design (the somewhat infamous General Electric Mark II) is completely outdated, see further Sterner (1991b). Several leaks have been confirmed and strontium 90 has been found in shrimps, iodine 131 in milk and so forth, see also Martinez (1990). The plant is located in a seismically very unsafe area where there have been at least two serious earthquakes during this century and the dominant winds come from the East carrying any pollution in over the country.

Considering the way other radioactive wastes have been treated in Mexico, the risks of incidents at the Laguna Verde plant are a cause for very serious concern. In 1983 an obsolete piece of radiotherapy equipment containing cobalt 60 was stolen from a hospital, sold to a scrapyard and ended up being melted and thereby incorporated into the production of steel rods. A part of this was used to make 17,000 table supports and innumerable building reinforcement rods that were spread across the country and no-one would have known unless a Mexican lorry with exported rods had not driven past a US nuclear weapons facility and set off the alarms: they thought someone was stealing plutonium and that is how the story unravelled, but most of the rods were never found and are still being used in Mexico.

4 AIR POLLUTION AND URBAN ENVIRONMENT: MEXICO CITY

The environmental problems of Mexico are epitomized by the air quality of the major urban centers and particularly of the capital. Mexico City has the added problem of being at a high altitude, surrounded by mountains and with a dominant wind blowing from the North where industry is located into the city where unfiltered factory smoke mingles with the exhausts from constant traffic congestion. 99% of the old lake on which the City was built is gone (and what remains is far from clean...). 75% of the forest cover is gone and the erosion by wind of the remaining sea-bed areas is a major source of dust in the capital.

Mexico City has about a quarter of the country's population but over 40% of the "economically active population", 40% of industrial investments and 40% of the cars. The second two cities, Guadalajara and Monterrey have about 3 million inhabitants each and a total of one million vehicles. In the capital, however, a total of over 4 million vehicles, according to official figures contribute an estimated 80% to air pollution. Most of these are old cars, practically all lack catalytic converters and most of them lack even elementary maintenance. In general, carburetors are not even adjusted for the altitude which immediately condemns the car to unnecessarily high fuel consumption and emissions.

Mexico City has an excellent French metro which runs silently, frequently and in general reliably, but due to the prodigious growth of the City, it now only serves its center whilst very large parts are dependent on busses to even get to the end-stations. The busses are far from being silent, reliable or ecologically acceptable since they run on diesel and their notorious black clouds of exhaust indicate that they lack the most elementary exhaust controls.

Given its high altitude and the predominance of motor vehicles in air pollution, it is not surprising that some of the most severe problems concern ozone and NO_x. Official Ozone norms were exceeded on average 254 days a year 1987-89 while ozone norms are exceeded almost constantly (95% of days during the same period). For SO_x "only" 35 days. The lead content of gasoline has been reduced and is being further reduced now but still lead concentrations exceeded norms during the first and third quarters of 1989.

5 RECENT ENVIRONMENTAL POLICY INSTRUMENTS

Environmental threats and degradation in Mexico have become very serious and this has led to considerable debate, see for instance Leff (1990). Quite a number of environmental pressure groups and NGOs have been formed and both public and scientific opinion has obliged the government to take a number of policy measures. This activity goes back to the days of the Stockholm Conference, in preparation for which the Mexican authorities prepared a White paper on environmental issues which later was the basis for new legislation in march 1971. In 1983 a ministry for urban development and environment (SEDUE) was set up and due to the general lack of knowledge it explicitly set out to collaborate with a number of earlier independent environmental NGOs.

In 1987 a new General Environmental Act was passed and the SEDUE set itself a program of "One Hundred Necessary Actions". Many of these were ambitious but also in general vague and/or impracticable such as (No 18) "...moving people so as to minimize transport..." or (no 71): "Protecting forests and encouraging reforestation". Others were in principle excellent measures such as No 2 which ordered a compulsory program for vehicle inspection and maintenance but they have then failed to be implemented. This depends partly on the change of government in 1988 which (although it is always the same party) implies a complete reshuffle of all posts and a general change of plans. The new government, under Salinas has put forward a "National Action Plan for the Environment 1990-94" which does contain a number of concrete policy measures, see SEDUE (1989 & 1990).

For Mexico City, its goal was to reduce air pollution drastically in four years at a total cost of 3.3 billion US$. Part of this is to be financed by PEMEX and part by loans from the US, the World Bank and Japan. The goals were operationalized by Ortiz Monasterio (1991) as implying an average of 37.5% reduction in all emissions or more specifically as shown in Table 1.

Table 1 Planned reductions for various pollutants

NO_x	- 5%	HC	- 26%
SO_x	- 79%	PST	- 55%
CO	- 36%	Pb	- 40%

One of the more drastic programs initiated by the new government is the "Day without the Car" in Mexico City which implies that each car is banned one day a week (basically registration numbers ending 0 or 1 are banned Mondays, 2/3 Tuesdays or something equivalent). Initially this program led to a noticeable reduction in traffic but the effect has quickly dissipated as certain families have compensated themselves by buying an additional car (or sometimes just an additional number plate). The number of cars sold has soared, since the program started, from 80 000 new cars a year in 1989 to 275 000 in 1991 and although rising income is part of the explanation it would seem likely that the "day without a car" is a major factor. Regression estimates by Eskeland (1991) do not find any significant effect for the program. As a matter of fact the number of cars in Mexico City increased considerably as a result of the "day without a car" program. There was a big immediate increase of "new" cars - but, in fact, most of them were old cars brought in from other places. However, just as the program did raise considerable protests it also heightened consciousness about the problems of traffic induced pollution and for a number of motorists it implied their first contact with public transport. For some this proved that public transport is actually a viable alternative. In many cases the effect was the opposite, but thereby the deficiencies of the public transport system came to be the focus of greater public attention and this might conceivably be one of the main long-run advantages of this program.

New standards for vehicle emissions (applicable to new cars from 1991) are very stringent, almost the same as new US requirements (see Chapter 14). They will require the use of catalytic converters and PEMEX has therefore been obliged to introduce unleaded gasoline called "Magna Sin". Also the conventional leaded gasoline (Nova Plus) has had its lead content cut in half (from 1 to 0.5 g/l). The oxygenating agent MTBE has also been added (5%); this provides an octane increase and is particularly valuable for reducing emissions of volatile organic compounds and carbon monoxide at the high altitude of Mexico City. Unfortunately the unleaded gasoline is priced considerably above the ordinary leaded Nova and although this price differential was recently reduced somewhat (from 40 to around 15%) there is still a strong and perverse incentive to use leaded gasoline. This is unfortunate in itself and furthermore implies a considerable risk that many new catalytic converters may be ruined by "lead poisoning" (which eliminates their catalytic effect).

Public transport is also being improved in a number of ways: extension of the metro; 3500 municipal busses ("Ruta 100") are having their engines replaced to meet

California 1989 standards, taxis older than 1985 will have to be replaced by new models meeting the latest emission standards. Taxis and minicabs also face a series of other more detailed regulations. Parking is being restricted and parking fees increased. Finally a new, and this time more seriously intended, inspection and maintenance program for all vehicles is being built up. Experience to date of getting this type of system to work in Mexico is, however, not encouraging.

For industry and other sectors a number of additional measures are foreseen: 250 industrial plants were closed on April 3 1991 and, at the end of May, allowed to reopen only if satisfactory filtering equipment had been installed (or, in some cases, if the cost of such equipment was deposited). The large and severely obsolete refinery Atzcapotzalco was closed while other refineries in Tula, Cadereyta, Salamanca, Ciudad Madero and Minatitlán were upgraded to produce the new gasolines and to reduce sulphur from diesel and fuel oil.

Industry is also being required to change from fuel oil to diesel or natural gas and to install anti-pollution equipment in general. Since this will not suffice, further investment in polluting industries (or heavy water-consumers) will be stopped and a number of heavy industries will be relocated.

Funds will also be supplied for reforestation (the official goal is one million trees in the "Valley of Mexico" - the area surrounding the capital) and for the clean up of environmentally affected areas. An area of 727 Ha in the Ajusco has been expropriated to guarantee water supplies to the capital.

As for more general environmental issues and nature conservancy, the government has prohibited the capture of the marine tortoises and created a nature reserve for the white doves. It has also prohibited the irrigation of vegetables and fruit with untreated sewage water (!) and imposed a system of charges for sewage water depending on the level of contamination. The latter, together with some moderate taxation of gasoline appears to be the very first step towards using any form of economic policy instruments (except subsidies) for environmental purposes.

REFERENCES

Cervantes, J., M. Martinez, O. Masera and F. Schutz, 1984. "End Use Oriented Energy Strategies for Mexico", presented at the Global Workshop on End-Use Oriented Energy Strategies, Sao Paulo, Brasil.

Eskeland, G.S. 1993. "A Presumptive Pigouvian Tax on Gasoline: Analysis of an Air Pollution Control Program for Mexico City". Policy Research Working Papers, The World Bank WPS 1076.

Grupo de Energética (Facultad de Ciencias, UNAM). 1989. Energy Use Patterns and Social Differences: A Mexican Village Case Study. Manuscript Report 215, International Development Research Centre, Canada.

Kandell, J. 1990. La Capital: La historia de la Ciudad de Mexico, Javier Vergara, ed., Mexico.

Leff, E. ed. 1990. Medio Ambiente y Desarrollo en Mexico, Centro de Investigaciones Interdisciplinarías en Humanidades, UNAM, ed. Porrúa, Mexico.

Margulis, S. 1992 "Back-of-the-Envelope Estimates of Environmental Damage Costs in Mexico", World Bank, Working papers (Agr. Operations, Country Dept II) WPS 824, January.

Martinez, M. 1990. *No a Laguna Verde*, edición de la Campana Contra Laguna Verde Nuclear, Mexico.

Meyer, M.C. and W.L. Sherman. 1979. The Course of Mexican History, Oxford University Press, New York

Ortiz Monasterio, F.P. 1991. Contaminación en la Ciudad de Mexico, ed. Milenio, Mexico.

Ramos-Oliveira, A. (1952). Historía de España, ed. Compaña General de Ediciones, Mexico.

SEDUE. 1987. LE87 (Ley General del Equilibrio Ecológico y la Protección al Ambiente), Secretaría de Desarrollo Urbano y Ecología, Mexico.

SEDUE. 1990. Programa Nacional para la Protección al Medio Ambiente 1990-94, Secretaria de Desarrollo Urbano y Ecología, Mexico.

Sterner, T. 1985. "Structural change and Technology Choice", *Energy Economics*, April.

Sterner, T. 1989. "Factor Demand and Substitution in a Developing Country: Energy use in Mexican Manufacturing", *Scandinavian Journal of Economics,* vol 91 no 4, Nov.

Sterner, T. 1991a. "The Development of Nuclear Power and Sustainability in Latin America", in *The Other Side of Paradise: Sustainable Development and Latin America,* eds. D.Goodman and M. Redclift, Manchester University Press, May.

Sterner, T. 1991b. "The Development of State Oil Companies in L America: From Conflict to Collaboration", *The Journal of Energy and Development,* vol 15 no 1.

Toledo, V.M. 1983. *Como Destruir el Paraiso: El Desastre Ecologico del Sureste,* Centro de Ecodesarrollo, Ediciones Oceano, Mexico D F.

Toledo, V.M. 1990. "El proceso de Ganaderización y la destrucción biológica y ecológica de Mexico", in Leff.

Tongeren J., S. Schweinfest, E. Lutz, M. Gomez Luna and F. Guillen Martin, "Integrated Environmental and Economic Accounting: A Case Study for Mexico", The World Bank, Environment Working Paper no. 50.

CHAPTER 11

Sustainability, Deforestation and Policy Implications for Africa

by

Gunnar Köhlin*

Abstract

A series of adverse economic and social trends for Africa are paralleled by a number of environmentally related problems. Both local problems such as erosion, reduced supplies of food, fodder and fuel, and global concerns regarding the greenhouse effect, imply that deforestation is a key variable in the present process. The causes behind deforestation are therefore analyzed as well as a number of policies to improve the situation. It is argued that the fundamental challenge is to encourage the adoption of policies that create a favourable incentive structure for investments in soil conservation, agro-forestry and reforestation. Such policies would include secure user-rights, reasonable taxation and institutions that secure properly functioning markets.

* The author is indebted to Tom Alberts, Alemu Mekonnen, Steve Mugerwa, Robert Nygård and Thomas Sterner for their valuable comments on earlier drafts.

T. Sterner (ed.), Economic Policies for Sustainable Development, 192–211.

1 INTRODUCTION

The catchword "sustainable development" implies in a third World context, some material improvements in the present without compromising the ability of future generations to meet their own needs. Unfortunately, many African countries have lately experienced the opposite; a deterioration in living standards (UNDP, 1990), combined with a degradation of the environment.

In this chapter we will show that a series of adverse economic and social trends for Africa are paralleled by a number of environmentally related problems. Both local problems such as erosion, reduced supplies of food, fodder and fuel, and global concerns regarding the greenhouse effect, imply that deforestation is a key variable in the present process. We therefore will take a closer look at the causes behind deforestation and give special attention to policy implications.

Avoiding deforestation would lead to both global benefits, in terms of reduced CO_2 emissions and more importantly, national and local benefits in terms of climate stability, watershed protection and increased long-term productivity of the land. However, this can hardly be achieved only through the dissemination of technical solutions. We argue that the fundamental challenge is to encourage the adoption of policies that create a favourable incentive structure for investments in soil conservation, agro-forestry and reforestation. This exemplifies a process where an improved and more sustainable use of the environment also implies increased economic productivity, thus dodging any possible contradiction between sustainability and development. Since poor people are most vulnerable to environmental degradation such policies should also have favourable distributional effects.

2 UNSUSTAINABLE TRENDS FOR AFRICA

Although real GDP increased by an annual average of 2.1% in sub-Saharan Africa from 1981 through 1990, increase in population made the GNP/capita decrease by 4.4% per year (World Bank, 1991b). The debt crisis has many countries in a firm grip and the debt ratio (the ratio of total outstanding external debt to exports of goods and non-factor services) for Africa has increased from 85 to 331% since 1980. Despite debt rescheduling the debt service ratio (the ratio of actual interest and amortization payments on external debt to exports of goods and non-factor services) was still 27% in 1987. During the 1980's the terms of trade have deteriorated drastically by 25% which makes the countries no better off, despite the fact that they have increased exports by 16% and decreased imports by 17% (Stymne, 1991).

The balance of payments problems have had implications for other sectors, too. Gross domestic investment as a percentage of GDP has decreased from 19.9% in 1980 to 15.5% in 1990. The lowest rate of capital formation, 10.8% of GDP, was reached in 1984. In per capita terms the decrease is even greater - from an average of USD 90 in 1980 to USD 50 in 1990. Such averages of course disguise even more dramatic reductions. Côte d'Ivoire, for instance, saw its per capita gross domestic investments plummet from USD 460 in 1980 to a mere USD 50 in 1990. One also notes that many Sahelian countries have a below average domestic investment (World

Bank, 1991b, All figures expressed in 1987 USD). Low-income economies have fared especially badly. Their gross domestic investment decreased by an average of 9.9% per year between 1980 and 1987 (World Bank, 1989b).

A trend that should give rise to considerable concern can be found in food production. Despite a 16% increase from 1980 to 1988, population growth was faster so that per capita food production decreased by 5% in the same period. This is, unfortunately, a trend that can be traced back to the 1960's and which is in contrast with other developing regions (WRI, 1990).

Even in education, where such great advances were made in previous decades, the trend turned against sub-Saharan Africa in the 1980's. While 79% of the eligible age group was enrolled in primary education in 1980, this had decreased to 73% in 1986.

These economic and social trends are paralleled by a series of environmental and resource problems. When social and economic infrastructure is being run down, the same applies to natural resources. Rapid population growth in combination with urbanization leads to overutilization and degradation of resources such as land, fresh water, biomass etc. We will exemplify this later with the deforestation around cities due to fuelwood shortage.

Social and environmental trends are often very closely related. Overgrazing or extensive agricultural practices reduce vegetative cover, thus leading to less percolation of rain-water to recharge the ground water and instead contributing to reduced productivity through soil erosion.

The greatest threat to large parts of Africa, from the point of view of sustainability, is the alarming pace of this erosion. There are many factors affecting the rate of soil erosion, such as topography, type of soil, etc. The most important factor, however, is the degree and kind of vegetative cover (Repetto, 1988). This points at the problem of excessive rates of deforestation experienced by many countries and is underlined by the high rates of erosion reported from countries such as Ethiopia, Lesotho and Madagascar. These countries have also experienced serious deforestation (WRI, 1988).

3 ENERGY USE AND CO_2 EMISSIONS

Energy production and consumption is often closely related to environmental issues both locally and globally. On the global scale the greenhouse effect is often mentioned. In this context Africa's energy consumption is marginal today. With more than 12% of the world's population, Africa only consumes about 2.6% of the world's commercial energy. This gives the African continent the lowest per capita consumption of commercial energy, half that of Asia and less than 5% of the per capita consumption of the United States (WRI, 1990). Still, this includes the consumption of South Africa Customs Union[1] and Northern Africa which made up 43% and 36%, respectively, of a total consumption of 7,300 petajoules in 1987. Another clear indication of the skewed distribution of commercial energy in Africa

[1] South Africa Customs Union consists of South Africa, Botswana, Lesotho, Swaziland, and Namibia (WRI, 1990).

is the consumption of oil. Four oil producing countries[2] use up about half of Africa's oil consumption while South Africa, the next six[3] and the rest share the other half equally (Sterner, 1992). If we also take into consideration the unequal distribution of energy consumption between sectors and social groups it is evident that while some parts have a high consumption of commercial fuels the majority of the continent has an extremely low consumption. In a comparison with how other continents have developed, it is likely that many of the countries that now have a very low consumption of commercial energy would face a fast increase if the present foreign exchange constraint were eased and growth rekindled. However, there should also be a substantial potential for energy conservation in the oil producing countries.

With increasing consumption in the large regions in Africa that hardly consume any commercial fuels today, such conservation could be both cost effective and important when attempts are made to reduce global greenhouse gas emissions. In 1987, Africa only contributed 155 million tons, or 2.7% of world carbon emissions from commercial fuels. With a population growth of 3% and a doubling of average per capita commercial energy use this would increase to over 500 million tons in 2005. This would equal 14% of OECD emissions (Leach, 1990a).

Commercial energy is only part of the energy sector in Africa. The share of biomass in total primary energy consumption has been estimated to 60 - 95% in sub-Saharan Africa. Most of these fuels are consumed by households, especially in rural areas where they typically account for 90% or more of total energy use (Leach, 1990b). A number of biomass consumption surveys indicate that annual per capita consumption amounts to between 1 and 2 m^3 of wood in rural sub-Saharan Africa. For the whole of Africa this would mean a biomass consumption in the range of 160 - 240 million tons of oil equivalent or 80 - 120% of Africa's commercial energy consumption (Leach, 1990a).

The use of biomass as energy is not a major cause of CO_2 emissions. Much of the biomass that is used regenerates on a sustainable basis, while some come from deforestation for other reasons, notably clearing for agriculture. The net addition to CO_2 emissions comes from unsustainable harvesting of wood, especially around urban centers. However, there are two implications of the current patterns of use. First, that the burning of dung and crop residues can decrease fertility and carbon content of the soil, and secondly, that even if deforestation was to be halted for other reasons, fuelwood needs would still need to be met, implying a hidden threat for net deforestation due to energy needs.

Net deforestation and other land use changes are by far the greatest factors behind atmospheric CO_2 emissions from Africa. In 1980, biotic emissions from Africa were around 700 million tons of carbon (Leach, 1990a), i.e. more than four times the carbon emissions from fossil fuels.

This is one reason for our focus on the process of deforestation. This focus implies that we deal with global sustainability, in terms of reducing the greenhouse effect, as well as an environmental factor of production that is used and abused in the pursuit of economic development both at local and national levels .

---

[2] Egypt, Nigeria, Algeria and Libya.

[3] Morocco, Tunisia, Angola, Côte d'Ivoire, Cameroon and Zaire.

4 CAUSES BEHIND DEFORESTATION

Africa has about 700 million ha of forests and woodlands. Almost 70% of these are open forests. During the 1980's the average annual deforestation rate was 0.7% or 5 million ha (WRI, 1992). The most rapid deforestation is taking place in Côte d'Ivoire which has lost 75% of its forest cover since 1960 (Repetto, 1990) and is still experiencing a closed forest deforestation rate of 6.5% per year (WRI, 1990). This change in land use could of course be consistent with a sustainable strategy if the alternative use is enduring and the returns to society higher. However, there are a number of factors that complicate the choice of optimal land use and that tend to bias the decision towards other uses than forestry, even when the latter would have been more beneficial.

The first reason relates to the fact that a forest is a multi-purpose resource. Forests are a source of a multitude of amenities at local, regional and global levels. For the global community, deforestation, especially of the moist tropical forests, means a reduction of the genetic pool, carbon fixing capacity, climate regulation and aesthetic values. At the regional or national levels deforestation can seriously affect the micro-climate and the protection of watersheds. This has implications at the local level in the form of flooding or drought, less groundwater and increased erosion. In addition, the local population may experience shortages of wood for fuel and buildings, as well as decreased availability of fodder, fruit, game, medicinal herbs etc.

Many of these benefits are difficult to measure and to aggregate into one flow of benefits over time. They are also dispersed in time and space. As long as there is a lack of institutions for all the people affected, now and in the future, to express their willingness to pay for tropical forests there will be a bias towards other uses where the benefits are captured privately instead of in terms of positive externalities.

The second bias against keeping land under forests is that forests often are *de facto* open access although they are often *de jure* state lands. State ownership with insufficient control can lead to overuse particularly if combined with increased population pressure. It is also associated with rent-seeking behaviour and myopic interests. The result is underinvestment and overutilization of forest areas.

A third reason is the long rotation period for harvesting timber from the forests. In societies with political unrest, insecure property rights or simply a high preference for present consumption, other land uses will often be preferred to forestry. The society then needs to correct for the difference between private and social rate of discount either through legislation, incentives or own management of forest resources.

Table 1 shows the extent and cause of deforestation in selected African countries. It highlights the large disparity in extent of and reasons for deforestation between countries. Worth noting is the combination of logging and shifting cultivation in many of the heavily deforested countries with tropical forest. The expansion of both shifting cultivation and permanent crops is much facilitated both by the infrastructure created for logging and the clearing that is the result of logging. Easier access in combination with high population pressure, as in Nigeria and Ghana, leads to rapid deforestation. In both countries this expansion has been accelerated even

Table 1 Extent and causes of deforestation in selected African countries

Region/country	Closed forest[c]/ total area	Deforest'n percent per year	Cause of deforest'n	Comments
West Africa				Heavy logging, fast deforestation
Côte d'Ivoire	14	6.5	A,L	Highest deforestation rate
Ghana	7	1.3	P,A,L	
Guinea	8	1.8		
Liberia	21	2.3	A,L	Very little remaining rainforest
Nigeria	7	5.0	P,L	Most areas disrupted
Sierra Leone	10	0.8	P,L	Very few undisturbed areas
Central Africa				Largely undamaged tropical forests
Cameroon[b]	36	0.1		
Central African Republic[b]	6	0.1	A	Southern forest largely untouched
Congo[b]	62	0.1	L	Except for South, largely untouched
Equatorial Guinea	46	0.2	A	Relatively untouched
Gabon[b]	76	0.1		
Zaire[b]	44	0.2	A,L	10% of world total of raw forest, large areas untouched
Tropical Southern Africa				Only 4% of forests are closed
Angola	2	1.5	P	Continued deforestation in the coastal belt has led to ecological crisis
Mozambique	1	1.1	P	Deforestation esp. around urban areas
Tanzania	2	0.7	P	
Zambia	4	1.3		
West Sahelian Africa				Less than 6% of forests are closed
Burkina Faso	1	1.1		
Guinea-Bissau	23	2.6		
Niger	0	2.5		
East Sahelian Africa				About 10% of forest are closed
Ethiopia	4	0.2	P,A	Only remnants of natural forests
Kenya	2	1.7		Biomass problem in arid arable areas
Somalia	2	0.2		
Sudan	0	0.6		
Uganda	4	1.3		
Insular Africa (Madagascar)[a]	20	1.2	A	Fragments of rainforests remain
Africa (40)[a]	27	0.8		

Principal causes of deforestation: P, population pressure, fuelwood scarcity; A, population pressure, shifting cultivation; L, logging.

Sources: [a] FAO, "Second Interim Report on the State of Tropical Forests", paper presented at the 10th World Forestry Congress, Paris, September 1991. Forest area in 1990, deforestation 1981-90.

[b] Schmidt, "Sustainable Management of Tropical Moist Forests" quoted in Burgess (1991). The rest of the data from WRI (1992) mostly based on FAO, Interim Report on the state of Forest Resources in Developing Countries, 1988. Comments from White, 1983 in Repetto and Gillis, 1988; O'Keefe et.al., 1989.

[c] Closed forest is land where trees cover a high proportion of the ground and where grass does not form a continuous layer on the forest floor (FAO, as above).

further by economic policies and political instability that have led to drastic reductions in the standard of living. In Côte d'Ivoire the combination of an active policy to support timber exports and rapid population growth, due to fertility rates of 6.6% and high rates of immigration from the poorer neighbors, have led to the highest deforestation rate of closed forests. Indeed, it has been estimated that "for each five cubic meters of logs harvested in the Ivory Coast, 1 hectare of forests disappears at the hands of the follow-on cultivators" (Myers, 1983).

In the South and in the Sahelian areas closed forests only make up a small fraction of the total forests, that mostly consist of open forests or savannah. The thinning of these forests is hard to monitor but can be disastrous in the long-term for eco-systems prone to desertification. The reasons for deforestation in these areas are more linked to overgrazing, extensive agriculture and fuelwood needs, especially around cities.

Let us now look closer at the three alleged major direct causes of deforestation: (1) clearing of land for agriculture, (2) logging for commercial sale and (3) the use of biomass as a source of energy both for domestic and commercial uses.

4.1 Clearing of land for agriculture

According to IFPRI (1989), 90% of all tropical forest depletion is caused by agricultural expansion. The World Bank (1991a) attributes 60% of the reduction of tropical moist forest to agricultural settlement.[4]

There has been a secular trend of conversion of forests to agricultural land in all developing regions, as can be seen in Table 2. In tropical Africa this process has been pronounced with large changes in both absolute and relative numbers. The forests and woodlands of tropical Africa have decreased by about 20% or 260 million cultivated ha since 1850. During the same period the area with crops has increased by four times. Worth noting is also that grasslands and pasture have increased at the expense of forests and woodlands in Africa, a process otherwise mostly attributed to Latin America. In more recent times, 1965 - 1987, this conversion has stopped and has in some countries been reversed. Still, for the same period 30 out of 45 African countries experienced decreasing forest areas and increasing agricultural areas (World Bank, 1989b).

A change in land use from forestry to agriculture can be an optimal strategy in places suitable for agriculture. However, in many areas agriculture is unsustainable and leads to land degradation. The crucial factor is the quality of the land. With a total land area of more than 3 000 million hectares, Africa would seem to be well endowed with agricultural lands to feed its 650 million people. This is, however, complicated by a number of physical and chemical soil constraints, limiting the area without such constraints to less than 15% of the total, or 440 million ha. Of these 15%, almost 85% are in arid areas, which leaves us with less than 70 million ha of land suitable for agriculture. Despite these constraints 185 million ha are used as cropland (WRI, 1990). This means that much marginal land is used for this purpose. When steep slopes are used, massive soil erosion is often the result.

---

[4] These are global figures but they are reported to be relevant for densely populated countries in West and Central Africa.

Table 2 Land use for selected regions, 1850-1980

Region	Forests and woodlands			Grasslands and pasture			Croplands		
Area (million hectares)	Area 1850	Area 1980	% change	Area 1850	Area 1980	% change	Area 1850	Area 1980	% change
Tropical Africa	1,336	1,074	- 20	1,061	1,158	9	57	222	228
North Africa and Middle East	34	14	- 60	1,119	1,060	- 5	27	107	294
Latin America	1,420	1,151	- 19	621	767	23	18	142	677
China	96	58	- 39	799	778	- 3	75	134	79
South Asia	317	180	- 43	189	187	- 1	71	210	196
Southeast Asia	252	235	- 7	123	92	- 25	7	55	670
Rest of the World	2,465	2,296	- 7	2,437	2,258	- 7	282	631	124
Total	5,919	5,007	- 15	6,350	6,299	- 1	538	1501	179

Source: Adapted from Repetto and Gillis, 1988.

Policy failures

Although limited appropriate soils and erratic precipitation is a constraint to productive agriculture, the situation could have been much better if corrective policies had been implemented. Instead mistaken politics include inappropriate tenure regimes and misdirected market interventions.

The effect of a specific tenure regime on land use is an important but often complicated question. There is no single system that is appropriate for all uses and cultures. From a forestry-policy point of view it is useful to analyze the incentives for deforestation, reforestation and soil conservation that result from a specific tenure system.

The establishment of an informal or formal tenure right is often connected with the clearing of forests (Southgate et al., 1990). When incentives and subsidies are linked to settlement programs this has the potential for inducing very uneconomic behavior. Well-documented examples of this aspect can be found in Binswanger (1989), and Mahar (1988).

Inequality in land distribution is forcing the landless to encroach on forest lands. According to Myers, landless peasants clear three-fifths of the rain forests lost annually (Brough, 1991). The reasons for the skewed land distribution range from the colonial heritage to the establishment of large state farms and market forces in instances of extremely uneven income distribution.

Ill-defined or badly-enforced tenure rights, leading to open access of common land, is a "classical" reason for sub-optimal behavior. However, in the rebuttals of Hardin's "The Tragedy of the Commons" it has been emphasized that this was probably less common than generally believed since many traditional, communal and informal systems for the allocation of user rights did provide appropriate incentives for the long-term economy of the resources. Unfortunately, such traditional systems, guiding common resources, are seen to break down in the face of population pressure, market integration, technological change, migration and the weakening of local authorities (Lawry, 1990).

With political instability ravaging many developing countries, people are sometimes left with a mixture of an old system, that has been largely disabled, while the new system is not yet fully functional, or inappropriate. Local action is stifled by limited economic incentives for individual users' participation and eroded legitimacy of traditional authorities. Direct state management, on the other hand, has rarely worked well either, due to reasons such as lack of information on resource conditions and use practices, capricious and arbitrary enforcement of rules and a state authority too weak to fill the void of traditional rules (Lawry, 1990).

In cases where user rights are insecure, we can hardly expect investment to raise the output of the land or to plant trees. In cost-benefit terms the loss of title to a specific piece of land means that the flow of benefits from an investment in conservation is terminated at the time of the loss. If such an event is likely to happen, then the expected value of the investment is, of course, reduced. This intuitive cost-benefit analysis leads peasants to invest less in tree-planting and soil-conservation at times when land holdings are insecure. Instead extensive land use and further expansion of the agricultural frontier follows.

Ethiopia, during the eighties, was an extreme example of insecurity in land use rights. The fact that the Marxist state was the official owner of all land was, however, not the key issue. Instead it was the implementation of a series of policies that made the incentives for investment in soil conservation, agro-forestry and tree-plantation perverse. Local "Soviets" or peasant associations were formed. They became the focus of many allegedly socialistic reforms. First of all they were in charge of the allocation of land to the peasants. Peasants could subsequently be moved from one plot belonging to the village to another plot. This authority was not only used and abused on the local political arena. It was also instrumental in carrying out a range of broader policy goals such as resettlement, cooperativization, and villagization programs. The most drastic of the three was the resettlement program. During the 1984 - 1986 drought, 600,000 people were moved from the central highland (Wollo, Shoa, Tigray) to the South-west (Wollega, Illubabor, Gojjam, Kaffa) See Karlsson, (1987). In the case of Wollo, this meant that almost ten percent of the population was moved (Wilkens, 1986). Some of these managed to return to their old homes, only to find their land redistributed to others or incorporated in producers' cooperatives.

The establishment of producers' cooperatives was heavily subsidized by the government. The best land was assigned for cooperative production. If the farmers, who previously had used the land, did not want to join the cooperative their land was expropriated and they were often compensated with marginal land.

The villagization program meant that hundreds of households were moved, often from far away, to a single rectangular area. The only piece of land that was large and flat enough for such a village was usually prime farming land, which was then expropriated for the purpose.

In combination with massive drafts to the civil war these programs created such distortions in the communities and such insecurity in the user-right to a specific plot, that soil-conservation, based on self-interest, became very difficult to propagate. This is very serious, considering the fact that large parts of the Ethiopian highlands are denuded and hence prone to erosion. In the mid-1980's the FAO initiated Ethiopian Highlands Reclamation Study made detailed estimates of erosion on different soils and resulting costs. It found that the average soil loss for the highlands was 0.3% of 1985 soil depth and that it inflicted an annual yield decline of 2.2% on crops and 0.6% on grass (SIDA, 1987).

The agricultural sector is often given a lower priority than urban sectors such as industry and public administration. This can be seen in pricing and marketing policies that subsidize urban consumption and tax agricultural exports. The situation for the Sahelo-Sudanian region is described by Southgate et al. (1990):

> "The region's governments maintain low food prices for the benefit of urban consumers and ignore marketing bottlenecks responsible for price instability, generally, and the collapse of farm-gate prices at harvest time, specifically. In addition, agricultural research and extension are not strong. Incentives to adopt high-yield, sustainable crop production systems, then, are weak. Farmers opt instead for extensive production, generally on fragile lands."

Unfortunately, this description is also valid for many other regions in Africa. Price controls on agricultural products have been commonplace and the political influence of urban population strong (Harvey, 1988). Although agriculture still contributes about 35% of GDP in sub-Saharan Africa, and in some countries more than 70%, this is seldom reflected in the proportion of government expenditures going to this sector. All factors that make agriculture more extensive also tend to aggravate deforestation due to the expansion of agricultural land.

Structural adjustment programs tend to strengthen the rural sector by liberalizing the economy from these biases. On the other hand, if the stabilization part of the program implies drastic reductions in employment and income in urban areas, then the urban sector cannot ease the pressure from a growing population in rural areas. It can even lead to migration from the cities increasing the pressure on the countryside (Reed, 1992). This effect depends, however, greatly on the absorptive capacity of the informal sector, thus compensating for the decreased output from the formal sectors (Cornia, Hoeven and Mkandawire, 1992).

4.2 Logging

The tropical forests of Africa have been the object of commercial extraction of hardwood for centuries. At the beginning of the sixties one-third of world tropical timber exports originated from West Africa. By the mid-eighties this had shrunk to less than a sixth because of the expansion in Southeast Asia. The highest volumes, between seven and eight million cubic meters per annum, were reached in the seventies. The main exporters have been Côte d'Ivoire, Ghana, Liberia and Gabon (Repetto and Gillis, 1988).

The viability of tropical logging depends on how it is done, the silvicultural practices applied and the following land use. Whether logging of tropical natural forests could be sustainable is debated.[5] A common alternative in West Africa is to

[5] At the centre of the controversy is the statement by Poore et al. (1990) that tropical moist forests are managed sustainably only on one fifth of one percent of their extent.

establish hardwood plantations, especially teak. Still, logging is often a venue for expansion of agriculture. This could be a rational strategy if its discounted value is greater than the discounted flow from a retained forest. To find out if this is the case, one would need to establish how much of the revenues remain in the country, how these are invested and if the quality of the land is such that grazing and agriculture are profitable in the long-term.

Unfortunately, the policies that have led to deforestation in West Africa, directly or indirectly induced by logging, have not been based on a thorough analysis of long-term costs and benefits of logging. Instead a series of policy failures can be identified. They range from centralized property rights, limited capture of rents and short concession terms to non-forest policies.

• ***Property rights*** are usually highly centralized to the government. This limits the possibilities for traditional local groups to hold on to communal practices for managing the commons. It also alienates the affected groups from the decision of the best trade-off between benefits from keeping the forest intact and those from having it exploited. The impact of centralized property rights is often aggravated by limited government resources to control the areas.

• ***Concession terms*** of longer duration are generally thought to be more conducive to good forest management practices. The five-year contracts granted in Côte d'Ivoire obviously do not give any incentive to maintain the forest. However, in Ghana, where concessions before independence were granted for 50 or up to 99 years, there is little evidence that this has led the concessionaires to maintain forests. Long-term contracts must therefore be supplemented by other measures, such as silvicultural treatment, royalties that reduce high-grading, penalties for noncompliance with felling rules, etc (Repetto and Gillis, 1988).

• ***Rents*** accruing to the government from the felling and the export of tropical timber have differed between countries and over the years but have generally been lower than those in, e.g. Malaysia. Liberia and Gabon have fared especially badly, leaving loggers with double the profit from certain species compared with Côte d'Ivoire. Even so, Côte d'Ivoire did not come close to capturing the rents that Southeast Asian countries did. The available tools for rent capturing are royalties, taxes and fees. Royalties are generally set at very low levels. A World Bank mission estimated the stumpage value to be 20 to 60 times the royalty rates in Ghana in 1986. Although different schemes are in effect in different countries in West Africa, they all seem to have one thing in common - a marginal impact on the way the forests are exploited (Gray and Grut, 1992). Low rent capture by the government means high profits for the logging firms. In a situation when profits are high and the future policy is uncertain, loggers can be expected to try to reap their profits as fast as possible. Lack of management plans and government control exacerbate the situation. The combined effect is excessive and uneconomical clearing.

• ***Other policies*** are sometimes as, or even more, important than forestry policies in affecting the deforestation induced by logging. The deteriorating economy of Ghana has already been mentioned. In Côte d'Ivoire the road network and harbor facilities have received much investments, primarily to expand the logging industry. At the same time the government has also encouraged small-scale commercial farmers to clear forest areas for cash-crop production (Repetto and Gillis, 1988).

As a first step towards a better management of commercial tropical forests in West and Central Africa, a recent World Bank study had the following recommendations (Gray and Grut, 1992):

- Introduction of annual concession rental fees at a significant rate. This annual concession rental should be the major revenue source, replacing the present multiplicity of forest fees.

- Concession contracts to be sold by bidding in sealed tender or auction.

- Forest management concessions to replace logging concessions.

- Each forest concession to have a forest management plan.

- Inspection of concessions to be done by independent, private firms, selected by international competitive bidding, on behalf of governments.

4.3 Biomass as a source of energy

Already in section three we noted that biomass is an important and often dominating source of energy in many African countries. This dependence on fuelwood is often associated with local deforestation around urban centers. An early example of this is Pankhurst's (1966) description of the foundation of the Ethiopian capital Addis Abeba in the late 19th century. The center of the Abyssinian highland culture had then moved southward throughout the centuries. In 1887 the first houses were erected in what would be Addis Abeba. However, the new town soon suffered from acute shortages of supplies, especially fuelwood. A foreign traveller wrote that "for two or three days before reaching the capital, we had to do without wood in the camp, for there was scarcely a tree to be seen. Every shrub that could possibly be used for firing has been cleared." Already in 1900 a new town, Addis Alem, was established as a possible successor of Addis Abeba. The reactions to a new move were generally negative, especially from foreign legations, and King Menelik decided in 1902 that Addis Abeba would remain the capital. Instead of moving the capital he ordered road construction to facilitate transportation of wood and food from nearby areas and major afforestation schemes using the newly introduced eucalyptus tree. Indiscriminate cutting of forests was also prohibited.

These fuelwood plantations around Addis Abeba have spread during the century and cover now more than 20,000 ha. The management has changed over time. During the Marxist years, 1975 - 1991, the right to harvest was given to the urban "soviets", the kebbeles. They could give permits to the members to harvest and sell the wood. More common, however, was that the kebbele organized wood harvests and also took care of the proceeds. This management was not without problems. The low salaries and the impersonal nature of the property rights made the guards corrupt which led to overuse of the plantations.[6]

The large dependence on fuelwood in combination with reports of widespread deforestation and increasing difficulties to find wood pointed at fuelwood as a major reason for deforestation. The energy approach to deforestation was widely disseminated in Eckholm's paper "The Other Energy Crisis" in 1975. This view was reinforced by a series of energy studies including gap-models that showed how fuelwood demand, increasing with the growth of population, widely exceeded the growth of forests, thus leading to a fuelwood gap that was assumed to be met by a reduction in the stocks of forests. It was in this spirit the UNDP/World Bank energy surveys summarized in Table 3 were made at the beginning of the 1980s.

The energy approach to deforestation led many donor agencies, and indeed developing countries, to embark on a triad of countervailing actions:

- Increase the supply of fuelwood through major afforestation projects, especially in peri-urban areas;
- Decrease the demand of wood through use of more efficient stoves;
- Decrease the demand of fuelwood through substitution to other fuels, notably through subsidies on kerosene and Liquid Petroleum Gas (LPG).

Lately, much of the conventional wisdom has been questioned regarding fuelwood consumption, its contribution to deforestation, the method of analysis and the policy prescriptions.

The conventional wisdom that high population pressure and resulting high demands for fuelwood would induce deforestation, as in our example of Addis Abeba, is moderated in a series of empirical studies. A study of the Kano region in Nigeria shows that "the area closest to the city and that which is under the greatest potential urban and rural fuelwood demand pressure supports high and increasing farm tree densities" (Cline-Cole, Main and Nichol, 1990). They also quote similar findings in the Kenyan highlands. Likewise, Dewees (1989) refers to a study by du Toit et al., 1984, that shows that in a heavily deforested area in Zimbabwe with increasing demands for wood, further clearing had been insignificant during a 20-year period and the residual woodland appeared to be more densely forested now than before.

These examples show that there are no simple truths in this respect. A situation of increased demand would, with proper land entitlement, be expected to lead to increased, rather than decreased, supply. It should also be remembered that other uses of the trees than fuelwood often dominate decisions on plantation, management and harvest.

A second possible reason for disjoining the relationship between use of biomass as energy and deforestation, is that there might not be a perceived lack of energy. With reduced forest stocks the perception could rather be a lack of poles for construction or of fodder or household labor. When the availability of wood appropriate for fuel decreases, the response is not necessarily to chop down the last living trees, or plant new trees to be used for fuelwood. A number of other strategies have been observed.

---

[6] I am indebted to Alemu Mekonnen for this insight.

Table 3 Biomass dependence and fuelwood situation in selected African countries

Country	Biomass as % of total energy	FAO fuelwood classification	Situation
Burundi	93	5	Rapidly dwindling supply of fuelwood
Ethiopia	93	4,5,6	Deforestation for fuel biggest issue facing country
Kenya	77	4,6	Forests being overexploited by about four times sustainable growth for fuelwood
Lesotho	56	5	Fuelwood currently only viable alternative to imported fuel
Malawi	94	4	Fuelwood consumption greater than sustainable supply
Morocco	36	2,3,6	Severe problem of forests being exploited by three times sustainable fuelwood production
Niger	86	3,4,5,6	Severe shortage of fuelwood causing massive overexploitation of forest particularly near population centers
Nigeria	59	2,4,5	Shortage of fuelwood serious problem throughout country with severe imbalances in northern states
Rwanda	94	4,5	Severe shortages of fuelwood. Fuelwood expected to provide over 50% of total energy in foreseeable future.
Senegal	64	4,6	Overexploitation of forests for fuelwood has resulted in loss of 90% of forest area
Sudan	82	1,3,6	Existing forest resources rapidly declining and causing localized shortages of fuelwood
Uganda	95	4	Forest capital being eroded and local fuelwood supplies nearly exhausted in some areas
Zambia	45	4	Fuelwood expected to continue to be major household energy for some years, local excessive fuelwood cutting leading to widespread deforestation
Zimbabwe	30	3	Fuelwood most important source of urban and rural household energy; forest resources depleted to critical levels in some areas

FAO fuelwood classification:

1: Satisfactory situation; resources considerably exceed present and foreseeable needs.
2: Satisfactory situation, but decreasing resources could become inadequate, at least locally in the foreseeable future.
3: Prospective deficit; present resources higher than requirements, but evolving towards crisis situation in year 2000.
4: Deficit situation; present resources below requirements obliging population to overexploit.
5: Acute scarcity; resources so reduced that population no longer able to ensure minimum supply.
6: Desert and arid areas in scarcity situation with few resources and low population.

Sources: UNDP, FAO and the World Bank in World Bank, 1989a.

Conservation through improved fire management is often the cheapest step to take. Fuel consumption may be a quarter or less in areas where wood is traditionally scarce compared to areas with much wood (Foley, 1991). This is also a reason why urban fuelwood and charcoal consumption generally is smaller than rural consumption. The size of the consumption unit is also very important, with markedly decreasing per capita consumption of fuelwood as the consumption unit increases to about 14 people (Cline-Cole, Main and Nichol, 1990).

Substitution to crop residues, twigs and other scrap woody biomass as well as dung is another cheap possibility. However, they are often considered to be inferior fuels because they smoke, smell and burn too fast (O'Keefe and Munslow, 1989). There is a concern that this practice would decrease agricultural productivity because of loss of nutrients and structure to the soil. However, this is not always true. Some stalks decompose too slowly to be left in the fields, others spread plant diseases if not burnt. There could even be competition between the decomposing material and crops for microorganisms and minerals (Dewees, 1989).

So far we have shown that the assumptions underlying the expected causal relationship between fuelwood and deforestation are tenuous. What has this implied for the success of the policy prescriptions?

On the supply side, while the plantations around Addis Abeba were moderately successful, other peri-urban plantations have not been as successful. One main reason is that fuelwood produced by such plantations is very expensive compared to small-scale biomass production. The main difference is in the high establishment costs of formal plantations (Leach and Mearns, 1988). It can therefore almost always be undercut by fuelwood and charcoal from rural areas where wood has low stumpage fees or is in effect in free access. In addressing this issue regarding a peri-urban forestry fuelwood program for Lusaka, the World Bank suggested that stumpage fees be raised ten-fold. The Zambian government refused to do this because it would hurt the rural population (O'Keefe and Munslow, 1989).

Communal woodlots, being a scaled-down version of fuelwood plantations, have suffered from similar problems. The interest among farmers has often been limited because of uncertainties regarding ownership and access and more fundamentally because it has not addressed their main concerns. "The Tanzanian experience suggests that people do not give priority to communal woodlots unless wood is high on the list of problems that they face." (O'Keefe and Munslow, 1989).

On the demand side the improved stoves programs have received most interest. Most rural stove programs had little impact. In most cases rural people showed themselves unwilling to abandon the open fire and construct or purchase stoves which would help them economize on fuelwood (Foley, 1991). This is not surprising in the light of what has been described above.

Urban stove programs, on the other hand, have been somewhat more successful. An often cited example of this is the Kenya Ceramic Jiko (KCJ). This improved stove was developed at the beginning of the 1980s. At the end of the decade well over 50% of the stoves sold in Nairobi were KCJs and the annual production was over 165,000 stoves (Karakezi, 1990). Part of the success can be attributed to the efficiency of the stove in combination with the use of simple and familiar technology. This was also essential for its commercial dissemination. No subsidies were given and the first stoves were sold at a price of USD 15, giving high profits. More entrepreneurs and artisans were attracted, boosting output, and the price decreased to USD 3, thus ensuring popular acceptance.

Policy makers must consider that bio-energy is a byproduct of a number of economic activities such as fruit, timber and pole production, clearing of land, agriculture and animal husbandry. At times the concentration of demand for fuel in combination with inappropriate property rights and low productivity (esp. dry areas) may aggravate deforestation. Accordingly, when forests are depleted for other reasons, then this is reflected in deteriorating accessibility to bio-energy. However, a frontal attack on the symptom defies the solution. The multi-functionality of trees and woody bushes must be taken into consideration and be reflected in policies regarding forestry, agriculture as well as energy. Such an approach to woody biomass management would be the antithesis to earlier plantation approaches. It would entail an indirect intervention with low capital costs, broad goals and multiple outputs (O'Keefe and Munslow, 1989).

Substitution between different fuels usually occurs because of scarcity of the preferred fuel or a change in income. As we have seen the change is not seldom to a less preferred fuel. Subsidies on kerosene and LPG are intended to facilitate a move away from biomass to commercial fuels which have less disruptive effect on the environment. We have already seen that sub-Saharan Africa is characterized by low per capita income, high proportion of biomass in household energy consumption and a very low consumption of commercial fuels. Since lower income households prefer to spend any incremental income on food and other necessities rather than fuel, subsidies on fuel cannot be expected to be effective until income has risen (Hosier, 1985). Subsidizing kerosene and LPG is also difficult as long as neighboring countries do not follow the same pricing policies. This is evident from the extensive illegal exports of such subsidized products in West Africa. A similar problem is the possibility to use the products for other purposes than household consumption (Sterner, 1989).

5 CONCLUSION

In this chapter we have touched upon a series of interrelated problems. Per capita food production has a secular deteriorating trend. To increase agricultural production, forests and marginal lands are cultivated at the expense of fuelwood gathering and ecological stability. Direct, large scale attempts to fulfill fuelwood needs have been expensive and often missed the target. Similarly, with economic stagnation, aggravated by decreasing terms of trade and staggering foreign debt, foreign exchange is sought through exports of timber. The set of policies in place has neither been able to reap the full economic benefit of these exports, nor to prevent further uneconomic behaviour that follows, e.g. unsustainable cultivation of poor forest soils. Over and above the human suffering now afflicting the African continent the present trends also pose a threat to global initiatives to come to grips with various environmental problems including global warming.

A sustainable path that would lead out of the present vicious circle of decreasing output -> increased use of marginal lands -> reduced vegetative cover -> decreasing output, would be one that stimulates the "grass-roots" to intensify their production of food, fodder and fuel. This would meet their needs, decrease the pressure on marginal lands and even give a small global positive externality in binding more carbon in biomass.

There have, of course, been numerous technical solutions to achieve this during the last decades. Improved seeds along with fertilizers, pesticides and intensified extension services belong to the standard prescription. Improved land-use management is, of course, another general answer. More specifically, agroforestry has been put forward as a way to operationalize these ideas. Integrating woody biomass with agricultural production has the potential of reducing soil erosion and maintaining soil fertility. It can increase the productivity of agriculture substantially (Leach, 1990a) at the same time as it provides fruit, fodder and fuel. However, agroforestry could be very broadly defined as all practices that combine woody biomass and crops in space and time. This includes many traditional cropping systems that were abolished when Western mono-cultures were introduced. From a farmer's point of view, agroforestry is a risk averse strategy, spreading both the risk of crop failure on many crops and the risk of volatile markets by producing more for subsistence. It often also has positive effects on fertility, reduced risk of pests etc.

Agroforestry is often viewed as a technical solution (changed cropping system) to a technical problem (low farm productivity and high erosion). This fits well the organization developed to deal with the problem, all the way from the agricultural divisions of the aid donors to the governmental organizations and extension agents in the implementing countries. It could be argued that the fact that forestry and agricultural staff are more integrated is a major accomplishment. Still, technical solutions such as a recommendation to plant hedge-rows of *Leucaena sp.* with maize will have little impact on the farming community as long as the incentive structure affecting the people is not conducive for long-term investments in the land and production for a surplus.

This brings us back to the importance of policies - that user-rights are secure, that taxation is not excessive and that institutions are established to secure properly functioning markets. In a secure policy climate where people have faith in the future, the present short-sightedness of both policy-makers and individuals would be reduced and new land-use management systems can be expected to develop.

REFERENCES

Binswanger, H.P. 1989. *Brazilian Policies That Encourage Deforestation in the Amazon*, Environmental Department Working Paper No. 16, World Bank, Washington, D.C.

Brough, H.B. 1991. "A New Lay of the Land", *World Watch*, pp. 12-19 vol. 4 no 1.

Burgess, J. 1991. *Economic Analysis of Frontier Agriculture Expansion and Tropical Deforestation*, Masters thesis, University College London.

Cline-Cole, R.A., H.A.C. Main and J.E. Nichol. 1990. "On Fuelwood Consumption, Population Dynamics and Deforestation in Africa" *World Development*, vol. 18, no. 4, pp. 513-527.

Cornia, A.C., R. van der Hoeven and T. Mkandawire. 1992. (eds.) *Africa's Recovery in the 1990's: From Stagnation and Adjustment to Human Development*, St. Martin's Press, New York.

Dewees, P.A. 1989. "The Woodfuel Crisis Reconsidered: Observations on the Dynamics of Abundance and Scarcity", *World Development*, vol. 17, no. 8, pp. 1159-1172.

Eckholm, E. 1975. "The Other Energy Crisis: Fire Wood". World Watch Institute, Washington, D.C.

Foley, G. 1991. *Energy Assistance Revisited*, Paper presented at Stockholm Environment Institute, April.

Gray, J., and M. Grut. 1992. *Pricing and Management of Tropical Forests in West and Central Africa*, Paper presented at the conference Forestry and the Environment: Economic Perspectives, Alberta, Canada, March.

Harvey, C., (ed.). 1988, *Agricultural Pricing Policy in Africa*, Macmillan, London.

Hosier, R. 1985. *Energy Use in Rural Kenya: Household Demand and Rural Transformation*, Energy Environment and Development in Africa 7, The Beijer Institute and the Scandinavian Institute of African Studies.

International Food Policy Research Institute (IFPRI). 1989. *Environmental Policy for Agricultural Sustainability*, Washington D.C., Draft.

Karakezi, S. 1990. *Energy Issues in Sub-Saharan Africa: the Case of the Kenya Ceramic Jiko*, Paper presented at Stockholm Environment Institute, November.

Karlsson, M. 1987. *Landrapport Etiopien*, Planeringssekretariatet, SIDA.

Lawry, S.W. 1990. "Tenure Policy and Toward Common Property Natural Resources in Sub-Saharan Africa", *Natural Resources Journal*, vol. 30, pp. 403-422.

Leach, G. 1990a. *Carbon Dioxide Emission Strategies: Africa*, Research Memorandum, Stockholm Environment Institute.

Leach, G. 1990b. *Woodfuels and Farm Trees*, Research Memorandum, Stockholm Environment Institute.

Leach, G., and R. Mearns. 1988. *Beyond the Woodfuel Crisis*, Earthscan, London.

Mahar, D.J. 1989. *Government Policies and Deforestation in Brazil's Amazon Region*, World Bank Environment Department Working Paper no. 16.

McGranahan, G. 1990. *Fuelwood, Subsistence Foraging and the Decline of Common Property*, Research Memorandum, Stockholm Environment Institute.

Myers, N. 1983. "The Tropical Forest Issue" in *Progress in Resource Management and Environmental Planning,* T. O'Riordan and R.K. Turner (eds.), New York: John Wiley and Sons.

O'Keefe P. and B. Munslow. 1989. "Understanding fuelwood", *Natural Resources Forum*, vol. 13, no.1, (Feb). pp. 2-19.

O'Keefe P., J. Soussan, B. Munslow, and D. Spence. 1989. "Wood Energy in Eastern and Southern Africa", *Annual Review of Energy*, 14:445-68.

Pankhurst, R. 1966 *State and Land in Ethiopian History*, The Institute of Ethiopian Studies and Oxford University Press, Addis Abeba.

Poore, M.E.D., Burgess, P., Palmer, J., Rietbergen, S. and Synnott, T. 1990. *No Timber Without Trees: Sustainability in the Tropical Forest*, London, Earthscan [for ITTO].

Reed, D., ed. 1992. *Structural Adjustment and the Environment*, Westview Press, Oxford.

Repetto, R. 1990. "Deforestation in the tropics", *Scientific American*, vol. 262, no. 4, pp. 36-42.

Repetto, R. 1988. *Economic Policy Reform for Natural Resource Conservation*, World Bank Environment Department Working Paper no. 4.

Repetto, R. and M. Gillis eds. 1988. *Public Policies and the Misuse of Forest Resources*, Cambridge University Press, New York.

SIDA. 1987. "Proposed SIDA support for agricultural development in Welo Region", SIDA SC/CF Welo Mission, 12 January.

Southgate et al. 1990. "Resource degradation in Africa and Latin America: Population pressure, policies, and property arrangements", in Chapman, D., (ed.), *Arresting Renewable Resource Degradation in the Third World*, World Bank Environment Working Paper no. 44.

Sterner, T. 1992. "Economic and Environmental Policies for Sustainability" in *Society and the Environment: A Swedish Perspective*, Svedin, U. and B. Aniansson, Kluwer.

Sterner, T. 1989. "Les Prix de l'energie en Afrique", *Revue de l'Energie* no 415, Nov..

Stymne, J. 1993. "Reducing Africa's Debt Burden" in *Economic Crisis in Africa, Perspectives on Policy Responses,* M. Blomström and M. Lundahl Eds.Routledge, London.

UNDP. 1990. *Human Development Report*, Oxford University Press, Oxford.

Wilkens, A. 1986. *Katastrofbistånd för utveckling*, Liber, Stockholm.

World Bank. 1991a *Forest Policy Paper*, Washington, D.C.

World Bank. 1989a. *People and Trees*, Washington, D.C.

World Bank. 1989b. *Sub-Saharan Africa: From Crisis to Sustainable Growth*, Washington.

World Bank 1991b. *World Tables 1991*, Johns Hopkins, Baltimore.

World Resources Institute (WRI). 1988. *World Resources 1988-1989*, New York.

World Resources Institute (WRI). 1990. *World Resources 1990-1991*, New York.

CHAPTER 12

Environmental Considerations for Chinese Energy Policy

by

Torleif Haugland and Kjell Roland

Abstract

China faces two main challenges in its energy policy: 1) to provide adequate energy supplies to foster economic growth, and 2) to limit environmental damages from energy production and consumption. This paper examines energy supply options and conservation opportunities which could alleviate the conflict between economic growth and environmental protection. The abundant coal reserves provide the cheapest alternative for further expansion of energy supplies. Alternatives to coal (notably hydropower) require large financial funding and technological skills and also involve a number of environmental problems. Alteration of the current emphasis on coal supply expansion will therefore depend critically on financial support and transfer of technology from industrialized countries. Energy conservation potentially offers a forceful policy option for combatting environmental degradation and alleviating the energy supply shortage. China achieved impressive results in energy efficiency improvements during the 1980's. Despite this, the partial market reforms introduced during the 1980's had little impact on energy efficiency improvements. In fact, there is some evidence that the reforms encourage energy supply while large energy consumers did not perceive benefits from saving energy. The report concludes that comprehensive economic and political reforms are required to harvest the vast energy efficiency potential and to balance the conflicting targets of economic growth and environmental protection.

T. Sterner (ed.), Economic Policies for Sustainable Development, 212–226.

1 ENERGY CHARACTERISTICS AND CHALLENGES

A basic aspiration of the Socialist revolution in 1948 was to promote industrialization in order to improve living standards and reduce poverty. To this end, the first Five Year Plan (1953-57) was decisive in laying the foundation for the structure of the Chinese economy. During this period the rate of investment was exceptionally high with an ensuing boost in production capacity, particularly in heavy industries.

Subsequent Five Year Plans did not to the same extent guide the development of the Chinese economy. A lack of consensus within Chinese leadership on the development strategy strongly influenced the political and economic development. The result has been important shifts in sectoral emphasis and the role of centralized versus decentralized decision-making. Consequently, over the last 40 years China has undergone periods of strong economic growth followed by years of political turmoil and economic setback.

Despite large fluctuations in economic activity the average annual growth in GDP from 1953 to 1980 was 6%. In response to the Open Door Policy and the economic reforms pursued in the 1980's economic growth accelerated and reached an average annual rate of 9% for the decade.

1.1 Strong growth in energy consumption

A characteristic feature of the entire post-revolution period was the tremendous growth of the energy sector. Production of commercial energy products increased from 54 million tons of coal equivalent (mtce) in 1953 to 602 mtce in 1980, i.e an annual average increase of 9.3%. Hence the energy intensity (gross energy consumption per unit of GDP) more than doubled from 1953 to 1980. During the 1980's energy consumption growth decelerated to 5.5% despite strong economic growth. Hence energy intensity in 1990 was recorded to be 30% below the level of 1980. Nevertheless, the current energy intensity in China is still higher than in any other large country, developing or developed, see Table 1.

China belongs simultaneously to both the categories studied in this book: it is an LDC and it is a planned economy. The high and wasteful use of energy can be attributed to a number of factors of which the following seem to be the most important:

1. Regional and local self-reliance has been a major priority in Chinese economic policy. Hence the economy is largely based on small units which do not enjoy the full benefits of economies of scale, nor have they the financial power or the technical skills required to use modern technologies.

2. The manufacturing industry, in particular energy intensive sectors, represents an exceptionally large share of GDP.

Table 1 Energy consumption, population and GNP in selected countries (1989).[1]

	GDP/pop (USD 88)	Energy Cons. (Mtoe)	Energy cons./pop	Energy cons./GDP
China	330	631	580	1.76
India	340	172	211	0.62
Japan	21020	406	3306	0.16
USA	19840	1883	7655	0.39

Source: World Development Report 1990, World Bank

3. The central planning system with physical production targets and irrational pricing of energy and other products has discouraged energy saving. Even recent price increases have had little impact on energy consumption since managers do not perceive clear benefits from such efforts as long as industry is not granted greater autonomy from state interventions.

4. Limited access to energy efficient equipment inhibits energy savings both in industry and households. Consequently coal, which is the dominant fuel available to consumers, is utilised directly for cooking, space heating and industrial heating purposes at very low efficiency.

1.2 Energy shortages and economic losses

Paradoxically, major energy waste in China runs parallel with widespread energy shortages which generate major economic losses and create hardship for private households all over the country. As in many other developing countries, the most critical part of energy scarcity is the lack of adequate supplies of electricity. According to a report by the International Energy Agency (IEA (1989)), Chinese authorities evaluated the annual loss in industrial production due to electricity shortages in the early 1980's to Yuan 100 billion. Ironically, annual investments in the electricity sector during the same period were only Yuan 5 billion a year. Shortages of oil supplies also hamper economic productivity. Part of the vehicle fleet is kept idle for substantial periods and lack of diesel oil has adverse effects on productivity in agricultural production. Shen and Liu (1991) claim that currently 20 percent of the country's production capacity is under-utilized due to shortages and disruptions in electricity supply. Other reports suggest similar or even higher estimates of economic losses. However, the energy shortage should be considered in the light of the persistent strong economic growth during the 1980's. It is hardly surprising that energy deliveries become a bottleneck during periods of economic

[1] Compare also Table 1 in Chapter 5. Poland has an energy intensity of 0.98 TOE/$1000.

growth close to 10% (World Bank (1990)).

China still faces serious energy shortages and will for many years to come though there are obvious economic gains to be made from various policy measures which could narrow the gap between supply and demand.

1.3 Local, regional and global environmental problems

Environmental damage related to energy use in China reflects the structure of energy supply and use. Due to heavy reliance on coal in energy consumption, and in particular its direct, local use in the domestic and commercial sectors, environmental effects of energy use are dominated by the coal sector.

Environmental issues have over the last few years gained increasing political attention in China. Local air pollution in the big cities is appalling and leads to major health problems. Regional consequences of energy production and consumption (acid rain), are also starting to influence environmental policies.

While local and regional environmental problems related to coal use can be alleviated by more advanced coal treatment techniques (e.g. coal washing and briquette production) and cleaner combustion technologies, curbing CO_2 emissions calls for limitations to the overall volume of coal use. China currently contributes 10% of global CO_2 emissions.

China's share of CO_2 emissions will inevitably increase. If energy consumption grows by 3.5% per annum (which is low in historical comparison), China's share of global CO_2 emissions could reach 15% by the year 2010, see ECON (1990). The development of energy consumption in China will therefore become an issue of great concern in relation to international initiatives to combat global warming. But as Chinese officials rightly claim, if they were to avoid this while relying exclusively on their own resources, it would seriously hamper economic growth.

1.4 Two targets - two sets of policy measures

The energy situation descibed above shows that energy policy in China is faced with two challenges: **1) to foster economic growth** and **2) to promote environmental protection**. The policy measures required to attain and balance these partly conflicting targets can be categorized in two classes: **energy supply expansion** and **energy conservation.**

Two characteristic features of the Chinese energy consumption pattern underscore the strong rationale for both supply and demand side measures (see Table 1 above). *The energy consumption per capita* in China is less than 10% of that in the USA and 17% of the average energy consumed by the Japanese (which is the lowest among OECD countries). In the course of economic development per capita energy consumption will tend to increase if Chinese consumers adopt some of the lifestyle of industrialized societies. Furthermore, China will be faced over the next 20 years with an increase in population of close to 300 million. Hence, energy production would have to be increased substantially, and this in turn would conflict with environmental goals.

Another striking feature shown in the table is the extraordinarily high *energy intensity* in China; 10 times higher than in Japan, 4 times the level in USA and nearly

3 times higher than in India which is much like China in its stage of development and economic structure. This figure illustrates the large scope for inexpensive energy conservation opportunities. Energy conservation can therefore make a significant contribution both to environmental protection and economic progress.

Energy supply expansion on the other hand may seriously conflict with environmental goals. One major challenge for Chinese authorities is therefore to balance the energy requirements against the environmental considerations that are also of vital importance for the modernisation of China. In the following we review the characteristics of China's supply options and relate the discussion to the environmental issues involved.

2 ENERGY SUPPLY OPTIONS

2.1 Vast coal reserves but poor infrastructure

In 1983 China surpassed the United States as the world's leading coal producer. In 1990 coal production in China was 1080 million metric tons of raw coal, representing nearly 30% of world production. The attractiveness of coal is based on a vast resource base and low extraction costs.

Proven reserves of coal in China are estimated at 770 billion tons (World Energy Council), i.e. more than 700 years of production at the current level. The coal beds are generally thick and relatively flat and conditions for modern mechanized operations are good.

China's mining techniques cover the whole spectrum from modern mechanized mines to primitive mining based on manual coal winning by hand picks and shovels and transportation by human or pack animals. The abundance of manpower provides a rationale for labour-intensive techniques, as does the seasonality of small operations which are closely tuned to local needs.

The average total cost of production is around 45 Yuan per metric ton (Doyle (1987) and the World Bank (1985)). In comparison, mine-mouth costs for steam coal production in Wyoming, USA and Transvaal, South Africa were in 1989 $ 9 per ton and $ 12 per ton respectively, according to Coal Information, IEA (1990). Using the offical exchange rate of Yuan/$ = 4.9 (1987-rate), average Chinese coal production costs are $ 9 per ton, i.e. on the same level as the cheapest available surface-mine coal in other parts of the world.

Though the reserves are vast and mining costs are moderate, coal supplies are hampered by inadequate infrastructure. A major part of the mining is located in the North and the Western part of the country while the populous South and East are in deficit of cheap coal reserves. Transportation of coal to the consuming areas is of vital importance to the country's energy supplies.

Currently the railway system is a chronic bottleneck in the Chinese coal supply system. Some 40% of the country's railway cargo capacity is earmarked for coal transport but even this is inadequate and leads to major supply disruptions for power stations, industry and households. Plans for further expansion of the railway system are ambitious but transport may still remain as much of a problem to the coal supply system as it was in the 1980's.

China suffers from a lack of coal-washing facilities. In 1985 16% of all raw coal produced was washed, against 80 and 60% for OECD and the Soviet Union, respectively (IEA (1989)). Coal-washing has the advantage of improving the efficiency of coal use and reducing ash content, and thereby air pollution during combustion. Expansion in coal-washing capacity would in addition alleviate some of the burden on the railway system, as several million tons of rock would not have to be moved with the coal. However, coal-washing is hampered by lack of water supplies in the large coal provinces. The burden on water supplies also impedes the construction of mine-site power plants which are intended to reduce the pressure on the coal transportation system.

Despite the difficulties with the coal supply infrastructure, prospects for further increases in coal production are generally good. The official production target for the year 2000 is 1400 million metric tons, which implies an annual growth rate of 2,6% during this decade. In comparison the growth rate in the 1980's was above 5%.

The increase in coal production experienced during the last 10 year period was largely a result of the economic reforms which in particular benefited small local mines. Coal producers were allowed to sell part of their production at unrestricted prices. This was combined with a higher degree of local responsibility for investments.

Table 2 Production in state and local mines in China. (Million tons), 1980-1989

	1979	1980	1985	1986	1987	1988	1989
State mines	357	344	406	414	420	434	458
Local Mines	278	276	466	480	507	545	596
Total	635	620	872	894	927	979	1054

Source: Ministry of Energy, PRC (1989)

The effect of the policy change came rapidly and was strong; local mines (run by local governments at the provincial, county or prefecture level, or as collective enterprises) showed an annual growth rate of 12% from 1981 to 1985 which decelerated to 6% per annum from 1985 to 1989. The local mines which accounted for 45% of total production in 1981 increased their share to 57% in 1989.

The large centrally-controlled mines also benefited somewhat from the reform, but in general coal prices were, and still are, below production costs. Consequently the industry is drained of financial resources with ensuing low investments and productivity. However, if the larger mines eventually are granted greater autonomy from state interventions, both productivity improvements and expansion in production capacity can be expected to make a leap forward.

2.2 Oil - large reserves, bleak production prospects

China has sedimentary basins comparable to the United States. It is, however, only in recent years that China has become a major producer and exporter of oil. The current production level of 2.7 million barrels/day is still low in consideration of the large reserves that are expected to be found in Chinese geological structures.

Major oilfields are located in the Northeast (Daqing) and the East (Shengli), both fairly close to major consuming areas and export ports. Daqing and Shengli were developed in the early 1960's and now contribute 65% of the country's total production.

During the 1980's foreign companies started oil exploration in China, mainly offshore. Only a very small portion of the offshore fields turned out to be commercially viable. Therefore many foreign companies pulled out, some rather hastily. This in turn had a negative impact on Chinese policy towards participation in exploration in potentially promising areas onshore.

The most attractive territory is in the Xinjiang Province in the Northwest of China. So far only Chinese teams have been allowed in the area and they have made encouraging discoveries in the Tarim and Junggar Basins. However, these petroleum reserves are in inhospitable areas far away from the market place. Oil from Tarim would have to be piped 3000-4000 km to the East. Exploration and development are also hindered by lack of transportation and communication infrastructure.

The Xinjiang Province is known to harbour major ethnic conflicts. This may be an important motive behind the government's hesitation to start large-scale exploration and development of the area and may also explain its reluctance to give foreign companies access.

In the early 1980's the target for crude oil production by the year 2000 was set at 200 million tons (4 mill. barrels/day). The authorities now admit that this production level will not be reached. Production from the two major fields, Daqing and Shengli, will at best remain constant. The prospects for significant additional production from other fields are at the moment bleak. Offshore production, mainly in the Bohai Sea, reached 3 million tons in 1990 and current development projects do not indicate any notable increase above this level. Production prospects for the next 10-20 years are therefore not very encouraging.

Friedley (1990) presents an outlook for production in 2000 at a level of 3.5 mill. barrels/day (175 million tons) as the high case and 3.15 mbd as the low case. Haugland and Roland (1990) argue that 3.15 mbd should be considered a mid-case prediction. Production could very well remain at the current level of 2.7 mbd until the turn of the century, as it will become increasingly difficult to sustain the current production level of 1.8 mbd in Daqing and Shengli.

Looking at the oil balance as a whole, China is moving inevitably in the direction of becoming a net oil importer. As mentioned, crude oil production will at best reach 3.5 mbd in year 2000. If the country succeeds in maintaining an annual GDP growth rate above 5%, which seems likely in light of current growth rates, it will become extremely difficult to keep the growth in oil consumption below 3%. With all of the current suppressed demand for oil, growth rates for oil demand could become higher than the GDP rate. Hence, China may well be a net importer of oil by the turn of the century. Towards the year 2010, a further increase in net imports seem likely.

Substituting oil for coal in residential and industrial sectors, as part of an environmental policy, is therefore inconceivable. On the contrary, strong measures will probably be imposed to substitute coal for oil, as has been successfully done over the past 10-15 years.

2.3 Natural gas - the neglected sector

Proven reserves of natural gas in China are estimated at 900 billion m^3 (bcm), which is less than 1% of the world total. With the current annual production level of 14 bcm, the R/P ratio (reserves to production ratio) is 65 years. Natural gas exploration has traditionally been considered a low priority in Chinese energy sector investments, and the present reserve estimate should be regarded partly as a result of this neglect (Li and Friedley (1990)).

Natural gas has been produced primarily to cover local use. The main area of gas production is in the Sichuan Province, and in conjunction with oil in the Daqing and Shangli oil fields. In recent years some encouraging new discoveries have been made in Sichuan and on the Hainan Island. With development of these fields underway a doubling of production by the year 2000 seems feasible. However, natural gas will still remain a minor product in the Chinese energy balance. In 1988 natural gas contributed 2% towards total energy supplies. The major part of production was either used in the industrial sector or in oil and gas exploration. Natural gas as a substitute for coal in residential cooking and heating cannot be justified with the current scale and geographical location of proven reserves and production.

From a geological viewpoint, the Xinjiang province in the Northwest is probably the most likely area for large natural gas discoveries. Recently, discoveries have been made in the huge Tarim Basin. It is, however, unlikely that these discoveries will play any important role in Chinese energy supplies before the turn of the century given the long distance from Tarim to any major consuming area.

2.4 Hydroelectric power - large potential

Exploitable hydropower resources in China are estimated at 380 GW, believed to be among the largest in the world. The potential output from this resource base is some 1900 Twh on an annual basis, i.e. more than 3 times current total electricity production in China. There exist major financial and technical obstacles to a large-scale exploitation of hydropower resources. Most of the resources are in the Southwest and the Northwest of the country and would need to be transmitted some 2000-3000 km to the large consuming regions in the East.

Harnessing China's large hydro potential also involves a number of environmental problems. Traditional problems such as salinization of river deltas, erosion and siltation of dams etc. are often experienced. Furthermore, several of the large projects involve massive farmland flooding and forced migration of large numbers of people. Smil (1989) estimates the loss of farmland by the current official hydro program to be 100-150 000 ha and that 1-1.5 million people will have to be resettled.

Within China, there is a considerable disagreement between those who argue in favour of concentrating the country's resources on a few mega projects, and those who favour construction of many smaller projects. Already, a large number of small rural hydro stations supply local markets. However, even a large number of these power stations will not be sufficient to lay the foundation for an integrated and reliable power network that can fuel the economic modernization of large areas.

Despite difficult environmental and social issues and large capital requirements related to an ambitious construction program, hydro power probably offers the best alternative to coal consumption. An acceleration of the hydro power construction program (20 GW currently under construction) would, however, seriously conflict with social and environmental considerations and would divert key resources from other ends. To address these problems, and in light of regional and global environmental considerations, additional financial support and technological transfer from industrialized countries seems particularly relevant in this case.

2.5 Nuclear power - too expensive

China possesses reserves of uranium in excess of what is needed to support the current program for installation of nuclear capacity. Currently China has two nuclear plants. Plans for building nuclear plants have been scaled down compared to the ambitious plans of the early 1980's. The down-scaling of the nuclear program was motivated by cost considerations. Environmental and safety arguments do not seem to have played a major role. If the current government plans are fulfilled, total nuclear capacity will reach 4.5 GW by the year 2000.

2.6 Energy in rural areas: Biomass and coal

About 800 million people live in rural areas in China[2]. A large part of energy consumption in these areas is met by traditional (non-commercial) fuels. Since production and consumption are quite dispersed, regular statistics on consumption are not available. Yet, comprehensive surveys have been undertaken in order to map the structure of rural energy consumption (Wu and Chen (1982), World Bank (1985), Smil (1988)). Total rural energy consumption in 1984 was close to 400 million tons of coal equivalent. Biomass accounted for 60%, coal 30%, liquid fuels 4% and electricity 6%. Most of the liquid fuels and coal are included in official energy statistics while biomass and to some extent hydro-generated electricity are not included as commercial fuels.

Households are the dominant consumer of biomass fuels. Slightly more than half are crop by-products (straw, stalks and other vegetal or animal waste). The portion of crop by-products used as fuel has gradually increased to 60-80% (World Bank (1985)). The result of this development is that less of these products are available as animal fodder and organic input for soil improvement. This development is clearly unsustainable in the deforested and intensively farmed lowlands.

---

[2] According to official statistics in China, about half the population are considered to be rural inhabitants. This low share is a result of an administrative upgrading of large villages, towns and peri-urban zones. However, in relation to the discussion of rural energy supply and demand a different definition of rural is normally applied.

Biogas generated from animal, human and plant waste has for years attracted attention as a promising renewable energy source. Mass construction campaigns were initiated and there were plans to build 70 million units by 1985. Construction problems and resistance by peasants have, however, resulted in only 5 million being built by 1989.

The limited forestland in China cannot support the current rate of tree-felling for fuel purposes. Deforestation, soil erosion and desertification are problems of great concern in China. Great efforts have been made in afforestation projects but information about the results is inconsistent. There have been problems applying the appropriate incentives in afforestation work. Since 1980, private fuelwood lots have been allowed. Together with dissemination of fast-growing trees this may counteract the unsustainable development in some areas of the country.

Coal from small-scale local mines has eased the energy supply shortage in rural areas in the 1980s. Some 79,000 small mines produced 352 million metric tons (Mmt) of coal in 1988, while the same mines produced only 113 Mmt in 1980, (Ministry of Energy (1989)) i.e. an annual growth rate of 13.5%. A large part of the supply has gone to the booming small-scale industry in villages throughout the country and to households that have spent part of their additional income (rural household income doubled in the 1980s) to purchase coal in the free market. Safety and the rate of coal recovery from local mines are usually poor and the coal quality often makes it unsuitable for anything but households and small manufacturing.

Small-scale hydro represents a valuable energy source in rural electrification in China. Exploitable resources are estimated to be 71 GW. In 1988 more than 63,000 small hydro power stations with a total installed capacity of 11.8 GW were in operation. Production in 1988 was 31 Twh which represents 2600 hours of operation (30%) per year. Production from the full exploitable resource-base would with the same utilization rate (30%) yield 186 Twh in annual production.

Conditions for solar energy and windpower are good in some areas. Development of these technologies has started and financial support has been granted for installation of solar cookers and solar water heaters. Pilot projects have also been launched for wind power and utilization of geothermal energy. However, these energy forms will play no more than a marginal role in the near future.

Data on biomass consumption from surveys undertaken in different years does not give a clear indication of the development over time. However, most analyses suggest that there has been an increase despite a massive substitution to coal, expanded electricity supplies and improved fuel efficiency in household stoves. Consumption of biomass is primarily constrained by physical supplies, and consumption is in many areas unsustainable and environmentally destructive. The need for a reduction or at least a stabilization of biomass use seems to be pressing. On the other hand, fuels available for cooking and water heating are often inadequate to meet basic needs. It is estimated that the 1984 consumption was 20-25% below minimum annual needs.

As income rises, demand for commercial fuels will probably increase steeply in rural areas. Coal and hydro-based electricity seem to be the fuels that will have to meet this demand.

3 ENERGY CONSERVATION

3.1 The 6th Five-Year plan (1981-85)

When China launched the Open Door Policy and later in 1980 announced the target of quadrupling GDP by the year 2000, a looming fear arose that lack of energy supplies would inhibit economic growth. Furthermore, the harmful environmental effects of China's predominantly coal-based energy sector became more apparent. Together with evidence of major energy waste, this initiated a comprehensive energy conservation program as part of the 6th Five-Year Plan (1981-85). The program contained the following main elements:

1. Specific efficiency requirements and standards, including mandated installation of energy-consumption-metering equipment. Enterprises could face penalties for non-compliance, and receive bonuses for energy consumption below quota levels.

2. Creation of investment funds for energy management and efficiency investments. The Chinese authorities recognized that investments in "technology modernization" or "capital equipment projects" to a large extent could save energy at a far lower cost than the cost of providing additional energy to the consumer. A total of 10 billion Yuan was allocated to these projects during the period of the 6th Five-Year plan, i.e. some 15% of total investments to the energy sector. An interesting and well-documented account of the success of this program is given in Levine and Liu (1990).

3. Policy measures to shift industrial production to less energy-intensive processes and products.

4. Price reforms and elimination of subsidies.

5. Propaganda campaigns and the establishment of energy conservation centres throughout the country. Furthermore, enterprises consuming more than 50,000 tons of coal equivalents on a yearly basis had to create energy conservation units to evaluate and implement conservation measures and to undertake long-term energy planning and training.

In addition to these measures, which were primarily aimed at improving the energy efficiency in the industrial sector, large programs were implemented to replace old and inefficient stoves in rural and urban households.

China achieved impressive results in energy efficiency improvements during the 1980's from this program and similar initiatives during the subsequent Five Year Plan. Energy consumption grew on average only 5.5% per annum from 1980 to 1990, while the GDP growth-rate for the same period was close to 9.5%. Hence, energy efficiency improved by more than 4% per annum.

It is difficult to fully assess how much of the decline in energy intensity should be attributed to direct policy measures, and it is even more difficult to quantify the effect of each of the factors listed above. However, the Energy Research Institute in Beijing estimates technological improvements, including improvement in management procedures, to account for 1/3 of the drop in energy intensities, while changes in sectoral composition of the economy generated more than 2/3 of the improvement. Price increases seem to have played a negligible role in efficiency improvements during the first part of the 1980's despite the introduction of some price reforms in 1982-83. This may depend on the problems related to "soft budgets" typically found in planned economies, see Chapters 4-7.

3.2 Recent developments

As illustrated in Figure 1, the slower growth in GDP during the last few years has only partly been accompanied by a similar slow-down in energy consumption growth. This is primarily explained by the substantial **energy demand surplus** which has prevailed during the 1980's.

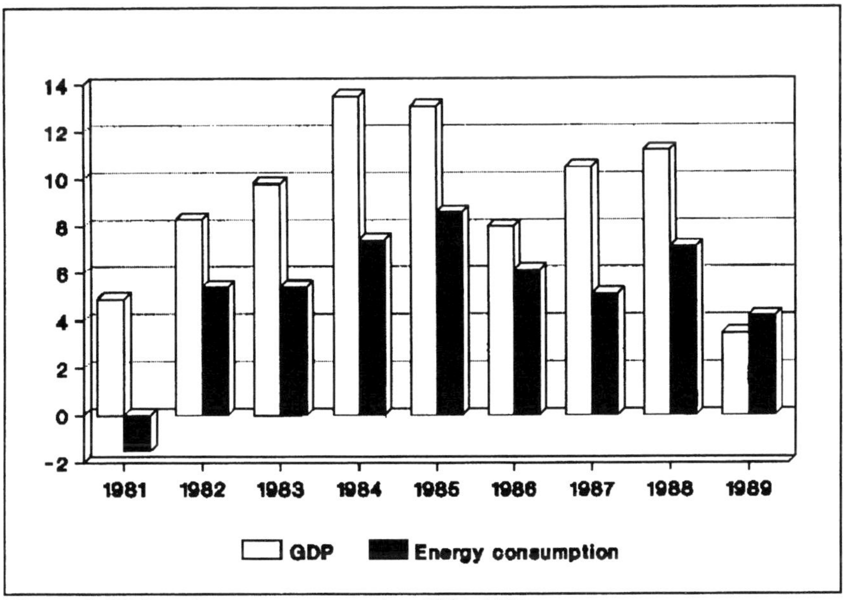

Figure 1 GDP and energy consumption 1981-1990

Though detailed end use data after 1985 are sparse and comprehensive analyses of the energy efficiency improvements of different sectors of the economy are lacking, there is reason to believe that the energy conservation programme may have had less of an effect during the latter part of the 1980's. The cheapest and most obvious conservation opportunities were exhausted in the course of the 6th Five-Year Plan (1981-85). Hence, the costs of energy conservation programs increased, i.e. energy saving gained per Yuan invested was lower than in the early 1980's. Moreover, the 7th Five-Year Plan (1986-90) allocated relatively less resources to investment funds for efficiency improvements while allocation of funds for expansion of energy supplies increased substantially, Levine and Liu (1990).

3.3 Market reforms and energy efficiency improvements

If China is to maintain a high economic growth-rate and high rate of improvement in energy efficiency (the two are probably interdependent), comprehensive market reforms are needed. Some steps in this direction were taken during the 1980's, but they have so far had little positive impact on energy efficiency. In fact, there is some evidence that the reforms contributed to higher energy consumption:

a) De-regulation of markets created incentives for investment in small-scale industries, in particular outside big cities. Such plants are often characterized by poor performance in terms of energy efficiency. Higher production from such plants consequently contributed to a slow-down in overall energy efficiency improvements.

b) The two-tier price system that was introduced in the early 1980's raised prices on energy products in segments of the market. The price increases encouraged higher production, particularly in small-scale coal mines which at the same time were granted greater autonomy. However, the impact of higher prices on consumption was negligible since few of the large energy consumers (industry) perceived any benefits from saving costs. Furthermore the substantial demand surplus implies that increased supplies easily get absorbed in the market irrespective of price increases.

The experience gained from the partial market reforms of the 1980's is therefore that they do not promote the market behaviour required to harvest the vast energy efficiency potential which exists in China. Political and institutional reforms will be required which radically alter the incentive structure of the economy. If enterprises are granted more independence from state interventions and markets are allowed to function in a flexible manner, industrial managers may soon feel encouraged to save on costs and consequently respond to the large energy saving opportuinities.

Market flexibility is also closely related to the chances of acquiring and making efficient use of new capital equipment. Like other developing countries, China is notoriously short of capital. Furthermore, political barriers still exist (though to a lesser extent then before 1979) for inflow of modern foreign capital equipment. The availability of engineers and other technical staff may be better than in many other developing countries but managerial performance is often poor due to inadequate incentive schemes.

Residential energy consumption may be somewhat more responsive to price increases than industry as procurement of energy is largely paid out of these households' own income. However, as energy at the current stage of development meets basic needs and because the availability of energy-efficient equipment and appliances is limited, the demand response (price elasticity) is probably low. Price elasticities for rural coal and kerosene consumption may be somewhat higher as households have the option of switching between traditional fuels (wood and crop residues) and commercial fuels.

4 CONCLUDING REMARKS

Energy market developments and the state of the environment will be decisive for economic growth and modernization of Chinese society. Lack of adequate energy supplies could in the future seriously impair the growth potential of the economy, as it has partly done during the 1980's. Abundant coal reserves provide the cheapest alternative for further expansion of energy supplies. Inevitably China's energy requirements will continue to show a considerable increase (probably above 3% per annum) and such prospects clearly conflict with global environmental objectives, see further Chapter 16.

Local and regional environmental problems can be alleviated through introduction of advanced coal treatment techniques and clean coal combustion technologies. Global warming, on the other hand, calls for energy conservation and fuel substitution measures. Hydropower offers the best alternative to coal, but harnessing China's large hydro potential involves a number of environmental problems and requires large financial funds and technological skills. Large investments in hydropower will therefore critically depend on financial support and transfer of technology from industrialized countries.

Environmental challenges and the objective of providing adequate energy supplies to foster economic growth can only be jointly achieved through comprehensive economic and political reforms. The old centralized command and control system, which still is omnipresent in the Chinese economy, represents a major obstacle to the elimination of vast energy waste and environmental degradation. The Chinese people demonstrated during the partial reform process in the 1980's that they are able to respond very rapidly to new opportunities. However, reforms which trigger economic growth and development are considered by Chinese political leadership to be policies subordinate to political stability and continuity. The disruption of the political and economical reform processes in 1988-1989 was largely motivated by a perceived fear of political instability and disintegration of the Chinese state. There may, therefore, exist some degree of conflict between the objective of strong economic growth and the existing "social order and stability". Balancing the potential conflicts inherent in this development process is a big challenge to Chinese society for the coming decades.

REFERENCES

Doyle, G. 1987. "China's Potential in International Coal Trade". IEA Coal Research, London.

ECON 1990. "Virkninger av klimapolitikk på Olje- og Gassmarkedene". (Report to the Norwegian Dept. of Energy on the effects of a CO_2-tax on international oil and gas markets). ECON-report no. 10/1990, Oslo.

Friedly, D. 1990. "China's Oil Industry: A Decade in Review and Challenges Ahead". A report of the China Energy Study, Energy Program, East-West Centre, Honululu, Hawaii, March.

Haugland, T. and K. Roland 1990. "Energy, Environment and Development in China". EED-publication no.17, Oslo.

IEA. 1989. "China" IEA/IER (89)5, presented to the Adhoc group on International Energy Relations, Paris, March.

IEA. 1990. Coal Information 1990. Paris, June.

Levine, M.D. and X. Liu 1990. "Energy Conservation Programs in the Peoples Republic of China" Lawrence Berkeley Laboratory and Energy Research Institute, Beijing.

Li, A. and D. Friedly. 1990. "China's Natural Gas: A Disappointing Decade". A report of the China Energy Study, East-West Centre, Honululu, Hawai.

Ministry of Energy. 1989. "Energy in China". Ministry of Energy, People's Republic of China.

Shen, L. and L. Liu. 1991. "Energy Development and Environmental Protection: Dual Challenges for China", in *Energy and Environment* vol. 2 no. 4.

Smil. 1988. "Energy in China's Modernizations". M.E Sharp, Armonk, NY.

World Bank. 1985. "The Energy sector". Annex 3 to China Long-Term Development Issues and Options.

World Bank. 1990. "China: Country Economic Memorandum Between Plan and Market". Report no. 8440-CHa, Country Operations Division, China Department, Washington DC, May.

Wu and Chen. 1982. "Our Views on the Resolution of China's Rural Energy Reqiurements". Guangzhou Institute of Energy Conservation, Guangzhou.

CHAPTER 13

Acid Rain in Asia: Regional Analysis and Policies

by

W.K. Foell

__*Abstract*__

With the notable exception of China, the potential impacts of acid deposition are only just beginning to be recognized in Asia. The expected high growths of economic activity and its associated energy production suggest SO_2 emissions scenarios for Asia which could have serious long-term and Asia-wide impacts on ecosystems, health and materials along with associated political ramifications of trans-boundary environmental pollution. Because of these future high emission levels, there is an urgent need to develop inventories with higher spatial resolution as well as a region-wide atmospheric transport model to assess strategies and agreements for reduction of acid rain impacts. Strategies for mitigation of the acid rain problem would appear to be closely linked with many of the policies under discussion for addressing the issues associated with emissions of greenhouse gases and the associated problems of the global change. The combined benefits of policies that will mitigate global warming, in addition to providing protection of ecosystems and public health from the damaging effects of sulfur and nitrogen oxides, may be seen by policy makers as very attractive options. An international collaborative Project on Acid Rain and Emissions in Asia has been established to address the above issues.

T. Sterner (ed.), Economic Policies for Sustainable Development, 227–239.

I INTRODUCTION

Many of the environmental problems that have emerged in the last two decades can be characterized by two factors: they are triggered by rapid socioeconomic development and the spatial resolution of their impacts is usually well beyond the local and often even the national scale. These two important factors argue persuasively for the establishment of a policy analysis framework and an environmental management program, both of which address regional (multi-nation) impacts.

Both of the above two factors are particularly relevant within the Asian context. In addressing the first factor, socioeconomic development, attention must be paid not only to the costs of abating but also to the costs of not abating. Especially in developing countries it is important to point out that benefits of abatement do exist. Concurrent with the explicit recognition of these benefits has been the emergence of the concept of sustainability, as introduced by the World Commission on Environment and Development.

Development policies, which in the long run are not sustainable because of their increasingly negative impacts on the productivity of human and natural systems, are proving costly for industrialized countries. Except for the case of China, the possibility that acid deposition could in the coming decade reach a level having widespread and diverse impacts throughout Asia has only recently begun to be addressed. It is well-known from experience in Europe and North America that acid deposition can damage fresh water ecosystems, terrestrial systems including crops and forests, man-made structures and human health. However, in Asia, there is little specific information available on the possible consequences of acid deposition.

The second factor, namely, the increasing tendency of environmental impacts to extend their domain to points at greater distances from the pollution source, has been strongly demonstrated by the nature of acidification problems in Europe and North America. In North America the acid precursor emissions of the Midwestern industrial heartland of the U.S. inflict their damage on the states of the Northeastern part of the U.S. or on Canada, hundreds or even a few thousand kilometers distant. In Europe some 30 countries influence each others environment so that national solutions are not adequate. An environmental decision in one country can greatly influence the situations of its neighbors. Preliminary analysis indicates that the same national interdependence may exist in the case of acid deposition and impacts in Asia.

In most Asian countries there does not seem to be a strong scientific nor public constituency to address the potentially serious problems in the future for long-range transport and deposition of sulfur and nitrogen species and consequent damage to ecosystems, health and materials. The long-term and regional implications of potential impacts of this type touch not only the natural environment but also have implications for important economic and cultural activities such as forestry, agriculture and tourism. The political ramifications of transboundary environmental pollution in Asia are also likely to be serious.

This paper addresses the environmental issues surrounding the problem of acid rain in Asia, within the context of the need to develop regional policies and institutional frameworks for environmental management. The emphasis will be on the regional nature of the problem and on the need for a strong policy assessment program in the region in order to establish and coordinate national and regional strategies for addressing the emerging problem.

2 BACKGROUND OF THE ACID RAIN PROBLEM IN ASIA

Fossil fuels are used in large quantities in Asia such that local air pollution is becoming a serious problem and high pollutant deposition levels are being measured in an increasing number of locations. Emission regulations in many countries (with the notable exception of Japan) are not very stringent. Energy plans in many countries (particularly China, India, Thailand and South Korea) call for accelerated development of fossil fuel energy systems. Most of these would involve coal combustion, which would entail greatly increased emissions of acid deposition precursors. Because these would likely be emitted from large energy facilities with high stacks, they could increase the transport of these acidifying substances to sensitive geographical area.

An overview of some of the key elements of the acid rain situation in Asia was developed from information presented at the 1989 Workshop on Acid Rain in Asia (Report of 1989 Workshop on Acid Rain in Asia). A graphic summary of this information is sketched in Figure 1. Relative sulfur dioxide emissions in 1985 by country or region are indicated by vertical bars. Emissions are significant in China, India, Japan, and the Koreas, and are small but very rapidly growing in several other countries of South and Southeast Asia.

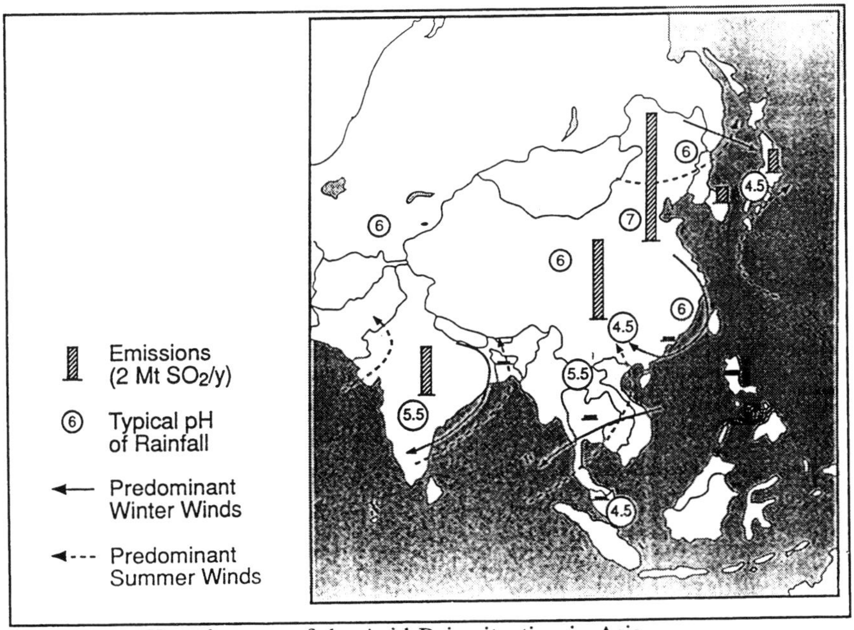

Figure 1 Key elements of the Acid Rain situation in Asia

Deposition patterns of emissions are largely determined by wind flow patterns, shown by arrows in the figure. In Winter (January) the flow is generally from the land mass to the ocean, while in summer (July) the reverse is true. Typical monitored values of pH are shown in the circles. Low pH values, e.g., 4.5, occur in Japan and southern China where emissions are large; elsewhere the pH values are 6 to 7. Because of the paucity of monitoring sites, we cannot discount the possibility of low-pH values at other unsuspected locations.

2.1 Meteorology of Asia

Most of the air pollution problems previously identified in the nations of Asia are confined to localized areas of high emissions which are usually associated with the densely populated cities of this region, such as Beijing, Bombay, Calcutta, Seoul, Bangkok, Hong Kong, Manila and Kuala Lumpur. The few attempts to address air pollution issues in the developing world to date, have, therefore, focused on these localized urban pollution problems. However, the projected very high emissions and the particular meteorological conditions of Asia are causing reconsideration of this perception for a number of reasons (Bhatti et al., 1990):

1. The increased use of very high smokestacks will result in increased residence time and greater potential for long-range transport of acid rain.

2. The higher temperature and sunlight intensity generally present in Asia increase the efficiency of atmospheric chemical reactions, particularly those transforming SO_2 and NO_X to acidic sulfates and nitrates (Chatfield and Crutzen, 1984).

3. Stable air masses in Asia during large portions of the year may increase the residence time of pollutants, there allowing greater opportunity for conversion to secondary pollutants. In addition, the strong mixing of the lower portion of the atmosphere, characteristic of much of the tropics and subtropics, would transport pollutants to higher altitudes (thus mimicking tall smokestacks) where they would have longer residence times and be carried farther afield (Chatfield and Crutzen, 1984)

4. High rainfall rates (at least seasonally) would increase the proportion of SO2 and NO_X that is converted into sulfates and nitrates by aqueous-phase reactions. These sulfates and nitrates can then be coupled to large-scale precipitation producing weather systems and deposited farther from emission sources than the same acidic substances produced via gaseous-phase (dry) processes. Also the greater amounts of rainfall in these regions would contribute to larger total hydrogen ion deposition than that predicted on the basis of precipitation pH alone (McDowell, 1988).

Clearly the above factors are complex, and their unambiguous interpretation would require further analysis. However, the potential for acid precursor transformation and transport to regions beyond the local areas of concern is clearly a strong possibility and warrants serious consideration of preventive measures.

2.2 Environmental Quality and Impacts on Receptors

Ultimately it is the impact that acid deposition has on the natural and man-made environment that is of greatest concern to society. From a public policy perspective, the most important issue is not whether acid deposition does or can occur, but whether the environment of the area is vulnerable to its potential effects. In Europe and North America there is now substantial accumulated evidence on the capacity of acid deposition's damage on a number of components of the environment. Unfortunately in most of Asia there is an absence of both research and empirical evidence.

Soils, through their differing ability to process and neutralize acidic inputs, determine to a large extent how acid deposition will affect the terrestrial and aquatic ecosystems. Soil sensitivity to acidification is based on a number of factors, the most important of which are texture, base saturation and cation exchange capacity (CEC), organic matter content, anion mobility, thickness of vegetation cover and rainfall rate. Various areas of Asia would appear to satisfy one or more of these conditions.

The impact of acid deposition on the natural environment is dictated by the sensitivity of the flora and fauna of a region as well as the sensitivity of its soil. Any change in productivity of the flora or fauna of Asia could have severe consequences because of the large human population dependent on these resources. However, very little research has been done on species extant in Asia. Among the general concerns, two points have been raised which are particularly relevant. It is possible that in the tropical and subtropical climates of Asia, with the associated longer leaf life, the cumulative effects of acid deposition could be large enough to cause direct damage, although this has not been observed in temperate climates. Secondly, some of Asia's forests are located in mountainous areas where exposure to acidic species is potentially higher than at lower levels, as experienced in Europe and North America.

Acid deposition corrodes man-made surfaces such as those of statues, monuments, buildings and vehicles. Due to the prevalence in Asia of a vast number of significant cultural, religious, and historical relics, often hundreds or thousands of years old, deterioration due to acid deposition could be of great concern, both because of deep cultural values and because of potential long-term negative impacts on tourism.

In summary, Asia's acid rain situation is becoming increasingly similar to that which many industrialized countries experienced one to two decades ago, when they first recognized the seriousness of the problem. At that time, those countries responded with varying degrees of preventive actions and further investigation. Their experiences should provide some valuable guidelines for Asia. However, the particular conditions in Asia may provide some significant differences.

Developing and implementing approaches to reduce anthropogenic emissions will require the efforts of many organizations, both public and private. Currently there is little regional coordination. However, as national regulators and the development community become increasingly aware of this issue and the consequences of no action become clear, sound programs and projects could be developed in the region.

In order to reduce the emissions of acid precursors, the Asian countries will have to shift their energy policy through:

-Expanded use of cleaner fuels and renewable energy resources
-Upgrading of older inefficient facilities
-Instituting energy efficiency measures
-Industrial restructuring for regional energy efficiency
-Installation of pollution control devices

Strategies to reduce acidifying emissions will also result in reduction of other pollutants such as greenhouse gases. There are two major international initiatives underway to address greenhouse gas emissions: the Intergovernmental Panel on Climate Change (IPCC), under the auspices of UNEP and WMO; and the Global Environmental Facility (GEF), administered by the World Bank in association with UNEP and UNDP. Similar initiatives for acid rain in Asia may be needed because of the regional and global implications and to obtain regional agreement.

In response to the above recognition and growing concern about acid rain in Asia, a small group of international specialists has held a series of workshops on this topic and established a project to address the problems. The focus of the project is the development of an integrative program for the purpose of formulating and assessing long-term strategies to confront the emerging problems of acid rain and the anthropogenic atmospheric emissions of a wide range of substances of concern at both the national and Asia-wide levels (see Workshops on Acid Rain 1989 and 1990).

One of the initial outputs of the above project is the development of Asia-wide economic, energy, and emission scenarios which will provide an assessment of region and country-specific future energy emissions and control strategies. These scenarios have been used to assist in the development of an awareness and understanding of the magnitude of the acid rain problem. The scenarios and the analytic technique upon which they are based also are being used to develop the more detailed methodology which will be used to provide emissions with a higher spatial resolution in a later phase of the above project.

The following section summarizes the results and the implications of these initial scenarios.

3 COUNTRY-SPECIFIC CURRENT AND FUTURE ENERGY USE

3.1 Current Situation

The current energy system which has evolved to fuel Asia's economic development is striking in many respects. First, it is almost completely dependent on fossil fuels (more than 95% of its commercial energy). Second, approximately 60% of the consumed fossil fuel is in the form of coal, with most of the remainder being fuel oil. Both of these fuels contribute significantly to the emissions of acid rain precursors in Asia. Equally important from an environmental perspective are the extremely high growth rates of Asian energy systems. During the past decade these annual rates have greatly exceeded (by factors of 2 to 4) those in Western industrialized countries, which are now relatively stable at a few percent or less. There is little reason to expect that per capita energy use in the developing countries of Asia will stabilize anywhere near its present level of approximately 0.5 tons of oil equivalent per year, which is approximately ten percent of the per capita use in North

America and Europe. If the Western experience can be used as a guide, even with strong conservation measures we can expect continued very high energy growth in Asia for many years.

Of particular concern is the continued growth of coal use. Coal use in the region in 1987 was approximately 1360 million metric tons with the three largest users being China, India, and Japan. Preliminary data and estimates presented at the 1989 Workshop indicated that regional coal use in the year 2000 could be as high as 2 300 million metric tons, with very large growth increments in China and India, and significant growth rates in several other countries, including Indonesia, Thailand, and the Koreas.

3.2 Framework for Emissions Analysis

Described briefly below is a framework developed by Foell and Green to calculate a range of emissions scenarios for 13 developing Asian countries for a range of energy scenarios based on a variety of socio-economic and technical assumptions. From these energy scenarios, national values for sulfur emissions from fossil-fuel combustion were calculated, based on fuel characteristics, combustion technology and emission control assumptions.

The objective of the analysis was to calculate SO_2 emissions resulting from fossil fuel consumption in a base year (1986) and two future years, 2000 and 2010. Energy use in the scenarios is disaggregated into 5 sectors (industry, residential, commercial and agriculture transportation, energy-sector energy use and other) and three fuel types (coal, oil, and natural gas) for each country. A uniform emission factor for SO_2 is applied to each fuel type in each sector. Such methodology is often adopted in national studies to account for the variations in sulfur, ash, and energy content with fuel types and differences in combustion technology. Additionally, the emission factor used will be influenced by the control strategy for each sector. The resultant emissions are then summed to give the total SO_2 emissions for each country.

The energy consumption scenarios which were developed for this analysis were in general based upon scenarios taken directly from the literature, e.g., from a country report developed by an energy agency in the country of interest. This approach was used as much as possible for the so-called base case scenarios. Wherever possible, both the assumptions and the resulting energy consumption patterns were compared with available related studies. In essentially every case, the "alternative scenarios" required a considerable amount of supplementary analysis because of the need to introduce different assumptions on a sectoral or fuel-by-fuel basis. The general scenario assumptions are described below. (For a more detailed description, see Foell and Green, 1990).

3.3 Scenario Assumptions

Four main scenarios were developed.

S1: Base Case Scenario

S2: Efficiency Case: Energy improvements are introduced by sector in the residential, industrial, and transportation sectors as well as the electricity distribution network. Significant improvements over the base case values were introduced progressively in 2000 and 2010. These improvements were in general on the order of 15 to 30 percent, depending on the country and sector involved, and were assumed to be in part price-induced and in part through other interventions. A further assumption, probably reasonable in comparison with the gross assumptions made for such a long time horizon, is that these efficiency improvements occur equally across all industrial fuels, i.e., they are fuel independent.

S3: Low Carbon Emission Case: This scenario combines the energy efficiency improvements of S2 and shifts to fuels with low carbon and acid-precursor emissions. The study examined the availability of natural gas, and where judged appropriate, assumed substitution for a fraction of the coal or oil used for electricity generation in the year 2010. In addition, new and renewable electric generating sources which are free from all precursor emissions were introduced in that year to a small degree.

S4: Control Scenario: Sulfur controls were assumed to be implemented on electric power plants in a phased approach. In this approach, 50 percent of all new power generation between 1986 and 2000 was assumed to have 90 percent sulfur removal and all new power generation between 2000 and 2010 was assumed to have 90 percent sulfur removal. The controls were assumed to be applied to the Base Case energy and emission figures.

3.4 Scenario Results

Of particular interest in the results of this analysis are the continued high growth rate of primary energy consumption and the continued dependence on fossil fuel energy sources, particularly coal and oil. In aggregate, commercial energy consumption for the region as a whole in the Base Case scenario is expected to grow at above 4.5 percent per year from 1986 through 2000 and only slightly less than 4.5 percent per year from 2000-2010. As a result, primary commercial energy is expected to reach approximately 2000 million tons of oil equivalent (Mtoe) in 2000 and 3000 Mtoe in 2010.

Even when considering significant improvement in energy efficiency, energy growth in the region remains at relatively high levels. Efficiency improvements assumed in S2, the Efficiency Scenario, result in a net savings of about 250 Mtoe in 2000 and 600 Mtoe in 2010 from the base case. However, energy growth rates for both periods remain at about 3.5 percent per year, still far higher than those of industrialized western countries.

Also of interest is the continued dominance of China's energy use in the regional totals. In 1986, China was responsible for nearly 55 percent of the region's total primary energy. Despite the assumption of a significant decrease in China's overall growth rate for energy (from 5.2 percent in 1980-87 to 3.9 percent in 2000-10), China is expected to comprise 48 percent of the region's total energy use in 2010. Coal has supplied about 75 percent of China's commercial energy needs during the 1980s, and this situation is not expected to change during the 1990s or into the next century.

The regional sulfur dioxide emissions are shown in Figure 2 for the Base Case and for the three alternative scenarios. The total emissions for 1986 are approximately 28 million tons of SO_2. By comparison, the estimated U.S. sulfur dioxide emissions in 1985 were 21 million tons. Notable in 1986 were the emissions of China (19 million tons), India (3.2 million tons) and the Republic of Korea (1.2 million tons). By far the largest portion of the 1986 emissions is from coal-based facilities.

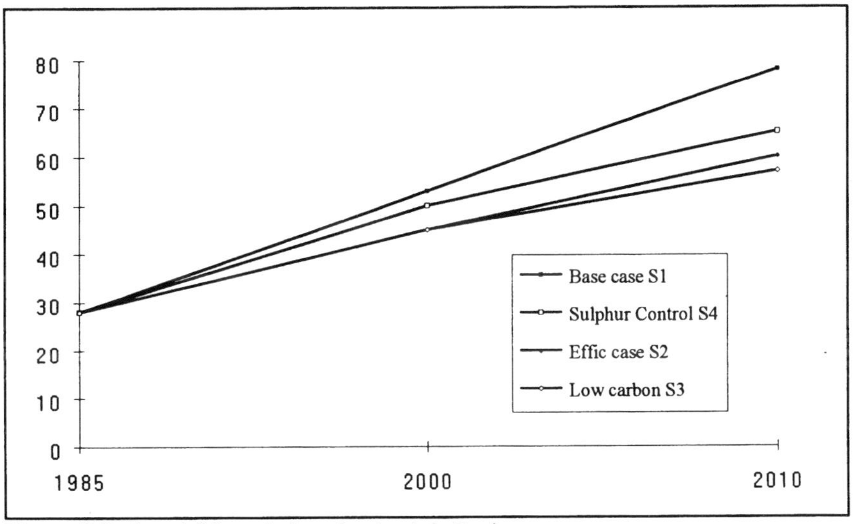

Figure 2 Projected SO_2 emissions for the Asia Region

The base scenario shows very high growth rates of the emissions, as might be expected from the scenario assumptions described above, and in particular the continued or growing reliance on coal in several of the major countries. Coal is responsible for the largest part of the emissions and, in both the base year and in 2010, accounts for approximately two-thirds of the total, followed by petroleum which accounts for around thirty percent. The contribution of natural gas is very small. By the years 2000 and 2010, total emissions for the 13 countries have grown to 53 and 76 million tons, respectively. Annual growth rates of SO_2 are 4.6 and 3.7 percent in the periods 1986-2000 and 2000-2010, respectively. Of this total, coal is responsible for 35 million tons in the year 2000 and 50 million tons in the year 2010, nearly 65 percent of the total emissions in 2010.

The above emission magnitudes are large by almost any standard, although it is clear that the emission densities and the meteorology will be critical factors in determining the severity of the resulting deposition. Nevertheless, it is our opinion that serious consideration will be given to emission control strategies during the coming decade. This may occur out of concern about acid precursors alone, or it may result from a combined concern about acid precursor and other emissions such as greenhouse gases, e.g. carbon dioxide. On this basis the other scenarios described above, i.e., S2, S3, and the sulfur control scenario, S4 are of considerable interest.

The sulfur control strategy, S4, leads to a reduction of 3 million and 12 million tons in 2000 and 2010, respectively. Interestingly, this pollution control strategy, although quite ambitious in its rate of implementation, does not ultimately lead to the magnitude of reduction achieved by efficiency improvements and fuel shifts. Of course, the economics of these alternatives need to be investigated in some detail. If efficiency improvements, fuel shifts, and emissions controls were all implemented, it appears that the emissions could possibly be stabilized between 2000 and 2010. However, reduction in the absolute level would require more drastic measures. Similar analyses for emissions of NO_X are described in Foell and Green, 1990.

4 SUMMARY AND CONCLUSIONS

With the notable exception of China (e.g., Zhao and Xiong, 1988), impacts of acid deposition are only just beginning to be recognized in parts of Asia. Given the future economic and energy outlooks presented here, the situation is likely to deteriorate rapidly in the not so distant future. The long-term and regional impacts on ecosystems, health, and materials, along with the associated political ramifications of trans-boundary environmental pollution are likely to be very serious. The time has come to develop a dialogue to raise environmental awareness in the region with respect to this emerging problem. Such awareness, coupled with analytic and policy development experience gained in the West, could help to ameliorate the problem in its early stages.

This paper addresses one of the major components of the assessment of the potential problem, namely, the development for Asia of a country-specific and regionally-aggregated emissions inventory of acid rain precursors, i.e., SO_2 and eventually NO_X. The above analyses of energy use and acid precursor emissions in developing countries in Asia have led to a number of conclusions.

1. The scenarios developed for the region reveal extremely high emissions of SO_2 and NO_X within the next one or two decades. These emissions are shown to exceed current emissions in both North America and Europe. There appears to be the potential for considerable in-country acidic deposition as well as concern about transfrontier pollution.

2. Because of these high values, there is an urgent need to develop inventories with higher spatial resolution so that adequate atmospheric modelling and long-range pollutant transport analysis can be conducted. The existing preliminary region-wide studies in Asia need to be compared and incorporated into a framework which will be useable and useful for widespread application within the countries in the region.

3. Development of a regional atmospheric transport model is needed. Many countries will be both importers and exporters of trans-frontier pollution. The costs and benefits of various emission reduction strategies will be unevenly spread across the countries. In Europe, the use of atmosphere transport models within the framework of policy-friendly models has been a valuable input to negotiations and the development of strategies and agreements for

reduction of acid rain impacts. A similar program would appear to be extremely beneficial for Asia.

4. Because of the high growth rates, much of the emissions control strategy and technology would likely be applied to new facilities. This situation may provide an opportunity for extensive application of modern clean coal technologies in the region. Serious considerations should be given to the application of indigenous clean coal technologies as well as those currently being applied and developed in Western countries.

5. Strategies which implement energy efficiency improvements have potential for substantial reductions in emissions of acid precursors. These reductions may have greater potential to limit emissions than ambitious control strategies. If emission control measures are implemented, it is essential that their costs be incorporated in a timely way into energy prices, to provide appropriate pricing signals to consumers, encouraging greater long-term efficiency in consumption.

6. Experience in Europe and North America has shown that lead times are extremely long for the development and implementation of policy and control strategies. It is therefore imperative to begin now with analysis, design and development of technological, economics and institutional strategies. Among these might be the development of frameworks for the application of programs of emission targets, technology transfer and assistance from industrialized countries, as well as exploration of economics-based approaches such as emissions trading, etc.

7. Strategies for mitigation of the acid rain problem would appear to be closely linked with many of the policies under discussion for addressing the issues associated with emissions of greenhouse gases and the associated problems of global climate change. The analysis described above should carefully consider the interrelationships between the two concerns. The benefits of international cooperation in addressing complex multi-faceted problems are often significant. Cooperative efforts have in most cases resulted in less-costly overall solutions than would have resulted from individual actions, necessarily addressing only partial solutions. Even given the extremely high predicted growth rates of acid precursor emissions predicted, the associated impacts alone may not be sufficient to influence policy-makers regarding future energy choices. However, the combined benefits of policies that will mitigate global warming, in addition to providing protection of ecosystems and public health from the damaging effects of sulfur and nitrogen oxides, may be seen by policy-makers as very attractive options.

5 CURRENT AND FUTURE RESEARCH

The international collaborative Project on Acid Rain and Emissions in Asia, briefly described in Section 2, has established the following as its broad goals (Second Workshop on Acid Rain in Asia, 1990):

- To develop approaches that assist in deriving regional and sub-regional policies to avoid the rapidly emerging problems of atmospheric emissions in Asia.

- To provide basic assessments needed to catalyze the process of inter-governmental policy dialogue on acid rain precursor emission control in the Asia Region.

- To develop basic strategies for policy advice, institution building, and investment incentives in countries of the Asia Region to deal with problem of acid rain precursor emission control.

In recent years, integrated assessment models have been utilized for international negotiations on acid rain. The purpose of these models is to provide negotiators or regulators with a full regional picture of the problems associated with the entire causal process from energy systems and emissions through to the ultimate impact on natural and man-made systems. The model user can analyze the regional and national implications of various scenarios, which include options for energy use, control strategies, and mitigation policies. Such an effort for the acid rain problem in Europe has led to the Regional Acidification INformation and Simulation (RAINS-EUROPE) model (IIASA, 1990).

The Project on Acid Rain and Emissions in Asia has established as its initial objective the adaption of the RAINS-EUROPE model to the Asia region. RAINS-ASIA will be developed by integration of the following modules applied to the Asian situation:

(1) Energy and Emissions Module
(2) Atmospheric Transport and Deposition Module
(3) Ecosystem Sensitivity Module

Initially, RAINS-ASIA will be used to conduct a preliminary analysis of different energy and emission scenarios. The impact of these energy and emission scenarios consists of (a) acid deposition and (b) comparison of acid deposition to the best estimates for sensitivity of ecosystems in Asia based on the European and North American data. The subsequent phases of this project will allow for refinement of the impact data based on specific work on critical Asian ecosystems, more detailed scenarios analysis and inclusion of other pollutants.

Specific sub-objectives of this initial project phase are to involve scientists and policy-makers from Asian countries and development institutions in all aspects of the project to increase their awareness and to transfer the model RAINS-ASIA and associated technologies to participating Asian governments and organizations.

REFERENCES

Bhatti, N., D.G. Streets, and W.K. Foell. 1990. "Acid Rain in Asia," In: Foell, W.K. and Sharma, D. (Eds) *Proceedings of the Second Annual Workshop on Acid Rain and Emissions in Asia.* pp. 5-33, Asian Institute of Technology, Bangkok, Thailand.

Chatfield, R.B. and P.J. Crutzen. 1984. "Sulfur Dioxide in Remote Oceanic Air: Cloud Transport of Reactive Precursors", J. Geophysical Research, 89:7111-7132.

Foell, W.K., and C.W. Green. 1990. "Acid Rain in Asia: An Economic, Energy, and Emissions Overview": In: Foell, W.K. and Sharma, D. (Eds) *Proceedings of the Second Annual Workshop on Acid Rain and Emissions in Asia.* pp 123-145, Asian Institute of Technology, Bangkok, Thailand.

International Institute for Applied Systems Analysis. 1990. "The Rains Model of Acidification: Science and Strategies in Europe". Alcamo, J., Shaw, R., and Hordijk, L. (Eds). Kluwer Academic Publishers, Dordrecht, the Netherlands.

McDowell, W.H. 1988. "Potential Effects of Acid Deposition on Tropical Terrestrial Ecosystems", in: *Acidification in Tropical Countries*, SCOPE 36, Rodhe, H. and R. Herrera (eds.), Wiley and Sons, Chichester, U.K.

Second Workshop on Acid Rain in Asia: November 19-22, 1990. "Report of the Second Workshop on Acid Rain in Asia." Asian Institute of Technology, Bangkok, Thailand.

Workshop on Acid Rain in Asia: November 13-17, 1989. "Report of the Workshop on Acid Rain in Asia," Asian Institute of Technology, Bangkok, Thailand.

Zhao D. and J. Xiong. 1988. "Acidification in Southwestern China," In: Rodhe, H. and Herrera, R. (Eds) *Acidification in Tropical Countries*. SCOPE Report 36, John Wiley and Sons, Chichester, U.K.

CHAPTER 14

Environmental Regulation of Transport: US, OECD and Global Trends in Legislation and Policy

by

Michael P. Walsh

Abstract

Vehicle exhaust emissions are distinguished from other environmental problems by a number of characteristic features. Firstly they are caused by large numbers of mobile sources. Secondly technology, fuel, driving habits and many other factors influence in a rather complex way the character of the emissions. When studying total vehicle exhausts, as opposed, for instance, to carbon emissions, it is therefore natural to rely quite heavily on detailed technical norms. This chapter describes how these norms are formulated in different countries and traces how successively more ambitious norms appear to spread from California and Japan across to other industrialized countries and then, with varying speed, be adopted also in Third World countries.

T. Sterner (ed.), Economic Policies for Sustainable Development, 240–260.

1 INTRODUCTION

Motor vehicles have been and remain a dominant pollution source in most areas of the world, emitting significant quantities of carbon monoxide, hydrocarbons, nitrogen oxides, fine particles and lead. In an effort to minimize the motor vehicle pollution problem, emission rates from cars in highly industrialized countries have been limited by legislation since the 1968 model year. Over time, these requirements have gradually been tightened. Today virtually every OECD country requires the availability and use of unleaded gasoline in new cars and by the end of this year virtually all new cars sold in these countries will be equipped with catalytic converters. Increasingly, the same problems which led to the adoption of tight standards in the highly industrialized countries have been noted in developing countries and many of these countries have taken steps to lower their vehicle emission rates. While most of these requirements have taken the form of mandatory regulations, they have frequently been complemented by or even replaced by economic incentives.

The purpose of this chapter is to review the status of motor vehicle pollution control efforts with particular emphasis on the emerging efforts of developing countries.

2 THE PROBLEM

Worldwide, cars, trucks, buses, and other motor vehicles are playing an ever increasing role in global climate change and air pollution. As large oil consumers, motor vehicles are major sources of carbon dioxide; volatile organic compounds (VOCs) and nitrogen oxides, the precursors to tropospheric ozone; carbon monoxide (CO); and chlorofluorocarbons (CFCs). All of these gases contribute to greenhouse warming either directly or indirectly; CFCs also contribute to depletion of the stratospheric ozone layer. Many of them also contribute directly to adverse health effects.

2.1 Tropospheric Ozone

Although ozone in the lower atmosphere does not come directly from motor vehicles, they are the major source of the ozone precursors, hydrocarbons and nitrogen oxides, throughout the industrialized world. Over the past 100 years, "background" ozone levels have approximately doubled (Volz and Kley, 1988), and monitoring data suggest that ozone concentrations are increasing by about 1 percent per year in the northern hemisphere (Ciborowski, 1989).

Besides contributing to the greenhouse problem, ozone pollution also adversely affects human health, crops, other vegetation, and materials. Eye irritation, coughing and chest discomfort, headaches, upper respiratory illness, increased asthma attacks, and reduced pulmonary function can all plague people exposed to ozone (American Lung Association, 1989). Widespread and pervasive, smog looks to be a long term problem in many areas of the world unless more stringent controls are adopted (US EPA, 1991).

2.2 Carbon Monoxide

Carbon monoxide -- an odorless, invisible gas created when fuels containing carbon are burned incompletely -- poses a serious threat to human health. Participating in various chemical reactions in the atmosphere, it also contributes to smog formation and the buildup of methane.

Exposure to carbon monoxide results primarily from motor vehicle emissions, though in some locales wood burning is also an important source (for example from cooking in poor households, see Chapter 11). People with coronary artery disease who are exposed to carbon monoxide during exercise experience chest pain (angina); exposure also alters their electrocardiograms (American Lung Association, 1989). Although ambient carbon monoxide levels have been reduced across Europe, Japan, and the United States, the problem is far from under control (US EPA, 1991). Global carbon monoxide concentrations in the lower atmosphere are increasing by between 0.8 percent and 1.4 percent per year (Khalil and Rasmussen, 1988).

Carbon monoxide can elevate concentrations of tropospheric ozone and methane in several ways. First, carbon monoxide helps convert nitric oxide (NO) to nitrogen dioxide (NO_2) -- a crucial step in ozone formation (US EPA, 1986). Second, the hydroxyl radical (OH) that eventually removes carbon monoxide from the atmosphere is also the principal chemical that destroys ozone and methane. If carbon monoxide levels increase, OH concentrations will fall and regional concentrations of ozone and methane will rise.

Comprehensive data are not available on global air pollution emissions from transportation and other activities. For the twenty-four OECD countries, however, motor vehicles are the dominant source of emissions of carbon monoxide, oxides of nitrogen, and volatile organic compounds. (See Table 1).

Table 1 Motor Vehicle Share of OECD Pollutant Emission (1000 tons, 1980)

Pollutant	Total Emissions	Motor Vehicle Emissions	% Vehicles
NO_X	36,019	17,012	(47%)
HC	33,869	13,239	(39%)
CO	119,148	78,227	(66%)

Source: OECD Environmental Data, Organization for Economic Cooperation and Development, Paris, 1987.

2.3 Carbon-Dioxide

Virtually the entire global motor vehicle fleet runs on fossil fuels, primarily oil. For every gallon of oil consumed by a motor vehicle, about 19 pounds of carbon dioxide (containing about 5.3 pounds of carbon) go directly into the atmosphere.[1] In other words, for a typical fill up at the service station (estimated at 15 gallons of gasoline), about 300 pounds of carbon dioxide are eventually released into the atmosphere. Globally, motor vehicles account for about a third of world oil consumption and about 14 percent of the world's carbon dioxide emissions from fossil fuel burning.

2.4 Chlorofluorocarbons (CFCs)

Highly potent greenhouse gases, CFCs also reduce the protective stratospheric ozone layer (Gribbin, 1988). During the Antarctic spring, the ozone hole spans an area the size of North America. At certain altitudes over the Antarctic, the ozone is destroyed almost completely.

If CFCs continue to deplete the world's stratospheric ozone layer, ultraviolet radiation would increase and so would ground level ozone formation. Even a moderate loss in the total ozone column would significantly boost peak ozone levels at the earth's surface. By allowing more ultraviolet radiation through the ozone shield, such a loss is also expected to increase the number of skin cancers and impair the human immune system. Increased ultraviolet radiation might also harm the life supporting plankton that dwell in the ocean's upper levels, thus jeopardizing marine food chains that depend on the tiny plankton.

A major source of CFCs in the atmosphere is motor vehicle air conditioning, and in 1987 approximately 48 percent of all new cars, trucks, and buses manufactured worldwide were equipped with airconditioners (UNEP Technology Review, 1989). (CFCs also are used as a blowing agent in the production of seating and other foam products, but this is a considerably smaller vehicular use.) Annually, about 120,000 metric tons of CFCs are used in new vehicles and in servicing air conditioners in older vehicles. In all, these uses account for about 28 percent of global demand for CFC-12. As agreed under the Montreal Protocol, CFCs are to be completely phased out of new vehicles by the turn of the century, a welcome but long overdue step. CFC's emitted over the next decade will cause damage to the planet for the next two centuries.

2.5 Toxic Chemicals

Historically, stationary industrial sources of air toxics have been the first subject of air toxics regulations and guidelines, in part because of existing permitting authority at the state and local level. However, over time as the vehicle population has grown, mobile sources have become recognized as a major contributor to the overall health risks associated with air toxics. A variety of US EPA studies have documented that in individual metropolitan areas mobile sources are one of the most important and possibly the most important source category in terms of contributions to health risks associated with air toxics. Most recently, EPA has concluded that motor vehicles cause approximately 54 to 58% of nationwide cancer cases associated

---

[1] This applies to direct tail-pipe emissions only. Transportation, refining and distribution account for perhaps 15 to 20 percent of total emissions.

with toxic air emissions. "Area sources are found to contribute approximately 75% of the total number of annual cancer cases (including those from secondary formaldehyde) with point sources contributing approximately 25 percent of the total. Of the area sources, the major source is mobile sources, contributing 78 percent of the total annual incidence attributed to area sources". In looking at the sources of the motor vehicle problem, Table 2 indicates that diesel particulate and various organic compounds stand out. In addition, the EPA projections indicate that strategies designed to reduce especially diesel particulate and hydrocarbon emissions will lower many of the risks in the future.

Table 2 Summary of risk estimates

US CANCER INCIDENCES/YEAR			
Motor Vehicle Pollutant	1986	1995	2005
Diesel Particulate	178-860	106-662	104-518
Formaldehyde	46-86	24-43	27-30
Benzene	100-155	60-107	67-114
Gasoline Vapors	17-68	24-95	30-119
Other Gas Phase Organics			
1,3-Butadiene	236-269	139-172	144-171
Acetaldehyde	2	1	1
Gasoline Particulate	1-176	1-156	1-146
Dioxins	ND	ND	ND
Asbestos	5-33	ND	ND
Vehicle Interior Emissions	ND	ND	ND
Cadmium	<1	<1	<1
Ethylene Dibromide	1	<1	<1
Total	586-1650	355-1236	374-1099

Dealing with the above problems requires aggressive government and industry action and increasingly this action is taking place. The next section reviews some of the progress made to date in developing technological solutions to reduce emissions and the trend toward introduction of these technologies in both developed and developing countries.

3 VEHICLE POLLUTION CONTROL TECHNOLOGY

3.1 Gasoline Fueled Vehicles

Significant progress has occurred during the past two decades in the development of a wide variety of emissions reduction technologies for gasoline fueled vehicles.

Before controls were required, engine crankcases were vented directly to the atmosphere. Crankcase emissions controls which basically consist of closing the crankcase vent port were introduced on new cars in the United States in the early 1960's with the result that today, control of these emissions is no longer considered a serious technical concern.

The hydrocarbon evaporative emissions result from distillation of fuel in the carburetor float bowl and evaporation of fuel in the gas tank. To control these emissions, manufacturers generally feed these emissions back into the engine to be burned along with the other fuel. When the engine is not in operation, vapors are stored, either in the engine crankcase or in charcoal canisters which have a strong affinity for these emissions, and then burned off when the engine is started. Technology to control these vapors is now readily available but its overall effectiveness is dependent on the fuel volatility for which it has been designed.

Exhaust emissions of hydrocarbons, carbon monoxide and nitrogen oxides are related to the air/fuel mixture inducted, the peak temperatures and pressures in each cylinder, whether lead is added to the gasoline, combustion chamber geometry, and other engine design parameters. Variations in these parameters are, therefore, capable of causing significant increases or decreases in these emissions. The most important parameters are probably air/fuel ratio and mixture preparation, ignition timing, and combustion chamber design. Variations in these parameters are usually key elements in vehicle controls when modest light duty vehicle emissions standards are imposed.

Dilution of the incoming charge has been shown to reduce peak cycle temperature by slowing flame speed and absorbing some heat of combustion. Recirculating a portion of the exhaust gas back into the incoming air/fuel mixture (EGR) thereby lowering peak cycle temperature is therefore used to lower NOx.

Improvements in mixture preparation, induction systems, and ignition systems can increase dilution tolerance. It can also be increased by increasing the burn rate or flame speed of the air-fuel charge. Techniques to do this include increased swirl and squish, shorter flame paths, and multiple ignition sources.

With so many interrelated engine design and operating variables playing an increasingly important role in the modern engine, the control system has taken on increased importance. Modifications in spark timing must be closely coordinated with air-fuel ratio changes and degrees of EGR test significant fuel economy or performance penalties result from emissions reductions, or NOx emissions increase as CO goes down. In addition, electronic controls which can be much more selective depending on engine load or speed have been found beneficial in preventing widespread adverse impacts.

Therefore, electronics have begun to replace more traditional mechanical controls. For example, electronic control of ignition timing has demonstrated an ability to optimize timing under all engine conditions and has the added advantage of reduced maintenance and improved durability compared with mechanical systems. When coupled with electronic control of EGR, it has been demonstrated that NOx emissions can be reduced with no fuel economy penalty and in some cases with improved fuel economy.

When stringent exhaust emissions standards (especially hydrocarbons or nitrogen oxides) are mandated, exhaust aftertreatment devices such as catalytic converters tend to be used to supplement engine modifications.

An oxidation catalyst is a device which is placed on the tailpipe of a car and which, if the chemistry and thermodynamics are correct, will oxidize almost all the HC and CO in the exhaust stream.

Three-way catalysts (so called because of their ability to lower HC, CO and NOx levels simultaneously) were first introduced in the United States in 1977 by Volvo and subsequently became widely used when the US NOx standard was lowered to 1.0 grams per mile. To work effectively, these catalysts require precise control of air/fuel mixtures. As a result, three way systems have indirectly fostered improved air/fuel management systems such as advanced carburetors and throttle body fuel injection systems as well as electronic controls.

Starting with 1975 model year cars, catalysts have been placed on upwards of 80 per cent of all new cars sold in the United States; in the last few years, either oxidation or three-way catalysts have been placed on all new gasoline fueled cars. In Japan and Canada, catalysts are also widely used to meet emission standards. Many cars in Austria, the Netherlands, Sweden and Germany are starting to be sold with these systems and they are required on new cars in Australia and Switzerland.One of the unique advantages of catalysts is their ability to selectively eliminate some of the more unhealthy compounds in vehicle exhaust such as aldehydes, reactive hydrocarbons and polynuclear hydrocarbons.

Since many of the two-wheeled vehicles which are prevalent in many developing countries are powered by two stroke engines, a few special comments are in order. As a general matter, most of the solutions to reduce emissions from four stroke engines can be applied to two strokes. However, in addition, since much of the HC emitted comes from the lubricating oil this deserves special attention. It is known that visible smoke can be reduced by the use of engine oils containing polyisobutylene, and also by leaner fuel oil ratios. Therefore the separated lubrication system, which brings about overall leaner fuel/oil ratios, seems to be favorable for smoke reduction (Sugiura and Kagaya, 1977). Further, Since 1986 mopeds with catalysts have been available in Switzerland and in Austria (Laimboch and Landerl, 1990). It is a fair conclusion to state today that the historical problems of high smoke and unburned hydrocarbons from two stroke engines technology are no longer technologically necessary. New technology promises to resolve these concerns. As examples, direct cylinder electronic fuel injection, electronic computer control, and catalytic exhaust conversion are now commonplace solutions (Wyczalek, 1991).

3.2 Diesel Fueled Vehicles

While the major technical problems associated with reducing emissions from gasoline cars are solved, it is apparent that reductions from these vehicles alone are not sufficient to solve the air pollution problems in many areas. Diesel trucks and buses have therefore been receiving increased attention as significant sources of particulates and NOx. The US has adopted standards for these vehicles which will foster technological developments similar to those which have already occurred for gasoline cars. These developments are receiving close attention from other countries. Basic approaches to diesel engine emission control fall into three major categories:

* engine modifications, including combustion chamber configuration and design, fuel injection timing and pattern, turbocharging and EGR;

* exhaust aftertreatment, including traps, trap oxidizers and catalysts; and

* fuel modifications, including control of fuel properties, fuel additives, alternative fuels.

NOx control techniques being phased into the diesel population include variable injection timing and pressure, charge cooling, and exhaust gas recirculation. Retarding injection timing, while a well known method of reducing NOx formation, can lead to increases in fuel consumption, particulate and hydrocarbon emissions. These problems can be mitigated by varying the injection timing with engine load or speed. Also, high pressure injection can reduce these problems. If coupled with electronic controls, it appears that NOx emissions could be reduced significantly with a simultaneous improvement in fuel economy (although not as great as could occur if electronics were added without any emission requirements).

4 PROGRESS IN LOWERING VEHICLE EMISSIONS - OECD

Advances in automotive technologies have made it possible to dramatically lower emissions from gasoline fueled motor vehicles. Increasingly, countries around the world have been taking advantage of them. Initial crankcase HC controls were first introduced in the early 60's followed by exhaust CO and HC standards later that decade. By the early to mid 1970's, most major industrial countries had initiated some level of vehicle pollution control program. For a variety of reasons -- differing types and degrees of air pollution problems, varying vehicle characteristics, economic conditions, etc. -- the emissions control approaches differ significantly between countries.

Because of the various problems associated with diesel smoke and particulate, control programs have also been started for trucks, buses and other diesels. In general, the initial focus was on smoke control because it was clearly visible and a nuisance. As the evidence has grown in recent years regarding the serious health and environmental risks of diesel exhausts, more attention has focused on control of the particles themselves for health reasons. For reasons of space, we will however concentrate on gasoline vehicles.

4.1 Gasoline Vehicles

4.1.1 Japan and the United States

During the mid to late 1970's, advanced technologies were introduced on most new cars in the US and Japan. These technologies resulted from a conscious decision to "force" the development of new approaches and were able to dramatically reduce CO, HC and NOx emissions beyond previous systems. As knowledge of these technological developments on cars spread, and as the adverse effects of motor vehicle pollution became more widely recognized, more and more people across the globe began demanding the use of these systems in their countries. Simultaneously, in 1990 the US Clean Air Act was amended to tighten requirements. This landmark law will pave the way for progress throughout the US for the remainder of the century. Among the most far reaching aspects of the new law are substantial tightening of the light duty vehicle standards along with several aspects of the compliance program.

4.1.2 California - the world leader

Culminating a year long process, on Friday September 28, 1990 the California Air Resources Board decided to adopt the most advanced motor vehicle emissions controls in the world. Their intention is to gradually tighten standards to the degree that by the end of the decade vehicles will be 70% cleaner than the 1993 cars and a small proportion of zero emissions (electric) vehicles will be in mass production.

Specifically, an average standard has been adopted for each manufacturer which would effectively require at least 10 percent of new vehicles in 1994 through 1996 would have to meet a hydrocarbon standard of 0.125 gpm when fueled with conventional gasoline (so called "transitional low emission vehicles" or TLEVs). Starting in 1997, these vehicles would be replaced with "low emission vehicles" (LEV's) emitting only 0.075 gpm HC and 0.02 gpm NOx. Starting that year, 25% of new cars sold in the state would have to be LEV's with that number increasing each year until it encompasses a maximum of 96% in 2000. In 1997, manufacturers also would have to begin selling "ultra low emission vehicles" (ULEV's) which emit no more than 0.04 gpm HC. Sales of these vehicles should reach 2% by the year 2000 and 15% by 2003. Also starting in 1998, 2% of all new vehicles will be required to be "zero emission vehicles" (ZEV's), rising to 10% by 2003. The staff also indicated its intention to propose rapid improvements in gasoline, including removal of benzene and other modifications similar to those contained in ARCO's EC-1 gasoline.

4.1.3 Other OECD

During the mid 1980's, Austria, the Netherlands and the Federal Republic of Germany adopted innovative economic incentive approaches to encourage purchase of low pollution vehicles. Since then, Australia, Canada, Finland, Austria, Norway, Sweden, Denmark and Switzerland have all decided to adopt mandatory requirements.

Within the European Community, at the European Council of Environmental

Ministers meeting on June 12th, there was unanimous agreement to adopt the 1992/1993 auto standards provisions which have been on the table the last several years along with an additional step to be introduced in approximately 1996. However, the details of the "second step" will need to await subsequent action since the European Parliament was unable to muster sufficient votes to resolve the question.

4.2 Developing countries

4.2.1 Hong Kong

After years of study and evaluation, the Hong Kong EPA took decisive action to reduce vehicular pollution during 1991. Unleaded gasoline was made available for the first time in Hong Kong on 1 April 1991. Simultaneously, the Government decided to impose new car standards as from January 1992 as follows:

Table 3 Hong Kong emission standards 1992

Vehicle types	Standards	
	Gasoline	Diesel
Private car, taxi	US 1987, FTP75 Japan 1987, 10-mode	US 1987, FTP75 Japan 1990, 10-mode
Light goods vehicle, light bus not more than 1.7 tonnes	US 1990, FTP75 Japan 1988-90, 10 mode	US 1990, FTP75 Japan 1988, 10-mode
Light goods vehicle, light bus more than 1.7 tonnes but not more than 2.5 tonnes	US 1990, FTP75 Japan 1988-90, 10-mode	US 1988-90 FTP75 Japan 1988-90, 6-mode

As planned, Hong Kong was able to accelerate the use of unleaded gasoline following its mandatory introduction as of April 1, 1991. Almost immediately, sales increased dramatically, spurred not only by the widespread availability but also by the "subsidy" created by lighter taxation which implies price advantage (approximately $1 HK per liter) relative to leaded gasoline. On May 1, catalytically equipped new cars made their entry into the marketplace and plans remain on track for all new cars to be so equipped by the beginning of next year.

4.2.2 Singapore

The Government of Singapore is also moving rapidly to introduce state of the art pollution controls. Following a series of sweeping decisions, the country will carry out the following measures:

1. As of October 1991, all new motorcycles were required to comply with US 1980 emissions standards. Second hand motorcycles brought into the country have been given a one year grace period, until January 1992 before the requirement will go into effect across the board.

2. As of January 1, 1991 all new diesel vehicles have been required to comply with ECE R 24.03.

3. The tax on leaded gasoline, as of February 4, 1991 was increased by 15 Singapore cents per liter; in effect, unleaded gasoline is now approximately 10 cents per liter cheaper than leaded.

4. After July 1, 1991, no car was allowed to be imported unless it can operate on unleaded gasoline.

This series of measures follows an earlier decision designed to reduce car use in Singapore. Effectively, drivers who committed to only use their vehicles between the hours of 7PM to 7AM or on weekends qualified for a substantial reduction in road taxes. As a result, individuals are encouraged to only use their vehicles during off peak hours when the potential adverse environmental consequences are at a minimum.

Unleaded fuel was only recently introduced at service stations throughout this island nation, even though 300,000 of the 332,000 cars on the road in Singapore can run on lead-free gasoline. Service stations will continue to sell leaded fuel for older cars.

To prevent Singapore motorists from crossing the border to Malaysia to fill their tanks with cheaper gasoline, the Singapore government also has imposed a so-called three-quarter tank rule. At a border checkpoint, Singapore's officials now check each departing car to see if the fuel gauge shows that the tank is at least three-quarters full. Violators can be fined up to S$500 (US $292). Because of lower prices and the weakness of Malaysia's currency, the ringgit, gasoline as well as many other consumer products can be purchased at substantial savings over Singapore's prices.

The three-quarter rule became effective Feb. 4, replacing a similar, half-tank rule, which was enacted in 1989. Finally, the Ministry of the Environment announced that all gasoline driven vehicles which are to be registered from July 1, 1992 will have to comply with either the new ECE consolidated Directive or the Japanese JIS 78
emission standards. According to their press statement, the use of catalytic converters will generally be required for compliance with these new standards.

4.2.3 Malaysia

While it is not yet mandated, the fuel industry appears certain to introduce unleaded gasoline on its own into Malaysia in the next few years. Shell in particular appears to have decided that unleaded gasoline is the wave of the future and will voluntarily introduce it and encourage it, in a similar way to in Bangkok (see below).

In Malaysia the government is beginning to take action on air pollution issues.

The minister of environment is planning to develop regulations this year to require the use of catalytic converters and unleaded gasoline. However, intense debate has occurred over the phase-in period, which at this point looks to be about 1995.

In support of the upcoming rules, plans are underway for developing a $1 billion unleaded gasoline refinery in Malaysia. It will be the first in Southeast Asia and is expected to be finished in three or four years.

Malaysia continues to move toward the adoption of vehicle emissions standards and to increase the use of unleaded gasoline. The Department of the Environment decided that beginning January 1, 1992, all new private vehicles must comply with the current EC requirements. Further, the government reduced excise or import duties on unleaded gasoline from December 1. This will be for nine months after which it will take "appropriate steps" to discourage oil companies from producing and selling leaded gasoline. After December 1, unleaded gasoline was to be retailed at the same price as leaded, but according to the government, users of leaded will eventually have to pay more for its use.

4.2.4 Thailand

Having achieved more than a decade of strong economic growth, Thailand is now looking at ways to improve quality of life, which is being threatened by rapid environmental decline. Thailand's, seventh economic development plan, for 1992-96, had an environmental component to ensure that economic development is sustainable in the long run. Among its new initiatives, the government wanted to establish standards for waste water discharges, require environmental impact studies, and promote imports of energy-saving devices and environmental equipment through favorable tariffs. Local refineries will be required to produce lead-free gasoline starting in 1993 and new cars must install catalytic converters according to the plan.

A report prepared by TDRI (Thailand Development Research Institute) concluded that if the current status quo continued, air pollution would increase to disturbing levels over the next 20 years. Sulfur dioxide emissions would increase more than five times to 3 million tons by 2011 and carbon dioxide would more than quadruple to 389 million tons by 2011, according to the report, Industrializing Thailand and Its Impact on the Environment.

The air quality conditions in Bangkok have already exceeded or are about to exceed the national and international standards for health. The doubling and, in many cases, quadrupling of emissions over the next 10 to 20 years from their already critical levels will have severe health impacts, on a population which will be at least double its current size.

The Thai government has moved to spur competition in the domestic car industry by slashing import duties on complete knockdown kits and fully assembled vehicles. The action would reduce the tariff on kits to 20 percent of assessed value from 112 percent now, and to 60 percent from 180 to 400 percent on assembled cars. The tariffs, which have made Thailand one of the most protected vehicle markets in the world, have guaranteed the profitability of local assemblers, regardless of efficiency. Prices of locally produced vehicles are expected to fall as much as 30 percent due to stiffer competition from imports. At the same time, the government has resurrected plans for vehicle inspection. The plans remain quite vague with no specific date set.

4.2.5 South Korea

The motor vehicle related air pollution problem in South Korea is unacceptable with diesel smoke and particulates standing out as the major concern. In addition, ambient ozone concentrations frequently exceed acceptable levels during the summer.

In 1987, motor vehicles were responsible for approximately 25% of the CO, 85% of the NOx, 57% of the HC, 8% of the SO2 and 8% of the particles. (The reason for the lower than normal contribution rate of CO by motor vehicles is the major contribution attributed to the burning of charcoal briquettes in Korea.) In addition, the vehicle contribution to the more harmful particles is higher than the contribution to total particles since they, as very fine respiratory particles, remain suspended in the air for a long time without being washed out or deposited. Diesel particles raise a special health concern because they are very small in size (averaging about 0.2 microns) and up to 10,000 chemicals may be absorbed on the surface of them.

By adopting stringent passenger car standards and introducing unleaded gasoline, Korea believes it has made significant progress with Otto cycle vehicles. However, in spite of significant progress, they can still barely keep pace with the high rate of growth in the domestic vehicle population. From a current total of approximately 3 million vehicles throughout South Korea, the domestic population is expected to grow to about 15 million by the year 2000. In addition, while gasoline vehicles are gradually being controlled (with 50,000 mile durability requirements for US 83 standards introduced in 1990) diesels remain a serious unsolved problem. Approximately 45% of the annual kilometers in the country are accumulated by diesels, mainly trucks and buses.

4.2.6 Taiwan (Republic of China)

Vehicles are the dominant source of emissions in Taipei. NOx, HC and CO emitted from motor vehicles account for about 50% of all emissions, respectively According to Shen Shu-Hung, 1989. An especially important source, unique to Taipei is motorcycles. Taiwan has the highest density of motorcycles in the world. Because 80% of motorcycles are equipped with two-stroke engines they contribute about 33% and 10% of HC and CO emissions respectively. To significantly improve the air quality in the Taiwan area, something must be done to control vehicular pollution, especially for motorcycles.

As a result of rapid industrialization and motorization, Taiwan is experiencing severe environmental problems particularly in Taipei. The most severe air pollution problem is again total suspended particulate. While many sources contribute, the importance of the motor vehicle has been highlighted by a recent review of existing coefficient of haze air quality data. While the area wide trend lines are flat for the last several years, the problem continues to deteriorate in traffic areas. A clear correlation exists between the growth in diesel bus traffic and the increase in the coefficient of haze. Ozone is also a serious problem. In 1987 alone, a total of 80 violations of the air quality standard were noted at 4 monitoring stations. Further, carbon monoxide air quality levels are also excessive.

In their analysis of the air quality problem in Taipei, the Taiwanese make an especially perceptive observation. Because so much of their population is located so close to high traffic situations throughout the day (either as a result of their residences or the widely prevalent use of motor cycles and motor bikes as a means of travel) public exposure to high levels of vehicle exhaust is probably greater than in highly developed countries. There are a number of efforts underway to solve the problem. These include cleaner fuels as well as improved controls of cars, motorcycles and diesels.

Since August 1, 1988, unleaded gasoline of 92 octane has been available throughout the entire country. Further, a 95 octane fuel was introduced in July 1990. The lead content in leaded fuel has been reduced from 0.8 grams per liter to 0.12 since 1988. A gradual reduction in lubricating oil mixed with unleaded gasoline for motorcycles has been underway since 1984. And finally since September 1983, on road diesel fuel has a maximum sulfur content of 0.5%.

Since July, 1987, all new cars have been required to comply with European standards as contained in R 15-04. Starting July 1990, all new models and all imported cars were required to achieve US auto standards. Domestically produced new cars are required to meet the same requirements but they are allowed waivers for up to three years. By 1994, the US standards will apply to all new cars. While it is very difficult to determine the actual sales, it is estimated that about 15% of new cars met US standards in 1990, rising to about 40% in 1991. In an effort to accelerate the transition, the EPA is considering the introduction of a tax incentive package similar to the German and Dutch programs.

Two levels of controls have been imposed on motorcycles. The first, relatively modest stage went into effect in 1988; more stringent standards were introduced on July 1, 1991. This latter requirement is intended to either require substantial control of or the elimination of two stroke motorcycles. The new motorcycle standards are 4.5 grams per kilometer for CO (from 8.8), and 3.0 for HC and NOx combined (from 6.5), based on the ECE R40 test procedure. In anticipation that two stroke engines will still be able to comply, the EPA is considering an additional tightening of motorcycle standards in 1993 or 1994.

Random roadside inspection has been conducted by local officials for many years. Free motorcycle and city bus emissions tests have also been encouraged. The EPA intends to propose that all new vehicles achieve California standards by 1993. No diesel taxicabs are allowed in Taipei. They are considering a change in their regulations to allow but not require LPG to be used in their taxicabs.

4.2.7 Mexico

Mexico City remains a place of extremes. In a short period of time, they have made dramatic progress in putting an aggressive motor vehicle pollution control program in place; on the other hand, the pollution problems remain severe. Whereas peak ozone readings generally occur during the high inversion winter months, and usually in limited portions of the city, readings during the month of July have been extremely high and appear to be spread throughout the entire city. For example, on July 17, ozone levels of approximately 290 ppb were recorded in the city; two weeks earlier, levels over 300 occurred.[2] This is in spite of the fact that very significant

[2] By way of comparison, the US air quality standard is approximately 120 ppb.

steps have been taken including:

1. Stringent new car emissions standards have been introduced for 1991 model cars. While not as stringent as the current US standards which will go into effect during the 1993 Model Year, many manufacturers have in fact put the more advanced systems on their vehicles already.

2. Higher octane unleaded gasoline has been introduced (so called Magna Sin was introduced in September 1990) and is widely available. Leaded Nova gasoline has had the lead content reduced from about 1.0 gram per liter to about 0.54. Both leaded and unleaded fuels contain approximately 5% MTBE. According to data supplied by PEMEX, a fleet test using Mexican vehicles in the MCMA showed a 14.7% reduction in HC and an 11.6% reduction in CO compared to leaded gasoline without MTBE. The addition of 5% MTBE also provides an octane increase equivalent to approximately 0.25 grams of lead per gallon of fuel,or about half of PEMEX's recent reduction in lead content.

3. Pre-1985 model year taxicabs have started to be replaced by new models meeting 1993 standards. Approximately 65,000 taxis should be upgraded over the next two years; several thousand minivans and suburban buses will also be upgraded.

4. 3 500 buses have had their diesel engines replaced with new engines meeting 1989 California standards.

5. A one day a week ban on the use of each individual vehicle has been in effect for over a year.

6. An inspection and maintenance program was put in place for all vehicles in 1989.

In addition, over 36,000 additional gasoline cargo vehicles will shortly be replaced with LPG fueled systems containing three-way catalysts. Stages 0, 1 and 2 vapor recovery are also planned and PEMEX has given its full support.

In spite of this progress, the pollution problem remains severe and may actually be getting worse. There appear to be several reasons beyond the fact that it will take time for many of these strategies to have their full impact:

While unleaded fuel is widely available it has been priced approximately 40% higher than leaded gasoline. In 1991 the cost of regular leaded gasoline was 710 pesos per liter compared to 1 000 pesos per liter for magna sin unleaded. Just before the end 1991, on November 12, the Mexican government raised gasoline prices dramatically. However, it selectively raised leaded fuel by 54% and unleaded by only 25%, thereby reducing the differential between them to 14%. This is still considered unacceptable by many who fear that it will encourage misfueling in the next few years as catalytic converters are introduced on a growing proportion of the vehicle fleet but it is clearly a big step in the right direction.

The actual composition of the fuel is not independently verified and is suspected by some of actually increasing VOC emissions. The state owned oil company, PEMEX, and its major contractor, IMP, have the exclusive right and capability to measure fuel quality - lead, RVP, MTBE composition, aromatics, etc. - and there is widespread skepticism regarding the actual composition as opposed to the reported composition. Further, there is no assurance that the correct fuels are being distributed to the correct pumps.

While the "Day Without A Car" program appears to have initially reduced the use of vehicles, over the past year the population has "adjusted" by buying large numbers of second cars. As a result, the program may actually be increasing overall traffic at this point. For example, in 1989 when the program first went into effect, 80,000 new cars were sold; in 1991, this rose to 275,000. (Certainly, the improvement in the economy also contributed to this increase).

The I/M program has not yet been very successful. It was first established in Mexico City (DF) by SEDUE (the ministry of the environment) in the 1970's, with 13 fixed and 17 mobile Government run testing sites. It has since then been expanded to include 750 test sites in the DF and an estimated 180 in the State of Mexico. The program design follows that of early US I/M programs, consisting of a measurement of CO and HC concentrations in the exhaust at idle and 2 500 RPM. The program uses manually adjusted emissions analyzers, and data recording and analysis are by hand. For heavy trucks a non-loaded snap acceleration smoke test is used with uniform standards of 60% opacity. The current vehicle regulations are given in table 4.

Table 4 Mexican Passenger car and light truck pass limits

Model year	HC(ppm)	CO (%)
Pre 1980	700	6.0
1980-1986	500	4.0
1987-1990	400	3.0

In the 1970's, the program was only voluntary in the DF, and in the mid-1980's it experienced significant cuts in program support. Reacting to the air quality emergency levels of late 1980's, the DF and State of Mexico expanded the program in 1989 to include private licensed garages and a mandatory semi-annual testing requirement for all vehicles.

4.2.8 Brazil

Presently, the major problems in Brazil's motor vehicle pollution control program seem to be fuel specification and quality. Due to the alcohol crisis, the ethanol content in Brazilian gasohol was lowered from 22% to 13% nationwide, with exception made to the Sao Paulo Metropolitan Region. However, in some regions, the ethanol content went down to zero. In order to maintain octane quality, PETROBRAS has increased aromatic and olefinic compounds in the fuel. As a result, vehicles have experienced excessive carbon buildup on EGR valves, spark plugs and combustion chambers. In addition, the "new" gasohol has shown a great tendency to gum formation and to elastomer membrane attacks. These problems have resulted in significant engine failures and, consequently, increases in emissions and fuel consumption. Both CETESB and the automakers have been putting pressure on PETROBRAS to solve these problems.

On the positive side, ninety-seven percent of the Brazilian gasoline (gasohol) is already unleaded. Only one small refinery in Rio de Janeiro is still producing leaded gasoline, but this was expected to be phased out soon (end of 1991). Just before the global environment conference in 1992, Rio was embarrassed into abandoning plans to keep using some leaded gasoline because of the image it would project. Most 1992 model year vehicles will be equipped with catalytic converters in order to attain the second stage emission standards (12 grams/kilometer CO, 1.2 HC, 1.4 NOx, 2.5 % CO at idle and 0.15 g/km aldehydes). Certification data indicates that 1992 vehicles will attain these standards with a great safety margin. On June 10, General Motors Brazil presented the first alcohol fueled vehicle equipped with electronic fuel injection. CETESB is planning an I/M program for in use vehicles, probably in 1993. In May 1991 CETESB also proposed a motor vehicle noise emission control program. The goal is to achieve present EEC standards by 1995. CETESB, the automotive industry and IBAMA (the Federal Environmental Protection Agency) are in the process of discussing the feasibility of the proposal and preliminary agreement is expected soon.

Brazil produced approximately one million vehicles in 1991. Most of these, from 7 to 800,000 were intended for the domestic market while the remainder are for export to the US, Europe and the rest of Latin America. As import taxes have been reduced, imports have been gradually increasing. The tax is presently at 65% of the new car price and is expected to be reduced to 40% soon. Lada has become the largest importer. Hyundai is expected to make a big push soon and the rumor is that Toyota will both expand imports and build a manufacturing capability. Feeding the latter rumor is the fact that Toyota has purchased a large parcel of land adjacent to GM's facilities.

Citroen has already had a model approved for 1992 as has Alfa Romeo. Most major luxury cars are expected to get type approval and be imported into the country. The municipal government in Sao Paulo has developed a 10 year plan to convert 10,000 buses to CNG. PETROBRAS has a large surplus of natural gas. They have stopped flaring and constructed a pipeline from Rio to Sao Paulo. The first CNG station will be in operation next year - for 200 buses. Also DB has developed a CNG bus with low HC, CO, particulate and noise. NOx levels will increase by 15%, initially since the buses will not be equipped with catalysts. DB has indicated that it intends to add catalysts at some later date.

CETESB is investigating whether or not it makes sense for the natural gas to be used in vehicles as CNG or whether it should be converted to methanol and then used. The major advantage in their eyes is that the use of a liquid fuel would be less disruptive to the existing infrastructure. In addition, when equipped with a catalyst, the overall emissions should be lower.

GM has indicated that it will produce two models in 1992 with catalysts and two others with fuel injection. Autolatina will use catalysts across the board as will Fiat.

Diesel fuel sulfur levels in Brazil average about 1%. CETESB is trying to get PETROBRAS to introduce a lower sulfur fuel, initially in the cities, starting with buses. PETROBRAS says the best they can do is to introduce 0.5% in the cities, several years from now. To get to 0.05% would require about 1 billion dollars in investment, according to PETROBRAS, and they are expending all available capital on increased exploration.

There are no motorcycle regulations in Brazil and no plans to adopt any. About 200,000 motorcycles a year are sold with Honda dominant. Most are four stroke (125cc engines) and used as rapid delivery vehicles. The major problem is perceived to be noise.

4.2.9 Argentina

Argentina at present has no EPA. Its vehicle manufacturing industry, once very successful, has been in some decline and was expected to only produce about 160,000 vehicles in 1991. Major manufacturers include Autolatina, Sevelle (a combination of Fiat and Peugeot) and Renault. Unleaded gasoline is not available in Argentina; the lead content of gasoline averages between 0.6 and 1.0 gram per liter. The government is considering a plan to reduce lead by offering a tax incentive for "green fuel".

All taxis in Buenos Aires are currently fueled by natural gas. In theory ECR 15-00 is in effect in Argentina but there is no enforcement, even in theory.

4.2.10 Chile

The air pollution problem in Santiago is already severe and appears to be worsening. Total suspended particulate levels routinely exceed safe levels by a factor of 2 to 3; many of these particles, especially those emitted by diesels, tend to be sub micron in size and therefore of even more concern from a health standpoint. Ozone levels are also very high during summer months and are increasing. On the other hand, during winter months, CO concentrations are generally very unhealthy.

The particulate problems are gradually improving. The number of times, peak levels have exceeded 50 micrograms per cubic meter has declined from 12 in 1989 to 7 in 1990 and it appears to be less in 1991. Alternatively, CO levels have increased by from 10 to 25% in the past year. NOx levels remain below unhealthy levels but have increased since 1985.

Motor vehicles are a major source of the air pollution problems. For example, gasoline fueled vehicles emit approximately 79% of the CO, 59% of the NOx, 44% of the VOC's, and 5% of the respirable particles. Diesel vehicles emit 31% of the NOx and 19% of the respirable particles.

In some cases the impact of vehicle emissions on health effects is out of proportion to their percentage because vehicles frequently emit their pollutants directly into the breathing zones of people. While diesels emit only 19% of the particles, they cause 70% of the respirable particulate problem.

The government has decided to introduce catalytic converters on all new cars starting next year. The US 83 requirements go into effect in 12 months, starting in September 1992. In addition, taxicabs will possibly be retrofitted with catalytic converters and about 6 000 to 7 000 diesel buses may be equipped with traps.

A catalyst retrofit test program has been underway for some time. In fact 40 vehicles are on the road equipped with 6 different types of devices. The oxidation catalysts far exceeded the others achieving 60 to 90% reduction.

In Santiago, diesel fuel contains about 0.2 to 0.4 Wt. % sulfur. Gasoline contains about 0.04 g/liter. US 83 standards are going to be mandatory for the 3 central regions of Chile from this year and for the rest of the country in 94-95.

As for buses in particular and heavy duty vehicles in general, opacity standards (as part of the I/M program) are being tightened (23% big buses and 18% small buses at 50% load) in a 4 year schedule. Some people (bus owners and trap suppliers) want a technological standard to be mandated by law. Government officials are against that, preferring performance standards as the main instrument and freedom to comply with them whatever way you want.

5 CONCLUSIONS

The development of petroleum-powered motor vehicles has truly revolutionized society over the past century. The benefits of increased personal mobility and access to goods and services previously beyond the grasp of individuals cannot be denied. And, yet, the relentless growth in motor vehicle use has a dark downside with a broad array of adverse public health and environmental impacts that many have been slow to acknowledge.

The environmental damages caused by motor vehicle emissions are no longer debatable, and on a global basis they are increasing. The cars, trucks, and buses that make life better in so many ways emit more than 800 million tons of carbon per year. From their tailpipes come virtually all of the carbon monoxide in the air of our cities. Less directly, they cause much of the ozone and smog. And motor vehicles play a significant role in stratospheric ozone depletion. All of these pollutants contribute directly or indirectly to global warming.

Over the last forty years, the global vehicle fleet has grown from under 50 million to more than 500 million, and there is every indication that this growth will continue. Over the next twenty years, the global fleet could double to one billion. Unless transportation technology and planning are fundamentally transformed, emissions of greenhouse and other polluting gases from these vehicles will continue to increase, many relatively clean environments will deteriorate, and the few areas that have made progress will see some of their gains eroded.

The worldwide challenges that these problems pose for motor vehicle manufacturers and policy-makers are unprecedented. Nothing less than a revolution in technology and thinking at least as profound as the initial mechanization of transportation is needed. Manufacturers will come under increasing pressures to produce petroleum-powered vehicles that are ever cleaner, safer, more reliable, and more fuel efficient. At the same time, they will need to develop new kinds of vehicles that will emit no pollution whatever. The amount of capital needed to accomplish these goals will be large and, making matters even more difficult, the pressures for these changes will arise not so much from traditional market forces but from public policies adopted in response to climate and other threats.

While development of appropriate policies and technologies progresses, countries can benefit from adoption of currently available policies and technologies.

Various steps can be taken to reduce air pollution emissions from motor vehicles. These include incentives to remove older, highly polluting vehicles from the road; tightening new vehicle emission standards for nitrogen oxides, volatile organic compounds, and carbon monoxide; developing and using cleaner fuels with lower volatility and fewer toxic components; enhancing inspection and maintenance (I&M) programs, including inspections of anti-tampering emission-control equipment; and extending the useful life for pollution-control equipment to ten years or 100,000 miles rather than the current five years or 50,000 miles. The potential overall impacts of tighter standards, enhanced inspection and maintenance, and extended useful life are especially significant because they help ensure that the benefits of clean-air technology will persist for the vehicle's full life.

Additional reductions in vehicular emissions can be achieved by reducing dependence on individual cars and trucks and by making greater use of van and car pools, buses, trolleys, and trains. Improving urban traffic management by installing synchronized traffic lights, reducing on-street parking, switching to "smart" roads, banning truck unloading during the day, and so forth can also improve transportation system efficiency (US Congress, 1989). Providing efficient, convenient, and affordable public transportation alternatives worldwide would produce multiple benefits. For every 40 persons who get out of their cars and onto a bus for a ten-mile trip to work, some 50 to 75 pounds of carbon are not emitted to the air. Greater use of public transportation would reduce congestion, cut fatalities and injuries from traffic accidents, and greatly improve air quality. Fortunately, such transportation improvements can be phased in over time. For example, roadways initially dedicated to bus traffic can later be upgraded to light rail or heavy rail if circumstances warrant.

Motor vehicle related air pollution problems are not limited to the highly industrialized countries of the OECD nor is the search for solutions. Countries as diverse as Brazil, Taiwan, Singapore and Mexico as well as many other developing countries are rapidly moving to introduce state of the art pollution controls. In instituting these requirements, the primary strategy remains mandated standards for both vehicles and fuels but there has been no lack of creativity in using a variety of economic instruments as well. Most countries realize that tax policies must be designed to reduce any price differential that favors the use of leaded gasoline and many see economic incentives as a viable approach to accelerating the introduction of state of the art controls such as catalytic converters in advance of mandatory requirements.

REFERENCES

American Lung Association. 1989. *Health Effects of Ambient Air Pollution*, New York, N. Y.

Ciborowski, P. 1989. *Sources, Sinks, Trends and Opportunities, The Challenge of Global Warming*, ed. Dean E. Abrahamsson, Island Press, Washington, D.C.

Gribbin, J. 1988. *The Hole in the Sky, Man's threat to the Ozone Layer*, Bantam Books, New York.

Kang Rae Cho. 1990. *Motor Vehicle Emission Control in Korea.*

Khalil, M.A.K. and R.A. Rasmussen. 1988. "Carbon Monoxide in the Earth's Atmosphere. Indications of a Global Increase". 332 *Nature* 245.

Laimboch and Landerl. 1990. "50cc Two-Stroke Engines for Mopeds, chainsaws and Motorcycles with Catalysts" *SAE 901598*, September.

Shen Shu-Hung and Huang Kuang-Huei. 1989. "Taiwan air Pollution Control Program: Impact of and Control Strategies for Transportation-induced Air Pollution", UN Conference, Ottawa, Canada.

Sugiura and Kagaya. 1977. "A Study of Visible Smoke Reduction from a Small Two-Stroke Engine using Various Lubricants", *SAE 770623*, June.

UNEP Technology Review. 1989. "Technical Progress on Protecting the Ozone Layer". *Refrigeration, Air Conditioning and Heat Pumps Technical Options Report*, July 30.

US Congress. 1989. "Advanced Vehicle/Highway Systems and Urban Traffic Problems", Staff Paper, Science, Education and Transportation Program, Office of Technology Assessment, September.

US EPA. 1986. "Air Quality Criteria for Ozone and Other Photochemical Oxidants" vol II, EPA/600/8-84/020bF, pp 3 -15.

US EPA. 1991. "National Air Quality and Emissions Trends Report, 1990", EPA-450/4-91-023.

Volz, A. and D. Kley. 1988. "Evaluation of the Montsouris Series of Ozone Measurements made in the nineteenth century", *Nature 332* pp 240-243.

Wyczalek. 1991. "Two-Stroke Engine Technology in the 1990's", SAE 910663, March 1991, contained in SP-849 *Two-Stroke Engine Design and Development.*

CHAPTER 15

Environmentally Sustainable Energy for Development

by

Mohan Munasinghe*

Abstract

The rapid growth rate of energy demand for economic development, large investment requirements and scarcity of resources, coupled with emerging need to protect the environment, have placed severe burdens on the developing countries. This paper sets out an integrated analytical and conceptual framework for identifying sustainable energy strategies and options within the national context. It also discusses potential areas for South-North collaboration to meet future energy-environmental challenges.

* The author is grateful to Noreen Beg for assistance in preparing this paper. The opinions expressed herein are those of the author and do not necessarily represent the views of any institution or government.

T. Sterner (ed.), Economic Policies for Sustainable Development, 261–282.

1 INTRODUCTION

Energy has been a major international issue since the 1970s, following the oil crisis. More recently, a wide range of local and transnational environmental issues, as well as potential global climate change induced by excessive greenhouse gas accumulation in the atmosphere have emerged as problems that further complicate energy decision making. In this paper, we will focus on energy-related environmental issues in the developing countries. Energy is a fundamental requirement for economic development, and future prospects for growth are closely linked to the provision of affordable and reliable energy supplies. This is particularly important in the developing world, where present per capita energy consumption levels are relatively low, the demand for energy has been growing rapidly, and further increases in energy requirements are unavoidable in the years to come.

Decision makers in developing countries (LDCs), however, are faced with a difficult dilemma. Owing to the scarcity of financial resources, they have been struggling with formidable hardships to meet growing energy demand at acceptable costs. Inability to do so may slow down the rate of economic growth with corresponding deterioration in living standards. Meanwhile, this problem is compounded by growing concerns about the environmental consequences of energy production and use -- e.g., pollution, acid rain, radioactivity and global warming.

LDC decision makers share the worldwide concerns about environmental degradation, and most have already instituted policies to improve their own natural resource management as an essential step toward ensuring sustainable economic growth. But such efforts are constrained by the fact that they are also confronted with other urgent issues like poverty and malnutrition. The paucity of resources available to address such problems sets a limit on the ability of these countries to undertake costly measures for environmental protection. One can only expect that their response to environmental protection cannot extend much beyond measures that are consistent with their overall economic development goals.

The crucial dilemma for LDCs is how to reconcile development goals and the elimination of poverty -- which will require increased use of energy and raw materials -- with responsible stewardship of the environment, and without overburdening already weak economies. The per capita GNP of low income economies (with half the world population) averaged US$290 in 1987, or under one sixtieth of the US value ($18,530). In the two largest developing countries, India and China, per capita GNP was $300 and $290 respectively. Correspondingly, the US per capita energy consumption of 7 265 kilograms of oil equivalent (kgoe) in 1987 was 35 and 15 times greater than the same statistic in India and China respectively.

The disparity in both per capita income and energy use among different countries also raises additional issues in the context of current global environmental concerns, and the heavy burden placed on mankind's natural resource base by past economic growth -- fossil fuel-related CO_2 accumulation in the atmosphere is a good example. The developed countries accounted for over 80% of such cumulative worldwide emissions during 1950-86 -- North America contributed over 40 billion tons of carbon, Western and Eastern Europe emitted 25 and 32 billion tons respectively, and the developing countries' share was about 24 billion tons. On a per capita basis the contrasts are even more stark, with North America emitting over 20 times more and the developed countries as a whole being responsible for over eleven times as much total cumulative CO_2 emissions as the LDCs. The LDC share would be even smaller if emissions prior to 1950 were included. Clearly, any reasonable growth scenario for developing nations that followed the same material-intensive path as the industrialized world, would result in unacceptably high levels of future greenhouse gas accumulation as well as more general depletion of natural resources. (Se also Chapters 16-17).

Up to now, scientific analysis has provided only broad and rather uncertain predictions about the degree and timing of potential global warming. However, it would be prudent for mankind to buy an "insurance policy" in the form of mitigatory actions to reduce greenhouse gas emissions. Ironically, both local and global environmental degradation might affect developing countries more severely, since they are more dependent on natural resources while lacking the economic strength to prevent or respond quickly to increases in the frequency, severity and persistence of flooding, drought, storms, and so on. Thus, from the LDC viewpoint, an attractive low cost insurance premium would be a set of inexpensive measures that could address a range of national and global environmental issues, without hampering development efforts.

1.1 Evolving Trends in the Global Electric Power Sector

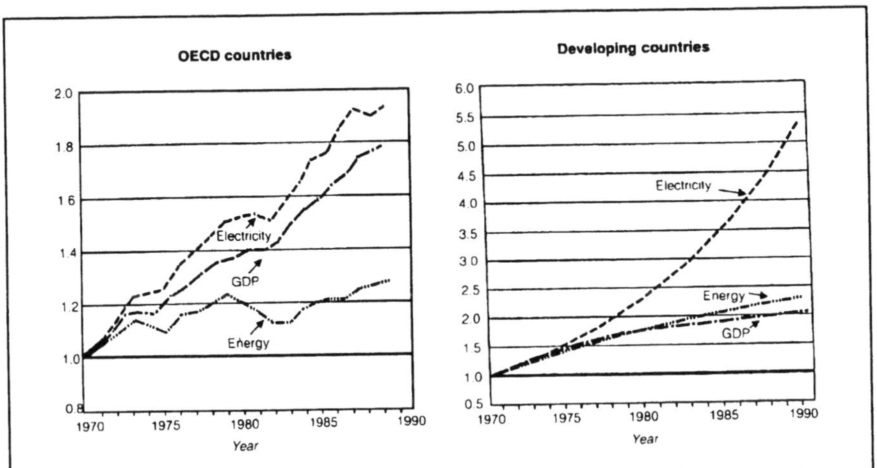

Figure 1 Energy, electricity and GDP in OECD and LDC countries

While the energy sector is an engine of economic growth, the highly capital intensive electric power sector in particular has a vital role to play in this development process, and we will focus our attention on it. Figure 1 summarizes the past relationship between GDP, commercial energy, and electricity use in LDCs in comparison with the OECD countries. Following the oil crises of the last decades, overall energy used per unit of GDP has declined dramatically in the industrialized countries, but dependence on electricity has not. Based on the OECD example, energy efficiency improvements could help to reduce the growth of demand for

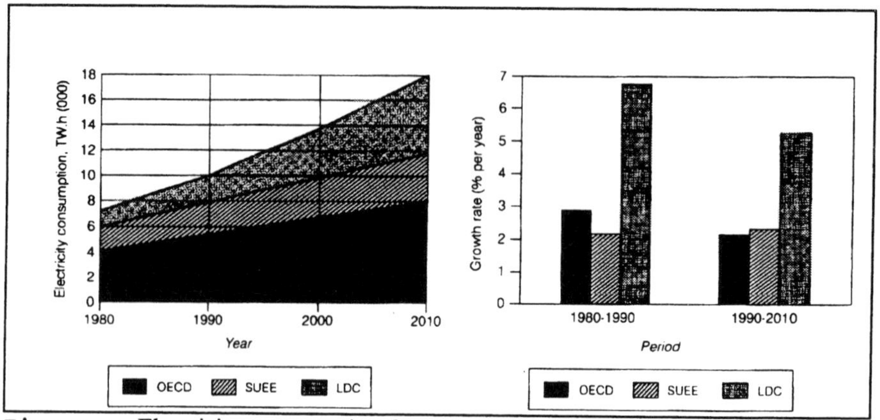

Figure 2 Electricity consumption forecasts for different regions

commercial energy in the developing world. However, the 1970-90 trend for electricity demand in LDCs, and the inability of the OECD countries to significantly decouple electricity use from GDP during the same period, suggest that the growth-related power needs of the LDCs will increase rapidly in the future. One recent long-run forecast of worldwide electricity consumption up to 2010 is shown in Figure 2, with the LDC growth rate expected to be significantly higher than for the OECD and Soviet Union-Eastern Europe (SUEE).

In the medium term, assuming no drastic changes with respect to past trends as refers to demand management and conservation, the World Bank's most recent projections indicate that the demand for electricity in LDCs will grow at an average annual rate of 6 to 7% during the period 1989-99 (Moore and Smith, 1990). This compares with average growth rates of 10% and 7% per annum in the seventies and eighties, respectively. Future growth rates correspond to additional total capacity requirements of 384 GW during 1990-99, and an annual energy consumption of 3,844 TWh by 1999. The needs of the Asia region dominate (see Table 1). Coal and hydro will be the primary sources of power generation, and are expected to supply over 80% of the additional capacity needed.

The investment needs corresponding to these World Bank projections are very large, totalling almost $750 billion (constant 1989 US$), or about $75 billion annually. The present annual rate of investment in LDCs is only around $50 billion, but even this is proving difficult to maintain because of increasing scarcity of fiscal resources and limited access to capital markets due to high levels of external debt. Developing country debt which averaged 23% of GNP in 1981, increased dramatically to 42% in 1987 and has not declined significantly since then. Furthermore, the environmental consequences of this projected expansion path are likely to be substantial. From both economic and environmental standpoints, therefore, it is important that continued emphasis be placed on measures that will improve efficiency in energy production and use (e.g., accurate demand forecasting, least-cost investment planning, electricity end-use management, etc.).

The developing countries feel that any attempts to mitigate environmental effects should not jeopardize the critical role played by electric power (and more generally, energy) in economic development. Similarly, the allocation of resources

Table 1. LDC Power Capacity Additions (GW) and Investments (US$ million) for 1990-99

	Asia	EMENA*	LAC**	Africa	Total
Incremental Capacity	244	69	66	5	384
(%)	(63.5)	(18.0)	(17.2)	(1.3)	(100)
Required Investment	455	124	155	11	745
(%)	(61.1)	(16.6)	(20.8)	(1.5)	(100)

* Europe, Middle East and North Africa (Mediterranean region), but excluding Eastern Europe and the Soviet Union.

** Latin America and the Caribbean.

Source: Moore, E.A. and G. Smith, Capital Expenditures for Electric Power in the Developing Countries in the 1990s, The World Bank, Industry and Energy Department, Washington, D.C., February 1990.

to environmental programs in developing countries cannot diminish the resources needed to fund projected expansion of supply.

2 THE ECONOMICS OF ENERGY-ENVIRONMENTAL ISSUES

The foregoing discussion has helped to identify the elements of a rational and equitable framework for addressing energy-environmental issues. In this section we present an economic efficiency framework which ties together the issue of environmental protection with the existing energy sector goals of energy efficiency and economic growth.

It is convenient to recall here that traditionally, the specific prerequisites for economic efficiency have included both:

(a) efficient consumption of energy, by providing efficient price signals that ensure optimal energy use and resource allocation

(b) efficient production of energy, by ensuring the least-cost supply mix through the optimization of investment planning and energy system operation (Munasinghe, 1990b).

A new issue which has emerged in recent decades as an area of particular concern, is the efficient and optimal use of our global natural resource base, including air, land and water. Since there has been much discussion also about the key role that energy efficiency and energy conservation might play in mitigating environmental costs, it is useful first to examine how these topics relate to economic efficiency. Specific issues dealing with the formulation and implementation of economically efficient energy policies are presented in Section 4.

Major environmental issues vary widely, particularly in terms of scale or magnitude of impact, but most are linked to energy production and use. First, there are the truly *global problems* such as the potential worldwide warming due to increasing accumulation of greenhouse gases, e.g., carbon dioxide (CO_2) and methane, in the atmosphere; high altitude ozone depletion because of the release of chlorofluorocarbons (CFCs); pollution of the marine environment by oil spills and other wastes; and irreversible loss of biodiversity. In particular, global warming is caused largely by the energy sector, which contributes 50-60% of greenhouse gases, mostly in the form of CO_2 (World Resources Institute, 1990).

Second in scale are the *transnational issues*, such as acid rain or radioactive fallout in one country, due to fossil-fuel or nuclear emissions respectively in a neighboring nation. These are generally subcontinental in scale, and typically require agreements between governments for their resolution, see in particular Chapter 13. The sulfur in coal, for example, is converted by combustion to sulfur dioxide (SO_2), which combines with water vapor to produce acid rain. Acid rain can travel long distances before falling to the earth, and results in health hazards to populations, damage to buildings, harm to forests and vegetation and destruction of wildlife. Nitrogen oxide emissions, produced in large amounts by motor vehicles during fuel combustion, also result in acid rain deposits.

Third are the *national and regional issues*, which are often at the river basin scale, such as those involving the Amazon Basin in Brazil or the Mahaweli Basin in Sri Lanka. River basin development is generally for multiple purposes, bringing energy planners and electric utilities concerned with hydroelectric development into contact (and often conflict) with agencies involved with irrigation and regional development.

Finally, there are the purely *local impacts* associated with specific activities: slag heaps from coal mines, resettlement problems at a hydroelectric dam, or the loss of wildlife habitat for a reservoir. Here the pressures for mitigation of the adverse environmental effects are generally driven by local concerns, such as public health (an example of this is the elimination of the Babaquara hydro project in Brazil after extensive public criticism).

While environmental problems of any kind are a matter for serious concern, those that fall within national boundaries are inherently easier to deal with from the standpoint of policy implementation. Issues that fall within the energy sector must be addressed through the national policy making framework. In cases where national energy policies have global consequences, one may expect that the most immediate pressures will come from local and national considerations. Nonetheless, significant efforts are now being made to improve international cooperation for implementing transnational and global mitigatory measures.

Given this background, we discuss next some of the principal points concerning energy use and economic efficiency (Munasinghe, 1990a). In many countries, especially those in the developing world, inappropriate policies have encouraged wasteful and unproductive uses of some forms of energy. In such cases, better energy management could lead to improvements in economic efficiency (higher value of net output produced), energy efficiency (higher value of net output per unit of energy used), energy conservation (reduced absolute amount of energy used), and environmental protection (reduced energy-related environmental costs). While such a result fortuitously satisfies all four goals, the latter are not always mutually consistent. For example, in some developing countries where the existing levels of per capita energy consumption are very low and certain types of energy use are uneconomically constrained, it may become necessary to promote more energy consumption in order to raise net output (thereby increasing economic efficiency). There are also instances where it may be possible to increase energy efficiency while decreasing energy conservation.

Despite the above complications, our basic conclusion remains valid -- that the economic efficiency criterion which helps us maximize the value of net output from all available scarce resources in the economy (especially energy and the ecosystem in the present context), should effectively subsume purely energy-oriented objectives such as energy efficiency and energy conservation. Furthermore, the costs arising from energy-related adverse environmental impacts may be included (to the extent possible) in the energy economics analytical framework, to determine how much energy use and net output society should be willing to forego, in order to abate or mitigate environmental damage. The existence of the many other national policy objectives -- including social goals that are particularly relevant in the case of low-income populations -- will complicate the decision making process even further.

2.1 A Graphical Exposition

The foregoing discussion may be reinforced by the use of a simplified static analysis of the trade-off between resource use and net output of an economic activity (see Figure 3).

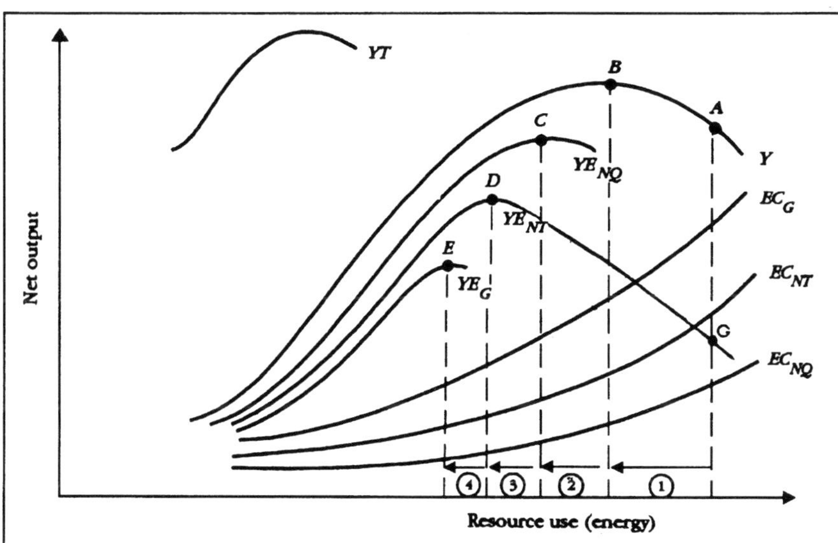

Figure 3 The trade-off between economic output and the environment.

2.1.1 Energy efficiency

Y represents the usual measurement of the net output of productive economic activity in a country, as a function of some resource input (say energy) -- considering only the conventional internalized costs, i.e., not accounting for environmental impacts. Due to policy distortions (for example, subsidized prices), the point of operation in many developing countries appears to be at A, where the resource is being used wastefully. Therefore, without invoking any environmental considerations, but merely by increasing economic and resource use efficiency (i.e., energy efficiency), output, as usually measured, could be maximized by moving from A to B. A typical example might be improving energy end-use efficiency or reducing energy supply system losses (see Section 4 for practical examples).

2.1.2 Quantifiable national environmental costs

Now consider the curve EC_{NQ} which represents economically quantifiable national environmental costs associated with energy use. The latter might include air pollution-related health costs of a coal-fired power plant or the costs of environmental protection equipment (like scrubbers and electrostatic precipitators to reduce noxious gas and particulate emissions) installed at such a plant, or the costs of resettlement at a hydropower dam site. The corresponding corrected net output curve is: $YE_{NQ} = Y - EC_{NQ}$; which has a maximum at C that lies to the left of B, implying lower use of (more costly) energy.

2.1.3 Non-quantifiable national environmental costs

Next, consider the "real" national output YE_{NT}, which is net of total environmental costs, whether quantifiable or not. The additional costs to be considered include the unquantified yet very real human health and other unmonetized environmental costs. These total (quantifiable and non-quantifiable) costs are depicted as EC_{NT}; and once again $YE_{NT} = Y - EC_{NT}$. As shown, the real maximum of net output lies at D, to the left of C.

2.1.4 Transnational environmental costs

Finally, EC_G represents the globally adjusted costs, where the transnational environmental costs (to other countries) of energy use within the given country, have been added to EC_{NT}. In this case, $YE_G = Y - EC_G$; and is the correspondingly corrected net output curve which implies an even lower level of optimal energy use.

For example, consider the costs imposed on other countries (such as transborder impacts of a major dam or global climate impacts of carbon dioxide emissions). If it is decided to reduce resource use within this country further in order to achieve the internationally adjusted optimum at E, then a purely national analysis will show this up as a drop in net output, i.e. from D to E. As other countries benefit, this drop in net output may justify compensation in the form of a transfer of resources from the beneficiary countries. Note that the transnational costs imposed by other countries on the nation in question will be a function of regional or global resource use rather than the national resource use shown on the horizontal axis.

The additional curve YT shows net output for a technologically advanced future society that has achieved a much lower resource intensity of production.

2.2 Policy Implications for the LDCs

The foregoing analysis illustrates the crucial dilemma for developing countries. In Figure 3, all nations (including the poorest) should be willing to adopt measures that will lead to shift (1) which simultaneously and unambiguously provides both economic efficiency and environmental gains. Most developing countries are indicating increasing willingness to undertake shift (2). However, implementing shift (3) will definitely involve crossing a "pain threshold" for many third world nations, as other pressing socioeconomic needs compete against the costs of mitigating nonquantifiable adverse environmental impacts.

We note that real economic output increases with each of the shifts (1), (2) and (3) -- shown by the movement upward along the curve YE_{NT} from G to D. However, these shifts are often mistakenly perceived as being upward only from A to B (energy efficiency improvements), followed by downward movements from B through C to D. It is therefore important to correct any misconceptions that environmental protection results in reduced net output. However, it is clear that shift (4) would hardly appeal to resource constrained developing countries unless concessionary external financing was made available, since this movement would imply optimization of a global value function and costs that exceed in-country benefits. In the foregoing, we have neglected considerations involving reciprocal benefits to the given country due to energy use reductions in other countries.

Therefore, we may conclude briefly that, while the energy required for economic development will continue to grow in the developing countries, in the short- to medium-run there is generally considerable scope for most of them to practice better energy management, thereby increasing net output, using their energy resources more efficiently, and contributing to the effort to reduce global warming. In the medium to long-run, it will become possible for the developing countries to adopt newer and more advanced (energy efficient) technologies that are now emerging in the industrialized world, thus enabling them to transform their economies and produce even more output using less energy.

In other words, the developing countries could be expected to cooperate in global environmental programs only to the extent that such cooperation is consistent with their national growth objectives. The role of the developed countries, on the other hand, is to incur the risks inherent in developing innovative technological measures which are the prerequisites for the next level in environmental protection and the mitigation of adverse consequences. These risks include the possibility that the more extreme measures may turn out to be unnecessary or inapplicable after all, given the prevailing uncertainty about the future impact of current environmental developments.

3 NATIONAL LEVEL ENERGY-ENVIRONMENTAL POLICY ANALYSIS

Section 2 introduced a way of considering energy-environmental issues in terms of four shifts. In this section a rational framework for energy-environmental policy analysis within a country is presented in terms of these shifts. This coverage is expanded to the global level in Section 5, focusing particularly on the interaction between developed and developing countries.

Developed countries generally differ from the developing countries in the extent to which the shifts have already been made. The LDCs are more likely to be characterized as being at point A in Figure 3, while at least some of the developed countries are somewhere between C and D. This means that for developing countries there is still considerable scope for environmental improvement by undertaking programs that are consistent with the national objective of increasing overall output. The challenge for national decision makers and the international community is to find as many areas as possible where such consistency and complementarity exist, between growth and environmental protection goals.

3.1 Conceptual Framework for Integrated National Energy Policymaking (INEP)

Successful planning and implementation of national energy programs must explicitly take account of the role of the energy sector in economic development vis-a-vis those of the other parts of the economy. This will require an integrated approach that will help decision makers in formulating policies and providing market signals and information to economic agents that encourage more efficient energy production and use. Summarized in Figure 4 is an integrated approach to decision making which emphasizes a hierarchical conceptual framework for integrated national energy planning and policymaking (INEP) that can be implemented through a set of energy supply and demand management policies (Munasinghe, 1990b).

The core of the INEP framework is the integrated multilevel analysis shown in the middle column. Although INEP is primarily country-focused, at the global level it is recognized that there are transnational energy-environmental issues. Thus individual countries are embedded in an international matrix, and economic and environmental conditions at this global level will impose exogenous inputs or constraints on decision makers within countries. The next hierarchical level in Figure 4 focuses on the multisectoral national economy, of which the energy sector is a part. This suggests that energy planning requires analysis of the links between the energy sector and the rest of the economy. Such links include the energy needs of user sectors (e.g., industry, transport and agriculture), input requirements of the energy sector, and impact on the economy of policies concerning energy prices and availability. The intermediate level of INEP treats the energy sector as a separate entity composed of subsectors such as electricity, petroleum products and so on. This permits detailed analysis, with special emphasis on interactions among the different energy subsectors, substitution possibilities, and the resolution of any resulting policy conflicts. The most disaggregate and lowest hierarchical level pertains to analysis within each of the energy subsectors. At this level, most of the detailed energy resource evaluation, planning and implementation of projects is carried out by line institutions (both public and private).

In practice, the various levels of INEP merge and overlap considerably, requiring that (inter-) sectoral linkages should be carefully examined. Energy-environmental interactions (represented by the vertical bar) tend to cut across all levels and need to be incorporated into the analysis as far as possible. Such interactions also provide important paths for incorporating environmental considerations into national energy policies.

INEP facilitates policymaking and does not imply rigid centralized planning.

Figure 4 A framework for integrated national energy planning

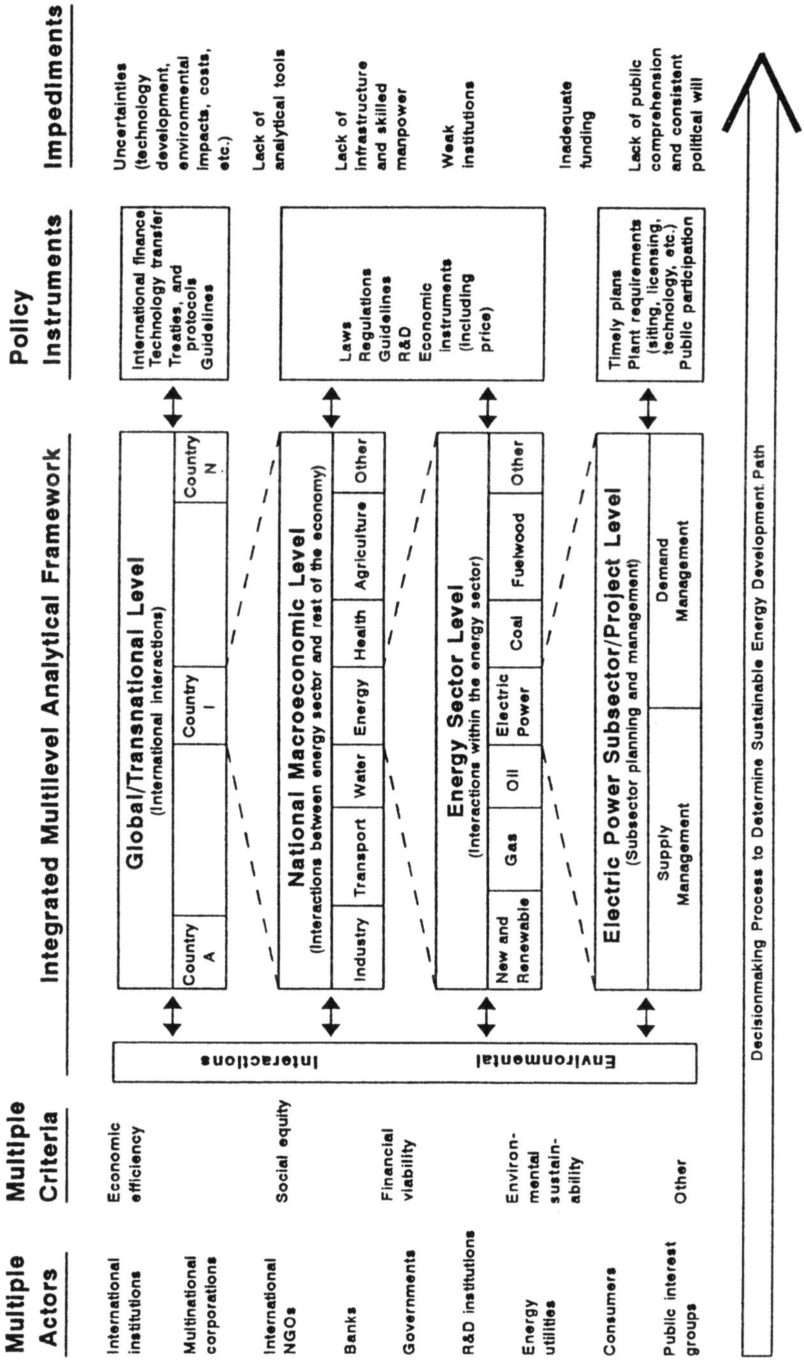

Thus, such a process should result in the development of a flexible and constantly updated energy strategy designed to meet national goals. This national energy strategy (of which the investment program and pricing policy are important elements), may be implemented through energy supply and demand management policies and programs that make effective use of decentralized market forces and incentives.

Consequently, INEP implies improvements in overall economic efficiency through better energy management. As shown in Figure 4, a variety of policy instruments are available to decision makers for instituting sound energy management. The figure also indicates the most important impediments that limit effective policy formulation and implementation.

4 ENERGY POLICY OPTIONS FOR SUSTAINABLE DEVELOPMENT

Energy sector measures which simultaneously improve economic efficiency (i.e., higher value of net output using same inputs), energy efficiency (i.e., higher value of net output per unit of energy used) and conservation (i.e., reduced absolute amount of energy used), together with environmental protection (i.e., reduced energy-related environmental costs), are particularly effective in ensuring sustainable economic growth. Where the energy required for economic growth will continue to increase, (as in the case of many developing countries), and financial resources for energy supply expansion are severely limited, better energy management provides the opportunity to achieve specific improvements in energy efficiency and conservation. Such improvements can result in substantial reductions in input requirements (both energy and raw materials) for development, and thus conserve resources and lessen the environmental consequences of energy-related economic activities.

Owing to inappropriate policies that have encouraged wasteful uses of energy and poor operational performance, there is generally considerable scope for most developing countries to improve management of their energy resources and achieve substantial energy savings even in the short run (Munasinghe, 1990a). On the supply side, better energy management will require more accurate demand forecasting, improved least-cost investment planning, and the optimal operation of energy systems -- that is, plant performance, operation and maintenance procedures, loss levels, etc. are optimized. On the demand side, better management will include efficient electricity end use, proper load management, and optimal pricing. All these options, as well as those discussed below, constitute attractive policy alternatives -- both in economic and environmental terms -- that LDCs may adopt.

4.1 Supply - Side Options

4.1.1 Energy Efficiency Improvements and Fuel Substitution

There is a spectrum of technological options which can be adopted as short- or medium-term measures for improving energy production efficiencies in the developing world. Energy supply technologies concerning the power sector, for example, may include plant generation improvement and rehabilitation, transmission and distribution loss reduction, fuel substitution, interconnections, etc. Among these technologies, reducing transmission and distribution losses, and improving generation plant efficiencies, are the most attractive in terms of yielding economic benefits that are several times the corresponding costs incurred (Munasinghe, 1990b). For example, transmission and distribution losses in Third World power systems are estimated to average in the 16-18% range (of which about one-third could be theft), although acceptable loss levels may be only about 6-8%. The economic consequences of reducing these losses can be quite substantial. A one percent reduction in losses per year would reduce additional capacity requirements in Third World countries by about 5 GW annually, and this corresponds to an estimated savings in capital investment of around US$10 billion per year. In Brazil, for example, the implementation of technical loss reduction programs in the power sector has shifted the emphasis of investment away from generation, and towards transmission and distribution, resulting in potential savings in investment requirements (World Bank, 1990b). The positive environmental implications of such measures are obvious, on account of reduced energy requirements and better production efficiencies.

Substitution of primary energy sources in power generation is another potential means of achieving both economic and environmental benefits. In the developing world, natural gas is the most likely candidate for coal or oil substitution. The economic benefit of natural gas substitution comes from either import substitution for petroleum products, or releasing the latter for export. On the environmental front, natural gas firing typically achieves reductions in various pollutants (e.g., lowering of carbon emissions of 30-50%). Fuel switching policies nonetheless must be carefully evaluated to ensure that there will be adequate long-term supplies of the fuels required.

In the long term, developing countries may have to rely on more advanced technological options which are currently being developed in the industrialized countries, for further improvements in energy efficiency and conservation, and reductions in environmental costs. Since power generation capacity in LDCs is expected to increase significantly, this provides future opportunities to add state-of-the-art technologies (e.g., clean coal technologies, cogeneration, gas turbine combined cycles, steam-injected gas turbines, etc.), which have been designed with regard to both economic and environmental criteria. Some of these options are summarized next.

4.1.2 Technologies to Mitigate Environmental Impacts

Clearly, the energy sector can potentially contribute to environmental and health hazards at all four levels of impact discussed in Section II: global, transnational, national and local. *Coal-fired power plants* are the worst offenders because coal may have a sulfur content as high as 5% or more and can be a severe pollutant. In addition, coal is an important source of total suspended particulate emissions, which usually constitute a health hazard in local and regional areas. *Large-scale hydropower*, another major source of energy, also has environmental drawbacks. It is an excellent source of renewable energy and does not cause global environmental problems, but hydro plants may suffer from local, regional, national and sometimes trans-national environmental problems (World Bank, 1990a). For example, they may inundate fertile valleys and population centers (requiring resettlement of the local population); alter the river flow and affect the downstream population (particularly the agricultural and fishing activities); change the river quality (typically the silt content and navigation); affect the reservoir area ecosystem; and flood historic sites. Other renewable energy options such as wind, direct solar, biomass and bagasse can make still modest but increasing contributions towards environmentally friendly energy development (Anderson, 1991), see also Chapter 8, 9 and 11.

Technologies are available to mitigate some of the environmental consequences associated with fossil fuels (Bates, 1991). For example, although coal may have large amounts of sulfur, there are ways to remove sulfur from the plant effluent: coal washing, scrubbing, and sulfur flue gas desulfurization (FGD). The sulfur problem can be addressed further through fluidized bed coal technology, coal benification, coal gasification, and coal liquefaction. Nitrogen oxide (NO_x) which is also produced during coal combustion can be reduced through combustion control (CC) using modern electronics. NO_x from stack emissions can be removed using the selective catalytic reduction (SCR) system, which is 90% effective. Most SCR applications to date are in Japan and Germany. Finally, total suspended particulates in stack emissions can be removed using either electrostatic precipitators or baghouse fabric filters.

However, there are certain limitations in using some of these technologies. For instance, FGD has large space requirements, large volumes of by-products, and high cost. While it removes 90% of the SO_2 from the stack emissions, it does not address the problem of carbon emissions at all. As of 1988, only about 140 GW of FGD equipment were installed in OECD countries. To illustrate the range of costs involved in mitigation efforts, Table 2 shows the typical costs of installing FGD, SCR and CC technologies in a coal-fired plant, compared with oil and gas. At 70% capacity factor and 10% discount rate, emission control costs amount to US mills 9.1/kWh, US mills 6.7/kWh and US mills 1.3/kWh for coal, oil and natural gas steam power plants, respectively. The emission control cost for gas steam is only one-seventh of that of coal steam.

Table 2 Cost of environmental control technologies on steam plants (1987 US mills/kWh)

	Coal	Oil	Gas
FGD, SCR, CC			
(Capital cost, $kW)	(215)	(177)	(25)
Capital	3.90	3.21	0.45
Operating Variable	0.86	1.11	0.49
Operation Fixed	4.32	2.35	0.35
Total	9.08	6.67	1.29

Source: Emission Controls in Electricity Generation and Industry, International Energy Agency, OECD, 1988.

Recognizing that future increases in world energy requirements are inevitable (Munasinghe et al., 1991), the associated negative effects of such a trend on the environment can be tremendous. Although mitigating measures are available, on the whole, they are not designed to resolve all major problems and the costs of adoption may very well restrict their application. It is crucial for decision makers to establish policies and institutional frameworks to improve the efficiency in energy production and use, especially in developing countries where most of the future growth-driven increases in energy consumption will take place, and where only limited use of mitigating measures has so far been made.

4.1.3 Institutional and Regulatory Reforms

Although many difficulties have plagued the energy sector in developing countries, perhaps the most pervasive has been excessive government interference in organizational and operational matters. Such interference has adversely affected least-cost procurement and investment decisions, hampered attempts to raise prices to efficient levels, mandated low salaries tied to civil service levels, and promoted excessive staffing. This in turn has resulted in inadequate management, loss of experienced staff due to uncompetitive employment conditions and poor job satisfaction, weak planning and demand forecasting, inefficient operation and maintenance, high losses, and poor financial monitoring, controls and revenue collection.

In order to address these difficulties, an important principle must be recognized -- i.e., given the complexity of energy problems and the scarcity of resources and managerial talent, each set of issues should be dealt with by that level of decision making and management best suited to analyzing the situation and implementing remedial measures. This hierarchical approach corresponds loosely to the INEP concept summarized earlier in this paper. Thus, political decision makers, senior government officials and ministry level staff should focus on critical macroeconomic and energy sector linkages and design policies to improve sector performance. Management of power utilities, for instance, may occur under the guidance of an independent board of directors, they may conduct their daily operations without government interference, but subject to overall national policy objectives and targets within regulatory guidelines. Such an organizational structure will still necessitate regular consultations with government, as well as consumer representatives, to achieve further improvements in operational efficiencies. Nonetheless, it will provide the power utilities a wider autonomy, and at the same time make them more accountable for their performance.

The natural monopoly characteristic of energy enterprises, combined with the willingness of those concerned to manipulate these enterprises for general policy purposes, are in many countries accepted as sufficient reasons for maintaining them as large centralized public sector organizations. While there may have been some rationale for this centralization in the past (e.g., economies of scale in production), it is becoming a critical barrier to greater management efficiency and improved flexibility. For example, in a recent survey of over 350 power utilities involved in projects financed by the World Bank during the period 1965-84, it was found that the financial performance of the electricity sector in several developing countries had deteriorated markedly up to the 1980s due largely to inadequate increases in tariffs

(Munasinghe et al., 1988). The consequences of a weak financial situation because of government control of energy prices can be widespread -- but perhaps the most important is that expenditures on such items as maintenance, power system loss reductions, and refinery upgrading (in the oil subsector) receive lower priority than increased production. There are foregone financial savings and positive environmental effects associated with these items. Improved maintenance reduces the fuel requirements for power generation; reductions in power system losses through investments in transmission and distribution result in lower total production requirements; upgrading of oil refineries produces better quality petroleum products which are also less polluting (McKeough, 1991).

The desperate circumstances of energy enterprises in many developing countries have generated pressures for re-organizing the sector. There is considerable interest in the scope for more decentralization, and particularly, greater private participation in the hope that it will bring significant gains in terms of infusion of new capital and innovative management methods. Options for private, and even cooperative, ownership of energy enterprises may include both local and foreign participation as well as joint ventures. As long as a given regulatory framework prevails, it can be argued that the form of ownership would not by itself affect management efficiency. The main point is that, to the extent possible, the introduction of competitive market forces should be encouraged. Governments may wish to divest themselves of either all or part of some government owned enterprises. This may create an environment in which governments, enterprise managements, and energy consumers are all better off.

Power sector officials in several LDCs have been actively studying the various options for decentralization and private participation. However, despite potential opportunities for their adoption in these countries, such options are likely to meet considerable difficulties. For instance, since the power sector occupies a central position among publicly-owned enterprises, changing this framework in a manner conducive to private participation is proving to be difficult. Furthermore, LDC utilities often operate in a climate which is economically weak and politically unstable. This increases the risk of expropriation and frequent disruptions, or the likelihood of adverse future regulatory changes. Meanwhile, there is no guarantee that enhanced private sector involvement will lead to economic and environmental benefits. With profit maximization goals, private participants can be expected to make full use of cheaper (but not necessarily environmentally benign) inputs like coal for power generation. In such cases, both environmental benefits and overall economic efficiency gains can only be ensured if there are regulatory measures that will internalize the pollution costs of energy production and use, and make them a part of the private production costs.

Consequently, energy companies in developing countries need to be supported by national policies and legislation that emphasize environmental issues. Environmental standards and regulations should be developed and executed in a manner that will facilitate the process of internalizing the environmental costs associated with energy sector activities. The INEP framework provides an appropriate starting point for this purpose. A number of techniques exist for valuing the environmental impacts of energy projects, and these can be used for incorporating quantifiable environmental costs into methodologies for least-cost investment planning and in estimating the long-run marginal costs of energy supply. However, one should be aware of the uncertainties in such estimates and be prepared to perform sensitivity tests where appropriate.

Going beyond the quantifiable environmental costs is of course problematical. Nevertheless, an attempt should still be made to assess the significance of non-quantifiable environmental costs rather than implicitly assume that they are negligible. Non-quantifiable environmental costs can be incorporated in various ways, such as adding new constraints on the investment program which reflect social concerns or absolute environmental standards. On the whole, internalization of environmental costs, and having them reflected in private decision making, serves as a means to reconcile economic development with the goals of environmental protection and sound natural resource management.

4.2 Demand - Side Options

4.2.1 Energy Price Setting

Energy price rationalization offers the most attractive demand-side option for improving energy sector efficiency. By providing the correct economic signals, energy prices that reflect the true marginal costs of supply assist in establishing optimal patterns and levels of energy consumption. However, energy prices in many developing countries are often set and regulated by the government rather than being based on the changing demand and supply situations in the market. This creates a system of prices which are inflexible to market pressures and opportunities, and incapable of providing correct economic signals. In a situation of rising international prices, this system of controlled prices has usually lagged behind, thereby resulting in significant price subsidies. Furthermore, to compensate for the financial losses in the energy sector, price increases, when instituted, have tended to be non-uniform across different energy substitutes, thereby creating severe interfuel price distortions and imbalances in consumption.

More precisely, energy pricing policy in developing countries is guided by a tradeoff between economic efficiency on the one hand and a series of financial and socio-political considerations on the other. There is a strong perception among decision makers that access to energy is a basic need which improves living standards of the people. This idea has driven a policy in which affordability competes with economic efficiency as the criterion for energy pricing. Consequently, in practice it has been difficult to separate socio-political and economic criteria within the same pricing structure, often leading to poorly designed policies that are both economically inefficient and socially regressive.

Energy prices themselves are an important demand management tool. Innovative pricing strategies such as time-of-use, spot pricing and priority pricing are increasingly being applied in the industrialized countries to achieve further improvements in energy end-use efficiency. Indeed there is a great potential for incorporating these pricing strategies selectively in developing countries whose power systems are still evolving and sufficiently flexible to adopt such technological know-how (Schweppe et al., 1988).

4.2.2 Other Incentives and Related Options

Apart from price rationalization, there is also scope for applying a coordinated package of other demand-side options aimed at improving the efficiency of energy use. These include taxes and subsidies (based on fuel type), end-use technology, research and development, retrofits, conservation programs, etc. In most instances these programs are likely to achieve desirable effects on both energy use and environmental impacts. Fiscal instruments such as emission fees and carbon-based user fees can be used to control environmental impacts more directly. However, the problems of implementing and monitoring these fiscal tools in developing countries can be significant.

Technological innovations through research and development have made available a new set of opportunities for demand side management in developing countries with increased potential for energy efficiency and conservation. Examples of such technologies are high intensity heating, high efficiency cooling devices, efficient lighting options, etc. In Brazil, the National Energy Conservation Program has advanced the development and commercialization of a number of energy-efficient technologies, e.g., improved refrigerators, energy-efficient lamps, reflectors for fluorescent fixtures, and building-control systems. These technologies are now manufactured and sold in Brazil, and their adoption provided approximately 1.2 TWh of electricity savings in 1989 (Geller, 1990).

5 GLOBAL ENERGY-ENVIRONMENTAL ISSUES FROM AN LDC PERSPECTIVE

Industrialized countries and LDCs differ in their capabilities in attending to issues concerning energy-environmental interactions, and this should be emphasized in devising means of cooperation for solving global environmental problems. The industrialized countries have already attained most reasonable goals of development, and thus, they can afford to commit resources to global environmental protection even at the expense of further material growth. By contrast, LDCs have limited ability to resolve even domestic environmental problems; they can be expected to participate in global environmental programs only to the extent that such participation is consistent with their national growth objectives. Technology and capital transfers from the industrialized countries are essential to enable the LDCs to contribute toward the protection of the "global commons" (Munasinghe and Munasinghe, 1991).

Currently, discussions are underway among world bodies and governments to define effective criteria and mechanisms for both generating and disbursing funds to address global environmental issues. While a broad workable agreement will not be easy to reach, global financing issues may be analyzed and resolved through a tradeoff involving several criteria: affordability/additionality, fairness/equity and economic efficiency.

First, since LDCs cannot afford to finance even their present energy supply development, to address global environmental concerns they will need financial assistance on concessionary terms that is additional to existing conventional aid. The latter will have to be increased also, to assist developing countries in dealing with local environmental degradation.

Second, the disparity in energy use (and therefore, per capita income) between the industrialized countries and LDCs raises issues in the context of current global environmental concerns, and the heavy burden placed on mankind's natural resource base by past economic growth. A good example of this is the accumulation of greenhouse gases, particularly CO_2, in the atmosphere due to the use of fossil fuels mentioned in the introduction.

Clearly, the development of industrialized countries has effectively exhausted a disproportionately large share of global resources -- broadly defined to include both the resources that are consumed in productive activity (e.g., oil, gas and minerals), as well as environmental assets that absorb the waste products of economic activity and those that provide irreplaceable life support functions (like the high altitude ozone layer). Indeed this development path has significantly indebted the industrialized countries to the rest of the global community (Brundtland Commission Report, 1987). If the division of responsibility in the worldwide effort to resolve global environmental problems were to be based fairly on the unbalanced use of common resources in the past, then the industrialized countries would be required to assume a bigger role than the LDCs in protecting the "global commons." This approach would also help determine how the remaining finite global resources may be shared more equitably and used sustainably.

Finally, the economic efficiency criterion indicates that the "polluter pays" principle may be applied to generate revenues, to the extent that global environmental costs of human activity can be quantified. If total emission limits are established under a permit system, then trading in emission permits among nations and other market mechanisms can be harnessed to increase efficiency.

The principle of international assistance to LDCs for environmental protection efforts, specifically in terms of technology transfer and financial support, is already well established. One assistance mechanism that has recently been established is the Global Environment Facility, which is a core multilateral fund of about US$1.5 billion to be implemented as a pilot program over the next three years. This fund would finance investment, technical assistance and institutional development activities in four areas: *global climate change, ozone depletion, protection of biodiversity,* and *water resource degradation.* Another is the Ozone Fund of about US$160-240 million, which has been set up to help implement measures to reduce CFC emissions under the Montreal Protocol. Both funds are being managed under a collaborative arrangement between the UNDP, UNEP and the World Bank. In particular, they would fund those investment activities that would provide cost-effective benefits to the global environment, but would not have been undertaken by individual countries without concessions because the measurable benefits to a national economy are too low to trigger own investment.

6 CONCLUSIONS

While energy is a vital prerequisite for economic growth, energy production and use can also create extensive and serious environmental effects which can retard the growth process. The crucial dilemma this poses to developing countries is how to reconcile development and poverty alleviation goals with responsible management of their environment, considering that such goals will require increased use of energy and raw materials. Only through this reconciliation can sustainable development be achieved.

There is a pressing need in LDCs to rationalize energy sector activities in view of rapid growth of demand, coupled with inefficient energy policies and factors that inhibit energy investments (e.g., scarce fiscal resources, severe debt constraints, controlled energy prices, etc). On this account, better energy management, primarily through technical means and price rationalization, provides the opportunity for improving energy efficiency and conservation. This in turn can lead to lower energy and raw material requirements for economic growth, as well as lessen the environmental consequences of energy production and use. Meanwhile, INEP provides a conceptual framework for formulating national energy policies with macroeconomic-environmental links, and presents a comprehensive approach to attaining improved energy management. The foregoing requires that in addition to dealing more effectively with environmental concerns, decision makers must improve power sector resource mobilization and financing, organizational and regulatory efficiency, efficiency of prices, targeting of socioeconomic subsidies and basic needs-related measures and traditional concerns like demand forecasting, least cost planning, and system operations.

International pressures to implement measures for the protection of the "global commons" place a heavy burden on developing countries in general. Because of the severe financial constraints that these countries already face, their response to environmental protection issues at the global level cannot extend beyond the realm of measures that are consistent with their short-term economic development and poverty alleviation goals. Just as LDCs will need more conventional aid to address local environmental issues, they will also require concessional funding to participate in solving global environmental problems. It is, therefore, important that the industrialized countries provide the financial resources that LDCs need today and engage in technological innovations to be used in the 21st century by all nations. The Global Environment Fund and Ozone Fund can facilitate the initial participation of developing countries in protecting the "global commons."

REFERENCES

Anderson, D. 1991. "Energy and the Environment - An Economic Perspective on Recent Technical Development and Policies", The World Bank, Washington D.C.

Bates, R.W. 1991. "Commercial Energy Efficiency and the Environment", Environment Department, Policy and Research Division, The World Bank, Washington, D.C.

Geller, H.S. 1990. "Electricity Conservation in Brazil: Status Report and Analysis", American Council for an Energy-Efficient Economy.

McKeough, K. 1991. "A Study of the Transfer of Petroleum Fuels Pollution," The World Bank, Washington, D.C.

Moore, E.A. and G. Smith. 1990. "Capital Expenditures for Electric Power in the Developing Countries in the 1990s", The World Bank, Industry and Energy Department, Washington, D.C.

Munasinghe, M., *Energy Analysis and Policy*, Butterworths Press, London, 1990a.

Munasinghe, M., *Electric Power Economics*, Butterworths Press, London, 1990b.

Munasinghe, M. et al. 1991. "Incorporating Environmental Considerations in Electricity Decision making", Proc. Senior Expert Symposium, Helsinki.

Munasinghe, M., J. Gilling, and M. Mason. 1988. "A Review of World Bank Lending for Electric Power", Industry and Energy Department, Energy Series Paper no. 2, The World Bank, Washington DC.

Munasinghe, M. and S. Munasinghe. 1991. "Energy Policy, Technology Cooperation and Capital Transfers to Address Global Climate Change Issues in Developing Countries", in T. Hanisch (Ed.), *A Comprehensive Approach to Climate Change*, CICERO, Oslo.

OECD. 1988. International Energy Agency, "Emission Controls in Electricity Generation and Industry".

Schweppe, F., M. Caramanis, R. Tabors and R. Bohn. 1988. *Spot Pricing of Electricity*, Kluwer Academic Publishers, New York.

World Bank. 1990a. "A Review of the Treatment of Environmental Aspects of Bank Energy Projects", Industry and Energy Department Working Paper, Energy Series Paper No. 24, Washington, D.C.

World Bank, Brazil. 1990b. "Electricity Transmission and Conservation Project", Staff Appraisal Report, LA Dept., LAC Regional Office, Washington, D.C.,

World Bank. 1988. "A Review of World Bank Lending for Electric Power", Industry and Energy Department Working Paper, Energy Series Paper No. 2, Washington, D.C.

World Commission on Environment and Development. 1987. *Our Common Future,* Oxford University Press, London.

World Resources Institute. 1990. *World Resources 1990-91*, Oxford University Press, London.

CHAPTER 16

Global Policies for Global Problems: the Case of Climate Change

by

Michael Grubb*

Abstract

Global environmental problems pose unique difficulties and climate changes poses the most daunting challenges. The impacts of climate change will differ greatly between countries but may be devastating for some, amplifying the political and legal complications associated with the impacts of transboundary pollution. The risks and inertia involved mean that steps to limit emissions must be taken despite considerable uncertainty, but extensive emisssions abatement may affect the structure of economic development and thus face major political obstacles. Many diverse countries contribute to emissions so international agreement is essential, but such an agreement has to meet many diverse requirements, including those of being reasonably efficient, flexible and equitable.

This paper explores different international approaches to quantified agreement on limiting emissions. It draws a clear distinction between agreement on fixed national commitments (such as agreement on fixed emission targets or domestic carbon taxation) and the more powerful but largely unprecedented use of international market instruments. The latter are not only theoretically appealing but overcome many of the practical difficulties of conventional approaches.

Of these, offsets could provide a useful extension of existing, geographical commitments (depending upon how they are formulated) but are limited by practical objections, arising from baseline and monitoring problems and political objections. Interest in growing in the possible use of tradeable permits, perhaps evolving from an initial system of offsets. In detail there are many variants upon such a system and its key characteristics (including its flexibility and equitability), would depend upon careful design. But despite initial resistance, it seems to be becoming more broadly accepted that the use of such instruments, if properly structured, offers the most promising approach to effective international control of global pollutants such as CO_2.

*This paper draws upon the author's contribution to Chapter 1 and 2 of UNCTAD (1992) and to M. Grubb and J. Sebenius, (1991). The helpful suggestions of various co-participants in the UNCTAD and OECD studies are gratefully acknowledged.

T. Sterner (ed.), Economic Policies for Sustainable Development, 283–308.

1 INTRODUCTION

In earlier chapters the main focus has been on the making of national environmental policy. Environmental problems, however, do not respect national frontiers and many serious environmental problems are inherently regional or global. In this chapter, the author addresses one of the most challenging problems for environmental policy: the regulation of Earth's atmosphere.

Without an atmosphere, the average temperature on Earth would be well below freezing. Various gases in the atmosphere absorb infra-red radiation and act as a blanket which helps to trap the heat absorbed and re-emitted from the surface. Human activity is increasing the concentration of these "greenhouse gases", and hence changing the radiative balance in a way that seems almost certain to increase the surface temperature.

The rate and extent of temperature rise, and its implications, is a matter of considerable uncertainty. A rise in temperature increases the atmospheric concentration of water vapour - itself the most important greenhouse gas - and changes the extent and nature of clouds, snow fall and ice cover; these and many other feedbacks, together with the uncertain role of oceans, greatly complicate assessment of temperature and related climatic changes.

We do not yet know whether human interference with the atmosphere has pushed the temperature beyond the considerable range of natural variability. However, the 1980s saw the six warmest years on record and some extreme climatic disturbances - the most important of which politically was the US drought of 1988 - which helped establish the greenhouse effect as a major political issue.

In response to widespread concerns, the Intergovernmental Panel on Climate Change (IPCC) was established in 1988. Its first report in the Summer of 1990 (IPCC, 1990) supported the growing scientific concerns. The basic theory - that increasing concentrations of greenhouse gases will tend to warm the planet's surface - seems unchallengeable. Also, the world has warmed in the last 100 years, and especially since the late 1970s. Natural variability and other factors mean that this cannot conclusively be attributed to the greenhouse effect, but it is consistent with current understanding of it. If trends in emissions continue as projected, global average surface temperature over the next century is likely to rise by several (1.5-4.5) degrees centigrade (compared with about 4.5 degrees difference between the present and the depth of the last ice age some 20,000 years ago). The changes would not be smooth and there would be considerable regional variations in both temperature and other impacts, most notably rainfall and soil moisture. Storm patterns might change, and sea levels rise.

Naturally not everyone accepted the IPPC conclusions. Some scientists argued that the likely rate of change is considerably smaller than the IPCC suggested, and that the IPCC report was unduly pessimistic. Others expressed the fear that the conclusions were dangerously cautious, and highlighted the possibilities of further feedbacks which would amplify the concentrations of greenhouse gases (GHGs). The IPCC report itself noted that "it appears likely that, as climate warms, these feedbacks will lead to an overall increase, rather than decrease, in natural greenhouse gas abundances. For this reason, climate change is likely to be greater than the estimates we have given."

The IPCC Impacts Working Group II found that, given the uncertainties concerning precipitation and other regional variations, it was not possible to reach clear conclusions about the impacts. Climate change would be combined with other environmental stresses caused by human activities and natural variations. Agricultural impacts could be considerable at the regional level, but "studies have not yet conclusively determined whether, on average, the global agricultural potential will increase or decrease". Natural ecosystems, both on land and in the oceans, would be altered. Water resources could be a particular concern because "relatively small climate changes can cause large water resource problems in many areas ... changes in drought risk represent potentially the most serious impact of climate change on agriculture". Such factors, combined with changes in disease patterns and the impact of sea level rises, "could initiate large migrations of people". Overall the Impacts report emphasised that a key determinant would be the rate of climate change; irrespective of whether a stable warmer world might be better or worse, rapid changes could disrupt both human societies and natural ecosystems.

Various gases contribute to the "greenhouse effect". Over half of the addition comes from carbon dioxide (CO_2), but CFCs and methane are also important, and there are smaller contributions from nitrous oxide and tropospheric ozone, which is created from a range of other human emissions. Because CFCs are being phased out under the Montreal Protocol and subsequent amendments, and CO_2 emissions from fossil fuel use are projected to continue growing rapidly, CO_2 emissions were projected to account for at least 70% of radiative change in the atmosphere over the next century in the IPCC 1990 "business as usual" scenario. Further research summarised in the IPCC 1992 update downgraded the projected impact of some of the non-CO_2 emissions, thus slightly reducing the projected rate of overall radiative change, but further increasing the projected dominance of CO_2.

Most of the climate modelling assessments performed to date have examined the possible consequences of atmospheric change equivalent to doubling the pre-industrial CO_2 concentration in the atmosphere. It is sobering to note that if emissions continue to grow as most analysts project without abatement policies, this level will be reached within about 40-50 years, with continuing and accelerating changes beyond this. Indeed, this level could be avoided only by substantial cuts in projected global emissions, especially of net CO_2 emissions; and cuts of 60-80% from current levels of CO_2 and other long-lived gases (CFCs and nitrous oxide) would be required to stabilize their concentration in the atmosphere. This contrasts with an underlying growth trend of around 2%/yr in global CO_2 emissions in the late 1980s.

2 OVERVIEW OF RESPONSE OPTIONS

The policy issues raised by global warming are complex and unique. The projected climatic changes outlined above are far from certain in any degree of detail, especially at the regional level. The changes could be less damaging than many fear. On the other hand, in changing the planet without fully understanding the consequences, humanity is clearly running a degree of risk that the changes could be worse, perhaps with potential surprises in the way the planet responds.

Nor does it seem wise to wait for observational certainty. The extent of natural variations, the buffering effect of the oceans, and the inertia in human systems responsible for the emissions means that by the time we can measure for sure how the climate system is responding to increasing greenhouse gas concentrations, it will be too late to prevent many decades of further and more rapid change thereafter. Doing nothing is a very risky strategy.

The three broad options in responding to this situation are adaptation, climate engineering and abatement. *Adaptation* strategies focus on accepting climate changes and seeking to minimize the damage involved by adapting to climate changes, both as they come and by measures taken in advance. Mechanisms include migration, development of drought resistant plant strains, construction of sea defences, etc. Because the changes are uncertain, emphasis would be on resilience and flexibility. People would have to become reconciled to warming and changing conditions. There could well be benefits in cold areas such as Alaska and Siberia, but changes might be particularly difficult to accommodate in countries which are poor, and already hot - which account for the great majority of the world's population. The international ramifications and stresses of such changes could be considerable.

Difficulties therefore include uncertainties about the overall cost and feasibility of relying wholly on adaptation, the widely differing impacts and ability to adapt between different countries, and the risk of large-scale surprises in the climate system. The risk of unexpectedly high levels of warming or other unexpected changes, when it is too late to stop them, pose another problem.

Climate engineering entails measures intended to offset directly the warming in the lower atmosphere. Examples include altering the reflectivity of the earth's surface, and screening the earth's atmosphere from the sun's rays. Preliminary estimates of the costs of these alternatives are low. But the uncertainties involved and their unknown and potentially damaging side-effects, and the political difficulties of assigning responsibility for such deliberate intervention with planetary systems and any unforeseen consequences thereof, suggest that this is unlikely to be a feasible or desirable option except in desperate circumstances.

Abatement refers to measures which moderate the growth of concentration of greenhouse gases in the atmosphere. *Sink enhancement* increases the rate at which greenhouse gases are re-absorbed; the main example is reforestation, though some other possibilities have been explored. *Emissions abatement* refers to preventing emissions of GHGs at source. These measures include phasing out chlorofluorocarbons, increasing energy efficiency, switching to fuels that generate less or no GHGs, reducing methane leaks and deforestation rates, and "scrubbing" the CO_2 out during fuel combustion for disposal probably in depleted gas fields or deep ocean. Thus a wide variety of cleaner technologies need to be used to abate emissions.

These options are not mutually exclusive. Some adaptation will be required irrespective of abatement measures, and climate engineering might prove essential as an emergency response if dangerous degrees of positive feedback do emerge. Sink enhancement could undoubtedly contribute, though all options considered to date are limited by land area, environmental impact and nutrient availability. But to reduce the costs and risks associated with continuing and accelerating atmospheric changes, emissions abatement must play a key role. To achieve goals of environmental protection and sustainable development, the current trend of rising emissions needs to be reversed to limit warming to acceptable levels, and emissions must eventually be reduced to a level at which atmospheric concentrations are stabilized.

Abatement measures need to be considered as comprehensively as possible, so as to include as far as practicable all important sources and sinks of GHGs. At present however, uncertainties concerning the role and magnitude of many of the lesser sources and sinks, difficulties in monitoring them, and problems in comparing consistently the different gases, make it difficult or impossible to include them in an overall quantified emissions agreement. Thus different approaches may initially be required for agreements on different sources and sinks according to their characteristics, though it would be desirable for measures to become more comprehensive over time.

Another complication is the different composition of GHGs and their economic sources in different groups of countries. As shown in Table 1 industrialized countries account for more total "warming" than do the developing countries (in spite of the LDC's much larger population). This is (at present) particularly obvious for the distribution of the use of fossil fuel. For other sources however, such as agricultural methane and changes in land use (deforestation etc) the LDCs account for relatively larger contributions, see further chapters 11 and 15.

Table 1 Contribution of different gases to total radiative change during the 1980s, Btons CO_2eq

Source	Industrialized	Developing
Fossil CO_2	14.2	6.8
CFCs	3.7	0.4
Agricultural methane	1.4	2.6
Fossil methane	0.9	0.5
Land use CO_2	--	6.9
Total (Btons CO_2 eq)	20.2	17.2

Source: Adapted by the author from World Resources Institute, World Resources 1990-1, with revised deforestation estimates, using 100yr GWPs estimated in the IPCC 1990 Report. Note that the 1992 IPCC update Revision revised estimates of non-CO_2 impacts downwards.

Negotiating an agreement on abatement to include fossil CO_2 emissions has to be a central component because it is the biggest single contributor, and it would be technically relatively easy because reliable statistics are readily available and fossil carbon can be relatively easily monitored. But because it would engage the major economic issues involved in energy supply it would be politically very difficult, and it raises starkly the issues of equity, efficiency and distribution in responding to climate change. For these reasons, most studies have concentrated upon fossil CO_2, but the ability of any control regime to expand to include other sources and sinks as the regime develops and knowledge improves is an important issue.

Limiting the build-up of greenhouse gases will not be like any other environmental issue. Apart from the CFCs, which are already being phased out, many of the sources of greenhouse gases are closely linked to basic human activities of agriculture and industrialisation. There may be options for reducing leakage of methane and other non-CO_2 gases from fossil fuel systems, and for some other "end-of-pipe" fixes. But particularly for CO_2, which forms the bulk of projected future radiative change, substantial steps would have major implications for some of the world's largest industries, and for land use policies especially in developing countries. Abatement could affect trade flows, and alter patterns of economic development.

3 NEED FOR AN INTERNATIONAL AGREEMENT

A number of countries and regions have made unilateral declarations, and some have passed legislation aimed at limiting CO_2 emissions. At the time of writing (early 1992) most OECD countries have declared intentions (some conditional) to stabilize CO_2 emissions at 1990 levels (Japan on a per-capita basis), and the US has stated it expects to stabilize overall greenhouse gas emissions, with the phasing out of CFCs and other measures offsetting growth in CO_2. These countries have acted from a variety of motives, for example: a desire to be leading the process, backed by a belief that nothing will happen unless some lead; domestic political pressure; and a conviction in some that in fact initial steps need not be economically damaging, and indeed that they could be beneficial to the extent that they help to reinforce efforts to promote things that are desirable anyway, such as improved energy efficiency. However, such unilateral actions are unlikely to be sustained beyond the point at which substantial economic costs or political difficulties are encountered, or the competitive position of domestic industries is damaged. Furthermore, as of February 1992 those countries which have already sought to stabilize CO_2 emissions only account for a limited fraction (about 20%) of global emissions.

The US is the largest emitter at about 24% of CO_2 emissions (and over 20% of all GHGs) followed closely by the former USSR, and the EC with 13%. These three together accounted for more than 50% of the global total. Adding the Eastern European countries and China raises this figure to over 70%. An international agreement could thus in principle have considerable impact even if it included relatively few key actors, at least if Russia and some of the former Eastern bloc countries can act together.

In practice this appears less promising. It is unlikely that such a group of countries would make an agreement without the participation of most of the rest of the world, in part because of fears about giving competitive advantages to non-participants. Also, limiting the use of fossil fuels in some countries would tend to lower the global price of fossil fuels, thus encouraging greater consumption in non-participants and partially offsetting the environmental benefits of the action. Furthermore the industrialized countries which account for the majority of current emissions by no means correspond to the regions of highest population - the developing countries in which there is great potential for future growth in emissions. Also, the distribution of other gases and sources (excepting CFCs) tends to be somewhat more even than fossil CO_2. For long term abatement it is crucial to gain long-term participation of major developing countries, especially China and India, because of the great increases in population and in consumption of soft coal (which has a high carbon content) projected in those regions.

Thus whilst including the developed world initially is crucial, the contribution of developing countries is already significant and for long term and substantial abatement they must be included over time. In practice, given that changes in energy systems and land use cannot occur suddenly but reflect the cumulative effect of policy over decades, it is highly desirable to include countries with large potential growth as soon as possible.

Recognizing the issues discussed above, negotiations towards a global Framework Convention on Climate Change started in February 1991 under the auspices of the United Nations General Assembly. This convention, due to be signed at the UNCED conference in June 1992, is intended to establish initial measures and the structure and principles on which subsequent protocols to the convention will be based. The convention itself may include some preliminary commitments, and will do much to set the options for subsequent negotiations on effective emissions limitation. An effective global system of control is unlikely to be created in one step, but it is important that the framework convention sets the right context and that subsequent protocol negotiations can consider the best options for structuring an evolving system for addressing the threat of climate change.

4 CRITERIA FOR AN ABATEMENT AGREEMENT

Clearly, trying to formulate an international agreement to address climate change is going to be an exceptionally complex task. The scale of the issue has been noted - human actions are changing some of the basic planetary systems which regulate the climate on which humanity depends; but some policy proposals for abating emissions have been estimated to cost many billions of dollars over just the next few decades. Rapid abatement could damage national economies and may be particularly burdensome to developing countries, especially if they are poorly formulated and inefficient; but inadequate abatement could prove still more damaging. Decisions made over the coming months and years will have consequences for decades ahead.

An agreement on limiting the accumulation of greenhouse gases needs to meet a wide range of demanding requirements. It must attract the participation of many diverse countries. It needs to be environmentally effective in achieving its goal, and thus needs to provide both adequate incentives for the use of cleaner technologies, and the resources required for the poorest countries to adopt them. It must be sufficiently robust for the overall structure to last decades in order to avoid repeated and damaging renegotiations of the fundamental deal, but flexible enough to adapt to developing scientific and economic understanding of the problem, with respect to its overall seriousness, the nature of the sources and sinks involved, and the costs of abatement.

Underlying these requirements there are two main general criteria for an international agreement. The extraordinary scale of the greenhouse problem means that an agreement must be efficient: the environmental goals must be achieved for the least possible economic cost, or at least, the system must not be inherently wasteful. An agreement which is economically efficient, and thus involves the least costly way of meeting a given abatement target, also has a better chance of being environmentally effective because it enables the greatest abatement to be achieved for a given expenditure. As the gap between projected emissions and those required to stabilize atmospheric concentrations is so large, this is of great importance. (Ideally, economic efficiency would suggest a cutback of GHGs to the level where global marginal cost of abatement equals global marginal gains in terms of avoided damage. In practice, the uncertainties concerning the impacts of climate change and how to evaluate them are so vast that an 'objective" consensus on the costs involved is highly unlikely. The debate is primarily about risk aversion, and thus the emphasis has to be on the cost-effectiveness of meeting politically-determined abatement targets).

Economic efficiency is also likely to be a major political requirement, especially for the richer countries which in any equitable agreement would bear most of the costs involved. Doubts are expressed not only about the political feasibility of large-scale resource transfers, but about the extent to which they would really be well spent in addressing the problem. The political prospects for reaching an agreement which does involve large-scale resource transfers will be much greater if the arrangement is seen to be economically efficient, with minimal waste of the resources spent. As noted below, and irrespective of equity considerations, global efficiency also implies a need for resource transfers to poorer countries which would not otherwise exploit globally cost-effective abatement opportunities.

A related requirement is for flexibility, with the ability both to amend the degree of control and to expand the range of sources and sinks of gases covered as knowledge grows. Whilst to be practicable an initial system of quantified control may have to focus on a few major and well-understood sources (notably CO_2 from fossil fuels, given their central role and relative ease of monitoring and verification), to enhance efficiency the system should also allow and if possible encourage, expansion to include additional sources and sinks of greenhouse gases as knowledge improves. It should also be able to expand to include new members, without complete renegotiation.

The other central requirement is that the agreement is broadly equitable. An agreement which is not widely perceived as fair, but which reflects principally current dispositions of economic and political power, is unlikely to gain widespread participation or to last as international circumstances change.

Naturally, the key difficulty is that there are many differing perceptions of what would be equitable. But there are some basic principles which can and should command broad support. The richer countries that have caused the vast majority of atmospheric changes to date, and which are still emitting at far higher per-capita levels than poorer countries, must bear most of the responsibility for slowing atmospheric changes. Those which are still struggling to meet basic needs for their citizens tomorrow, and which have made negligible contributions to the problem to date, cannot and should not be expected to bear significant costs in preventing impacts which will be felt most sometime in the next century. It follows that if developing countries are to bear significant costs in limiting emissions in the near term, equity demands that there be some resource transfers from the rich countries to the poor to help them implement the policies required to adopt cleaner technologies as they develop.

Indeed a system which is clearly inequitable would also be impractical. Developing countries would be unlikely to join a greenhouse control program that did not take account of differential ability to pay and differing responsibilities. Even if they did, the pressures of capital shortage and debt repayment make it politically impossible to divert existing resources towards preventing an uncertain and very long term threat, as recognized by the IPCC Special Committee on developing countries. An equitable agreement would thus also be one that provides the resources essential for globally more sustainable paths of development for poorer countries. The degree of assistance involved and the terms on which it is given are clearly contentious issues of negotiation, and any deal will have to face the constraints of political reality reflecting in part differing equity perceptions; but if developing countries are to be involved, an equitable arrangement involving some resource transfers appears not only fair but essential.

Many doubt the ability of equity to rally an agreement, especially since the majority of equity concepts require some degree of altruism. Sceptics may regard equity arguments as mere public relations cover for raw interests or underlying power relationships. But whilst the realities of self-interest and power will be important in constraining what is possible, in practice some degree of equity considerations have appeared as a consistent feature in a large number of negotiated international environmental and natural resource regimes (Oran Young, 1989; Morisette et al, 1991). There are also precedents for large-scale resource transfers for the common good, as with the Marshall Plan and current action and proposals for assistance to the Eastern European and former Soviet countries. But clearly, no effective agreement is going to be easy, and a structure which can deliver strong incentives in a framework which is both efficient and equitable is crucial. What are the options?

5 FIRST OPTION: FIXED NATIONAL COMMITMENTS

5.1 Emission targets (Non-tradeable quotas)

As noted above a number of countries or regional groups have already declared targets to limit emissions, with most them aiming to stabilize CO_2 emissions at 1990 levels by the year 2000. These have been very important in establishing the importance of the issue and creating the political impetus for negotiations, and some country targets have already precipitated policy measures which will help to limit emissions. Many expect an international agreement to be based fundamentally on agreement over national emission targets.

This is partly because the approach has many precedents. The Montreal Protocol, UNECE agreements on sulphur and nitrous oxides, and the EC's Large Combustion Plant directive on sulphur emissions, are all major environmental examples.

The use of emission targets is economically more efficient than procedural requirements which specify technical control mechanisms (e.g., mandated levels of energy efficiency or renewable sources, use of CO_2 scrubbing, use of particular methane abatement techniques), because it leaves countries free to decide on the most appropriate means for limiting emissions. But for CO_2 there are important drawbacks which must be considered.

Even within the developed world, widespread variations would make an agreement based upon equal percentage reductions (as used in most of the agreements cited above) difficult and inefficient. Some have already taken major measures to limit fuel use (as some did during the 1970s), and consequently have emissions substantially lower than average in per capita and per GNP terms, and they would argue for more lenient targets. By contrast, other countries have easier opportunities arising from greater current inefficiencies or extensive gas or non-fossil energy resources. Including deforestation and other sources would add further layers of variation. Some countries could thus incur substantial costs in achieving relatively modest reductions, whilst others could reduce by much more for lesser costs. If they were bound to equal reduction targets, many relatively cost-effective options for reducing emissions could go unexploited, so that such an agreement would be both inefficient and hard to negotiate; an efficient target system would require differentiated national targets. The possible need for revision as countries learn more about emission trends and abatement costs and opportunities adds further complexities.

Irrespective of efficiency considerations, differential targets would be unavoidable if developing countries were to be involved, for most of which the question is not how to reduce carbon emissions but how to limit their rate of growth while developing - and how to finance the programmes for such limitations. Furthermore, as discussed above, international transfers would have to be separately negotiated if developing countries were to take part, further magnifying the difficulties of negotiating country-specific targets.

A number of these problems arise from the fact that an agreement based upon national emission targets is inherently neither equitable nor globally efficient. Attempts to adjust targets to make the system more equitable - which in the absence of an additional agreement on resource transfers might mean largely excluding developing countries - also make it less efficient, and *vice versa*.

Finally, in negotiations all countries would endeavour to find some arguments why they should reduce emissions by less than the average sought, and inevitably there will be an abundance of "special cases"; the incentive in such negotiations will always be to prove how difficult it will be to limit emissions so as to gain a more lenient target. More complex target formulae can be suggested, but they all face considerable drawbacks, including more general questions about the timescale and revision of targets if national circumstances change.

A number of these points have been illustrated by the attempts within the European Community to reach agreement on how to share the EC's umbrella CO_2 stabilization target. The attempts broke down amid suspicions that some member countries were working from unrealistically high baseline projections, and/or not offering as much abatement as they should, so that the national targets did not add up to overall stabilization; and with insistence from the less developed members of Southern Europe that they would have to be compensated for any efforts, the EC instead has opted for a variety of Community-wide policy measures, with a central focus on a proposed harmonized carbon tax in all member countries.

Thus, despite the attention this approach receives it seems unlikely that a long-term agreement to limit climate change effectively can be achieved by a global agreement on national emission targets, and even if some initial agreement were reached the lack of flexibility would make it an inefficient outcome which might prove not very long-lasting. Other options need to be considered.

5.2 Agreement on domestic carbon taxes

Whatever form of agreement is eventually adopted, many countries may choose to use market-based instruments as part of efforts to limit emissions. These would penalize CO_2 emissions and provide an economic incentive to use more efficient and lower-CO_2 technologies.

Two main forms of economic instruments are possible for domestic pollution control. One is the use of tradeable permits, as applied particularly in the US; some of this experience is described in Chapter 2. Domestic tradeable permits might be a viable way of implementing unilateral or agreed emission targets. The other main option would be to use carbon taxes (see especially Chapter 3). Environmental taxes, if properly set, compensate for the social and environmental costs of activities that are not captured in the market price. For limiting emissions of CO_2 they would probably be applied to the consumption of fossil fuels in proportion to their carbon content. The revenues, which could be huge in addressing global warming, can be used to offset conventional taxes or for a host of other purposes.

A general discussion of market-based instruments for domestic control of greenhouse gas emissions is beyond the scope of this chapter (see Pearce *et al*, 1989, Dornbusch and Poterba, 1991). There are doubts expressed about their environmental effectiveness and possible impact on the poor (concerns addressed in the international context below). But many now recognize that provided the market concerned works reasonably well, such instruments can provide an effective and efficient means of control, and that distributional impacts on the poor can be mitigated.

As discussed in earlier chapters, increasing numbers of governments are using pollution taxes in domestic policy, and one suggestion for an international agreement is that it should focus on agreeing levels of domestic carbon taxes. An agreement to apply domestic taxes up to a certain level could well be favoured by many industrialised countries. It would not involve passing significant resources to international control, and globally if the markets worked well, and other things being equal, it would not be obviously discriminating between countries (Barrett, 1991).

The drawbacks arise because other things are far from equal and energy markets are far from ideal. Not only do stages of development differ, but so do economic systems, price structures, and existing taxation and other policies. Many countries, both developed and developing, already tax oil consumption and subsidise domestic energy production, to widely varying degrees. Meaningful agreement on domestic tax levels would be very problematic with such wide differences in national policies. The social and political implications of domestic carbon taxes would also vary considerably between different countries. In many areas of the world people cannot afford commercial fuel without subsidies, let alone if taxes were to be added. False pricing of fuels is responsible for many problems (see Chapter 17 and Kosmo, 1989) but in some cases there are good reasons for current practice, and in all cases the political obstacles to major changes are substantial.

Furthermore, such agreement would not have an equal impact on different countries and equal tax levels could hurt most those countries which are poor and which rely most heavily on coal. An agreement which just stipulated equal domestic CO_2 taxes would therefore not necessarily be efficient, and it would certainly not be equitable; on its own, not only would it fail to provide any resource transfers to help the poorest countries, but it could hurt them the most.

To overcome these difficulties, an agreement might be considered with different tax levels for different countries, together with separately-negotiated international transfers. Such possibilities could be further examined, but they might reduce the efficiency and would add considerably to the complexity of this approach, and imply that an agreement on domestic taxation cannot be the only international or perhaps even main international instrument used.

Agreements on carbon taxes could play an important role among some groups of closely-aligned countries, as with the recent EC proposals to introduce an energy/carbon tax throughout the EC, which may test the impact and practicality of such a system (Pearson and Smith, 1991). But for broader application there are important issues of sovereignty and differing economic circumstances and ideology to be addressed. In a world where social and economic conditions and beliefs vary so radically, it is hard to see how an agreement can be based primarily upon national carbon taxes, or indeed upon any other agreement which specifies domestic policy.

Although an agreement on domestic carbon taxes appears to be a market-based approach, it is so only in the sense that it obligates the countries involved to use carbon taxes. This is not the same thing as exploiting the potential efficiency and flexibility of market-based instruments internationally. Indeed, economically it has much in common with an agreement on national emission targets in which countries agree to implement their targets using domestic tradeable emission permits, and as such it faces many of the same problems. The real need is for mechanisms which provide the flexibility required to meet both equity and efficiency requirements internationally.

6 SECOND SET OF OPTIONS: INTERNATIONAL MARKET-BASED INSTRUMENTS

6.1 General features

It is possible to consider the use of market-based instruments internationally. Three main options have been advanced for achieving this: an international emissions tax; external offsets; and internationally tradeable emission entitlements (or "tradeable permits"). These three options are explained and discussed in turn below, but first a few general points common to all are considered.

Market instruments seek to deter pollution by making it more expensive, so that those involved decide to reduce emissions to avoid the associated costs. This contrasts with approaches that directly stipulate the degree of reductions by each party. Initial debate on the use of such instruments internationally has revealed at least two key concerns. One is that such an approach would be environmentally ineffective, because it would not directly mandate limits on each country's emissions. The other concern is that it would be inequitable, because it would allow richer countries to carry on polluting whereas poorer ones could not afford to.

The first concern, that a market-based instrument would be ineffective and could indeed be seen to "legitimise pollution", is no more valid at the international level than it is at the national level. Emission targets and all other approaches similarly "legitimise pollution"; the difference is that market-based instruments would not allow this to occur for free, but would penalize emissions and thus give a continuing incentive to reduce emissions as long as the costs of limitation were lower than the penalties imposed.

A market-based approach could give a general and flexible incentive: those involved can explore all the options for limiting emissions, both within their own country and elsewhere, and there is a direct incentive to explore abatement opportunities anywhere and to develop and deploy cleaner technologies which can avoid the pollution and consequent penalty.

As noted above, this economic efficiency can also lead to greatest environmental effectiveness, because it enables the greatest abatement for a given expenditure. Thus in practice, because countries have the freedom to decide how and where to pay for limiting emissions, they might agree to more stringent cutbacks than would be the case if all countries were bound to fixed targets which allowed no flexibility (and which provide no incentive to cut back beyond the target agreed if this did turn out to be cheaper or easier than originally envisaged).

Whether or not a market-based instrument is more or less equitable than any other approach depends entirely upon how it is structured. Because the system would be created from scratch by negotiated agreement, its form and distributional implications would be determined by negotiated settlement, rather than the "vagaries of the market". All international market-based instruments would of necessity involve international resource transfers (just as domestic markets involve the exchange of goods or money), and a market-based system could readily be structured to ensure that developing countries benefit from the international resource flows associated with globally efficient abatement - indeed, they would not take part unless this were the case. They would pay for their emissions ("at the margin" as emissions increase) but this could be more than offset by their overall receipts.

One of the key attractions of such an approach is thus that it can provide simultaneously an efficient incentive to limit emissions, and the resource transfers from rich to poor (reflecting international disparities in wealth and emissions) which would form an essential part of any equitable and practical agreement involving limitations in developing countries. More generally, a key feature of a market-based arrangement is that it can separate the question of efficiency from that of equity - and can in principle achieve both simultaneously. Negotiations on an equitable arrangement could thus proceed in the knowledge that money spent is less likely to be wasted, improving the political prospects for a more equitable solution.

It is important to note that one question which is *not* unique to international market instruments is that of deciding how to share the costs. This issue of allocating costs is unavoidable whatever control system is adopted, whether it be national emission targets, taxes, or other approaches. All systems that have much global impact will impose costs on participants, and must include some resource transfers if poor countries are to take part. The use of a market-based approach neither creates nor solves the problems of allocation and burden-sharing, which will have to be addressed in any substantive agreement. But if the political debates about the appropriate degree of abatement and burden-sharing can be resolved, such instruments might in principle offer a powerful and efficient way of implementing the intention. There are of course many complications and unanswered questions about how such systems could be created and would operate in practice. Toman and Gardiner (1991) give a recent review of literature on practical aspects; the rest of this chapter examines some of the specific options and issues raised.

6.2 International emission taxes

An alternative - or complementary - option to an agreement on domestic CO_2 emission taxes could be for some or all of the revenues from carbon taxation to be disbursed internationally. The revenues would thus be paid in proportion to emissions, and redistributed in such a way as to ensure a net transfer from richer to poorer countries. Governments would then face an equal incentive to exploit opportunities for abatement, ensuring efficiency; and this would be achieved independently of how the revenues were redistributed, which would reflect a negotiated equitable outcome. Although this might appear to imply agreement on using taxes domestically, this is not necessarily the case; in principle, taxes could be applied to countries on the basis of total national emissions, leaving governments with the freedom to determine the extent (if any) to which this would actually be passed on in fuel prices. Unlike an agreement on domestic taxes it separates the question of efficiency - which in principle follows from use of the tax instrument - from that of fairness - which depends upon how the revenues are disbursed.

There are two very different ways in which an international emissions tax could be implemented. One option would be for the revenues to go to a central international fund. This however raises major problems of scale and management. A carbon tax sufficient to make a serious impact on industrial choices could raise hundreds of billions of dollars globally (compared with the current registered budget of the United Nations of about $1bn). It seems implausible that countries would willingly hand over such amounts for an international bureaucracy to disperse perhaps on a project-by-project or plan-by-plan basis. Apart from the magnitude of the payments involved, it is hard to see how a bureaucracy managing such vast sums would operate in practice, deciding which countries should receive money, for which projects. Whilst this approach might be feasible for managing relatively small amounts, for the scale of resources which could be involved in any general agreement on carbon taxation for abatement, (or those which might be required to involve developing countries in substantial abatement efforts) it seems questionable whether such an approach would turn out to be efficient, or even fair; having all the money controlled by an international bureaucracy may be impractical and undesirable.

This is part of the reason for interest in a different approach, in which revenues from agreed taxes would be redistributed according to an allocation formula, or "reimbursement parameters", as suggested by Hoel (1991). This in fact is the only form of international agreement on taxes that Hoel considers a real possibility. It overcomes many of the objections to other carbon tax approaches, and deserves more study (this approach in fact has much in common with proposals for a global scheme of tradeable entitlements as discussed below). It is however important to recognize that it is not what many studies have in mind when referring to an agreement based on carbon taxes.

6.3 External Offsets

The idea of *external offsets* is that a given actor (which could be a firm, industry, region or country) has an initial target, but is allowed to "offset" this by investing in measures to reduce emissions by an equivalent amount elsewhere (*internal offsets* can also be considered, in which firms or countries can be credited with the radiative benefits of investing in abatement of emissions through sources and sinks which are within the territory of participating countries, but which are not formally part of the main controlled emissions). In the international context, external offsets would imply that countries with an agreed national emission target could meet this either by curtailing their own emissions to this level, or by investing elsewhere to reduce emissions such that the total of national emissions minus the amount saved by those external investments would meet the target. The idea would be to increase efficiency and flexibility by allowing countries to fund abatement in places where it might be cheaper than measures undertaken in their own country.

The great attraction of external offsets is that they would enable efforts to limit greenhouse gas emissions to be spread globally, without necessarily having a global agreement on commitments. For example, it would be quite possible for industrialised countries to agree to emission reduction targets on the understanding that offsets in other countries could contribute towards the target. Offsets would thereby broaden the scope of abatement investments and enable countries to look around for the cheapest abatement opportunities, and so it should be possible for the countries adopting targets to declare or agree greater cutbacks than would be possible without offsets. Thus offsets could in principle allow both greater abatement and a degree of resource transfers, without involving the developing world in multilaterally negotiated commitments (though obviously, offsets would require case-by-case agreement with the countries in which offsetting investments are made).

Offsets are potentially important policy tools, but in the international context they could be rather constrained by the problems of ownership, monitoring and measurement. Many forms of offset would imply a degree of direct investment and perhaps ownership of assets by one country or firm in another country. Difficulties of assigning responsibility could arise for example if a project failed to "offset" the emissions originally envisaged. The need for monitoring and guarantees could give rise to issues similar to those raised by conventional foreign direct investments. Debt-for-nature swaps have in some respects illustrated both the potential and the pitfalls. The implications would require careful consideration.

Another important feature is that an offset system requires that the emission reductions associated with individual schemes be measured. This could be problematic. How much would be saved by a given incentive to slow deforestation? How much would be saved by a household conservation scheme, renewable energy subsidies, or by public transport investments? In all cases, it depends upon the level of activity which would have occurred in the absence of those measures, which is often unknowable. Some particular projects may be more manageable. Perhaps the simplest might be investments in particular non-fossil energy facilities which directly displace fossil power. The CO_2 absorbed by specific forest plantations might be adequately measurable, though even this could raise difficulties. There are thus practical issues surrounding the use of external offsets which need not rule them out, but will constrain their scope.

Finally, since offset transfers would be primarily from countries which adopt emission targets (and offset them) to those which do not, a system based on offsets is relevant primarily in terms of industrialised country commitments, and would involve developing countries primarily in responding to proposals for offsets on their territories. This is unlikely to prove a satisfactory long-term basis for global control; it is also questionable how long industrialised countries would sustain such transfers if there were no subsequent commitments from receiving countries. However, because external offsets are a relatively simple extension of emission targets which would help to extend their coverage, and increase their overall efficiency, they could usefully be a feature in the earlier stages of an evolving control regime. In fact, they could act as a natural stepping stone towards more comprehensive forms of international control - notably a system of tradeable emission entitlements.

6.4 Tradeable emission entitlements

Tradeable emission entitlements (sometimes called internationally-tradeable or marketable emission permits) share some of the features of offsets, but differ in other respects. Negotiations would define an overall target for emissions for all the participating countries (which could vary over time) and "permits", or "entitlements", would be issued equal to this total, together with an initially agreed way of allocating them among the participating countries (in practice, the overall target and allocation would probably be negotiated together).

After the system comes into force, participants would have to hold permits equal to their total emissions. If their initial allocation was insufficient, they would have to obtain permits from others that had spare, through bilateral trading. As a result there would be a direct incentive on all countries to minimize emissions (either to minimize the payment for permits or to maximize the revenue from selling them) irrespective of whether they were meeting some predefined national target. Also, if the initial allocation results in developing countries having excess permits, permits could become a powerful mechanism for resource transfers: developing countries could lease or sell their excess permits to the industrialized countries which need them, in return for finance or technology.

The concept of tradeable entitlements has been attacked as giving immoral "permits to pollute". As noted in the general discussion above this criticism is not well founded. Emission standards and targets are themselves "permits to pollute": if making them exchangeable provides a more practical, desirable and efficient means of control, that is all to the good. That "if" is the useful area of debate. There are many complex questions which need to be addressed concerning allocation, management and practical operation of such a system, as compared with the alternatives, some of which are considered below.

In many respects, there are similarities between a tradeable permit system and an international tax system. The question of how permits are allocated initially is directly equivalent to the question of how tax revenues should be distributed. A process of repeated negotiations on country-by country allocations would have much in common with an international tax going in to a central fund with negotiations on its disbursement. An allocation formula for tradeable entitlements is closely tied to

Hoel's suggestion of "reimbursement parameters" for the redistribution of tax revenues.

There are, however, important distinctions. The most striking difference is that tradeable entitlements are a way of ensuring that a given emission target is met, and expenditures follow from the costs involved in achieving this. This contrasts with a tax which regulates expenditures, not emission levels directly (though targets or tax levels could and would both be adjusted with experience, so the distinction may not be as sharp as it seems). Another difference is that a tax would presumably involve direct monetary transfers, whereas permits could be exchanged in other kinds of deals, for example in return for specific kinds of technology and development assistance (see below). In general, a permit system could rely more upon arrangements negotiated between individual countries (or groups of countries) following establishment of the system itself, and could give governments more control in deciding how and where to conduct transfers. This additional degree of discretion could make tradeable permits more politically appealing, though obviously it is obtained at the expense of greater complexity and some loss in global economic efficiency (eg. if states eschew buying permits from enemies, as seems likely!). Tradeable permits, involving bilateral negotiations subsequent to the agreement, could also mar higher transaction costs than taxes. In principle, a tradeable permit system may thus not be as globally efficient as an equivalent tax and redistribution system, though it would still appear far more efficient than other proposals (probably including harmonized domestic taxes).

Unlike offsets, monitoring of a tradeable permit system would focus upon measurement of total emissions of the controlled gases by each participant, rather than the amount saved by particular investments. There is thus no need to estimate what emissions would have been in the absence of abatement measures, but only what they are. Thus the measurement and monitoring issues are much simpler than with offsets. Also, there are no problems concerning foreign direct ownership, because it is the permits which are transferred internationally rather than direct offset investments. But because it is a system which relies upon trades of quantified emission levels, it could (unlike a tax-based system) evolve relatively easily from arrangements involving external offsets (Grubb and Sebenius, 1992).

There are many other issues associated with the design and operation of an international tradeable permits system, many of which are discussed below. But a number of studies which have examined the options for implementing an agreement on limiting CO_2 emissions have concluded that tradeable entitlements offer the most promising approach (Bertram et al, 1989; Grubb, 1989; Epstein and Gupta, 1990). The IPCC Response Strategies Working Group committee on economic instruments (report IPCC/WG3-II/Doc.3) concluded that:

> "Of all the instruments examined, the system of tradeable emission rights [tradeable entitlements] came in for the most attention and was considered to be most promising. It offers the advantages of flexibility, efficiency in pollution abatement, direct control of total emission levels, a mechanism for trading reduction in different gases, and incentives for research into pollution abatement technology"

7 FROM THEORY INTO REALITY

7.1 Tradeable permits on to the political agenda

The possible use of international market instruments has risen in international discussions with remarkable rapidity. When tradeable permits for CO_2 control were first suggested by the US in the summer of 1989 in discussions of the IPCC committee on economics instruments, it was greeted by almost all outside a small circle with great suspicion, and widely seen as an attempt by the US to avoid any serious commitments. This was in part because the US, extrapolating from domestic experience, assumed a system in which permits would be allocated in proportion to current emissions ("grandfathering"); not surprisingly, few others considered this acceptable, least of all the developing countries who would stand to lose immensely under such a system, as they would then have to buy permits.

The tone of the debate changed considerably with the publication of two reports in the autumn of 1989 (Bertram et al (1989), Grubb (1989)) which pointed to the potential of tradeable permits not only as an efficient solution, but as a practical and equitable one which could generate and direct international resource transfers; one which explicitly rejected a "grandfathering" allocation. As analysts struggled to find any feasible way of structuring an agreement, such ideas became more widely discussed. The OECD sponsored research leading to a detailed workshop on the issue, and UNCTAD organised a study as the basis of their official position at the UNCED conference, that protocol negotiations should be opened on the basis of tradeable emission entitlements (see references).

Offsets have also entered the international discussions. For CO_2, they first made news when a US utility announced that it would plant trees in Guatemala sufficient to absorb the CO_2 output from a planned power station (an example which did not seem to be followed by many others). The US Environmental Defense Fund has lobbied for formal recognition of such offsets through US and international legislaton. Then in 1991 Norway, facing severe difficulties in trying to meet its CO_2 stabilization target, started pushing for the idea of offsets, or 'joint implementation", as a valid component towards meeting existing targets. There are concerns expressed about this being a way of evading, or watering down, commitments; but the potential advantages as compared with fixed national targets and the potential for intergovernmental offsets to evolve into a tradeable permit system, is leading to considerable interest.

International taxes have not really been seriously broached other than as a moderate international fund-raiser (notwithstanding the EC proposals for harmonized domestic taxes). The general aversion to taxes (especially applied internationally to governments); the fact that a tradeable permit system can be seen as a natural extension of existing targets by trading, (including extension via offsets) and the fact that tradeable permits give a greater degree of sovereign control (eg. over who one chooses to trade with and on what terms) have tended to make tradeable permits the focus of growing debate. But many issues need to be resolved.

7.2 Market arrangements and preventing distortion

Obviously, enacting any tradeable permit regime would require detailed management, monitoring, certification, and varied other provisions, required to make a workable system. A number of these issues are already being carefully considered (Dudek and Tietenberg, 1991), and clearly do not pose insuperable obstacles providing the range of sources is not made too broad. Over time, many extensions could be considered, such as central exchanges, futures markets, etc. Some of these elements and issues of institutional arrangements and market development are investigated in the UNCTAD study.

There could be important efficiency and other advantages if governments can pass some or all of their national permits through to private or state entities (either through allocation or auction) which can then themselves engage in international trades with companies in other countries whose governments have acted similarly, (eg. Bertram (1992) and Harrison (1990)). "Mixed" trading systems within which there are government-to-government trades of permits as well as unfettered trades among private players and governments might be possible. Governments would still have to be internationally responsible for ensuring that the total of government+corporate permit holdings matched the national total emissions, but allowing trading at a lower level could better exploit abatement opportunities. Providing that the managerial issues raised by having mixed ownership of permits can be overcome, the gains could be large.

Another issue concerns the "currency" of permit trading. There might be considerable political resistance to a system which generated large financial flows which could be spent on issues wholly unrelated to emissions control. In principle, economic theory favours unrestricted transfers to maximize efficiency (Oates and Portney, 1991); the politics and other factors may call for restrictions on "acceptable" trades, related clearly to agreed goals of sustainable development (Burtraw and Tomin, 1991; Grubb, 1989).

But perhaps the key concern about market operation is the fear that such a market could be subject to collusive and cartel-like action; either by poor countries which would start with spare permits or by the rich countries, which can wield great financial power. Specifically, developing countries fear that rich countries could "buy up the market", in which case the developing world would soon be in a position of having to try and buy back permits in order to develop. Since the effective permit price might well escalate with time as global targets are tightened, the result could be very regressive. As with other markets, the more numerous and diverse the participants, the more difficult it will likely be to form and sustain collusive rings. This is one reason why the more countries the better. It is also an additional rationale for governments to allocate directly or by auction some or all of their permits to private companies who can trade internationally. But other measures could also help mitigate this problem. As discussed below, continuing rounds to re-allocate permits will ensure a wider distribution, a more liquid market, and the flexibility required to adapt to changing conditions. In this scheme, the specific concerns of many developing countries - that the industrialised countries would "buy up" the market - is automatically alleviated if the allocation formula and replacement process reallocates permits back towards developing countries at a rate sufficient to match their likely rate of (revised) emissions growth.

Direct action against potential market abuse is also possible. Anti-monopoly rules could place limits on the holding of any excess permits and establish rules against price fixing and cartel-like action. Perhaps the final guarantee against market abuse is simply that a system can only operate on the basis of voluntary participation of sovereign states. The final sanction is thus simply that if countries are unfairly disadvantaged by market abuse, they may just withdraw, leaving all participants the poorer.

7.3 Introducing flexibility

Emission permits cannot last indefinitely. Although infinite-lived permits would not necessarily preclude revision of the target emissions, either by withdrawing some permits or by redefining their value, it would be very hard to introduce other revisions and there would be grave political difficulties arising from the fear on the part of developing countries that rich countries could "buy up" the market, as noted above. Additional practical problems could emerge if governments could profit by selling long term "rights" - for example, if governments emerge which consider their predecessors and their actions to have been illegitimate. At the opposite extreme, the suggestion for permits which are "leased but never sold", i.e. rented out for an annual payment (Grubb, 1989) overcomes the latter problem at least but does not offer a ready mechanism for revision or expansion of the system, unless expressed in terms of very frequent re-issue of permits. Also, and especially if permits were to be sublet to industry, many participants would want some degree of security for medium term planning, implying a permit lifetime of perhaps 20-30 years. But a system which started with permits all of this duration would be almost as unacceptable as one with infinite lifetime, given the pervasive fear that rich countries would still "buy up" the market for decades, and various revisions might be needed on a much shorter timescale than this.

A solution to this conundrum has been proposed by Bertram (1992), namely that permits should be *overlapping*. Bertram suggests ten-year permits of which a tenth would be withdrawn each year and replaced by a new issue using the agreed allocation formula. This can be usefully generalised. If permits last L years, a fraction P/L are withdrawn every P years, and a new set of permits with lifetime L are issued. At any time therefore, the market consists of a mix of permits, some of which will be retired shortly and some of which will last for much longer.

The permit value would vary according to the remaining lifetime. Countries and companies could hold a mixed portfolio, and for example if a company were constructing a fossil plant, and wanted a reasonable guarantee that it would be able to operate it for long enough to cover costs, it would be able to buy corresponding permits - at a price, which may well reflect quite a high premium on long term security. This would ensure that companies factored in the implicit costs and risks entailed in such long term investments in greenhouse gas emitting plants in early stages, discouraging such investments but ensuring that if companies went ahead the risk of wasted capital would be fairly small. A permit lifetime L of perhaps 20-30 years seems appropriate for this.

But the timescale for revisions would be the much shorter period P on which a fraction of existing permits were retired and new ones issued. At each re-issue, a number of items could be up for negotiation, for example: the overall acceptable emissions projected (and hence permits re-issued) for the next period, which will be a function of emission trends and the state of science and concern; the question of whether new sources or sinks could be brought in; and whether additional countries might join the system. Grubb and Sebenius (1992) show how, in such an overlapping permit system, the various different kinds of revisions could be achieved without seriously disturbing the existing market. In practice a revision period P of 2-4 years seems appropriate. This would be long enough to tie in with a cycle of scientific assessment of both the severity of the problem and degree of knowledge and trends in various sources and sinks, and indeed a cycle of political assessment concerning the operation of the system and the possibility of new countries joining it.

7.4 Allocation

The way in which permits are initially allocated is a key determinant of a tradeable permit system. Within limits, the global average efficiency benefits of an international market instrument can be obtained by trading irrespective of allocation; but the allocation will determine the distributional implications. The perceived fairness of the allocation system will be central to the political acceptability of the whole system. It will strongly influence the nature and breadth of participation, and could become a central mechanism of resource transfers.

Allocation will pose considerable political difficulties - so great that some have argued that the difficulties will make such a system politically impossible. But as noted above, the allocation problem is unavoidable whatever control system is adopted, whether it be national emission targets, taxes, or other approaches. All systems that have much global impact will impose costs on participants, and must include some resource transfers if poorer countries are to take part.

There are many different possibilities for allocation. One important division is that between burden-based criteria, which seek to reflect explicitly the burden which abatement would impose on different participants and to allocate permits to some notion of equitable burdens; and responsibility-based criteria, which seek a simple equitable formula reflecting some notion of entitlements and a "polluter pays" approach to abatement. In practice, any allocation system is bound to be heavily influenced by perceived burdens, but the practical obstacles to trying to define burdens on a case-by-case basis appear to make it implausible as an explicit basis (Grubb, 1989). Most of the debate has focused upon possible general allocation schemes which could encompass the great majority of nations, even if some might have to be recognized as special (and temporary) exceptions, such as the transition economies.

The search for an allocation formula has to some extent reflected the age-old divide between "realists" and "idealists". "Realists" have tended to argue that entitlements would have to be distributed roughly according to current emissions or GDP (e.g. Pearce et al, 1991) on the grounds that other allocations would result in large resource transfers that would make it politically unacceptable to the most powerful countries; and also that this starts from the "disagreement point" of the outcome if negotiations fail completely. But not only does this lack any plausible ethical basis (it directly rewards current pollution), in practice it also fails to exploit one of the key potential advantages of an international market system, namely that of generating resource transfers where needed. In fact as noted, above developing countries would simply not be interested in such a system since their emissions are growing more rapidly, it would lead to net outflows from them. The "realist" solution is thus not "realistic" at all, at least if the scheme is to attract any developing countries; as noted above, the issue has only come on to the international agenda at all because other allocation schemes are being considered.

Various authors have sought the opposite extreme, and argued for explicit inclusion of historical emissions as a reflection of "natural debt" (developed most fully by Smith et al (1992). A variety of other schemes have been suggested (reviewed by Grubb et al (1992)). Several are analyzed for their possible economic implications by Barrett, in UNCTAD (1992). But of all the suggestions, per capita allocations have probably the strongest claim to an ethical basis, and other attractive features (e.g., Grubb (1989), Epstein and Gupta, (1990), Bertram, (1992)). They imply that initial permit allocations should be directly proportional to national population. In its most basic presupposition--that each human being should have an equal right to an as-yet unallocated, scarce global common--this principle has considerable appeal. In practice, this approach would reflect some measure of historical emissions, because countries with higher per-capita emissions tend to have emitted the most in the past. Many of the practical consequences of a per-capita allocation--though not all--are equally appealing. The key feature would be that all the industrialized countries with higher-than-average per capita emissions would have to buy permits from developing countries at least for fossil CO_2. In a system with broader coverage, they would have to buy permits for most other sources and sinks as well, the main exception being deforestation.

One practical difficulty with per capita allocation is that, in its simple form, it rewards population growth, which itself is an important component of the problem. Various ways of breaking this link are, however, available by modifying the formula (eg. adult or historic population, or by adding a term related inversely to population growth rates). More serious are the potential political obstacles arising from the potential scale of the implied transfers. Even under very modest assumptions about permit prices, the net North-South flow would roughly offset the current international flows from South to North exacted in debt service, with transfers that would be similar in magnitude to current official overseas development assistance ("ODA")--more than that from the US, and about a third of that currently from the rest of OECD. For constant emissions and population, the transfers would change in proportion to the permit price; and most studies suggest that prices (and transfers) could be much greater than implied by these figures. Given this, most political analysts consider pure per-capita allocations to be infeasible.

The alternative is to search for a mixed formula which carries the right properties but which may be politically more feasible. It is in fact impossible for independent analysts to determine what is a feasible allocation: that will arise from the process of negotiation between sovereign states. What can be done is to search for approaches which help to keep negotiations as simple as possible and yet result in an effective and efficient agreement.

Starting from the observation that a tradeable permit system would be meaningless unless it involves resource exchanges between participating countries, a key requirement is for a formula which ensures that the general direction of transfers is from developed economies to developing ones rather than vice versa. The magnitude of the exchange must be (a) sufficient both to create a real incentive for all participants to limit emissions and to provide the resources to enable poorer countries to adopt more efficient technologies, while (b) not so large as to be politically impossible, in which case, however attractive the formula on paper, it will be of no practical use.

This implies an allocation which has many of the broad features of a per-capita system, but which carries the flexibility for negotiations to affect the scale of transfers implied by the allocation, without compromising the environmental target. One simple way of doing this is to combine directly the two main alternatives presented to date in the allocation debate: current emissions ("grandfathering") and per-capita. Permits could be allocated permits in proportion to a mixed weighting of current emissions and population (if appropriate, qualified as noted to avoid incentives to population growth). In this combination of the "realist" and "idealist" solutions, the direction of transfers under the per-capita scheme is preserved, but the lower the relative weighting accorded to population, the lower the transfers, and vice versa. In this simple scheme, the allocation negotiations would focus upon only two parameters: the total permit issuance (defining the overall target emissions), and the relative weight between population and emissions in the allocation formula.

If permit allocations did increase directly with higher contemporaneous emissions, this would weaken the abatement incentive. An important variant would be to use this formula applied to emission levels and population "lagged" by a few years, for example expressed as a moving average of the previous decade's emissions (which would also help to even out annual fluctuations). This would introduce an element of dynamic incentives, since payments by developed countries would reduce in proportion to the rate at which they could reduce emissions, while the receipts by developing would be increased to the extent that they could restrain the rate of population and emissions growth. This adds further scope for meeting the varying demands of the system.

Naturally, other variants can be proposed, for example, by introducing dimensions such as GNP, land area, or cumulative emissions. However, many of the objections to adopting these as the sole criteria (summarized in Grubb et al, 1992) would apply also to their inclusion as a dimension in a mixed formula, notably difficulties of definition, measurement, monitoring and perverse incentives. While recognizing that the one-dimensional formula presented here is probably insufficient to cover all requirements (for example, the current situation in the former Soviet Union), it may be preferable to encourage such countries to join the system with more traditional forms of "side payments," rather than to add further dimensions to the basic allocation formula with all the attendant complexities in both negotiation and a range of other aspects. Or, indeed, it may be preferable to accept that some countries will necessarily wait until conditions change sufficiently for them to consider entering.

Finally, there is no reason why an allocation formula and its coefficients should be immutable. Indeed, it could and probably should change over time. In the above scheme, the allocation could evolve from one which is sufficiently weighted towards current emissions to make it politically feasible so that the major economic powers would participate in the early stages, towards a much stronger per-capita weighting over a period of decades--that would offer a powerful inducement to major developing countries. The path taken could be specified in advance or left to subsequent negotiations - though the incentive for all countries to prepare long-term abatement strategies would be increased if it were clearly understood that the weighting accorded to contemporary emissions would fall steadily over time.

Obviously, many other allocations can be conceived (as discussed in the references), but this appears to be a particularly flexible and interesting one. At the very least, analysis of such options illustrates how international marketable instruments and the allocations involved can offer efficient solutions, and help to focus the unavoidable debate about equitable burden-sharing.

8 CONCLUSIONS

An international agreement on specific measures to limit climate change has to meet many diverse requirements, including those of being reasonably efficient, flexible, and equitable. There are several policy instruments available for structuring an agreement, but some appear much more promising than others. Those which exploit the flexibility of international-market based instruments, but which can leave countries with sovereign authority over the internal policies they use in responding to the resulting incentives, are of particular interest; they are not only theoretically appealing, but appear to overcome many of the practical difficulties of conventional approaches.

Of these, offsets could provide a useful extension of existing commitments (depending upon how they are formulated), but are limited; the greatest interest has focused upon tradeable permits, perhaps evolving from an initial system of offsets. Key issues remain to be resolved in analysis and negotiations, and great political resistance to such novel approaches needs to be overcome; the characteristics of a system, including its flexibility and equatability, would also depend upon its careful design. But despite initial resistance, it seems to be becoming more broadly accepted that the use of such international market instruments, if properly structured, may offer the most promising approach to effective international control of global pollutants such as CO_2.

As we have seen from this and other analyses of environmental policy instruments in previous chapters, we are still on the learning curve. Market instruments appear to offer powerful solutions to some of the national and international problems, but a great deal hinges upon their careful design and implementation, and their interaction. Experience is required, and we must learn to discuss, understand, harmonize and develop appropriate policy instruments at different geographical levels, and for different types of pollution in order to give "sustainable development" a chance.

REFERENCES

Barrett, S. 1991. "Global Warming: Economics of a Carbon Tax", in D. Pearce, et al.

Barrett, S. 1992. "Acceptable allocations of tradeable carbon emission entitlements in a global warming treaty", in UNCTAD.

Bertram, G. 1992. "Tradeable Emission Permits and the Control of Greenhouse Gases", *Journal of Development Studies*, vol.28 no.3, April.

Bertram, I.G., R.J. Stephens and C.C. Wallace. 1989. *The relevance of economic instruments for tackling the greenhouse effect.* Report to the New Zealand Ministry of the Environment.

Burtraw, D., and M.A. Toman. 1991. "Equity and International Agreements for CO2 Containment", Discussion paper ENR91-07, Resources for the Future, Washington.

Dornbusch, R. and J. Poterba, eds. 1991. *Global Warming: Economic Policy Responses.* MIT Press, Cambridge, MA. Papers including: W.Nordhaus, "Economic Approaches to Greenhouse Warming"; J.Poterba, "Tax Policy to Combat Global Warming: On Designing a Carbon Tax"; T.Schelling, "Economic Responses to Global Warming": "Prospects for Cooperative Approaches"; J.Whalley, and R.Wigle, "The International Incidence of Carbon Taxes".

Dudek, D.J. and T. Tietenberg. 1991. "Monitoring and enforcing greenhouse gas trading", in OECD (1992).

Epstein, J. and R. Gupta. 1990. *Controlling the Greenhouse Effect: Five Global Regimes Compared.* The Brookings Institution, Washington, DC.

Grubb, M. 1989. *The Greenhouse Effect: Negotiating Targets.* Royal Institute of International Affairs, London.

Grubb, M. and J. Sebenius. 1991. "Participation, Allocation and Adaptability in International Tradeable Emission Permit Systems for Greenhouse Gas Control," in OECD (1992).

Grubb, M., J. Sebenius, A. Magalhass and S. Subak. 1992. "Sharing the burden". In I. Mintzer (ed). *Confronting Climate Change*, Stockholm. Environment Institute/Cambridge University Press, Cambridge.

Harrison. 1989. *Policy Approaches for controlling greenhouse gases.* National Economic Research Association, Cambridge.

Hoel, M. 1991. "Efficient international agreements for CO_2 control", *The Energy Journal* 12:2.

Intergovernmental Panel on Climate Change, 1990. The IPCC First Assessment, WMO/UNEP, Geneva; IPCC Update, Geneva, March 1992.

Kosmo, M. 1987. *Money to Burn? The High Price of Energy Subsidies*. World Resources Institute, Washington DC.

Morrisette, P., J. Darmstadter, A. Plantinga, and M. Toman. 1991. "Prospects for a greenhouse gas accord: lessons from other agreements", *Global Environmental Change*, 1:209-223.

OECD.1992. *Tradeable permits for abating greenhouse gases*: practical options (Edited Proceedings of OECD Workshop, June 1991), OECD, Paris.

Pearce, D., A. Markandya and E. Barbier. 1989. *Blueprint for a Green Economy*, Earthscan, London.

Pearce, D., A. Markandya, E. Barbier and S. Barret. 1991. Blueprint 2: *Greening the World Economy*, Earthscan, London.

Pearson, M. and S. Smith. 1991. "The European carbon tax: an assessment of the European Commission's Proposals", Institute of Fiscal Studies, London.

Tietenberg, T. 1985. *Emissions Trading, Resources for the Future*. Washington, DC.

Toman, M.A. and S.M. Gardiner. 1991. "The limits of economic instruments for international greenhouse gas control". *Resources for the Future discussion paper ENR92-06*. Washington DC.

UNCTAD, 1992. "Tradeable Entitlements for CO_2 abatement", United Nations Conference on Trade and Development, Geneva, April.

Young, O. 1989. "The Politics of International Regime Formation: Managing Natural Resources and the Environment". *International Organization, 43:3, pp. 349-375.*

CHAPTER 17

The Price of Petroleum Products*

by

Thomas Sterner

Abstract

This chapter discusses tax and price policies applied to petroleum products. It shows that there is a very wide disparity in policy between different groups of countries due both to tax policies in general as well as to more specific energy or environmental concerns. Raising the consumer price of petroleum (and other fossil) products is likely to be, in one way or another, an important part of any policy to combat global warming. This is illustrated by reference to some analyses of the price sensitivity of demand showing that consumption could be reduced quite significantly at least in countries where effective taxation is today either low or absent, notably the (formerly) planned economies, the oil-producing LDCs and the USA. The inherent sensitivity of tax issues makes it particularly important to understand and analyze the differences in policy and the economic and political barriers to changing policies in this area. The chapter therefore incorporates some of the country experiences emanating from earlier chapters to discuss these issues.

* Thanks are due to Gordon Macgranaham and Mikael Franzén for very useful comments on an earlier draft.

T. Sterner (ed.), Economic Policies for Sustainable Development, 309–325.

1 INTRODUCTION

If we are to face up to such global environmental problems as those caused by greenhouse gases in general and fossil combustion in particular, we will all, as the previous chapter should have made very clear, be forced to implement some very serious policy measures aimed at economizing on fossil fuels. As Grubb emphasized, it is of considerable importance that all or at least a very significant share of countries really do collaborate: Since the problem is global, national solutions have relatively little effect and there is the additional risk that non-collaborators could even capture benefits by being prepared to increase their use of fossil fuels when others reduce them. In fact the fall in world fossil prices would itself be a powerful incentive for increased consumption if most major countries decided to cut back on their domestic consumption, for instance through national consumer taxes. The fear of losing in industrial competitivity to non-collaborators will probably turn out to be a major obstacle to environmental policies and negotiations in this area.

The previous chapter discussed a number of different policy instruments to cut back on the use of fossil carbon (and other global warming gases): emission targets, national or international emission taxes, external offsets and tradeable emission entitlements. The choice is, as discussed by Grubb, quite a complicated one with delicate tradeoffs between efficiency, equity and several other criteria. Combinations of different economic instruments are furthermore becoming more common. Even if tradeable permits are chosen at the international level, and even if, as suggested by Grubb, it is desirable that some major actors such as electric utilities be allowed to participate directly in such a permits market, this does not necessarily mean that all national implementation in the individual countries would be entirely through the same mechanism. In fact, efficient implementation at the consumer level is still likely, at least in the market economies, to make some use of taxes. This is particularly so for products used by many small consumers such as fuel for domestic heating or individual transport. It may turn out to be unpracticable to use a tradeable permits scheme at the level of the individual car since transaction costs would presumably be quite high. Instead decision makers are faced with a number of other options including road pricing, emission taxes or fuel taxes. This choice must take into account all the negative externalities related to, for instance, driving which are not only the global warming effects but also (regional) effects such as acidification and eutrophication as well as direct local effects such as smog, noise, accidents, crowding and so forth. Fuel taxes are in this context the simplest if not the most precise of the available alternatives[1]. Other possible instruments include (differentiated) vehicle taxes, emission standards, area pricing of permits, parking etc, and differentiated mileage taxes. The most commonly used instrument however and the easiest to compare is simple fuel taxation which will be our focus of interest in this chapter.

---

[1] Flexible vehicle and road pricing is in principle superior because it allows for a more direct targeting of the instrument to the problem. Thus vehicles could perhaps be required to pay not only as a function of how far they drive or how much fuel they use but actually as a function of what emissions they generate (and where these are emitted!).

1.1 Petroleum product prices

Most of the chapters of this book have been dedicated to analyzing the complexities of different aspects of national environmental policy making in individual countries. A couple of chapters have instead been dedicated to global policy making or to comparing national policies from a thematic viewpoint: deforestation, acid rain, vehicle emission standards or energy policy in general. This final chapter follows the latter strategy, comparing national strategies across countries but focusing on one particular area that we already have identified as being of particular interest from the viewpoint of global warming. By focusing on price and tax policies for one set of products derived from petroleum - and mainly on gasoline, we can cover more countries and make the comparison more systematic and perhaps illustrative of some of the dilemmas that will confront international endeavors in this area.

In principle we could study energy policy by looking at taxes and duties in different countries for different products. The trouble is that the information necessary is difficult to collect and compare systematically since tax rules are generally quite complex and in some countries quite unclear. There are at least two types of tax used: excise and value added taxes (VAT) but in addition national variations are very common. The VAT may be the same for all products in an economy, or differentiated. Several countries have higher VAT for petroleum products. Usually (but not in all countries) the VAT is refunded when the fuel is used for commercial purposes[2]. The excise tax is product specific and often includes a number of separate taxes and fees introduced for different motives such as emergency stockpiling. In general this is (of course) not refunded but again there are exceptions such as for industrial use of petroleum products in Denmark. Furthermore the very structure of taxes varies radically between countries, some relying on percentage mark-ups, others on nominal taxes, duties and other specific fees and charges while others again rely on taxing the profits (and labour income) of the oil companies. In some cases, particularly among the developing countries or in the planned economies it is even more difficult clearly to identify the tax-structure. For instance many LDCs have nationalized state oil companies that are (or at least were until recently) so integrated into the state that it is impossible to draw a line between the tax policy of the government and its (or the state company's) pricing policy. They simply set "political" prices and their losses or profits go straight into the treasury. There is nc practical difference between the setting of a higher price and the imposition of a nev tax and hence it is pointless in these countries to analyze tax policy withou simultaneously looking directly at final consumer prices in general.

Our approach is instead to focus directly on the difference between national consumer prices and international spot prices as being an indicator of the country's energy policy. It is this real difference in price that will influence both the national and the international allocation of resources; it is also this real margin that acts as an incentive to illicit trading. This means that we consider the relevant concept of cost to be the opportunity cost (i.e. the international market value) not the production cost. Differences in border price only stand for variations of around 5-10% except for the special case of certain landlocked importing countries (particularly for importers of

---

[2] Naturally the standard VAT is then applied to the final product price.

small volumes such as certain small central and southern African states).

In these countries very small volumes are refined, distributed and traded and consequently these cost items may become more important. Obviously, assuming that the whole difference in price depends on policy is an over-simplification because part of it is due to these factors and to differences in market structure, demand factors and differences in retail costs and so forth. In general however, pre-tax prices vary much less than the final market prices. At least for the case of the OECD for which we have extensive data on both taxes and prices, we know that the main cause for differences in consumer prices are the differences in tax, see further Sterner (1989 a & b) or Angelier & Sterner (1990).

The fact that the international spot prices for products do vary so little between ports and the world market for petroleum products is fairly homogeneous is the major reason for choosing to study the prices of petroleum products as an example of energy or environmental policies. The prices of electricity and natural gas also vary considerably between countries but this is obviously due to differences in local production costs. In the absence of a world market price (due to high transport costs) there is no clear opportunity cost for exports foregone and thus local prices cannot readily be interpreted as indicators of energy or other policy.

2 THE PRICE AND INCOME SENSITIVITY OF PETROLEUM PRODUCT DEMAND

Figure 1 shows just how big a difference there is both in final consumer prices and in quantities consumed of gasoline[3], particularly between the US and other OECD countries. US taxes on highway fuels are surprisingly low by European standards (particularly given US budget problems and resistance to income taxes) but presumably this is largely the result of public opinion on the subject. It seems reasonable to assume that US reticence over the whole issue of greenhouse gases is influenced by the motor-lobby and maybe the oil-producers lobby. Although the new Clinton/Gore administration does imply a new view on these issues it is clear that there is considerable and powerful resistance to their politics in this field. Note also that, even within a relatively homogeneous group of countries such as the EC, prices do vary considerably, see next section.

One of the reasons for the impopularity of gasoline taxes is presumably the fact that adaptation is complicated and takes a long time. In fact many people cannot imagine any adaptation at all and typically just see higher prices as an increase in the cost for a certain mileage that they perceive as necessary or inevitable. Experience shows, however, that people do change cars, car manufacturers do change motor design and car characteristics such as weight and aerodynamics. People even move closer to their jobs and start taking public transport! But all these processes take such a long span of time that people barely perceive them. In fact politicians have a hard time perceiving them (and benefitting from them) since the effect of a change in gasoline taxation is still very small within the usual time horizon of the politicians (the typical electoral cycle being 3-4 years). Using econometric techniques it is

[3]Our main attention is on gasoline, economically the most important of the petroleum products and furthermore the easiest to compare between countries.

however possible to analyze the way in which the consumption of gasoline depends on income and price levels.

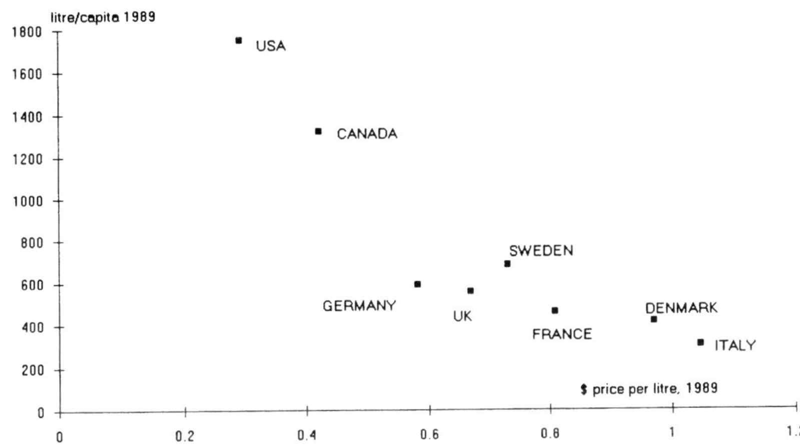

Figure 1 Price and consumption of gasoline in various countries 1989

Such techniques show that price differentials are in fact a powerful determinant of demand and do affect patterns of consumption not only for petroleum products but, indirectly for various energy using appliances (notably automobiles). Sterner (1990) has shown that long run price elasticities of demand for gasoline are close to -1.0 which implies that a 1% increase in gasoline price leads to a one percent (long run) decrease in consumption. The reader should note that long run in this context means a minimum of ten years. The short run elasticities (say for 1 year) may be just 0.1 - 0.2. This means that even a sizeable price hike of say 30% might just diminish consumption by a couple of percentage points. In fact such a small decrease will not generally be visible at all since it will typically be masked by the general increase due to increased income. The net result might thus be, for the first year, that consumption is stabilized instead of continuing to grow. Naturally this may lead to considerable disillusion among those who expected more immediate and tangible results. The fact that lead times are so long does, however, not decrease but strongly increase the urgency of taking appropriate measures immediately! The long run effects are very simply illustrated by the downward slope of the relationship between gasoline consumption levels in various countries and the corresponding prices-levels as in Figure 1. Naturally there are other differences between countries than gasoline price, notably income and population density. We do not want to suggest that the whole difference in gasoline consumption between the US and Denmark is explained by differences in gasoline prices, there are indeed other factors (such as there being more places to go to in the US!). Still we believe one of the main reasons for the differences in consumption level seen in Figure 1 is that there have been *permanent* differences in gasoline prices for long periods of time between these countries. As another illustration we can compare two countries which are much more similar, Italy and the UK. In Italy, which has for several years had a very high price of gasoline compared to the other EC countries, gasoline consumption is relatively low. The UK is a country of similar size, population density and income per capita: In the UK gasoline consumption per capita (1985) was 65% higher than in Italy, not because of the number of cars (on the contrary, Italy had a 35% higher per capita car ownership) but because of gasoline consumption per car which was 120% higher in the UK. Naturally the relative competitivity of different car manufacturers is strongly affected by the price of gasoline. Similar effects can be found in many industrial applications where the choice of production technology and equipment are closely related to the choice (and thereby to the price) of the available fuels.

In Sterner et al (1992) the consequences for transport fuel use and related carbon emissions of various tax policies in the OECD were calculated on the basis of individual price and income elasticities for each country. We started from the fact that there are strong forces at work at least within the EC to harmonize taxation (and thereby price levels) on gasoline and other petroleum products. Assuming that instead the whole OECD would harmonize its policies on this issue we found that, in the long run, OECD carbon emissions from transport would be three times as high if all the countries were to adopt US tax levels as if they all used the highest (current Italian) tax rates for gasoline. The US alone accounts for more than 60% of this difference.

3 HARMONIZATION OF PRODUCT TAXATION IN THE EC

An interesting illustration of the difficulties in changing product taxation is provided by the EC. As shown in Angelier & Sterner (1990), the differences in price and tax not only apply to gasoline but to diesel, as well as to light and heavy fuel oils and in fact all types of energy carrier. With the price levels that had evolved through national policy making and legislation on taxes etc, we found that there were a number of national frontiers, notably between France on the one hand, and Luxembourg, Germany or Spain on the other hand, across which price differentials were strikingly large. For gasoline they ranged from 20-40% and for diesel there was even a 55% price difference between France and Luxembourg. Other pairs of neighbouring countries with big price differentials include Spain/Portugal and Germany/Denmark. Comparing Denmark to Germany we found that gasoline was 65% more expensive but diesel 75% cheaper!

Such prices would lead to considerable cross-boundary trade if there were not relatively harsh control within Europe. Since the very idea of the Common Market is to abolish trade barriers between countries, the tax-induced price differences must also be abolished (or at least very much reduced). Seen in this perspective, one realizes what a challenge EC harmonization really is: according to the Commission all product taxes are to be squeezed into a very narrow wedge. In fact various proposals have been put forward but the general idea is a unique tax level for excise taxes based on the average country tax levels. Other specific taxes and charges are to be abolished as well as the variable excise taxes used in some countries to stabilize the fluctuations in world market prices. Implementation of these harmonizations is now leading to considerable tax and price changes on practically all the EC petroleum product markets. The final structure is not yet clear but unless the EC goes in for an ambitious environmental energy policy of its own, the consequences would be that some countries such as Italy and France would have to reduce taxes on almost all products thereby stimulating their domestic consumption. Other countries will anyway have to increase taxes on all products notably Luxembourg but also Spain and Germany (except for diesel). Many countries would find themselves drastically changing the structure of taxation by lowering taxes on some products and raising it on others. Denmark for instance would have to reduce taxes for private consumers and raise them for industrial users. Sweden has gone through rather dramatic changes just in anticipation of joining the EC. (See further Chapter 3).

Obviously changing tax-structures touches on one of the truly central points of the political process and will therefore meet with a good deal of resistance, see the case of the US. There are many factors shaping the tax structure in any one country and many vested interests in maintaining its structure. For instance many countries find it hard or at least expensive to implement efficient systems for direct taxation. In France and Italy for instance this appears to be one of the reasons for the heavy reliance on indirect taxes. Even Sweden has, as we saw in Chapter 3 given up a large part of its traditional reliance on direct (progressive) income taxation.

4 PRODUCT PRICING IN THE (FORMERLY) PLANNED ECONOMIES

The environmental record of the planned economies has been discussed in a number of Chapters (4-7 and 12) of this book. We have seen clearly that market failure is not the only explanation for environmental problems, government failure can be much worse. The over-utilization or abuse of natural resources and environmental degradation have put Eastern European and particularly Chinese industrial cities at the top of many pollution lists. It is typical that Germany, in its efforts to reduce carbon emissions finds it can reduce much more in the eastern Länder of the former GDR. (According to a recent report from the German Environment Ministry, quoted in Miljörapporter, 1993:8, total carbon emissions in Germany were reduced by more than 14% 1987-92 but all the reduction was in the East, in West Germany there was an increase of 3%)! The problems can generally be traced back to a couple of special features of these economies: their complete absence of incentives for efficiency and the bias towards heavy industry. Industrial plants lacked any reasonable incentives to economize on resources - whether human, man-made or, in particular, natural resources which were often "allocated" free of charge to the plants. Specific use of fuel, electricity, cement and steel in production are several times as high as in Western Europe. We will not, for these countries, go into any detailed discussion of prices since the non-convertability of currencies and the rationing systems used, as well as current instability make all comparisons with market economies very unreliable. However, according to Wilczynski (1990), the price of energy and natural resources in Eastern Europe was typically less than half or even a third of the corresponding in the West. As Żylicz shows in Chapter 5, the use of energy, natural resources and the resulting pollution was of the order 3-4-times[4] as much in relation to output as in comparable market economies. The world

[4] For China it was of course considerably more, see Chapter 12.

Development Report (1992) estimates that emissions of particles and sulfur dioxide could be reduced by about 60-80% by the year 2000 in Poland if European price levels were used for fuel instead of a continuation of the former Polish price policies. (The report also estimates that the savings effects would be roughly halved if just US instead of European price levels were used!).

Just as for industry, the same lack of incentives applies to individual consumers. Water and heat in residential areas have typically been "free goods" with no charge, no meters and indeed often no regulators so that the only way to avoid overheating in winter was to have the windows wide open! Now the planning system is gone but it still takes a long time to install regulators, meters and other energy saving equipment as well as to inform and reeducate numerous people in charge of issues related to energy efficiency. During the 1980s there was a considerable increase in fossil fuel use in spite of rather low growth at least towards the end of the period. At present consumption is falling but that is more the tragic result of supply interruptions, economic chaos and falling incomes rather than being the reflection of price-induced increase in efficiency.

The present transitory character of many of the East European economies between planning and market makes the choice of policy instruments quite complex. Although resource allocation in the past has been completely centralized, the actual idea of pricing natural resources is not new, and in fact some very advanced systems for pricing environmental degradation were discussed (see Chapters 4 & 7). Although the latter remained largely at the experimental stage (except in Estonia), the principle of using fees for environmental resources, such as water, was implemented quite early (by the GDR in 1969 and during the 1970s in Hungary and Poland, see (Sand 1990). The tax levels in these cases may not have been sufficiently high to make them effective but even if they had been higher much more fundamental traits of the planned economy, such as the famous "soft budget constraints" would anyway have rendered the taxes ineffective.

The main difficulty today in promoting a sustainable development in these countries seems to be not a lack of understanding or willingness, nor a lack of interest in appropriate policy instruments but simply one of economic resources. Still, if one were to venture a longer term projection, then a reasonable guess is that improvements in efficiency are inevitable as economic criteria are introduced into decisionmaking and thus there should be room for a significant amount of economic growth without too much growth in the use of energy. Recent work at IIASA (International Institute for Applied Systems Analysis) has studied energy efficiency in Eastern Europe for their Regional Acidification Programme, see Amann et al (1991). They compare two scenarios for energy consumption 2000. The first of these is based on the latest available official forecasts and, as usual, assumes a continued increase in the energy intensity of industry. Considering that this energy intensity already is more than three times as high as the corresponding values for west Europe, the second, energy-efficiency, scenario assumes that East European industry will be restructured and modernized so as to reach at least halfway towards western efficiency by the year 2000. According to their analysis, this would imply a reduction in energy use by 30% compared to current consumption instead of an increase by almost 20% according to the first scenario. Also emissions of sulphur dioxide and other gases could, in this way, be reduced considerably - and much more cheaply than by corresponding reductions in Western Europe.

5 PRICING POLICIES IN LDCS

When discussing the consumption of petroleum products in Third World countries we will find it useful to make a distinction between them according to two separate classifications: those with and those without significant oil (or other energy) resources of their own on the one hand and those with or without planning on the other. Oil consumption in the Third World accounts for less than a quarter of the world total or just over 20% if China is excluded (and put in the "planned economy" group). This is obviously quite a minor share - particularly considering their population share which is much larger. However, it is a percentage that is growing quite rapidly - the corresponding share was just over 10% in 1970. From the viewpoint of international equity this may be seen as a natural (and indeed desirable) development. If anyone should increase their use of our common fossil heritage it seems right for poor people in poor countries to do so. However one should be aware that at least 2/3 of the whole increase is accounted for by a small number of oil countries themselves. The OPEC countries together with a couple of other major oil-producing LDCs, principally Mexico and Egypt, themselves account for an ever-increasing share of LDC oil consumption and these countries with less than a quarter of LDC population (outside China) now account for over half their use of petroleum products. In these countries low domestic prices encourage (wasteful) use while the vast majority of poor countries are *not* seeing any increase in their use of oilproducts. See Sterner (1993) for a fuller discussion.

Figure 2 shows the relationship for a few countries between GDP per capita (1990) and energy consumption per capita (Kg oil equivalent, 1990). Most of the OECD countries can be found somewhere between the US and Switzerland while the formerly planned economies are to be found closely glued to the y-axis with sizeable

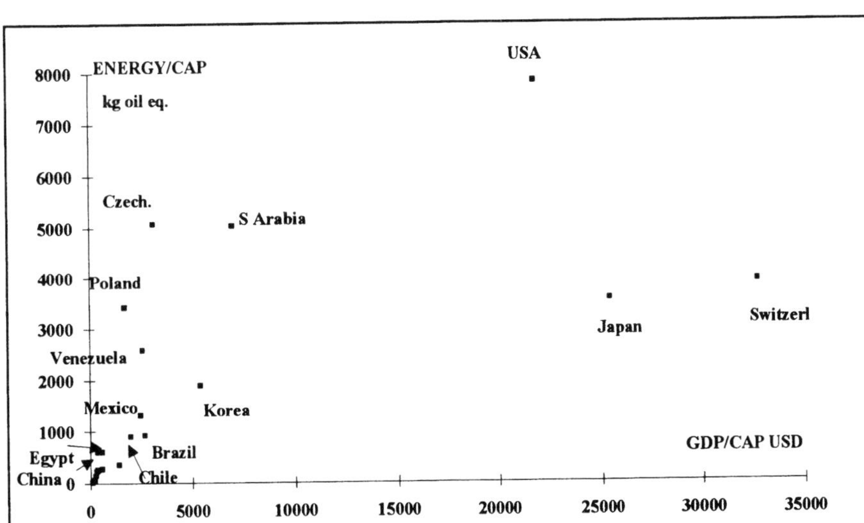

Figure 2 Energy intensity of GDP 1990

energy consumption and sadly little GDP. Although barely visible on the chart this is particularly the case for China which has the second highest relationship (after Poland) between energy consumption and GDP among the countries selected, see Table 1. The energy intensity of chinese GDP is almost three times that of India and six times that of Bangladesh.

Table 1 Energy intensities of GDP (Kgoe/$)

Switzerland	0,12	Korea	0,35	India	0,66
Japan	0,14	USA	0,36	Egypt	1
Ethiopia	0,17	Chile	0,46	Venezuela	1,01
Thailand	0,24	Indonesia	0,48	Czech.	1,62
Bangladesh	0,27	Nigeria	0,48	China	1,62
Brazil	0,34	Mexico	0,52	Poland	2,02

Aside from the formerly planned economies, the oil producing (and exporting) LDCs are the main group in which domestic energy consumption is large and this particularly applies to the big exporters with relatively little population such as several of the Gulf states but also to countries such as Venezuela. These countries contrast strongly with the energy importing countries - be they rich such as Switzerland & Japan, poor such as Ethiopia or in-between such as for instance Brazil.

The lack of incentives for energy management and the resulting waste of energy in the planned economies has already been discussed in detail. For the oil producing LDCs the situation is similar but perhaps not quite so extreme. Their high and growing share in world fossil energy is at least partly due to their low domestic prices for petroleum (and other energy) products. Even if they are market economies, they are economies in which the market has been subject to considerable political intervention and particularly this applies to the state-run sectors including, notably, the energy sector. The total span in product prices for developing countries is much greater than for the OECD. The cheapest products were to be found in the LDC oil countries such as S Arabia or Venezuela where they typically were priced at a fraction of even US prices. On the other hand the countries in which the products are most expensive (the land locked cou^ntries with big foreign exchange scarcities) have prices that are exorbitant even by North European standards (and hence unaffordable for most consumers of those countries). There is by now quite a significant literature on this subject including Kosmo (1987), Choucri (1986), Munasinghe (1985), Siddayao (1985) and Sterner (1989a & b). During the late 1980s and early 90s structural adjustment programs have striven to reduce these subsidies but as recently as 1992 Larsen & Shah estimate aggregate world energy subsidies at USD 230 billion and say that a mere removal of these would cut global carbon emissions by 9%. Most of these subsidies (around 185 billion) are for the former USSR and other Eastern European countries while China accounts for subsidies of 14 billion and another 15 are shared by Brazil, Venezuela, Mexico, Indonesia and S Arabia. The intricacies of energy politics in individual developing countries can be very complicated and it is quite hard to generalize. There are, however, a number of "stylized facts" that will generally (but not always) apply.

* Oil producing LDCs usually have a state oil company (like PEMEX as

described in Chapter 10) that has a local monopoly and in general they do not behave as profit-maximizing firms but more like ministries and thus can have political reasons to sell products very cheaply on their domestic markets. See also Chapter 15 for comments on similar behaviour in LDC electricity sectors.

* Product prices in these countries do not follow world market prices very closely. According to Sterner (1989a) there is even a tendency for domestic prices to vary counter-cyclically: when the world market is tight, oil exports give satisfactory income and the home market can readily be subsidized. When export earnings fall, however, due to falling world prices, the national oil companies start to try to cover their costs on the domestic market.
* These low prices tend to encourage the adoption of very wasteful technology in both industry, transport and the domestic sector.
* Subsidies vary from one country to another, and generally they vary very much between countries. Kerosene is for instance used for lighting and heating among poorer households in Latin America and thus income distribution criteria often dictate an extra subsidy for kerosene. Kerosene has even been heavily subsidized in some oil-importing countries such as Haiti and Nicaragua. To some extent, the same goes for diesel which is used for public transport and agricultural equipment. Attitudes towards gasoline, however, vary - in most Latin American countries popular pressure from the urban middle class appears sufficiently strong to secure considerable subsidies while in many African countries gasoline is quite clearly a luxury good and may be taxed quite heavily even in oil-producing countries, see Sterner (1989a & b).
* Large price differentials between different petroleum products are generally hard to maintain. They inevitably lead to the adulteration of the fuels (either by the sellers or by the users themselves). Cars and other machinery may be run on gasoline mixed with kerosene or diesel or whatever is cheapest but this does cause considerable increases in motor wear and other risks.
* Price differentials between countries also tend to lead to the smuggling of products and we have earlier described how various products such as kerosene and LPG may be found moving, sometimes in opposite directions across borders in response to differences in cross-subsidization, (see Sterner 1989b).
* Although in most LDCs subsidizing energy does imply a powerful incentive for waste and is therefore contrary to the interests of the environment, it has been argued that there might be conceivable exceptions where an environmentally sound policy could include subsidies on kerosene or LPG for poor people in areas very prone to deforestation or desertification. Actually the evidence on this is rather mixed since deforestation rarely depends in any simple way on the demand for firewood, see Chapters 9 and 11.
* We should also bear in mind that some importing LDCs face the opposite burden. For shortage of foreign exchange, imported products become even more expensive than on the world market and in some cases the fuel may be so expensive or even physically so hard to get hold of that this causes considerable economic costs, directly through standstills in industry and indirectly through efforts to substitute for oil by biomass which in some countries entails the risk of increasing the rate of deforestation or pushing up the prices of agricultural products etc.

6 FOSSIL ENERGY AND GREEN TAX REFORM

The literature referred to has made a pretty convincing case against the massive and systematic subsidies for all petroleum products with the general aim of promoting mobility and industrialization. Even though poor LDCs cannot be expected to give too much weight to the possible future costs of such global issues as climate warming, there are significant local externalities caused by excessive consumption of petroleum products as witnessed by the air in Mexico City or Cairo. Environmental economists have recently been focusing more and more on urban environmental problems, including in particular air pollution in the major cities. Eskeland(1993), for instance, recommends the use of economic instruments, including gasoline taxes, to curb air pollution in Mexico City.

Furthermore it is easy, as some populist politicians do, to make the point that many (practically all) products apparently "need" to be subsidized (in the sense that they are necessary for poor people) but unfortunately the state has very limited resources and taxation is very hard to raise. In many developing countries income taxes are too expensive to administer, and import duties or capital taxes would scare away foreign capital and distort consumption and investment decisions[5]. In these countries some form of differentiated product taxes are needed and if the bare necessities such as some basic foods, education and health are to be subsidized then what is there left to tax? Seen in this light it is not unreasonable to tax products which do have negative (local) externalities such as transport fuels and furthermore negative global externalities thanks to which the country may be able to attract international resources if it commits itself to abatement.

However, we should realize that matters are not quite so simple and before we count on political support for taxing carbon emissions from these countries we need to analyze very carefully why such policies as gasoline or other fossil fuel taxes may be so bitterly resisted. We will discuss three important factors; indirect effects through the international oil market, the power of pressure groups and cheap products as a means of distributing revenue.

6.1 A fall in the world crude price.

A crucial element in our argument in this chapter has been that products sold below world market prices can be thought of as subsidized since the world market in fact acts as an opportunity cost. Given that transport and storage costs etc are low and the planning horizon infinite this would seem impeccable. However, in practice, a reduction of world oil consumption, whether by taxes or through some other means, would actually have very uneven effects on different groups of countries. It is easy to see that the oil importing countries stand to gain heavily from this since it would inevitably exercise a heavy downward pressure on the spot market for crude. Figure 3 illustrates how a domestic tax τ in the OECD countries allows these countries to capture part of the "rent" (A) now captured by the oil producers (A+B) by lowering

---

[5] See the literature on optimal taxation for LDCs (for instance Newbery & Stern, 1987)

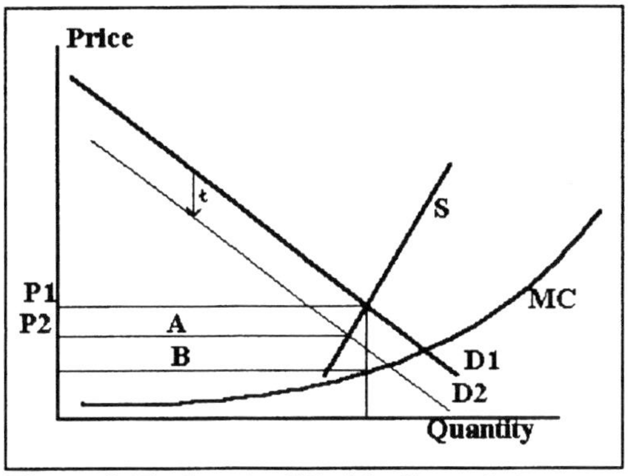

Figure 3 Taxing the World oil market.

demand from D1 to D2 and thus effectively lowering World prices from P1 to P2. (NB the reason there is a rent to be captured is that we assume the oil producers succeed in sticking to the supply curve S instead of following the marginal cost curve). Thus the consumers in oil importing countries would benefit from higher (instead of lower!) domestic taxation as a response to higher world crude prices.

By the same logic, however, the oil exporting LDCs obviously stand to loose from these policies and they are keenly aware of this. In fact they don't believe too much in the newly found environmentalism of Western leaders as shown by the quotation which is very typical of OPEC bulletin commentaries. As support for this position they can of course point to the lack of consequence when Western leaders want to tax oil but continue to subsidize much dirtier domestic coal production.

".. an energy tax, one that is carefully biased against oil ... (implies) ... the consumers of the world will be hoodwinked into paying an environmentally spurious tax, while the oil producers are stealthily deprived of their share of resources."
OPEC Bulletin March 93.

As illustrated by Figure 4, the situation for the oil-exporting companies is drastically different. This figure shows the domestic market in an oil exporting country. If, as is quite common in the short to medium term, they have some excess capacity then the relevant opportunity cost is not really the world market price P_w if this price is artificially elevated due to the market power of the producers on the world market. Selling an extra barrel of oil will then generally imply undercutting the cartel prices, is risky and does not give much extra revenue. Thus treating the world market price of oil as an opportunity cost may not appear correct. True the country could save oil for posterity but given imperfect foresight (and even more imperfect capital markets) this is hardly an easy option. If the countries, instead, choose to analyze their domestic markets separately then

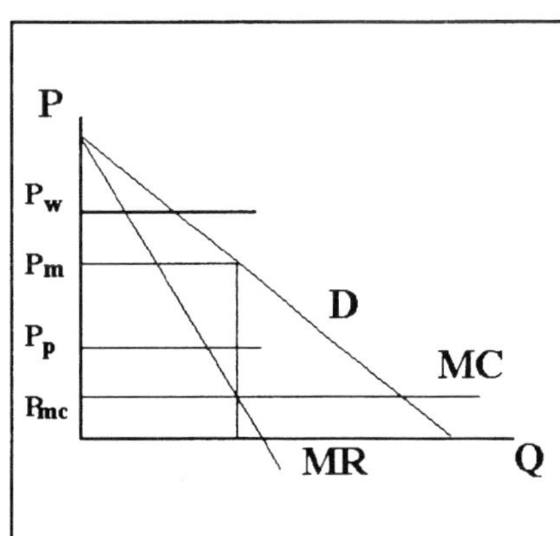

Figure 4 Domestic product pricing in an oil economy.

possible outcomes: anywhere from marginal cost pricing P_{mc} to a local monopoly price P_m. In fact the company generally has additional criteria in its decision making - it might be selling whatever is the residual between production and exports at say P_p or it might be maximizing popular support by setting low prices. It may be swinging between these two strategies, subsidizing the domestic market when exports are good but raising domestic prices when international demand is weak as discussed earlier. It is thus not easy to know which would be its preferred price but the point is that selling below the world market price is not necessarily contrary to *short run* profit maximization.

6.2 The power of pressure groups

It is worth noting that even in countries such as the US which would gain unequivocally and quite considerably from depressing the world oil price, there has still not been enough support to put even moderate domestic taxes on petroleum products. This evidently does tell us something about the strength of the lobby groups involved - including presumably both national oil companies and consumers' (motorists') organizations.

Naturally in the context of an oil-exporting country, these forces are stronger since the macroeconomic effect of consuming less oil (and thus maybe exporting more) would not necessarily be positive for the country. Furthermore for these countries to legitimate the very concept of domestic gasoline taxes could be thought of as tactically mistaken since it may again facilitate the adoption of higher domestic taxes in the importing countries. Instead countries such as Mexico will typically hope that their cheap oil will attract foreign investment in energy intensive industries or at least provide energy intensive companies in the importing countries with an arsenal of arguments against domestic taxation there. Obviously it is in the interests of for instance the main oil exporters that the US plastics industries oppose domestic oil taxes and threaten to relocate (for instance to the very oil-exporting countries). On the issue of domestic energy taxation there is thus a natural allegiance between the oil-exporters and the major energy users in the importing countries: both resist domestic taxation in the importing countries. Both will presumably resist global CO_2 taxation or permit schemes of the type discussed in the previous chapter. Considering the need discussed there of compensating the really poor countries as part of such programs, the prospect of also having to compensate the oil exporters and the energy intensive consumers to gain political support is clearly impossible.

6.3 Cheap petroleum products as a means of distributing revenue

Finally we should remind ourselves that cheap energy is after all fairly popular while raising prices can be politically very difficult. Several governments have met with widespread discontent after raising the prices of transport fuels. As economists we can perhaps envisage benefits of petrol taxes such as lower taxes on other goods, lower budget deficit (with less crowding out of investments, lower interest rates, less foreign debt etc) or even a better provision of public services and increased social benefits. In the best of cases we would have to devise ways of explaining this message more clearly. In some countries however, even a majority of citizens see the government as incompetent and in some cases even corrupt. In such a context our type of reasoning will seem naive and people will see cheap supplies of useful goods such as oil from nationalized monopolies perhaps not as efficient but at least as a reasonably effective way of distributing part of a national asset. Without knowing exactly what the alternatives are in practice we cannot easily judge, from the outside, whether this is right or wrong.

Finally we should note the asymmetry between responses in the importing and exporting countries. Individually the OECD countries might not gain much by taxing petroleum products (because of losses in competitivity). As a group, however, they surely stand to gain quite considerably and hence this policy option is relatively likely to materialize as the OECD countries start to coordinate their policies better. For the oil-exporting LDCs however taxing oil is even less attractive as a coordinated than as an individual response since the effect on world market prices will be stronger. Since higher taxes on these products and thus lower consumption and lower carbon emissions entails positive effects for the environment both at the local and at the global level it is not unreasonable to consider some form of payment from the industrialized countries as a support to this kind of policy as discussed in the previous chapter.

7 CONCLUSION

The use of fossil energy creates not only welfare but also a series of environmental problems both at the local, national and global levels. The policies to deal with these problems also need to be applied at different levels. The result is likely to be a mix of policy instruments at different levels. When you get down to the final consumer he is most likely to feel the result of these policies through higher prices. We have therefore in this chapter reviewed some of the literature that describes both the issues of energy pricing and taxation in different types of economy and also the work that analyzes the effects on consumption of different price (and income) levels. A large number of side issues complicate the picture, principally distributional ones, such as the use of the revenues collected and the distribution of taxes on different categories of product and final consumer. As emphasized several times above, the LDCs must be compensated for joining in on a fight against global environmental problems which, although it does concern them, can hardly be one of their top priority issues

REFERENCES

Amann M., et al., 1992, "Economic Restructuring in Eastern Europe and Acid Rain Abatement Strategies" *Energy Policy*, December.

Angelier, J.P. and T. Sterner. 1990. "Tax Harmonization for Petroleum Products in the EC", *Energy Policy*, July.

Choucri, N. 1986. "Domestic energy pricing: trends and Implications for the Arab World", *The Journal of Energy and Development*, vol. 11, no. 1.

Dahl, C. and T. Sterner. 1991a. "A Survey of Econometric Gasoline Demand Elasticities", *International Journal of Energy Systems.* vol 11, no 2.

Dahl, C. and T. Sterner. 1991b. "Analyzing Gasoline Demand Elasticities" *Energy Economics*, April.

Eskeland, G., (1992) "A presumptive Pigouvian Tax on Gasoline", World Bank.

Kosmo, M. 1987. *Money to burn? The high cost of Energy Subsidies*, World Resources Institute.

Krupnick, A.J. 1990. "Urban Air Pollution in Developing Countries: Problems and Policies" *Mimeo*, Resources for The Future, Inc.

Larsen, B. and A. Shah, "World Fossil Fuel Subsidies and Global Carbon Emissions", World Bank Policy Research Working Papers WPS 1002.

Miljörapporten, 1993 Nr 8. Published by Tomorrow Media, Stockholm.

Munasinghe, M. 1985. *Energy Pricing and Demand Management*, Westview Press, Colorado, USA.

Newbery, D. and N. Stern. 1987. *The Theory of Taxation for Developing Countries,* Oxford University Press.

OECD, 1989a. "The Application of Economic Instruments for Environmental Protection", Paris.

Sand, P.H. 1990. *Lessons Learned in Global Environmental Governance.* World Resources Institute.

Siddayao, C., ed. 1985. *Criteria for Energy Pricing Policy,* Graham & Trotamn, The East-West Center, Honolulu.

Sterner, T. 1985. "Structural change and Technology Choice", *Energy Economics*, April.

Sterner, T. 1987. "Mexico as a Regional Power" in *Middle Powers in the Third World: Towards South-South Cooperation or subimperialism*? Editors T. Shaw and J. Carlsson, (Coauthor B. Hettne). Macmillans, London.

Sterner, T. 1989a. "The Politics of Energy Pricing: Oil products in L America", *Energy Journal* vol 10 no 2.

Sterner, T. 1989b "Le Prix des Produits Pétroliers en Afrique", *Revue de l'Energie* 415, Novembre.

Sterner T. 1989c. "Factor Demand and Substitution in a Developing Country: Energy use in Mexican Manufacturing", *Scandinavian Journal of Economics*, Nov.

Sterner, T. 1990. *The Pricing of and Demand for Gasoline*, ISBN 91-8724 6-57-0. The Swedish Transport Research Board, Stockholm, May.

Sterner, T. and C. Dahl "Gasoline Demand Modelling: Theory and Application" in *International Energy Modelling*, London: Chapman and Hall, edited by T. Sterner.

Sterner, T, C. Dahl and M. Franzén. 1992. "Global Environmental Policies and Carbon Emissions from Gasoline" *Journal of Transport and Economic Policy*.

Sterner, T. 1992. "Economic and Environmental Policies for Sustainability" in *Society and the Environment: A Swedish Perspective*, eds., Svedin, U. & B. Aniansson, Kluwer,

Wilczynski, P. 1990. "Environmental Management in Centrally-Planned Non-Market Economies of Eastern Europe", World Bank Environmental Working Paper No 35.

World Bank. 1992. *The World Development Report.*

NOTES ON THE CONTRIBUTORS

Dr. Wesley K Foell is a policy analyst, researcher and educator who has worked for the past two decades on a wide variety of energy and environmental problems throughout the world. His professional activities in the US, which included twelve years at the University of Wisconsin-Madison as professor of engineering and environmental studies and Director of the Energy Systems and Policy Research Program, included the development of analytical tools and models for energy/environmental policy analysis. He has conducted energy and environmental policy work in North Africa, Iran, Mexico, Western Europe, the former Soviet Union, Eastern Europe (Czechoslovakia and the former GDR) and several countries in South and Southeast Asia. More recently he has been a member of the faculty of the Asian Institute of Technology in Bangkok where he initiated programs in energy conservation policy, private power and acid rain research. Dr. Foell is President of Resource Management Associates, an international consulting firm in Madison, Wisconsin.

Dr Michael Grubb conducted this research as Research Fellow at the Energy and Environmental Programme of the Royal Institute of International Affairs, where he directed the Institute's work on economic and policy aspects of climate change. He is also advisor to a number of international agencies concerned with the issue and has published widely in the field of energy policy and technology relating to environmental constraints. His latest book, *The Earth Summit Agreements: A Guide and Assessment* provides an overview of the outcome and implications of the Rio '92 UN Conference on Environment and Development. In April 1993 he was appointed as Head of the Energy and Environmental Programme at RIIA.

Torleif Haugland is Senior Economist and partner at ECON Energy in Oslo. Before joining ECON in 1989 he was a principal administrator at the International Energy Agency. Mr. Haugland has broad experience on international energy issues and environmental impacts of energy use. Torleif Haugland is an economist from the University of Oslo.

Tiit Kallaste, Phd in Economics, is Senior Research Fellow at the Stockholm Environment Institute - Tallinn Office. When writing this chapter he was at the Estonian Academy of Sciences. His main area of work has been on the quality of the environment and air pollution in Estonia.

Gunnar Köhlin is an economist at the Environmental Economics Unit of the department of economics, Gothenburg. Köhlin has done extensive research on economic evaluation of aid projects and his current main area of research is focused on the economic and social aspects of forestry in developing countries.

Dr. Marianne Löwgren is an associate professor at the Department of Water and Environmental Studies, Linköping University. Her research interests concern the implementation of environmental policies, particularly economical and ecological aspects of resource management and pollution control.

Dr Marco Antonio Martinez Negrete, Phd in physics from the Universidad Nacional Autonoma de México, is currently full time professor at the department of physics at the UNAM. His research and teaching have mainly been centered on thermodynamics and on the social and historical context within which energy efficient and sustainable technologies are adopted, both in rural Mexican villages and in the country as a whole.

Dr. Ammon Mbelle holds a Ph Dr. in economics from the University of Gothenburg and is a Senior Lecturer at the Department of Economic, University of Dar es Salaam. Dr Mbelle was also a former Economic Advisor to the Prime Minister of Tanzania. His main research interests are in industrial and natural resource economics.

Mohan Munasinghe has worked 18 years in the World Bank and is currently Division Chief for Environmental Policy. During 1982-86 he served as Senior Energy Advisor to the President of Sri Lanka. He has postgraduate degrees in physics, engineering and economics from Cambridge (UK), MIT (USA) and McGill (Canada). Dr. Munasinghe has authored over 40 books and several hundred technical articles. He has received several international awards for his work.

Kjell Roland is Managing Director and partner at ECON Energy in Oslo. Mr Roland is an economist from the University in Oslo and has served as section chief for energy studies at the Research Department of the Central Bureau of Statistics in Norway. He was a co-founder of ECON and his academic work covers a broad range from energy modelling to energy sector analysis and multidisciplinary environmental studies. Recently he has published widely on global environmental issues and the de-regulation of electricity markets.

Jürgen Salay is lecturer at Uppsala University, Sweden and consultant specialized o n energy and environment in Eastern Europe and the former USSR. In 1991, he published a book on environmental problems and policies in Eastern Europe. He is currently working on his Ph D thesis on energy policies and transition in East Central Europe.

Thomas Sterner, Phd in economics, is associate professor at the department of economics, university of Gothenburg and director of its Environmental Economics Unit. He has also been a visiting researcher at the Universities of Cambridge, Grenoble, Mexico (UNAM) and Montevideo. His main areas of research and teaching are environmental, development, energy, industrial and transport economics. He has published extensively in the areas of energy and development economics and is a member of the editorial board of several journals including *The Energy Journal* and *European Environment*.

Ann-Mari Sätre Åhlander has recently finished her doctoral thesis in Economics on resource use and environmental problems in the former Soviet Union. She is working at the Department for Soviet and East European Studies, Uppsala, where she is presently working on a book about the environmental disaster in Soviet Central Asia.

Dr Ruben Tansini is Professor of Industrial Organization at the Department of Economics of the University of Uruguay. He obtained his Phd in economics at the Gothenburg University, Sweden and at the present he is the Director of the Department of Economics of the University of Uruguay. He has conducted extensive research in Industrial Organization and Production Theory.

Tom Tietenberg is the author or editor of seven books (including ***Environmental and Natural Resource Economics,*** one of the two best selling textbooks in the field, and ***Emissions Trading: An Exercise in Reforming Pollution Policy,*** the most widely cited book on the American experience with marketable permits) and over fifty articles and essays on environmental and natural resource economics. Elected President of the Association of Environmental and Natural Resource Economists in 1987-8, he has served as a consultant on environmental policy with the World Bank, the U. S. Agency for International Development, the U.S. Environmental Protection Agency and the United Nations. He is currently Christian A. Johnson Distinguished Teaching Professor of Economics at Colby College, Waterville, Maine 04901 USA.

Michael Walsh is a mechanical engineer who has spent his entire career working on issues related to motor vehicle pollution control and energy consumption. For more than ten years, he managed significant government programs in this subject area and for the three years prior to his resignation from EPA in 1981, he headed the United States effort. Since leaving EPA, he has continued to work closely with the Congress on the Clean Air Act, serving as a technical consultant to the Senate Committee on Environment and Public Works.

Thomas Żylicz is an associate professor at the Economics Department, Warsaw University. Born in Lublin, Poland 1951, he graduated from Warsaw University (1974 - Economics; 1977 - Mathematics); Ph.D. (Economics) in 1979. He has for many years taught Environmental Economics, Mathematical Programming and Differential Equations. In 1989-91 he taught an "emergency" course in Microeconomics for Warsaw University economic students, who otherwise would have graduated without any contact with Western economic analysis. From October 1989 to September 1991, Director of Economics in Poland's Ministry of Environment. Since October 1991 has he served as an Advisor to the Minister.

Index

Economy & Environment

1. F. Archibugi and P. Nijkamp (eds.): *Economy and Ecology: Towards Sustainable Development.* 1989 ISBN 0-7923-0477-2
2. J. Bojö, K.-G. Mäler and L. Unemo: *Environment and Development: An Economic Approach.* 1990 ISBN 0-7923-0802-6
3. J. B. Opschoor and D. W. Pearce (eds.): *Persistent Pollutants: Economics and Policy.* 1991 ISBN 0-7923-1168-X
4. D.J. Kraan and R. J. in 't Veld (eds.): *Environmental Protection: Public or Private Choice.* 1991 ISBN 0-7923-1333-X
5. J.J. Krabbe and W.J.M. Heijman (eds.): *National Income and Nature: Externalities, Growth and Steady State.* 1992 ISBN 0-7923-1529-4
6. J. Bojö, K.-G. Mäler and L. Unemo: *Environment and Development: An Economic Approach* (revised edition). 1992 ISBN 0-7923-1878-1
7. T. Sterner (ed.): *Economic Policies for Sustainable Development.* 1994 ISBN 0-7923-2680-6

KLUWER ACADEMIC PUBLISHERS – DORDRECHT / BOSTON / LONDON